The York Chasseurs

The York Chasseurs

A Condemned Regiment of George III

Pete Lines

Francis
Boutle
Publishers

First published by Francis Boutle Publishers
272 Alexandra Park Road
London N22 7BG
Tel/Fax: (020) 8889 7744
Email: info@francisboutle.co.uk
www.francisboutle.co.uk

ISBN 978 1 903427 50 7

Printed by Cromwell Press Group, Trowbridge, Wiltshire

Contents

Dedicated to Gunner Ieuan Phillips,
8th Battalion Gordon Highlanders, 2nd Div,
and all Burma Star Veterans, past and present

Acknowledgements

First, my thanks to Dr James Thomas, University of Portsmouth, for his initial suggestion that I research the York Chasseurs instead of continuing on for a Master's Degree, and to Professor Roger Buckley, University of Connecticut, for his early comments of encouragement. For the invaluable contributions of Dr Hamish Maxwell-Stewart, University of Tasmania, Terry J Senior and Dr Therald L (Ted). Leonard DDS, Auburn, near Seattle, Washington, for supplying and allowing the publication of his pictures relating to Sergeant Thomas Leonard.

My appreciative thanks for the professionalism and courtesy received at Ottawa's National Archives, Perth Museum, Lanark County and Almonte Land Registry Office, Ontario, Canada, and to Mr and Mrs Willows, Bathurst, Lanark County, for allowing me to photograph the former farm of Thomas Leonard.

For the courteous assistance offered by the National Archives, Kew, Portsmouth City and Gosport Public Libraries, particularly Leila Smith and Kiran Shaughnessy, who for the past decade or so have tirelessly endured my obsessive ramblings. My thanks to Katy Ball, Local History Officer, and the Portsmouth City Museum, for permission to publish 'A Bird's Eye View of Portchester Castle, November 1817'; to the Curator, Green Howards Regimental Museum, Richmond, North Yorkshire, for his assistance in the successful search for the York Chasseurs King's and Regimental Colours, and the Curator of the Army Medical Services Museum, Keogh Barracks, Aldershot, for allowing the publication of the 'Spring Loaded Tattooing Machine'. To the Commanding Officer, Institute of Naval Medicine, Alverstoke, Gosport, for allowing me access to the Institute's library, and to Mrs J V S Wickenden, Librarian, for all her helpful assistance.

To Roger Hart, my constant companion during those long and frequent car trips to and from Kew, and most significantly for my ultimate survival, my sincere thanks and commiserations to my wife Margaret who, for the last decade or so, has seen her house constantly cluttered with books and loose papers. Not forgetting sons Kim and Peter for continually placating their mother on the never-ending subject of decorating: 'Come on mum, you know dad's a thinker and not a doer.'

Finally, my special thanks to all York Chasseur descendants who, through their correspondence, became a constant source of encouragement.

If any individual or institution copyright has been unwittingly infringed, then I sincerely apologise.

Unexpected postscript – My undying gratitude, possibly literally, to Doctor Strike, Sister Liz Clark and staff of Trafalgar Ward and the Cardiac Catheter Laboratory, Queen Alexandra Hospital, Portsmouth, and, even more specifically, to Staff Nurse Stacey Brown for all her attentive reassurance. A dedicated team of NHS professionals successfully ensuring that eleven years research and three years of writing didn't fall at the last hurdle

List of illustrations and tables

Hampshire Telegraph and Sussex Chronicle. July 10th 1815

The Amphion, Capt Purvis, is under orders for Barbadoes, to take under convoy six transports, having corps of York Chasseurs, (lately formed from soldiers condemned to perpetual foreign service) on board, and the William store-ship.

Gosport Public Library, where it all unexpectedly started.

Chapter One

Pardoned, Condemned, Commuted – or Volunteer

Tuppence I got for selling me cloak
Tuppence for selling my blanket
If ever I list for a soldier again
Devil shall be me sergeant
Poor old soldier – poor old soldier
If ever I list for a soldier again
Devil shall be me sergeant.

The Rogues March

Despite centuries of opposition, in April 1916 of the Great War, after months of attrition and a volunteer army virtually destroyed, compulsory military conscription finally became law. Yet, just a century or so earlier, while a partially press-ganged Royal Navy enjoyed primacy at sea, on land and confronting Bonaparte's oft-times conscripted masses, Britain's volunteer army had primarily recruited via silvery-tongued recruiters, the lure of the bounty or even the largesse of the magistrate.

So desperate was the need for 'volunteers' that allegedly, donning civilian clothing, recruiters would often try to persuade drink-befuddled new acquaintances to join them in enlisting. Pity the confused and luckless drink-sodden recruit, prey to tavern keepers, rapacious traders and accommodating females all waiting for his newly issued bounty.

> We worked hard at this business, and for three days and nights kept up the dance and drunken riot. Every volunteer got ten guineas bounty. Two were kept back for necessaries, but the rest they spent in all sorts of excesses till all was gone.[1]

As the 1802 Treaty of Amiens between Britain and France failed, conflict resumed, and with so many likely recruits lost when men were balloted for service in local militias, so dire was the need for recruits that, with the 1803 Additional Forces Act, legislation was enacted for the creation of a militia-style, compulsory balloted, national 'Army of Reserve', from which, optimistically, and with a persuasive additional bounty on offer, a further 55,000 recruits could be lured into the ranks of the regulars. With fewer than expected volunteering, however, and a ten per cent desertion rate amongst bounty takers within two years, all remaining recruits were transferred to three newly established Garrison Battalions, and the Army of Reserve was disbanded.

Although not before one young unfortunate, tempted by the highly lucrative but somewhat hazardous occupation of serial bounty jumping and desertion, would be singled out as an example, or, as the *Hampshire Telegraph* expressed it: 'The frequency of desertion having rendered strong examples necessary, and that occasioned in a great measure by the large bounties given for the Army of Reserve'.[2] On 6 December 1803, just as the Portsmouth clocks chimed nine o'clock in the morning, with local militia, yeomanry and regular troops all solemnly assembled, Stephen Carroll, private soldier of the 70th Foot and serial deserter marched out to his fate on Portsdown Hill, where, after a moment of prayer, a sixteen man firing squad raised grounded muskets to shoulders and – FIRED.

> The first fire wounded him in the thigh, the second, it was supposed, missed him, and the third deprived him of his feelings, though it did not entirely kill him; when three file marched close to him, and instantly dispatched him.[3]

While Carroll's death would have little effect over subsequent desertions, at least the spectacle was not lost on Benjamin Harris of the 66th Foot, and member of the firing squad: 'It was meant as a good hint to us young uns.' As for the unfortunate Carroll, the *Hampshire Telegraph* had nothing but praise for his final demeanour and scorn for the presence of so many female thrill-seeking spectators. 'We cannot but lament that principle, which could seek a momentary sight of the expiring struggles of a fellow creature, expiating by his death the offended laws of his country.'[4]

As the conflict in Europe continued, legislation was steadily making the militia less sacrosanct, so much so that, by 1809, voluntary militia transfers were in fact becoming a significant proportion of the army's annual intake. With one significant drawback, however: the exorbitant cost of additional bounties. None the less, whether militia volunteer or civilian recruit having accepted the King's shilling, each man would soon be paraded before the local magistrate or justice of the peace to swear the Oath of Enlistment, after which, providing he was neither an indentured apprentice, lame, deaf or indeed ruptured, he was now a King's soldier.

Whether escaping penury and deprivation, or merely in search of adventure, having taken the King's shilling, a soldier's only lawful escape was infirmity or death. From 1806, however, an infantry recruit was able to enlist for a seven year period, and if fit, for two further periods of seven years each; for cavalrymen, it was an initial ten years, followed by two seven-year periods; and artillerymen, twelve years of service, followed by two additional periods of five years apiece. For those desiring a lifetime of soldiering 'Unlimited Service' was still an option.

In spite of all the drawbacks volunteers in their thousands still faced Bonaparte's masses, of whom a handful later committed their experiences to paper. Men like John Shipp, ten years of age, thrilled by the 'finery and shrill music' of the recruiting party and encouraged by the Parish Overseer, who enlisted for the 22nd Foot[5] and, ten years later, received an ensign's commission. Benjamin Harris[6] of the 66th, so attracted by the dashing 95th Rifles that 'nothing would deter him from transferring'; and Thomas Costello[7] of the Dublin Militia, who, on volunteering into the 95th Foot 'became red-hot for a soldier's life'. Reputedly, it was the tales of great and heroic battles that drew Sergeant Thomas Morris of the 73rd Regiment[8] away from St George's Volunteer Militia, while William Wheeler's[9] career with the 51st Regiment began when voluntarily escaping the callous regime of the 2nd Royal Surrey Militia's colonel.

Tales of heroic battles, the stir of the drumbeat, or the cut of a uniform may have influenced some; yet in August 1800, amongst the convict-hulked residents of Woolwich and Portsmouth, talk was likely to be of Lieutenant Colonel John Fraser and the chance of a pardon in exchange for service with his new regiment. Four months later, his quest over, with suitable recruits selected and trained, Fraser's two companies strong 'Corps of Infantry' left Portsmouth Harbour one cold and wintry December for the West African island of Goree,[10] the first consignment of a ground-breaking concept – the expendable condemned regiment. Dregs of society dregs they may have been, but only overwhelming odds against them would drive Fraser's diseased and depleted command away from their island four years later.

Scarcely three months after that, with English Colours and red-coated figures visible on Goree's stone ramparts, a wary Captain Dickson aboard *H.M.S. Inconstant* prudently anchored his squadron well out of cannon range while dispatching a shore party to investigate. With darkness falling and all contact with the shore party lost, a returning ship's cutting-out party provided Dickson with crucial intelligence that a French force of about three hundred white and black troops now commanded the island. After a night planning an assault, Dickson was told that through the dawn's breaking light British Colours could now be seen flying over those of the French. Clearly the French defenders, with cannons trained from the sea and an armed party already ashore, considered surrender the better option. Goree was re-garrisoned by the reinforcements for Fraser's Corps of Infantry (now re-designated Royal African Corps) transported by Dickson's squadron – almost to the day that a French cartel deposited Fraser and his band of survivors safely ashore at Falmouth, Cornwall.

By November 1806, despite Fraser's temporary loss of his island, with convict-hulks and military prison ships filled almost to capacity and the Royal African Corps an unmanageable twelve companies, the British Army headquarters at Horse Guards decided on some serious restructuring, leaving the six companies on Goree as Royal African Corps, and reinforcements about to embark for West Africa being re-designated Royal West India Rangers and then dispatched to the West Indies.

Unlike military prison ships, conscription from the convict hulks administered by the Home Office was cumbersome, with the bureaucratic process allowing the War Office powers of recruitment, the Colonial Office responsibility for overseas shipping and the Home Office overall day-to-day management. So much so that, with 400 long-pardoned recruits still under confinement, and with the convoy season approaching, an exasperated Fraser eventually approached the Commander-in-Chief for assistance, only to receive the unhelpful reply that Fraser's 'corrupt recruits' were to remain in confinement until the Colonial Office could arrange the necessary shipping.

By 1808 the situation had become so precarious that a troubled Superintendent of Prison Hulks alerted the Home Secretary to the legality of continuing to confine those who, to all intents and purposes, were now the King's soldiers.

> As their pardons have been longed since signed by his Majesty, I dread the possible chance of it coming to their knowledge, and inducing them to claim to be let loose upon the public without regarding the conditions upon which the Pardons were granted.[11]

Yet, in spite of the personal intervention of the Home Secretary, an intransigent Commander-in-Chief steadfastly insisted that the fault lay not with Horse Guards but with lethargy at the Colonial Office. And fortunately for the administration no legal challenge appears to have been mounted.

Regardless of all bureaucrats and bureaucracy, recruitment still progressed at such a pace that by 1808 hordes of recalcitrant Royal Africa Corps reinforcements (now re-designated as Royal York Rangers) were reported as creating mayhem, not in the West Indies or even on Goree, but on the more tranquil island of Guernsey. With desertion rife, lawlessness widespread, and local able-bodied men being constantly under arms as a militia police force, even the island's fragile economy was reported as crumbling; a situation not helped by the War Office seemingly ignoring all the military governor's complaints about 'the calibre of men being sent to his island'.

Not until one May Sunday morning, following Private Robert Wilson's botched burglary and savage murder of a seventy-four-year-old widow, did the War Office finally take action. Too late for military governor, legislators and islanders, all angered not merely at the War Office's inaction but with the discovery that Wilson's original death sentence had previously been commuted to service as a Royal York Ranger. An episode on which the chief magistrate later commented:

There is not one of the ten thousand individuals spread over the County Parishes of the Island who does not say to himself, an old woman who could give no opposition to a robbery intended has had her throat cut, – what is to prevent the same thing happening to me or my wife or my children tomorrow. It is true the murderer is secured, but there are hundreds of the description in the same Corps.[12]

A week or so later, in spite of the War Office's assurance 'that all condemned soldiers would soon leave his island', an exasperated governor again complained that 'a fresh inundation of these desperadoes from the hulks had dashed all hopes of him pacifying the inhabitants'.[13] In fairness, arrangements were already in place for those on Goree to be reinstated as Royal African Corps, and the men creating mayhem on Guernsey to be dispatched to the West Indies as Royal York Rangers. These arrangements meant that once again there were three 'condemned' regiments: the Royal African Corps, Royal West India Rangers and Royal York Rangers.

Unsurprisingly, convict recruitment was not welcomed in all quarters, particularly by some parliamentarians, who, in a rather acrimonious debate, queried their excessive numbers, mode of selection and, importantly, the detrimental affect on esprit de corps and discipline if dispatched en masse to reputable line-regiments. In defence of the convict-hulk soldier, the Home Secretary simply quoted the words of a past Royal African Corps colonel.

Such men had conducted themselves well in his regiment and that another regiment, the Royal York Rangers had distinguished themselves well at the taking of Guadeloupe, and their conduct was noted in the Gazette in a manner that would have done honour to any regiment in the service.[14]

Despite opposition, however, so enthusiastically did Amy headquarters adopt deserter renaissance that, in the case of Trooper Seth Platt and 16th Light Dragoon deserter, the Adjutant General even recommended circumventing the mandatory court martial with a direct offer of 'Unlimited Service', which Platt rejected out of hand. Found guilty, Platt's punishment was in fact what the Adjutant General had suggested in the first place – 'unlimited service'. And in the case of Trooper Wallace, 7th Light Dragoons, it seems the Army may even have influenced the process of civil justice. On trial for forgery at Dorchester Assizes but with his prosecutor in abstentia, Wallace was conveniently dispatched to West Africa and the Royal African Corps 'in lieu of the punishment which would probably have been awarded him'.[15]

As the war against Bonaparte progressed, legislation eased the process of military offender recycling.

An Act for Punishing Mutiny and Desertion Geo III, 21st March 1808

Page 11. Section IV. And it be further enacted and declared, that in the

Case of any Non-Commissioned Officer or Soldier tried and convicted of Desertion whomsoever the Court-martial, which shall pass sentence upon such Trial, shall not think the Offence deserving Capital Punishment, such Court-martial may, instead of awarding Corporal Punishment, adjudge the Offender, according to the nature of the Offence, if they shall think fit, to be transported as a Felon for Life: Or for a Certain Term of Years: And also if such Court shall think fit, to be at the Expiration of such Term of Years at the disposal of His Majesty for Service as a Soldier, in any of his Majesty's forces at home or abroad for Life, or otherwise as His Majesty shall think fit.

On 13 September 1807 the *Hampshire Telegraph and Sussex Chronicle* reported:

Winchester. Passed through this city, 90 men from the 28th Regiment to the General Depot in the Isle of Wight; these were the men who inflicted on themselves the dreadful disorder of the eyes so as to occasion blindness, to prevent themselves from serving the King and Country. They are now to be conveyed abroad, to a condemned regiment for life. This day, passed through 20 deserters from London to the General Depot, in the Isle of Wight.

In fact, offending soldiers would now even have the 'Privilege' of commuting to unlimited military service:

I do hereby declare, that I am willing to serve, without limitation, in any regiment abroad, to which I may be attached, if the punishment, or the remainder of the punishment (as the case may be), awarded me for —— ——————————————, is remitted.

Nevertheless, in the case of Private Greenwood and Corporal Curtis of the Oxford Militia, even commuting seems to have been something of a lottery, particularly as Greenwood escaped his entire 500-lash sentence while Curtis, his fellow conspirator, endured 200 of a 1,000-lash sentence before commuting. Yet there were still those like Privates Taylor and Gillander of the Perthshire Militia who, in resolutely declining all offers of commutation had sent out their own defiant and unmistakable message – flog and be damned!

As desertion rates increased (see Table 1, below) – thirty-six per cent of all

Table 1 Total British Army Losses (1810–1814)[16]

	Deaths	Discharges	Desertion
1810	11,560	3,944	3,900
1811	11,670	3,289	4,060
1812	13,406	2,554	4,353
1813	15,012	3,621	5,822
1814	12,502	3,429	8,857

losses by 1814 – and the number of recaptured deserters escalating, what could the War Office do? Increase the number of prison ships, or offer the opportunity of redemption through the most suicidal and exposed positions of battle? When from Cadiz Lieutenant Colonel Fane of the 59th Regiment requested the return of his regimental deserters, however, the Adjutant General brusquely replied 'That His Royal Highness the Commander-in-Chief has directed that no Deserter shall be sent to join a Regiment in the Peninsula';[17] presumably the fear of contamination far outweighed the 59th's urgent need of replacements.

A solution seems partially to have been reached by mid-1813, when, with all military prison ships nearing capacity and three condemned regiments well above complement, 100 military miscreants apiece had been dispatched to the 14th, 34th and 89th Regiments serving in India. After which the remedy became obvious – simply to create a regiment specifically for military offenders.

> To select the Better Class of Culprit and Deserter at the Army Depot in the Isle of Wight, for the purpose of being employed at the Cape of Good Hope, or on any other Foreign Station. This Corps is to be styled 'The York Chasseurs' and is to be clothed in Green, with Red Collar and Cuffs.[18]
> Horse Guards. 13th November, 1813.

Yet why, out of 39 cavalry and 160 infantry regiments, was a solitary corps of military felons awarded a prestigious regimental title such as Chasseurs, the name of an elite French Light Calvary and Bonaparte's personal bodyguard? Is it possible that calling such incorrigibles Chasseurs was a deliberate, propaganda-directed slight on the French Army? (You have your Chasseurs and we now have ours, our condemned.) And why the missing Royal prefix bestowed upon the Royal African Corps, the Royal West India Rangers and the Royal York Rangers? Perhaps these disgraced former soldiers were thought unworthy of the title.

With his newly-appointed colonel, Major-General Andrew Hay, away with Wellington's Army in Europe, Lieutenant-Colonel Andrew Coghlan, the regiment's recently promoted commanding officer, left Scotland and the 2nd Battalion 21st (Royal North British Fuzileers) Regiment for the Isle of Wight in order 'to make a beginning of the Battalion'.[19] With his new regiment still under confinement experienced support was vital; it appears Coghlan was successful in persuading his former regiment's adjutant and four sergeants to accompany him.

One of the most valuable of travelling companions for Coghlan was Thomas Henshaw, the 21st Regiment's fearsome parade ground martinet, who, for all his years of service, had yet to see a shot fired in anger. Of the four sergeants, tragically, Henshaw and Sergeant Alexander McLacklan both died in Jamaica, and Quartermaster Sergeant Andrew Wilson returned to England an invalid, while Sergeant Edward Jordan was discharged at Quebec as a private.

Even as Coghlan and his cohorts travelled south, recruiting parties were already out seeking volunteers amongst the 1st and 2nd Battalions, Tower Hamlets Militia. It is be be wondered why they should concentrate on London's

Table 2 Tower Hamlet Militia Enlistment Roll

			Levy money
Cpl John Sewell	6 December 1813	2nd Battalion	Six Guineas
John Upcross	6 December 1813	2nd Battalion	Six Guineas
Richard Martin	6 December 1813	2nd Battalion	Six Guineas
John Wyman.	6 December 1813	2nd Battalion	Six Guineas
George Wheatley	6 December 1813	2nd Battalion	Six Guineas
John Dix	6 December 1813	2nd Battalion	Six Guineas
William Lusty	6 December 1813	2nd Battalion	Six Guineas
William Fletcher	6 December 1813	2nd Battalion	Six Guineas
John Fewkes	9 December 1813	1st Battalion	Eight Guineas
John Hollister	9 December 1813	1st Battalion	Eight Guineas
Anthony Carlow	9 December 1813	1st Battalion	Eight Guineas
Laurence Roovers	18 December 1813	1st Battalion	Eight Guineas
Cornelius Buyss	18 December 1813	1st Battalion	Eight Guineas

Isle of Dogs for a regiment about to be established 70-odd miles away on the Isle of Wight (see Table 2, above).

Of the volunteers from the Tower Hamlets Militia, Sergeants Upcross, Carlow, Wyman, and Corporal Martin all died in the West Indies, and Dutchman Sergeant Laurence Roovers at Tobago in 1816. Roovers had previously joined the Militia along with fellow Dutchman Cornelius Buyss from the York Light Infantry Volunteers (formerly Regiment of Barbados Volunteers) some time in 1812. On the disbandment of his regiment in Canada Buyss returned to England to a well deserved pension as a colour sergeant. It is not known if he stayed or returned to his trade as a shoemaker in Amsterdam.

Other former soldiers volunteered, whether in pursuit of certain employment or more merely for the eleven-guinea bounty. Hector Mackay was promoted straight away to sergeant. Years later, as his regiment departed to Canada, he transferred his unblemished record as colour sergeant to the recently arrived 50th Foot; but after less than two months he was invalided to England, thereby avoiding the yellow fever that raged through his new regiment, taking officers, men, women and children alike.

Just as war meant death by sabre, bayonet, musket ball or cannon shot, for the professional soldier peace might result in unemployed penury. In Jamaica, therefore, as his former regiment was about to be disbanded in Canada, Corporal James Darby, former 90th Foot private and York Chasseurs volunteer, continued his chosen career by transferring to the 58th Regiment, from which in November 1828 he was discharged with a sergeant's pension.

Unfortunately for Coghlan and his officers, not all volunteers were of the calibre of Henshaw, Buyss and Mackay, and certainly not the twenty-two-year-old

James Sitch-Voysey, corporal of the Royal Scots, who, following a voluntary transfer from Scotland and promotion to sergeant, soon joined the regiment's ever-growing list of deserters. Had this former 'Cutler of Middlesex' deliberately wangled a move south before deserting, where a London accent would be unexceptional? Did West Indies service with a condemned regiment no longer have an appeal? Whatever the motivation Sitch-Voysey was lost to the regiment for ever.

Christopher Ecklin's desertion appears to have been far more spontaneous, perhaps inspired by alcohol – why would a sergeant volunteer from the 5th Regiment with several years of Peninsular campaigning to his credit become a deserter at Portsmouth barely two months after volunteering? Nevertheless Ecklin, professional soldier, former volunteer sergeant, convicted deserter, arrived in the West Indies as a corporal, where some months later he was dispatched as a sergeant to the Bourbon Regiment.[20] When the Bourbon Regiment was unexpectedly disbanded he transferred to the 1st West India Regiment as a colour sergeant. A temporary stay, however, for within months he was charged with 'Unsoldierlike Conduct' and removed to the 25th Regiment as private. This transgression may indeed have saved his life too, as his new regiment soon returned to England and away from deadly mosquitoes of the West Indies. Not for this old soldier the raucous shouts of the parade ground; instead, the less onerous duties as a recruiter. In September 1819 Ecklin became due his fourteen-year long-service pay; the following month he successfully deserted.

If military experience and some degree of learning could guarantee the ideal recruit, then Thomas Jones undoubtedly qualified. Unfortunately, while this Gloucestershire clerk, 15th Foot and Royal Marine private, may have proved himself the better educated of a trio of Royal Marine volunteers, he was also the most troublesome. For the first three years of his service all seems to have gone well; promotion to sergeant, a short spell as schoolmaster sergeant – then came his downfall, reduction to private, an unsuccessful attempt at desertion and the almost inevitable flogging. Discharged at Quebec with a volunteer's right of free return passage, it seems Jones chose to remain in Canada.

The case of John Hartshone testifies to the fact that learning is no guarantee of reliability. Former Warwickshire schoolmaster, 89th of Foot sergeant and York Chasseurs volunteer whose 'Unsoldierlike Conduct' and 'Repeated drunkenness whilst a Hospital Steward' would twice cause his demotion to private. With his regiment on the point of departure he had taken his discharge while still in Jamaica, after which, who knows, a return to sobriety or the death of a drunkard?

On the other hand, volunteer John Fagan gained both promotion and a transfer without even leaving the regiment's Isle of Wight depot. A private of the York Chasseurs for two years he was promoted to sergeant, then immediately appointed sergeant major of the 2nd West India Regiment. Returning from the West Indies, Fagan served a further four years as 'Isle of Wight Staff,' until at thirty-three years of age and suffering 'Chronic Affliction of the Liver', he was discharged with a sergeant's pension.

Of all volunteers, however, the Jamaica enlistment in May 1816 of Charles

Willis and Henry Gurley as 'Gentleman Volunteers' is the least explicable. In *The Armies of Wellington*, Philip J. Haythornthwaite states that Gentleman Volunteers 'would carry a musket and usually fight in the ranks, but would live with the officers, until a vacancy occurred and he could be appointed to an ensign'. A convincing hypothesis when campaigning in Portugal or Spain, perhaps, but within Jamaica's class-ridden colonial society, it was unlikely that a York Chasseurs 'Gentleman Volunteer' private would stand piquet duty on a Friday to sup wine with his officers on the Saturday. In defence of the premise, however, while Gurley went 'Absent without Leave', seemingly never to be heard of again, Willis was commissioned 'Ensign without Purchase' in September 1817.

During the regiment's foundation (see Table 3, below), with an infrastructure still in its infancy and 600 prison-ship recruits being released in consignments on 1 and 5 February, 7 and 25 March 1814, and with only a small nucleus of non-commissioned officers, Coghlan needed to promote directly from confinement; with his lack of knowledge of the men difficult decisions had to be taken about selec-

Table 3 Proposed Establishment York Chasseurs Regiment of Infantry [21]

Colonel (1)	Sergeant Major (1)
Lieutenant Colonel (1)	Quarter Master Sergeant (1)
Major (1)	Paymaster Sergeant (1)
Captains (6)	Armourer Sergeant (1)
Lieutenants (12)	Schoolmaster Sergeant (1)
Ensigns (6)	Sergeants (30) (including 1 Colour Sergeant per company)
Paymaster (1)	Corporals (30)
Adjutant (1)	Drum Major (1)
Quarter Master (1)	Drummers (11)
Surgeon (1)	Privates (570)
Assistant Surgeon (1)	

tion criteria: whether by personal observation, general discussion, prison-ship recommendation, previous military experience and rank held, or maybe even personality and martial bearing. Whatever the criteria it made sense to promote a former Lancaster clerk to paymaster sergeant and Cork gunsmith to armourer sergeant, although more difficult to understand is the promotion of four cavalry and two artillerymen as company sergeants to a regiment of infantry.

Coghlan could hardly have envisaged that in spite all his best endeavours, of those instantly promoted who had survived to be subsequently discharged, all but three, at one time or another, had been reduced to private, several having deserted. One might compare the careers of Michael Fairlee of the York Chasseurs, deserter from the 70th Regiment and instant colour sergeant, with that of Colour Sergeant Thomas Savage, former 4th Garrison Battalion deserter; with Fairlee discharged at Quebec with an untarnished service record, Savage was a private soldier within weeks and a deserter within months.

With the benefit of hindsight, it is clear to see that for a number of those now released the York Chasseurs had almost certainly been seen simply as an avenue for desertion. With Robinson and Stevens in the vanguard (see Table 4, below), 160 desertion attempts had occurred on the Isle of Wight before the regiment departed for Guernsey in August 1814. As for the two aforementioned, they were

Table 4 Casualty Returns of NCOs, Drummers, Fifers and Privates of the York Chasseurs (vanguard of deserters from the Isle of Wight)[22]

			Joined	Deserted	Re-joined
Joseph Robinson	Boston	Seaman	1 February	4 February	February
Samuel Stevens	London	Labourer	1 February	4 February	20 February
Andrew Connell	London	Labourer	1 February	10 February	20 February
Edward Connery	Locklau	Labourer	1 February	10 February	–
Re-taken 11 February, no record of re-joining					
William Richardson	Swansea	Labourer	5 February	10 February	21 February
Thomas Counsell	Wicklow	Labourer	5 February	10 February	21 February
John Slaven	Longford	Labourer	5 February	10 February	21 February
Alexander Corcoran	Tipperary	Labourer	5 February	10 February	–
Re-taken 11 February, no record of re-joining					

soon apprehended, flogged and then re-incarcerated until the regiment embarked for the West Indies, where Stevens died and Robinson successfully deserted.

On the Isle of Wight desertion rates for the York Chasseurs were undoubtedly astonishing. On Thursday 7 July 1814, under cover of the 'National Thanksgiving for Peace in Europe Day', forty-two desertion attempts occurred, seventeen successfully. A trickle had suddenly turned into a flood (see Table 5, pages 24–25).

With desertion on the island commonplace, the *Hampshire Telegraph* did not hesitate in identifying the armed footpad waylaying the military paymaster's servant 'a deserter who wanted money to pay passage from the Island'.[23] This highlights the deserter's predicament: how to escape to the mainland. For most, swimming would be out of the question; to cross the watery miles of the Solent a deserter would have to beg, borrow or steal some kind of vessel. Even so, as in the case of three unfortunates – Rocklidge, Pearce and Sanderson – escape was still not a certainty, particularly when intercepted mid-Solent by Thomas Gloge, Chief Boatman of Coastguard: if only the trio had delayed their crossing for a week or so when Gloge, rheumatic and partially blind, was no longer in the Service!

If deserting the regiment and escaping the Island was not difficult enough there was still the little matter of a 'Twenty Shillings Bounty' and its attraction to opportunist and professional alike. Few, it seems, evaded the entrepreneurial and

List identifying York Chasseurs deserters from the Isle of Wight

Courtesy of The National Archives

...ters from the York Chasseurs —

...d at Landown this 8th day of July 1814.

Signature of Commanding Officer ; And Cophlen Lt Col.

	Head	Face	Eyebrows	Nose	Mouth	Neck	Shoulders	Arms	Hands	Height	Legs	Feet	Hair	Face	Waist	Trousers	
	oval	oval	Lark	prop	prop	prop	Square	Long	prop	Stout	Stout	Large	Sabra	Grey	White	Grey	Well
	oval	oval	brown	large	large	prop	Square	Long	Large	Stout	Stout	Large	Copters	Dry	White	Grey	Stout
	long	long	dark	Prop	Prop	Prop	Square	along	Prop	Stout	Stout	Prop	brown	White	Yellow	Blue	Stout
	Long	Long	Brown	Prop	Prop	Long	Square	Prop	Prop	Prop	Prop	Prop	Sabra	Grey	White	Grey	Prop
	Long	Long	Brown	Prop	Prop	Prop	Square	Prop	Small	Stout	Stout	Prop	brown	Grey	White	Grey	Stout
	Long	Long	Brown	Prop	Prop	Prop	Square	Prop	Prop	Stout	Stout	Prop	brown	Grey	White	Grey	Stout
	Long	long	Grey	Chief	Prop	Prop	Square	Prop	Prop	Stout	Stout	Prop	brown	Grey	White	Grey	Stout
	Long	Long	Fair	Prop	Prop	Chief	Square	Stout	Small	Stout	Stout	Small	brown	Grey	White	Grey	Stout
	Long	Long	Fair	Long	Long	Oval	Square	Stout	prop	Stout	Stout	Small	Sabra	Grey	White	Grey	Stout
	Round	Round	Dark	Stout	Small	Short	Round	Stout	Stout	Long	Stout	Large	brown	Grey	White	Grey	Stout
	round	round	Light	Small	Small	Long	round	Long	Small	Stout	Stout	Small	brown	Grey	White	Grey	Stout
	round	round	Grey	Prop	Prop	Chief	Square	Small	Large	Stout	Stout	Small	Sabra	Grey	White	Grey	Stout
	Large	oval	brown	Prop	Prop	Strait	Square	Large	Small	Stout	Stout	Small	White	Grey	White	Grey	Stout
	Long	Long	brown	Prop	Prop	Long	round	Large	Stout	Stout	prop	prop	Sabra	Grey	White	Grey	Stout
	Long	Long	brown	Large	Large	Long	Square	Long	Large	Stout	Stout	Large	brown	Green	White	Grey	Stout
	Small	Small	brown	prop	prop	Long	Square	Long	prop	Slender	Stout	prop	mill bright	Green	White	Grey	Slender
	oval	oval	Brown	prop	prop	prop	Square	prop	Small	prop	prop	Long	timber	Green	White	Grey	Small
	Small	Small	Brown	Small	prop	prop	round	Stout	prop	Slender	Slender	Small	Sabra	Green	White	Grey	Slender
	Small	Small	Brown	prop	prop	Short	round	Stout	prop	Slender	Slender	Large	Sabra	Green	White	Green	Slender
	round	even	Brown	prop	prop	Stout	Square	prop	Dry	Slender	Slender	Large	Cotton	Green	White	Green	Slender
	round	round	Brown	Large	Large	Long	Square	Long	Large	Stout	Stout	prop	Sabra	Green	White	Grey	Stout

Table 5 Casualty Returns of NCOs, Drummers, Fifers and Privates of the York Chasseurs (showing desertions National Thanksgiving Day, 7 July 1814)[24]

			Deserted	Re-joined
Thomas Harris	Leicestershire	Woolcomber	4 July 1814	No record.
Joseph Walker	Worcester	Labourer	4 July 1814	? date
James Reilley	Essex	Labourer	4 July 1814	15 July
George Thomas	Monmouth	Collier	4 July 1814	No record
William Hamilton	Amagh	Weaver	5 July 1814	No record
Michael Cooney	Queens County	Labourer	5 July 1814	No record
Edward Sweeny	Donagal	Labourer	5 July 1814	No record
Elias Flanders	Glamorgan	Labourer	7 July 1814	No record
Michael Louth	Amagh	Labourer	7 July 1814	No record
David Evans	Montgomery	Labourer	7 July 1814	No record
Charles Thornton	Sligo	Wheelwright	7 July 1814	No record
Timothy Murphy	Kerry	Labourer	7 July 1814	
	Recaptured and confined in the Savoy Military Prison – Rejoined in the West Indies 5 November 1815.			
Joseph Booth	Chester	Carpenter	7 July 1814	15 July
Joseph Chamberlain	Shelton, Leics	Labourer	7 July 1814	15 July
John Hall	Kimbling, Staffs	Tailor.	7 July 1814	20 July
Thomas Cowan.	Tynemouth	Labourer	7 July 1814	15 July
William Philpot	Salop	Labourer	7 July 1814	20 July
James Hartigan	Waterford	Weaver	7 July 1814	No record
John Sanderson	York	Labourer	7 July 1814	15 July
William Lane	Gloucester	Labourer	7 July 1814	27 July
Henry Reeve	Kerry	Shoemaker	7 July 1814	No record
John Farnon	Rosclare	Hatter	7 July 1814	No record
Michael Louth	Amagh	Labourer	7 July 1814	No record
Robert Griffiths	Middlesex	Weaver	7 July 1814	No record
John Haveran	Antrim	Carpenter	7 July 1814	No record
Patrick Kinsella	Carlow	Carpenter	7 July 1814	No record
Thomas McDonald	Donegal	Labourer	7 July 1814	No record
Charles Thorn	Sligo	Wheelwright	7 July 1814	No record
Thomas Lyons	Galway	Labourer	7 July 1814	No record
William Rocklidge	Hants	Labourer	7 July 1814	15 July
John Pearce	Worcs	Labourer	7 July 1814	15 July
Pheonix Gallagher	Sligo	Labourer	7 July 1814	17 July

Table 5 Continued

			Deserted	Re-joined
Michael Kelly	Mayo	Shoemaker	7 July 1814	17 July
William Maine	Devon	Labourer	7 July 1814	24 July
Dmr John Casscallian	Amagh	Frame Work Weaver	7 July 1814	22 July
William Beck	Gloucstershire	Sailor	7 July 1814	22 July
William Gain	Northumberland	Labourer	7 July 1814	22 July
John Hacking	Lancaster	Weaver	7 July 1814	22 July
Owen Hay	Monaghan	Labourer	7 July 1814	22 July
James Jarvis	Nottingham	Labourer	7 July 1814	24 July
George Laroyd	York	Labourer	7 July 1814	24 July
Thomas McGovern	Tyrone	Weaver	7 July 1814	24 July
John McManus	Dublin	Weaver	7 July 1814	24 July
Isaac Mills	Dublin	Blacksmith	7 July 1814	24 July
John Simpson	Derby	Plaisterer	7 July 1814	22 July

professional clutches of Henry A. Brooks – fifteen bounties claimed in a single day – or indeed the illiterate William Brading.

Even John Barrett, private of York Chasseurs, financially benefited by the capture of Private James Patching, a deserter of the 99th Foot. How was Barrett able to identify Patching as a deserter? Simple: he too had deserted from the same regiment just three months earlier. There was some truth to the old adage 'no honour amongst thieves'. Barrett would, perhaps, have cause to be apprehensive of Patching rejoining him in the ranks later on, but how would he be greeted in the barracks: ostracised or congratulated as a shrewd opportunist?

In June 1814 the West Indies Fleet assembled off Cork and while the Island's desertion rate snowballed – 'several men have lately deserted and it's probable that many more will speedily follow this example'[25] – the York Chasseurs' intended destination was suddenly changed from the Cape of Good Hope to the West Indies. As a consequence the regiment exchanged its coarse white drill uniform of recruits for York Chasseurs green, and departed for the island of Guernsey and a transit stay of six weeks, during which ten men deserted, including former colour sergeant, Thomas Savage, now a private, recaptured seventeen months later at Warwick. While men deserted, their benevolent commander, Andrew Coghlan, was encouraging his young officers to party, 'Pooh, pooh! D–n the parades; you must all go – you must all go.'[26] The enjoyable officers' sojourn only ended when, as their young female party companions looked on, the *Camden*, *Sir William Bensley* and *Cyrus* left Guernsey for Falmouth, Cornwall.

They left behind seven successful deserters and five men sick in hospital, of whom four would desert later; these included the indomitable Robert Cottrell,

County of Southampton
~~Borough of~~
~~Portsmouth~~ } to Wit.

To the Collectors of the Land Tax of
the Parish of *Hayling South*
in the said ~~Borough:~~ *County*

WHEREAS *John Pearce* — a *Private* in His
Majesty's *York* Regiment of *Chasseurs* — was this Day apprehended
in the said Parish, and Brought before me, whose Hand and Seal are hereunto
set, One of His Majesty's Justices of the Peace of and for the said ~~Borough~~ *County*, by

Thomas Gloge

for deserting from the said ————— Regiment, and was by me committed for
the said Offence to the Common Gaol of the said Borough, whereupon the said
Thomas Gloge ————— is intitled by Act of Parliament
to the Sum of Twenty Shillings, to be paid by the Collectors of the Land Tax
of the Place where the said Deserter was apprehended, which is to be allowed
them by the Receiver General of the Land Tax, upon passing their Accounts.

These are therefore in His Majesty's Name, and in pursuance of the Act, to
require you upon Receipt hereof to pay unto the said *Thomas Gloge*
the Sum of Twenty Shillings for apprehending the aforesaid Deserter; and for
your so doing, this shall be your sufficient Warrant. Given under my Hand and
Seal this *thirteenth* Day of *August* ————— in the Year of
our Lord One Thousand Eight Hundred and *fourteen*.

Received of Mr. *Thos. Bone*
one of the Collectors of the Land Tax of the
Parish of *South Hayling*
in the said Borough, the above-mentioned Sum
of Twenty Shillings, by me *Gloge*

15 Aug 1814

*Document showing the payment of twenty shillings bounty to Thomas Gloge
for apprehending the deserter Private John Pearce, 1814*

Courtesy of The National Archives

recaptured in Cornwall, who nevertheless managed to escape a second time. Of the five left sick on Guernsey, only the Prussian, Peter Leitner, arrived eventually at St Vincent in November 1815 – only to die six months later. Whereas Private Henry Nunn's extended stay on Guernsey occurred, not through desertion or sickness, but from a drunken escapade attempting to scale the wall of the barrack canteen. Nunn's punishment was twelve months solitary confinement and a transfer to the Royal African Corps on Goree.

Table 6 Casualty Returns of NCOs, Drummers, Fifers and Privates of the York Chasseurs at Cork[27]

Thomas Kingsley	Carlow★	Tallow Chandler	Deserted 30 September 1814
William Adams	Queens County★	Labourer	Deserted 30 September 1814
James Barry	Limerick	Painter	Deserted 30 September 1814
Coffee Edward	Cork★	Shoemaker	Deserted 30 September 1814
Cpl William Duggan	Cork★	Papermaker	Deserted 8 October 1814
John Sullivan	Dunncloe★	Minor	Deserted 8 October 1814
Patrick Fines	Kildare★	Labourer	Deserted 8 October 1814
John Sullivan	Cork★	Minor	Deserted 8 October 1814
Thomas Cowan	Cork★	Butcher	Deserted 10 October 1814
John Sullivan	St Anns, Cork★ _Rejoined at St Vincent or Grenada. 5 November 1815_	Nailor	Deserter 10 October 1814
William Townsend	Oxford	Butcher	Deserted 15 October 1814
William McDougal	Caithness _Recaptured at Barbados 13 April 181_	Labourer	Deserted 15 October 1814
John McManus	Dublin★	Weaver	Deserted 15 October 1814
Isaac Mills	Dublin★	Blacksmith	Deserted 15 October 1814
John Driscol	Waterford★	Labourer	Deserted 16 October 1814
John Watson	Leicester	Stocking maker	Deserted 16 October 1814
John Flannigan	Clare★	Labourer	Deserted 17 October 1814
John Shannegan	Tipperary★	Labourer	Deserted 17 October 1814
John Henry	Not recorded		Deserted 25 October 1814
James Ryan	Sick General Hospital, Cork		Deserted 27 October 1814

★_Irish_

After Guernsey, and a short period at anchor off Falmouth, with the loss of three further deserters, the regiment finally joined the convoy bound for the West Indies assembled off Cork. Before leaving on a short personal visit to Cork himself, Captain Joseph Anderson, the senior regimental officer aboard _Cyrus_, mindful of the proximity of the Irish coastline and the large Irish contingent on board, took the precaution of banning all shore leave. In his absence, however, using his master's laundry as a ploy to persuade a young and inexperienced duty officer to allow him on shore, Anderson's personal servant, John Henry, promptly deserted. On his return to the *Cyrus* and informed of his servant's desertion, a frantic Anderson dashed below to his cabin where, deep in his sea chest, nestled the £400 regimental fund. Finding the door locked but with a regimental officer outside with the key, Anderson learnt to his relief that Henry had handed the keys to the officer, stressing that 'none but his master should receive them'. With not a coin missing it suggests that despite the gulf between condemned soldier and regimental officer the esprit de corps of the 24th of Foot ensured Henry's loyalty .

At Cork, although anchored offshore, with posted sentries, vigilant commissioned and non-commissioned officers, when the regiment finally departed there were twenty more lost to desertion, fourteen of whom were Irish (see Table 6, page 27). One, the unfortunate John Sullivan, was later recaptured in the city of Bristol. Of the fifteen men left sick, two died, five successfully deserted, seven rejoined later in the West Indies, and a chronically unfit Private John Tully was sent to the Isle of Wight for discharge. As for James McDougall, either he was inept, stupid or simply unfortunate. What explains the action of a man who, having successfully deserted to spend six months as a mariner, with practically the entire world to hide in, manages to get himself recaptured stepping ashore at Barbados 'disguised as a sailor'? What made him go ashore? Surely he must have known the regiment's destination prior to his desertion. And yet for all his undoubted foolhardiness, and with a back scarred from four further unsuccessful desertion attempts, he at least survived the West Indies.

Two days out from Cork gale force winds forced the Fleet to seek the sanctuary of Bantry Bay's calmer waters; then tragedy struck, when the *Baring*, with the 40th Regiment aboard, hit the rocky entrance, went broadside and was totally wrecked within minutes. With each ship fighting for its own survival, Captain Joseph Anderson looked on helplessly as fifteen men, women and children perished, and a near naked officer's wife, baby clasped close to her breast, desperately pleaded for rescue. The mother survived but her infant was lost.

In late October the *Baring*'s replacement arrived; 200 merchantmen under the protection of *H.M.S. Sultan*, the fifty-gun frigate *Shamrock* and the gun-brig *Crescent*, finally sailed for the West Indies where the York Chasseurs disembarked at Carlisle Bay, Barbados, and occupied St Ann's Barracks seven weeks later.

In June 1815, with Europe ostensibly at peace, but with all Isle of Wight military prison ships filled nigh to capacity, further 'unattached deserters' were now released to the York Chasseurs depot, but with a regimental infrastructure now able to cope with a large influx. On this occasion, rather than chance their mass desertion before the regiment sailed for St Vincent in September, a wary Commander-in-Chief would order their removal to the added security of Fort Cumberland, Portsmouth. Even Fort Cumberland failed to contain Privates Dunlop, Gilroy and John Guest, however, of whom only Guest would be subsequently re-captured, flogged, returned to the hulks, dispatched to St Vincent to die in Jamaica.

Before the recruits had even landed, with adverse winds impeding the ship's short passage to Portsmouth, for safety reasons forcing it to anchor overnight in Stokes Bay a mile or so from the harbour's entrance, five determined escapees slipped overboard. At night, facing a long cold swim in strong tidal waters, it may be that only William Garney, recaptured seventeen months later in Norfolk, was the sole survivor.

When in November 1815, *Mary*, *Boadicca*, *Mariner* and *Promise* finally arrived at St Vincent, in addition to the regiment's new commanding officer, Lieutenant Colonel John Ewart, there were also twenty-three sergeants, twenty corporals, eleven drummers and 487 privates as augmented reinforcements. While the Regimental Monthly Record efficiently records six men dying at sea, no notation exists regarding desertions prior to departure. At St Vincent, Ewart now had command of a regiment, ten companies strong, but only temporarily as it turned out, as the *Mary* and five companies under the command of Major Dumas, were soon on their way to Grenada, a two-day sea passage.

Table 7 Nationalities of Officers and Men of the York Chasseurs[28]

	Officers	Sergeants	Drummers	Corporals	Privates
English	20	31	10	28	413
Scotch	5	6	4	8	77
Irish	9	15	5	10	342
Foreigners	-	1	1	-	2
Total	34	53	20	46	834

Of particular interest is the Inspection Report of 6 November 1815, the day after the regiment's additional replacements arrival at St Vincent, a report revealing not only the regiment at an absolute peak of 987 officers and men, but also its composition of nationals, of whom the most interesting were the Irish – less than fifty percent of the whole, but consistently to the fore of offences, particularly desertion (see Table 7, above). In addition the Report also provides a brief but interest-

Table 8 Recorded Height and Age of York Chasseurs[29]

(Three companies of the Right Wing – height in feet and inches)				
Height	*Sergeants*	*Corporals*	*Drummers*	*Privates*
6'	1	-	-	
5' 11"	1	-	-	1
5' 10"	3	2	-	2
5' 9"	4	1	12	
5' 8"	3	1	-	25
5' 7"	6	2	2	20

Table 8 Continued

Height	Sergeants	Corporals	Drummers	Privates
5' 6"	2	2	1	35
5' 5"	-	2	1	39
Under	1	3	1	54
Total	21	13	6	188

Ages	Sergeants	Corporals	Drummers	Privates
40	2	-	-	-
35	5	-	-	-
30	-	4	2	6
25	9	3	1	78
20	3	4	3	85
18	2	2	26	-
Under	-	-	-	-
Total	21	13	6	195

ing insight into the general stature of the early nineteenth-century British soldier (see Table 8, above).

As for the condemned soldiers, Scots, Irish, English or other nationals, whether serving in Africa, East or West Indies, by late 1815 the term of enlistment became a little less daunting. At least now a transfer into a reputable line regiment became possible, providing of course a commanding officer could attest as to his 'Seven years of confirmed Good and Faithful Service since joining the regiment'; in reality, in a regiment where of the 49 new arrivals in June 1816 twelve deserted within weeks, two within months, and three within the year, it would appear few York Chasseurs would have qualified. Most certainly not Andrew Leonard and William Pugh, both sentenced to 'Life in the Royal Navy for Highway Robbery' within the very first month of their arrival.

It was a regimental reputation hardly to be enhanced when the *Trave, Dover* and *Thames* transport vessels, with a seriously depleted 2nd (Queen's) Regiment aboard, took 300 prison ship 'unattached deserters off from Cowes as reinforcements'. Three months later in Barbados, plagued by desertion, the Queen's commanding officer rather ill-advisedly and without permission transferred thirty-three of his incorrigibles to the York Chasseurs, admittedly not before inflicting 1,000 lashes on thirteen, 800 on one and 600 on another (see Table 9, opposite). Several months later, when news of the action finally reached Horse Guards, the Queen's erring commanding officer suffered the distinct displeasure of a distant, but extremely infuriated, Commander-in-Chief.

It is quite impossible to approve of an arrangement of this nature, and I am to observe that were it not for the inconvenience which must attend the Measure, HRH would give Orders for those Men being returned to their former Regts. It is presumed that these Men are part of the Numbers attached to the Queens on its leaving the I.O.W, and this Regt is but recently arrived in the West Indies. It is not understood on what principle or ground they have been transferred to a Regt employed on the same Service, unless it was considered that they were more likely to be brought to a sense of duty in the York Chasseurs, than in the Queens Regt, an admission on the part of the Commanding Officer, which would be in no respect creditable to himself, or in favor of the discipline of the Regt.[30]

Table 9 Deserters and Punishment s in 2nd (Queen's) Regiment of Foot[31]

Name	Regiment	Where	Date	Offence	Punishment
James Lee	2nd Foot	Barbados	20 June 1816	Desertion	800 lashes
John Doyle	2nd Foot	Barbados	22 July 1816.	Desertion	1000 lashes & D★
George Tanner	2nd Foot	Barbados	22 July 1816	Desertion	1000 lashes & D★
Joseph Morris	2nd Foot	Barbados	23 July 1816	Desertion	1000 lashes
William Burns	2nd Foot	Barbados	23 July 1816	Desertion	1000 lashes
John Byrne	2nd Foot	Barbados	23 July 1816	Desertion	1000 lashes
James Long	2nd Foot	Barbados	23 July 1816	Desertion	1000 lashes
William McIndoe	2nd Foot	Barbados	24 July 1816	Desertion	1000 lashes.
Thomas Watson	2nd Foot	Barbados	24 July 1816	Desertion	1000 lashes & D★
Thomas Redman	2nd Foot	Barbados	25 July 1816	Desertion	1000 lashes & D★
John Johnson	2nd Foot	Barbados	25 July 1816	Desertion	1000 lashes & D★
James Cahill	2nd Foot	Barbados	25 July 1816	Desertion.	1000 lashes & D★
Peter Burns	2nd Foot	Barbados	25 July 1816	Desertion	600 lashes
Edward Dunn	2nd Foot.	Barbados	30 July 1816	Desertion	1000 lashes & D★
William Dodd	2nd Foot	Barbados	31 July 1816	Desertion	1000 lashes & D★

★*Tattoed with the letter 'D' under the left armpit.*

In fairness to the Queen's much-maligned commanding officer, what regiment would not want to rid itself of an incorrigible like Edward Dunn, a man who in spite of a 1,000 stroke lashing and a transfer still made six further attempts at desertion until he eventually succeeded. As for William McIndoe, the cat-o'-nine-tails may have lost its powers of persuasion, for, having received 1,000 lashes from the Queen's and an additional 800 from his new regiment, he still successfully deserted. And who would not be in awe of the resilient James Lee who, with 800 lashes from the Queens and then an unspecified number as a fivefold York Chasseurs unsuccessful deserter, almost certainly carried the scars of at least 2,000 lashes into discharge.

Upholding the traditions of the regiment, of the 231 men to arrive in the West Indies between June 1816 and May 1817, many had attempted desertion, and 75 deserted successfully. A good number of these almost certainly returned to Britain, although we can only identify eight of those recaptured; of these only John Martin (alias Vensmore) and James Slattery returned to Jamaica and the regiment. Martin went on to successfully desert within months; Slattery, with two failed desertions behind him and scars of the floggings on his back, reluctantly stayed until his discharge; and Edward O'Reilly, confined in London's Savoy Military Prison suffering a debilitating leg ulcer, after a 'Surgical Examination' was given his 'Certificate of Discharge'.

In December 1816 survivors of Waterloo, John McLeod, formerly of the 79th Regiment, James Stewart the 32nd Regiment and Michael Galvin, of the 40th Regiment, stepped ashore at Jamaica as condemned soldiers. McLeod would be dead inside two years, James Stewart successfully deserted, and Michael Galvin, with one unsuccessful desertion at Jamaica behind him, was later discharged at Quebec.

While the 104-strong consignment arriving at Jamaica in May 1817 had been the last of the major reinforcements, when the *Brailsford*, *Glory* and *Christian* conveyed the 6th Battalion of the 60th Regiment away from Jamaica in August 1817, twenty-seven men, presumably under constraint of previous sentencing, had been left behind as Chasseurs. One consequence was that the regiment now assumed a decidedly more cosmopolitan flavour, with two Germans, a Prussian, a

Table 10 Desertion Record of Mathew Schwartz

5th Battalion. 60th Regiment		
Deserted 5 February 1810	Rejoined 28 February	No punishment records held
6th Battalion, 60th Regiment		
Deserted 29 April 1813	Rejoined 30 April	No punishment record held
Deserted 20 July 1814	Rejoined the same day	No punishment record held
Deserted 13 January 1815	Rejoined 16 January	No punishment record held
Deserted 19 March 1815	Rejoined 23 March	Awarded 800 lashes, 600 lashes remitted
Deserted 1 November 1815	Rejoined 3 November	No punishment record held
Deserted 12 January 1816	Rejoined 30 May	No punishment record held
Deserted 29 August 1816	Rejoined 28 September	600 lashes, 4 October
Transferred to the York Chasseurs 25 May 1817		
Deserted 6 June 1817	Rejoined the same day	No punishment record held
Deserted 25 August 1817	Rejoined the next day	300 lashes, 2 September
Deserted 3 October 1817	Rejoined the next day	300 lashes, 10 October
Deserted 2 May 1818	Rejoined 13 May	No punishment record held
Deserted 2 October 1818	No record of rejoining	

Table 11 Men joining York Chasseurs – from Pay and Muster lists

	Date	Number	Cumulative Total
Released from military prison-ship and volunteers	1 February 1814	211	211
Released from military prison-ship and volunteers	5 February 1814	196	407
Released from military prison-ship and volunteers	7 March 1814	121	528
Released from military prison-ship and volunteers	25 March 1814	152	680
Arrived at Arrived at St Vincent	November 1815	535	1215
New Brunswick Fencible Infantry. From Canada	February 1816	1	1216
Arrived at St Vincent	June 1816	49	1265
Transferred from the 2nd (Queen's) Regiment	September 1816	33	1298
'Gentlemen Volunteers' at Jamaica	September 1816	2	1300
Arrived at Jamaica	December 1816	78	1378
From 101st Foot at Jamaica	December 1816	1	1379
From 101st at Jamaica	February 1817	3	1382
Arrived at Jamaica	May 1817	104	1486
Transferred from the 6th Bn 60th Foot at Jamaica	May 1817	27	1513
Transferred from the 1st European Garrison Company	May 1817	11	1524
Volunteer from the 101st at Jamaica	June 1817	1	1525
Arrived at Jamaica	January 1818	4	1529
Transfer from the 99th Foot	June 1818	1	1530

Spaniard, a Frenchman, a Dutchman, a Pole, a Hungarian and a Turk, not forgetting Alexander Orleff and William Krutzhous, of unknown nationalities.

Standing head and shoulders above even such persistent deserters as George Hamilton and Charles Nowland, both of whom had received an estimated 1,800 lashes apiece, was the German, Mathew Schwartz (see Table 10, opposite), who,

Table 12 Effective Strength of the York Chasseurs 1814–1819

	Jan	Feb	March	April	May	June	July	Aug	Sept	Oct	Nov	Dec
1814	–	360	517	604	603	571	528	525	505	484	At Sea	494
1815	483	487	499	484	479	453	NR	NR	NR	NR	NR	944
1816	NR	NR	917	NR	903	NR	892	906	908	810	NR	877
1817	864	849	835	831	820	955	941	926	904	884	865	850
1818	836	837	835	818	811	809	NR	786	773	765	750	NR
1819	729	717	NR	654	617	575	At Sea	Disbanded				

N.R. – Not Recorded

having enlisted at Halifax, Nova Scotia, for the 5th Battalion, 60th (Loyal American) Regiment in May 1803, had first deserted in Portugal in February 1810, and, five months later, classified a 'Suspected Man', was sentenced to the Isle of Wight prison ships, whence he had been shipped to Jamaica and the 6th Battalion the following year.

Schwartz, a persistent deserter with the 60th Regiment but now of the York Chasseurs, unsuccessfully deserted on four separate occasions before his fifth – and thirteenth overall – succeeded. A man apparently proficient in the art of deserting, but deficient in the skills of evasion, with a back scarred from minimum of 4,000 lashes, considered freedom worthy of great pain.

With the twenty-seven men from the 60th Regiment, eleven 'volunteers' from a recently disbanded 1st European Garrison and six late transfers from England, recruitment into the York Chasseurs would now cease. And as a consequence of men joining, being transferred, discharged, successfully deserting, being recaptured, getting sick or dying, the number available for duty, or 'Effectives', can best be described as being in a constant state of flux (see Tables 11 and 12 on page 33).

Chapter Two

Prison-hulks and Castle Walls

With desertion rife at the British Army's main receiving depot at Chatham in July 1801, 3,000 new recruits had been marched through Kent, Sussex and Hampshire, towards Portsmouth, to ship them on to the Isle of Wight, where 'with its newly constructed accommodation and surrounding waters would prove a bar to desertion and an ideal site for the training of new levies'.[32]

During the march, despite the ever-vigilant eyes of non-commissioned officers, a number of recruits may very well have deserted, those being re-captured most likely continuing their march in the column's wake alongside those deserters already under sentence from Chatham. Their march finally over, recruit and deserter would now separate, the recruits to the Isle of Wight and their new custom-built barracks and deserters to remain at Portsmouth under strict confinement.

While the origins of the Portsmouth and Woolwich convict hulks are all pretty well known, arising from the collapse of the convict markets in Virginia and Maryland after the American War of Independence, where convicts were sent as cheap labour, little is known of the early military prison ship system. Evidence suggests that by late 1803 the 6th Rate★ frigate *Medea* had been employed as a military prison ship on the Isle of Wight's river Medina, betwixt East and West Cowes, presumably to accommodate an anticipated increase in offenders.

> Hampshire Chronicle, Saturday November 12th 1803
> The punishment of flogging for desertion seems now to have been abolished and a wise regulation substituted in its stead, that of confining deserters on board a prison ship, until an occasions offers for sending to the West Indies or some settlement abroad.

From the much fragmented records, however, it is clear that the *Dido*[33] replaced

---

★ Ships were rated according to their armaments: 1st rate, 100 guns or above; 2nd Rate, 90–98 guns; 3rd Rate, 64–80 guns; 4th Rate, 50–60 guns; 5th Rate, 32–44 guns, and 6th Rate, 20–28 guns.

the *Medea* in 1804 and the much-travelled New South Wales penal colony supply vessel *Buffalo*[34] became the second prison ship in 1809; finally in January 1814 the *Volorous*[35] hulked sloop became the third.

In spite of the dearth of evidence, sufficient exists to suggest that despair and desperation had not been the sole privilege of the convict hulk, particularly after the success of Lieutenant Whalley of the 18th Regiment in preventing a mass breakout of prisoners who 'To show the length they intended to go, if necessary to affect their purpose, had actually sworn themselves to secrecy, by drinking their own blood in cold water'.[36]

With the Adjutant General's office pleading for funds 'Just to preserve their health during the forthcoming sea passage, as Arrangements are now in progress for transferring about 1000 Deserters to the Corps Stationed Abroad',[37] while also requesting surplus and obsolete clothing 'As the deficient state of clothing that deserters generally arrive in, makes such articles indispensably to the Health and Cleanliness of their wearers'[38] conditions had undoubtedly been dire. As for the prison ships' victuals, comparing the Home Office's salt pork and beef, thick oatmeal porridge (burgoo) enjoyed by the hulk convict with the bread, beef, pork, peas, and, occasionally, butter, cheese or rice of the soldier, even a confined prison-ship soldier, it seems that trained soldiers, albeit deserters and thieves, were still regarded as useful and worth keeping fit and healthy.

In terms of accommodation, the relatively unwholesome Portsmouth-based ships *Captivity* and *Portland*, both 3rd Rates, and the 4th Rated *Laurel* contained a mere 1,000 convicts between them; three smaller, 6th Rated military prison ships, confined more than 1,700. Despite such disparities, military discipline, scrubbed and regularly aired hammocks, reduced length of confinement and the robustness of a soldierly constitution, seemingly avoided any outbreak of hulk fever.

Like the Home Office hulk convict, had the military prisoner also been shackled? Maybe the witness of Sergeant Morris of the 73rd Regiment provides an answer; escorting a deserter to the *Dido* and unexpectedly meeting an old comrade, he commented on his plight but failed to mention the presence of manacles. And surely only a madman would jump into the sea heavily shackled.

> On Sunday last four prisoners confined on board the Buffalo Prison-ship stationed at the entrance of the River, attempted to make their escape by jumping overboard and swimming the shore. The sentinels gave alarm by firing at the prisoners; and a number of the inhabitants of East and West Cows assembled on the shore, and saw three of them secured, and the forth, unfortunately, drowned. – This is not the instance of the prisoners confined on board the Dido and Buffalo prison-ships attempting to escape, to which they have been tempted by these ships being anchored so near the shore. The Number at present in confinement is nearly six-hundred.[39]

Unlike Home Office hulks where allegedly wary warders seldom ventured into the dark and dangerous world of the convict, aboard military prison ships military discipline would certainly have applied throughout. The last word goes to the

Hampshire Telegraph, always ready to advise the War Office on security: 'If the ships were moored further off, it would considerably decrease the temptation to escape, and the fears of the inhabitants for their safety would not be so often excited'.[40]

Towards the end of 1813, with victory looming in Europe, plans were already under way to replace timbered-hulked prison ships with the ten-foot thick walls of Portchester Castle. Positioned to the north of Portsmouth Harbour, the castle had proved a convenient prisoner-of-war camp since the mid-seventeenth-century and, up to 1802 and the Peace of Amiens, had served as a place of confinement for 'French Revolutionary' prisoners. Following eight years as an Ordnance Depot the castle now replaced the nearby wooden hulks as a place of confinement for French prisoners of war. With Bonaparte's defeat, abdication in 1814 and rapid repatriation of French prisoners, the castle became next a reception and hospital area for the army's sick and wounded arriving at Portsmouth.

With all the sick and wounded dispatched back to duty, hospitalised, invalided or dead, and with the Treasury ready to arrange a new lease with its private owners in August 1814 Colonel Mainwaring, 'an old and highly esteemed Officer,'[41] was given orders to investigate turning Portchester Castle into a 'Depot for Deserters'. Despite his best efforts and with so many 'previously superfluous' but now necessary internal fixtures auctioned, not until February 1815 did Horse Guards finally appoint a staff captain, two lieutenants and six staff sergeants to oversee the castle's transition. Delayed by a multitude of necessary alterations, it was not until September 1816 that Lieutenant Colonel Williams, the depot's new commandant, 200 men of the 28th Regiment and 1,000 former prison ship charges, were finally settled behind the castle's thick and forbidding stone walls.

A month before, an intransigent Mainwaring delayed the transition further when with 170 of his charges considered 'Unfit for Further Military Service' and loath to release so many 'potential beggars and thieves' onto the local community he doggedly procrastinated until additional funds ensured the homeward journey of each 'unfit' convicted soldier. Though Treasury Funds were tight, profit could always be made out of the suffering of others and while Colonel Mainwaring pleaded 'for even the barest of Necessaries', others had been doing quite nicely thank you.

> Messrs Pittis & Wadmore – Newport Town, Isle of Wight.
> 'For Necessaries supplied to sundrae Culprits and Deserters transported to regiments abroad. – £410.10s.10d'.[42]

While the majority may have been deserters, the castle would also contain a variety of offenders. Amongst them, eighteen men sent originally from Messina to Fort Cumberland, who, with the castle now 'prepared for the Reception of Deserters',[43] had taken up residence until leaving for the Royal African Corps; their offence, 'having willfully mutilated themselves'.[44] Men who, 'while not to be considered either as Prisoners or kept in Confinement, should nevertheless, not be allowed to quit the Barracks in which they are placed, or permitted to conduct themselves in an Irregular or Disorderly manner'.[45] Though not officially classified as prisoners, it seems their stay in the castle was intentionally made as unpleasant as possible, 'they are to be employed as Privivers and Scavengers'.[46]

Almost certainly joining the eighteen had been William Brown, marched from Durham as a deserter of the 91st and 'self mutilator'. A man it seems the military powers had thought worthy of special attention. 'William Brown being represented as a notoriously bad Character and known to have committed several Robberies, it will necessary that Special Measures be adopted to prevent his escape'.[47]

Fortunately, for both the mental and physical well-being of non-commissioned officers, perhaps even the men of the York Chasseurs themselves, of those joining from Portchester, the notorious Oliver would not be amongst them.

> Among the deserters is Oliver, a man of no less notoriety in Ireland, as a mail and coach robber, during the last ten years, than remarkable for his bodily strength and activity. He commenced his lawless career at the age of fifteen years, by robbing a mail coach of fourteen hundred pounds and is worth thousands of pounds. He at length became the Captain of a gang of twenty one, who in a rencontre in the woods with a party of the 35th Regiment, actually beat the soldiers off. He has often been indicted for such offences, but the terror which his desperate character has created, deterred witness from appearing against him. He was at last taken by strategy, and claimed as a deserter by two regiments, in which he served for a short time. He was handcuffed and pinioned, in the passage from Cork and until he arrived at Portchester.[48]

By early 1817, with Europe at peace for almost two years and a dramatic reduction of the military, plans were already under way to transfer the castle back to private ownership, but only after disposal arrangements could be made for the occupants. Therefore, during March, and with upwards of a 1,000 deserters incarcerated, 700 had been dispatched for the Cape of Good Hope and the West Indies, including 104 to the York Chasseurs at Jamaica and, a month later, a further 100 apiece to the 32nd Foot and Royal African Corps.

Towards the end of 1817, with a further 200 men dispatched to the Royal York

Table 13 Staff Pay and Muster Lists, Portchester Castle, 1819[49]

Lieutenant Colonel	D. Williams
Staff Lieutenants	A. Moorhead
	J. Paxton
Paymaster	Wm. Tinling
Staff Sergeants	Benjamin Putt
	John Hunter
	James Maxwell
	Thomas Murphy
	John Williams
	George Dodd
	Robert Whipp

'A Birds Eye View of Portchester Castle, November 1817' (Re-produced by permission of
Portsmouth City Museum), though amateurish, it still offers an interesting insight into the
castle. For, where once had stood stone prison buildings and enclosed airing yards, there is
now well-cultivated grass. Where now one might hear the thud of leather on willow, in years
past and under the eyes of non-commissioned and commissioned Staff Officers, condemned
red-coated infantry and blue-coated artillerymen had exercised. To the north, a cultivated
vegetable plot had perhaps supplemented a bland prison diet, and, to the east, where the
wooded palisade protects a seemingly derelict church, can be seen an officer exercising his
horse, perhaps Lieutenant Colonel Williams, the Commandant.

Rangers, 200 to the Royal West India Rangers and 60 to the Royal African Corps,
and with the Commander-in-Chief now ordering all new deserters back to their
regiment 'for the purpose of being proceeded against according to the custom of
the Service,'[50] the demise of Portchester Castle as a depot for deserters was now in
sight. Finally, July 1819, with all remaining prisoners dispatched to the 2nd and
3rd Battalions of the 60th, a vacant castle could now be transferred back to the private ownerships of the Thistlewaite Family.

Chapter Three

The West Indies and Saving Guadeloupe for Louis XVIII

On 14 December 1814, safely at anchor in Carlisle Bay, the newcomers could now gaze with interest, perhaps even apprehension, at the distant foliage-covered rolling hills of Barbados. Burdened down with kit, hastened by the raucous bellows of non-commissioned officers, soldiers vacated their vessels' cramp and oft-times damp accommodation for St Ann's Barracks, their new quarters overlooking Bridgetown, the island's capital.

Scrambling ashore, garbed in wholly unsuitable clothing for the West Indies, perhaps 'Old Hands' like the 'Hollanders' Roovers and Buyss, had already warned them of what lay ahead: a north-east to south-west wind from February to May that would keep the temperature both pleasant and healthy; of the more disagreeable, but not particularly unwholesome high sun from June through to early August; after which, having experienced August's destructive hurricane season, thinking life and conditions could not get any worse, along came the heavy rainfalls and oppressive atmosphere of September right through to December. Although the newcomer might at least take comfort in the knowledge that St Ann's Barracks would enjoy the benefit of a refreshing and constant sea breeze.

What's more, for the newcomer used to campaigning, 'O'er the hills and o'er the main. Through Flanders, Portugal and Spain',[51] service in the West Indies would be a far different experience. Away would go the long and fatiguing marches, and in their place, drill and parade in the early morning and evening coolness. At first light, usually between four and five o'clock in the morning, sleepy men would be cordially invited to the parade ground where, before the rising sun became dangerously unhealthy, under a drill instructor's watchful eyes, possibly even an early rising officer, they would labour with all the intricacies of small arms drill. Company upon company, formed in columns two deep, exhaustively performing the battlefield manoeuvres as stipulated by the 'Rules and Regulations for the Movements of His Majesty's Infantry'. At the practice-butts men bit paper cartridges, rammed ball, powder and wadding home, and, with muskets raised, waited the command – Volley Fire! – and God help the hapless individual who inadvertently discharged the ramrod along with the ball. Yet, in spite of all the parade ground manoeuvres and musketry practice, the Inspecting General had still seemed somewhat unimpressed by the York Chasseurs 'want of celerity and precision in the changes of position and formation and, as for the firing, loading and levelling, the regiment exhibited but little precision'.[52] In mitigation, he would at least concede that the confines of the parade ground were 'probably not conducive to good military precision'.[53]

Unimpressed by their prowess as British soldiers, his comments pale into insignificance when it came to their general calibre, 'holding out but small hope for reformation in their morals for, though in general, well sized, they had that appearance which disease and dissolute habits produce in the countenance'.[54] As for non-commissioned officers, 'though not of the first description', no criticism could be made of their 'attentiveness'. Praise was reserved for the fifers and drummers who, 'Attentive to their Duty, and considering the time the Regiment has been formed, were found perfect in their beats of the drum, and fifes play in correct time'.[55]

Unlike Spain and Portugal where men marched and confronted the enemy, garrison duty in the West Indies was, it seems, more of unmitigated boredom, interspaced with repetitive but disciplined drudgery. With both morning parade and breakfast over, if not allocated guard or piquet duty, the remainder of the working day had probably been spent on personal kit detail, scavenging, clearing or at times, construction fatigues. Although for the more exhausting of tasks there were always the freed and enslaved labourers of the Black Pioneers. Men with such fascinating names such as 'December', 'Dublin', 'Duke', 'Wednesday', 'Friday One', 'Friday Two', 'Friday Three' and 'Friday Four'.

> We do certify that the sum of One Hundred Seventy Seven Pounds 14/5d Army Sterling charged in the Public Accounts of the York Chasseurs from the 25th Day of December 1816 to the 24th Day of March 1817, inclusive, for Black Pioneers, has been received by us from John McIntyre Esq. Paymaster York Chasseurs. Dated at Kingston, Jamaica Seventh Day of April 1817.
> Adam Robertson – Contractors[56]

Campaigning, a soldier ate when and wherever, whereas on garrison duty in the West Indies a soldier appears to have enjoyed a more regular diet, with a breakfast consisting of cocoa and bread; at noon and for the last full meal of the day, a fresh meat broth or even a soup of boiled salt meat, presumably supplemented by local peas, yams, potatoes, mango, pomegranate and avocado. All at a cost of five pence *per diem* (12 pennies=one shilling); and if the punishment records are anything to go by, all washed down with rum at a cost of a penny a gill (quarter of a pint).

Unfortunately, like soldiers throughout history, in the West Indies they also suffered the dishonesty of merchants, the bumbling of bureaucrats, and in all probably both. In fact, so poor was the quality of flour and packaging, and so irregular was the dispatching, that Lieutenant General Sir James Leith urgently recommended:

1. The Flour should be of what is nominated the best Superfree.
2. That the same should be packed in good water-tight new casks, and if possible to be lined inside with paper in the manner in which the French pack their Flour.
3. That some better arrangements should be made for finding the supplies from England.[57]

As for a soldier's living conditions, while not as cramped as on board the vessel that brought him, with sleeping hammocks slung just twenty-two to twenty-three inches-apart, barrack-room life still meant a cheek by jowl existence. If fact, not until 1827, with the introduction of the iron bedstead, was a soldier's personal space increased to three foot three inches, so that 220 men slept where 344 had slung hammocks before.

While the York Chasseurs gradually accustomed themselves to life in the West Indies in far away Paris in March 1815 Bonaparte triumphantly returned and the newly restored Louis XVIII hastily departed. Six or seven weeks later at Barbados, with only unsubstantiated rumours to go on, General Sir James Leith now faced a dilemma: how could the French King's authority be safeguarded over the recently restored colonies of Guadeloupe and Martinique?

As days became weeks and news of events in Europe became more widespread, developments now turned on the character of Rear Admiral Linois, the Governor of Guadeloupe. Would he remain steadfast to the cause of King Louis, or succumb to revolutionary fervour? No such dilemma existed on Martinique where, with a trustworthy militia servicing the cannons, the seventy-five-year-old ardent Royalist and Quiberon veteran, Compte de Vaugiraud, read the latest dispatches to his 400 regulars. Urging them to stay and defend the island in the King's name, they answered, as anticipated, 'Vive l' Empereur'. Vaugiraud had them instantly disarmed, placed under guard of the militia, and marched towards a purposely-waiting homeward-bound vessel: 'So they could entertain a cause more dear to them'.[58]

With Martinique secure, an assertive Leith, having previously dispatched a British man-of-war to cruise off Guadeloupe, now cautioned an unpredictable Linois against any shift in allegiance. As crisis loomed, thankfully for the cause of the restored Bourbon's, two resolute British commanders were undoubtedly in the right place at the right time. On land, Leith, a general who had commanded a Brigade at Corunna, suffered wounds leading the 5th Division at Salamanca and again during the battle of Sans Sebastian; then, with his health fully restored and Europe at peace, appointed Commander-in-Chief of the Windward and Leeward station.

At sea was the indomitable Rear Admiral Sir Charles Durham, who, commanding a completely out-gunned *H.M.S. Defiance* at Trafalgar, overcame and captured a vastly superior French First Rate. Leaving Portsmouth for the West Indies aboard *H.M.S. Venerable* in December 1813, he could hardly have imagined the *Venerable* and the frigate *Cyane* arriving at Barbados six or seven weeks later shepherding two French frigates, the *Alcemene* and *Iphigenie*, captured en route off Madeira.

As each day passed, Leith was more concerned about the dependability of Linois Fully conscious that his or Durham's presence on Guadeloupe might inflame an already fraught situation, he astutely selected Captain Thomas Moody of the Royal Engineers, an officer well versed in the art of military topography and West Indies service, as his personal emissary. With no time to lose, Moody made preparations for departure, but not before carrying out Leith's instruction to tactfully inform Admiral Durham of his Commander-in-Chief's correspondence. Expressing approval, Durham nevertheless handed Moody his own, decidedly more robust communiqué. Moody, the subordinate officer, rather audaciously recommended the more cautious approach of his General.

> As the Rear Admiral, in this letter which I was to deliver, proposed to Compte de Linois that no Batteries should be erected at the Saintes,[59] – and that the Rear Admiral should keep a vessel of war there, on which point I had no instructions from your Excellency, therefore, I requested the Rear Admiral, to permit me to exercise the discretionary power of delivering the letter or not, as circumstances might be. His Excellency the Rear Admiral acceded to this proposal, and I took the letter.[60]

Moody, Linois, and his senior advisors met clandestinely on a Guadeloupe beachhead, though significantly Adjutant General Eugene Boyer, Linois's ardent Bonapartist deputy, remained conspicuously absent. The discussion led to Moody conceding that a British warship should patrol off Guadeloupe; then he negotiated the nearby safe haven of Saintes for the very same warship, of which, with the hurricane season nearly upon them and with Admiral Durham's letter still unopened, an elated Moody commented: 'That I regard this is one of the greatest consequence, in as much as the Saintes unquestionably may be considered as the Key to Guadeloupe, when the power possessing the Saintes, has, at the same time, a naval superiority.'[61]

Before parting, however, Linois took Moody aside to confide that because of his lost authority if Durham or Leith had landed in person an armed anti-British, anti-Bourbon revolt would almost certainly have occurred. Leith's choice of emissary certainly became justified after several English residents and a 'zealous French friend of Louis XVIII',[62] covertly approached with intelligence that the military, militia, artisans and seafarers had all been eager for revolt, though the free-trading planters had been neutral; that the efficiently officered regular garrison was in a constant state of reinforcement by former military colonists from France; and, more significantly, there was speculation that with the island's cannon finally repaired, a *coup d'etat* would hand command to Colonel Boyer.

Moody's attention was also drawn to the number of French vessels leaving the island, armed with American Papers, probably returning to France in support of the Empire. In fact, even as they spoke, it was rumoured that the frigate *L'Erigone* had been carrying plans for an intended revolt back to Napoleon. From all intelligence gleaned, Moody could but conclude 'That everything I saw and heard tended to prove that the present Government has not the power to support the Interests of Louis XVIII against the slightest movement in favour of Buonaparte'.[63]

Several weeks later, as Moody predicted, a compliant Linois raised the tricolour to a twenty-one gun celebratory cannonade. Also, as predicted, while the colonists greeted the appearance of 'long concealed regimental eagles',[64] with 'sheer unconstrained and unostentatious celebration',[65] it was Colonel Boyer they applauded for 're-establishing the island's Imperial Dynasty',[66] ironically on the very day British and French soldiers were dying at Waterloo.

With political upheaval on shore and *H.M.S. Venerable* cruising nearby, an overoptimistic Durham decided to dispatch a ship's officer ashore with orders to investigate and parley if possible. A mission doomed from the start, however, with Linois declaring 'we have all rallied round the tri-coloured Flag and are determined to support the Emperor'.[67] Durham's intimidated emissary, realising that further dialogue was futile, rapidly returned to his ship.

To make matters worse, almost simultaneously and to the great embarrassment of the Royal Navy, a small force of revolutionary insurrectionists, evading a patrolling British brig-of-war, had raised the 'Imperial Tricolour' over the nearby island of Saintes; a rebellious gesture extinguished by Lieutenant Colonel Starck and 200 of his Royal York Rangers.

At sea, while Durham cruised, back in Barbados Leith had been fully occupied planning his assault on Guadeloupe. With the hurricane season looming, concerned both for the safety of the fleet and the hazards of landing assault troops through Guadeloupe's heavy surf, Admiral Durham had proved far from enthusiastic. Returning to Barbados and learning of the large body of troops already assembled (including the York Chasseurs), and the number of flat-bottomed boats and mortar-bomb vessels constructed or purchased, utter commitment soon replaced the Admiral's vacillation.

With conflict now inevitable, forces gathered from the South American, Leeward and Windward Commands, military detachments en route from St Lucia and Dominica, and three 'Royalist' ships and loyal French troops already arrived from Martinique. On 31 July 1815 the order came: 'General Rendezvous at Saintes'. There on the 8 August 1815, with fifty-three sail, about five thousand troops, the hurricane season almost upon them and the defenders increasing daily amid rumours that, in seven days on Napoleon's birthday, all royalists faced execution, Leith launched his attack.

Convinced that both French commanders were now fully aware of Waterloo and its aftermath, Leith first pamphleted the island.

Map of Guadeloupe and adjacent islands

Inhabitants of Guadeloupe! – The misrepresentation and artifices which have been employed to deceive you with regard to the true situation of Europe, the principles resulting at the same time from despotism and anarchy by which your revolutionary chiefs have conducted you to the brink of the precipice on which you stand, can no longer prevail. The veil is torn – your eyes are opened.

You are not ignorant that it was the intention of our Sovereign to furnish every assistance for the support of your legitimate government; but these generous offers have been rejected by the men who have misled you.

Buonaparte has been defeated by the Duke of Wellington and Prince Blucher in a great and decisive battle fought on the 18th of June – his army annihilated, and all his artillery and baggage taken. The usurper fled with some of his perjured generals, and reached Paris, where, knowing how desperate was his situation, he abdicated the pretended Imperial Crown. The allies were at La Fere on the 24th of June, in full march on Paris, where they would arrive on he 26th; there was nothing to oppose them.

The Austrians and Russians were penetrating into France, in mass, by Italy, Switzerland, and Alsace. At the same time his Most Christian Majesty had re-entered France, and by the latest accounts was advancing on Cambray.

In response, under possible pressure from Boyer, Linois immediately replied 'urging the populace to oppose their enemies with fervent cries of VIVE L'EMPEREUR'.

Guadeloupe, a butterfly-shaped volcanic mass, with Basse-terre's jungle-clad mountain ridges in the west, and to the east, separated by the mangrove-lined Salle river, the foliage-clad ridges of Grand-terre. A land mass of such difficulty that Leith changed his plans at the very last moment, by ignoring the potential threat of Grand-terre and concentrating all available forces in a three-pronged assault on Basse-terre (see map on previous page).

As Leith's new plans for assault were in the process of execution, with British troops struggling through high-pounding surf, Durham, from his vantage point aboard *H.M.S. Venerable*, sent *H.M.S. Chanticleer* closer to shore to bombard the estimated 500 defenders threatening Leith's First Division as it landed.

With the First Division successfully ashore, Lieutenant Colonel Starck's 850 Royal York Rangers then landed relatively unscathed to protect the left flank from French reinforcements moving west from Grand-terre. With his flanks fully protected and with the devastating firepower of *H.M.S. Fairy, Colombia* and *Barbados* decimating a battery of 12-pounders, the 2,000 men of the 15th, 25th Foot, 1st West India Regiment and Royal West India Rangers under Leith's personal command landed at the planned second location.

Wading or swimming through Guadeloupe's monstrous surf, with one gunboat lost but no serious casualties, the attacking force moved rapidly inland and 'with a sharp fire of musquetry they obliged the defenders to retire'.[68] As day ended, on shore, in darkness and with piquet lines out, both sides waited for dawn, while at sea, in fading light and with his boats not yet returned, Durham postponed all further landings until the coming daylight.

As dawn broke the British attempted to dislodge the defenders from the volcanic heights of Morne Palmiste and Boucanier; Captain Leith Hay, the Commander-in-Chief's nephew and aide-de-camp, leading a Royal West India Rangers rifle company and a 6th West India Regiment light company, swept all defenders before him at bayonet point. Even so Leith possessed few illusions about the difficulties confronting him: 'Where every part is not only susceptible of defence, but is even difficult to access without resistance, especially under the heat of a tropical sun'.[69]

With Morne Palmiste and Boucanier Heights safely secured and the 63rd Regiment and York Chasseurs landing through fierce pounding surf, Admiral Durham, with his fleet in the lee of Basse-terre, signalled the cannons of *H.M.S. Columbia, Chanticleer* and *Muros* even closer inshore as protection. Unseen, however, from their maritime protection and in the heat of battle, an enthusiastically advancing 63rd Regiment's light company now faced annihilation from an overwhelming and well-entrenched force of defenders. They were only saved when Lieutenant Colonel Ewart and the bayonets of his York Chasseurs charged up and over the volcanic slopes to put the French to full flight. No 'battle honours' to boast about in their regimental history, maybe, but to their credit the York Chasseurs could boast of saving a regimental light company.

On the second night of assault, with the landings consolidated, several pieces of artillery captured, strategic ravines and high ground occupied as protection against any surprise attack, in fading light and torrential rain the British troops again bivouacked, fast in the knowledge that, with the dawn, would come the inevitable bloody assault up the formidable slopes of Morne Houel.

A little before midnight a French emissary suddenly appeared at the piquet line bearing Linois's terms of surrender. Leith summarily dismissed them 'as the only acceptable terms have already been published in my proclamation.'[70] Nevertheless, Leith did agree to a brief postponement of his forthcoming attack to allow the French time to reconsider. Captain Moody was sent with the French emissary to negotiate peace terms, but with dawn breaking and no French reply received, ignorant of the struggles of the emissaries in darkness, torrential rain and along foliage-covered jungle passes, Leith prepared to attack.

Fortunately for the lives of both sides, despite all their difficulties, Moody and the French emissary somehow managed to return before Leith ordered the advance. Even then, with the Royal Bourbon standard flying in place of the tri-colour as a signal of surrender, an intransigent Leith still ordered two of his offi-cers to approach the French lines carrying the Union flag and the message 'that the only signal which would stop the troops would be to see it displayed on the parapet'.[71] After which, defeated French officers surrendered their swords and the troops their regimental eagles and tri-coloured banners.

Of his Victory, Leith commented:

> When it is considered that this beautiful and extensive colony, with a pop-ulation of 110, 000 souls, with forts, and an armed force numerically greater than ours – when it is known that every sanguinary measure had been devised, and that the worst scenes of the revolution were to be re-commenced, that the 15th August, the birth-day of Buonaparte, was to have been solemnized by the execution of royalists already condemned to death, it is a subject of congratulations to see Guadeloupe completely shielded from Jacobin fury in two days, and without the loss of many lives.[72]

On Guadeloupe, death appeared in several guises: direct action, by wounds, fever or, as the pay and muster list mysteriously records, 'Seven of the Rank and File who died – Were supposed to be poisoned'.[73] Who knows, but for these seven death may have arrived through some perfidiously offered 'poisoned chalice', or from some virulent bacteria or virus, or merely through over-indulgence of illicit raw alcohol.

When compared to the slaughter at Vitoria, Talavera, Salamanca, the 'Battle for Guadeloupe' with a British casualty list of sixteen killed, fifty-one wounded and the French, approximately 200 killed or wounded, was little more than a skir-mish. The author would argue, however, that the real significance of Guadeloupe should be seen, not in its casualties, but in the fact that seven weeks after Waterloo, regular troops from both Britain and Imperial France, were still engaged in battle.

In light of the medical, surgical and anti-sepsis techniques of the period, with approximately 600 of the 7,000 or so of the Waterloo wounded succumbing to

Table 14 York Chasseurs Losses at Guadeloupe[74]

	Formerly		
Sergeant Samuel Glasse	21st Foot	Weaver of Derry	Killed in Action
Effects willed to his mother, Sarah Glasse of Armagh, County Tyrone. – £2. 17s. 10d.			
Corporal Thomas Norris	Royal Artillery	Cutler of Sheffield	K.I.A.
Private William Browne	Royal Wagon Train	Painter of Manchester	K.I.A.
Private James Doolan	59th Foot	Weaver of Neath.	K.I.A.
Private Robert Addingley	55th Foot	Weaver of Antrim	Died of Wounds
Private Michael Frayney	2nd Bn 21st Foot	Labourer of Mayo	Died of Wounds
Private Thomas Jones	69th or 2nd Bn 90th Foot	Labourer of Chester	Died of Wounds
Private James Street	1st W York Militia	Weaver of Lancashire	Died of Wounds
Private Patrick Carroll	51st Foot	Labourer of Roscommon	Died
Private John Golding	9th Bn Royal Artillery	Weaver of Antrim	Died
Private John Hughes	2nd Bn 25th Foot	Weaver of Manchester	Died
Private Dennis Mahoney	2nd Bn 37th Foot	Labourer of Cork	Died
Private William Page	4th Dragoons	Labourer of Devizes	Died
Private James Pilkington	Royal Horse Artillery	Weaver of Lancashire	Died
Private John Sadler	1st Foot Guards	Labourer of Berkshire	Died
Private Samuel Overhand	No record	Weaver of Leeds	Missing

their injuries, it is an intriguing possibility that James Street, 1st West York Militia deserter and York Chasseurs private, dying on 22 August 1815, may have been the last British casualty from almost twenty-five years of continual warfare. How ironic, that the death of a York Chasseur, not a guardsman, hussar or dragoon may have ended so many years of armed conflict.

By September 1815, with victory complete, three companies York Chasseurs left Guadeloupe for St Vincent and three for Grenada. Although not before Privates Counsell and Stewart each received a flogging 'for having in his possession a French coin'.

Defeated and under house arrest, Rear Admiral Charles-Alexander-Leon-Durand Linois and Colonel Eugene Boyer de Peyreleau now had time for reflection. For Linois, possibly his days as a young King's officer during the American War of Independence, or even as a revolutionary post-captain of the *Atlante*, where he had first been overwhelmed and then captured by the 74-gun *Swiftsure*; of his exchange (prisoners of equal rank were exchanged between combatants) and command of the *Formidable*, with half the crew dead or wounded and himself partially blinded, being forced to surrender his second exchange and striking the

Unite's colours to four British frigates.

Exchanged for a third time, promotion to vice admiral and roaming the East African and Indian waters aboard the *Marango* in pursuit of rich booty. The embarrassment of mistaking the China merchant fleet for British men-of-war, fleeing when they signalled, 'Give Chase'. An incident over which Bonaparte fumed and the British press gloated: 'Bonaparte should look for a new set of Admirals'.[75]

Despite Bonaparte's considerable displeasure it was not until March 1806 that Linois finally lost his command after the *Marango*'s encounter with *H.M.S. London*'s devastating broadsides; the admiral, his son and the ship's captain all injured, and the majority of the ship's company lying wounded or dead. Despite the years of allegiance to Bonaparte, barely two months after release from his eight years of paroled internment in England, the newly restored King Louis appointed him Guadeloupe's Governor.

(With grateful acknowledgements to Terry J Senior.[76]) Perhaps Colonel Eugene Boyer de Peyreleau also reflected on past glories: of the l'Armee d' Italie, his capture of an enemy cannon, the year in British captivity, exchange, promotion to major and the catastrophic retreat before Moscow. The pride in his Légion d' Honneur and elevation to Baron de l'Empire, the command of men who, unlike Bonaparte's invading Russian army, were so disciplined and well led that they retained their personal weapons in retreat; of January 1814 when, as a colonel attempting to stem the allies advance towards Paris, his exploits would earn him a General's Star, although it was never ratified because of the emperor's abdication. Of all his glory days, perhaps Boyer best remembered General Duhesme's shout of encouragement: 'Go on Boyer, go and earn your star, show us what you can do', when charging to eliminate a battery of Prussian cannon vigorously harassing the retreating French columns. Following the outbreak of peace and despite all Boyer's proven loyalty to Bonaparte, a restored Bourbon regime, possibly through the patronage of General Ney, had appointed him Linois's deputy at Guadeloupe.

Returned from Guadeloupe to France as 'Wellington's prisoners of war', and with their supporters already released from confinement, Linois and Boyer had eventually appeared before the King's Court in March 1816 where Boyer, in a robust defence of his actions, citing the King's hasty flight from Paris as precedent, steadfastly maintained that by Royal assent any subsequent submission to a returning Bonaparte had therefore been lawful. 'He acted under the influence of the circumstances in which he was placed as that the King, in leaving France, seemed to permit his subjects to the same course of events'.[77] In contrast, Linois defended his actions by insisting that having done his utmost to prevent insurrection all personal authority had gone following the enthusiastic welcome of Bonaparte's emissary by a revolutionary cockade-wearing military.

In his final address, Boyer pleaded his innocence by claiming he acted solely to save the colony from the fury of civil war and dramatically concluded: 'I do not fear death, Gentlemen, I have frequently braved its moments'.[78] In contrast,

Linois reminded the court of his loyalty to the Bourbon cause, declaring that though the raising of the tri-colour may not have expressed his true convictions 'He had always remained a devoted subject of the King'.[79]

Retiring on the evening of the third day, after fours hours of discussion, the judges returned with their verdicts. On Linois, the court accepted that circumstances had made it impossible for him to maintain royal authority, and therefore ordered his immediate acquittal. For Boyer, however, regarded as both the author and instigator of insurrection, the sentence was 'death,' although the Court did allow twenty-four hours for a plea of clemency.

Two weeks later, Boyer, colonel and temporarily a general, adorned with Legion of Honour and in full military regalia, attended the Royal Palace to be informed that his sentence of death was now remitted to 20 years of imprisonment. Fortunately, with friends still in high places, particularly the influential Duke d' Angoulême, Boyer would be released from imprisonment and granted a full military pension less than eighteen months later.

As for the victors on September 1816 General Leith sought Royal permission to accept a sabre and the Royal Order of Merit from the French, but by mid-October was dead from fever. Philip Charles Henderson Calderwood Durham was awarded the Grand Cross of the Order of Military Merit of France and went on to serve as MP for Devizes from 1834 to 1836 and Commander-in-Chief, Portsmouth, from 1836 until retiring 1839. He died on a visit Naples in April 1845. Captain Thomas Moody received a promotion to Brevet Major and the Cross of the Knight of the Royal French Order of Military Merit. Lieutenant Colonel Ewart, who led the York Chasseurs up and over the volcanic heights to the 63rd Regiment's rescue, warranted a special mention in Leith's dispatches to Horse Guards.

Having successfully 'wetted their bayonets' on Guadeloupe, and now dispersed equally between St Vincent and Grenada, the York Chasseurs had at least avoided the Barbados slave insurrection of Easter Sunday 1816, during which rampaging slaves plundered and burned a number of sugar estates and plantations, and militia and regulars dealt out instantaneous and merciless justice, with an estimated 1,000 slaves killed on the spot or executed later.

With a further 535 men arriving at St Vincent in November 1815, the York Chasseurs now peaked at 953 'Effectives' dispersed into 10 companies, and spread throughout St Vincent, Grenada and Tobago and unified in Jamaica in one single command in October 1816. There, according to *Tullock and Marshall*, unprepared and ill-clothed British soldiers could expect climactic conditions in which

> From December, the weather is generally clear, except for a few showers around Christmas. As a result of a prevailing north wind the mid-morning temperature often falls to eighty or possibly even seventy degrees Fahrenheit.
>
> By April the heat is oppressive, then, with the atmosphere cloudy a few transient showers ushers in the Spring rains. Rains that, during May, are likely to be accompanied by thunder and lightening and be of great

violence.

By June the weather is generally hot and dry and, by noon, the thermometer is usually well into ninety's Fahrenheit.

Very little changes until the onset of the autumnal rains about the middle of October, rains which continue for four – six weeks.

July to October can justifiably be classified – 'Hurricane Months'.

On the north side of the island, however, the seasons are somewhat different, with the rains being generally a month later and much longer in their duration. As a result of a greater rainfall and the mountainous vicinity, the weather remains cooler during the winter, although liable to considerable temperature fluctuation. In the interior highlands, the climate yet again differs and where, on average, the temperature ranges could well be perceptibly lower.[80]

On the face of it, where a soldier was stationed often meant the difference between survival and death: whether it was Jamaica's moderately healthy Stony Hill barracks, with its thick brushwood and absence of any unhealthy swamp or marshland, or Port Antonia, with its tolerable breeze, where lives were frequently lost through drinking nearby contaminated river water.

If Port Antonia's water supply was hazardous, that of Falmouth was lethal, with water so scarce that, as needs must, inhabitants and soldiers would draw from a local, low banked, sluggish but often seasonally flooded river. Farther to the west, however, life became even more perilous, with Montego Bay's lowlying ground or a fever-ridden St Maria, the latter so pestilential that by 1817 the military had completely vacated. On the other hand, Maroon Town, high on the Trelawney Mountains with an abundance of clear spring water contained all the advantages and few of the lethal drawbacks associated with life in the West Indies.

'And all on the quayside the weeping and wailing four thousand women left on that cold ground.'[81] If marriage to a soldier was fraught on home soil, it became even more taxing as a husband was sent overseas, where only four to six 'legal' families per company were allowed to accompany them, dependent on the luck of the ballot or the throw of the dice. For those 'lucky' families, a long and perilous sea voyage, communal barracks, the privacy of a slung army blanket and of course, the strong possibility of death from yellow fever, malaria or dysentery, while for those left behind, perhaps, penury, starvation, prostitution or a return to some native parish pleading for subsistence.

With death commonplace and in the best of military tradition, whether actively campaigning or garrisoning the West Indies, if a spouse happened to die, most widows would rapidly acquire a new benefactor in exchange for all the comforts of married bliss. Unfortunately, while the Regimental Casualty List painstakingly records the fate of all soldiers, no notation actually exists on the fate of their dependents. Did the York Chasseurs, for example, share in the tragedy of the 2nd (Queen's) Regiment, losing 200 officers, men, and half of all women and children to yellow fever in one three-month period during 1816?[82]

While little is known regarding dependents, the Six Monthly Inspection Report[83] does helpfully record the Isle of Wight presence in May 1814 of 37 wives,

12 male and 6 female offspring and in Jamaica in April 1817, 79 wives, 25 male and 35 female offspring. Obligingly, the 1822 Census of Perth Military Settlement, Lanark County, Ontario[84] also records the presence of ten former York Chasseur family units. On a more sober note we learn from the Regimental and Muster Lists of September 1818 of Private Patrick Loughman's execution for the murder of his wife.

While military females were by necessity, strong, sturdy and resourceful, who on earth could have surpassed the wife of the multi-alias serial deserter Edward Massey who, marching from Liverpool to Portsmouth, June 1807, not only managed a seventeen-mile a day march schedule but also delivered him a boy in the process.[85]

Incongruous as it may seem, though the military flayed the skin from the backs of their fathers, it would also instill a modicum of education into their offspring. Commander-in Chiefs-Circular (1811) – 'To implant in the children's mind early habits of morality, obedience and industry, and to give them the quality of learning which may qualify them for non-Commissioned Officers'.[86] Whether the York Chasseurs adopted all the Commander-in-Chief's recommendation, is of course, speculative.

> Each regiment should select the best-qualified and best-behaved women to instruct all the girls in plain work and knitting, while tailors, boot and shoemakers of each regiment should instruct the boys in their particular trade'.[87]

The first appointment as 'schoolmaster sergeant' went to William Greyson, a 'Painter from York' who, having enlisted for the 95th Regiment, March 1811, spent the following two years campaigning in Europe before returning to England as a sergeant. Within a year, accused of 'Conduct tending to produce insubordination in the regiment,'[88] he had been found guilty, reduced to private and sentenced to a 250 lash flogging. Successfully commuting to one of 'Unlimited Foreign Service,' Greyson had now languished in the depths of his prison ship from December 1813 until his release to his new regiment at one shilling and ten pence *per diem*, 1 February 1814.

Reduced to private, February 1816, Greyson died in Jamaica, November 1817. Following Greyson's death, the mantle of schoolmaster sergeant landed briefly on former Gloucester clerk Thomas Jones, then Hector Mackey, until finally resting with Terrence Gallagher, a former Innis Close schoolteacher, Donegal Militiaman and 45th Regiment deserter. A man obviously better educated than most, who, with service at Monte Video (1806–7), Spain, Portugal and France (1811–1814) and eleven-years as a regular, eventually made corporal. Within months of his promotion he became first a deserter then a prison ship inmate and finally, by June 1815, a York Chasseurs private. In the West Indies, with promotion to sergeant and spells as both paymaster and schoolmaster sergeant, it seems Gallagher finally regained both a niche and his dignity. As schoolmaster sergeant life was hardly onerous: 'The School is carefully attended to; and contains nine males and seven female children'.[89]

From the December 1814 drowning of Private James Kane to the death of Private John Bull in June 1819; from the February 1815 desertion of John Simpson to that of Daniel Donovan in June 1819, in the West Indies, men of the York Chasseurs, sweated, became more debauched, deserted, suffered the cut of the cat-o'-nine-tails and died. As with the many who served and died in their droves in the West Indies few monuments mark their passing.

Chapter Four

Desertion, Cat-o'-nine-tails or a Fevered Death

In a faraway Britain, threatened by a crowd of ironworkers hostile to the military, Sergeant Wheeler of the 73rd Regiment warned 'he'd shoot his prisoner dead if any attempt was to be made to free him'. In the West Indies, with many hands turned against him and a 'reward bounty' to contend with, where might a deserter obtain sanctuary? In urban areas he risked recognition and detention and around a plantation his presence would be highly suspicious. Perhaps freedom lay in the more isolated thick woodlands or mountainous regions, with the assistance of a native or freed slave. Of course a deserter could always attempt to escape the islands.

In spite of the difficulties in the West Indies it seems 'once a deserter always a deserter', a fact borne out by 683 attempts at desertion before the regiment finally

Table 15 York Chasseurs – West Indies Yearly Desertions

Year	Attempts	Successful
1815	42	14 (33%)
1816	90	44 (48%)
1817	136	40 (29%)
1818	150	41 (27%)

Table 16 Combined Monthly West Indies Desertion Rates (1815–1818)

	Jan	Feb	Mar	April	May	June	July	Aug	Sept	Oct	Nov	Dec
Attempts	16	19	49	21	37	48	56	61	32	22	27	30
Successful	5	8	13	7	15	11	23	19	10	11	10	7
Unsuccessful	11	11	36	14	22	37	33	42	22	11	17	23

Table 17 Regimental Casualty List – Desertions and Deaths by Month[90]

Name	Occupation	Deserted	Rejoined
George Hamilton	Carpenter of Dungannon	19 June 1817	25 June 1817
Alexander McLaren	Shoemaker of Perth	25 June 1817	Same day
Maurice Sullivan	Butcher of Limerick	25 June 1817	Same day
Thomas Ford	Joiner of Middlesex	26 June 1817	10 July 1817
John Gravell	Labourer of Tipperary	27 June 1817	No record
John Bogg	Weaver of Lanark	27 June 1817	7 July 1917
Thomas Carroll	Labourer of Limerick	28 June 1817	25 October 1817
John Doby	Shoemaker of Ayr	30 June 1817	No record
John Martin	Paper Maker of Taunton	30 June 1817	No record
Daniel Meades	Labourer of Cork	30 June 1817	No record
John Moales	Wheelwright of Somerset	30 June 1817	No record
James Lee	Labourer of King's County	28 June 1817	1 July 1817
James Cahill	Rope maker of Dublin	29 June 1817	1 July 1817.
Michael Cahill	Not known	1 July 1817	23 August 1817
Thomas Foley	Sailor of America	4 July 1817	No record
Edward Dunne	Labourer of Worcester	5 July 1817	10 July 1817
John Lynsky	Labourer of Galway	5 July 1817	21 July 1817
William McCarlin	Weaver of Tyrone	5 July 1817	8 July 1817
James Savage	Labourer of Cork	5 July 1817	8 July 1817
Michael Shane	Labourer of Cork	5 July 1817	7 July 1817
Cornelius Mahoney	Labourer of Cork	10 July 1817	Next day
Henry Potter	Labourer of York	11 July 1817	14 July 1817
Thomas Taylor	Labourer of Gloucester	11 July 1817	17 July 1817
Edward Moses	Labourer of Carnarvon	Died 12 July 1817	
Maurice Sullivan	Butcher of Limerick	11 July 1817 3 August 1817	17 July 1817 5 August 1817
John Frederic	Tailor of Hanover	13 July 1817	24 July 1817
Richard Dolton	Carpenter of Hereford	17 July 1817	No record
William Summers	Labourer of Berkshire	19 July 1817	1 August 1817
John Hutchinson	Labourer of Linton	21 July 1817	Same day
Michael Kelly	Labourer of Tipperary	23 July 1817	No record
James Brien	Butcher of Cork	Died 25 July 1817	
Michael Osbourne	Fisherman of Falmouth	Died 27 July 1817	
John Quinn	Labourer of Tyrone.	Died 27 July 1817	
James Weir	Sawyer of Sterling.	30 July 1817	3 August 1817

Table 17 Continued

Name	Occupation	Deserted	Rejoined
James Kelly	Carpenter of Cork.	31 July 1817	Next day.
Peter Scully	Labourer of Amargh	31 July 1817	2 August 1817
William Summers	Weaver of Lancashire	1 August 1817	5 August 1817
Robert Dore	Labourer of Derry	Died 3 August 1817	
Sgt William Neal	Labourer of Kildare	Died 4 August 1817	
William Williams	Gardener of Bath	4 August 1817	Recaptured in England
John Cook	Shoemaker of Chichester	4 August 1817	8 August 1817
William Scott	Labourer of Boston	4 August 1817	8 August 1817
Sgt Thomas McKibbon	Weaver of Derry	Died 4 August 1817	
James Jarvis	Labourer of Nottingham	7 August 1817	13 August 1817

departed for Canada, a prodigious number for any regiment. When desertions peaked, however, records show that they peaked, not during the prime sailing months of late December to May, but primarily in June, July and August, normally the start of the hurricane season (see Table 17, pages 55–56).

While desertion was rife between 1815 and 1818, their numbers pale into insignificance compared to the desertion rates from March to May 1819 (see Tables 18 and 19 below and graph opposite), the period during which the regiment prepared for passage to Canada and disbandment. Condemned to the West Indies was one thing, but forcible 'transportation' to Quebec was possibly an imposition too far.

Whether deserting through sheer obduracy, to obtain freedom from the disciplined life of a soldier, alcohol-fuelled bravado or the desire to return to family and homeland, success, perhaps even survival, surely depended on escaping the West Indies. In accomplishing such a feat, however, furtive deserting landlubbers were almost certainly beholden to complicit ships' masters. In the not too distant future, perhaps, some researcher will be able to identify the American sea captain

Table 18 Desertion Rates in Jamaica (1819)

	January	February	March	April	May	June
Desertion attempts	13	12	49	90	58	19
Successful	6	4	22	35	28	9
Recaptured in Europe	–	–	1	2	1	–

Table 19 Total Desertions (1819)

Attempts – 241	Successful – 104 (43%)

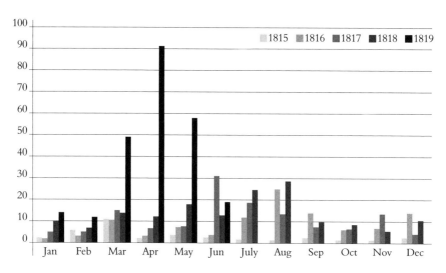

Graph of attempted desertions by month 1815–1819

only too willing to 'tweak the nose of John Bull' by assisting a deserting British soldier, or perhaps the British shipmaster who, with no questions asked had a penchant for signing on likely deserters, despite their obvious lack of seamanship.

If, like Thomas Foley, you were both a seaman and deserting American, finding a sea-going berth was probably less problematic; and for some hard-pressed ship's captain short of prime hands, Edward Murphy, experienced ship's carpenter, may well have appeared as manna from heaven, deserting a mere eight days after his arrival. Nor were Foley or Murphy, as mariners, the exception; James Everett (sailor of Middlesex), William Watson (sailor of Stonehouse) and Brian Cox (sailor of Yorkshire), all successfully deserted within weeks, or even days.

Logic undoubtedly dictates that, of the 232 York Chasseurs successfully deserting while in the West Indies, a good number had made a successful return to their homeland. Unfortunately, of those unlucky enough to have been recaptured only nineteen are identifiable, one the manifestly unpopular Sergeant William Anderson, who Private Thompson called 'a Damned Little Rascal' and received a 100-lash sentence for his insolence, and Private Gould who, in 'Making an attempt to strike William Anderson', got a 200-stroke lashing. Charged with 'Unsoldierlike Conduct and Drunk on Escort Duty' himself and reduced, Anderson later deserted, returned to England, was recaptured, confined at the Savoy Military Prison until marched to Portchester Castle, from where he returned to the West Indies, although not to his old regiment.

Then there was Michael Sweeney, a March 1817 Jamaica deserter who in voluntarily declaring himself a deserter in accordance with the Proclamation of Clemency, had first been confined in the Savoy Military Prison and then in January 1818, marched to Portchester Castle and dispatched to the Royal African Corps.

Even a 1,000-lash flogging from the 2nd (Queen's) Regiment failed to dis-

Table 20 Regimental Casualty List – Irish Deserters

Name	Occupation	Deserted	Rejoined[91]
George Hamilton	Carpenter of Dungannon	19 June 1817	25 June 1817
Alexander McLaren	Shoemaker of Perth	25 June 1817	Same day
Maurice Sullivan	Butcher of Limerick	25 June 1817 17 July 1817 3 August 1817	Same day Same day. 5 August 1817
Thomas Ford	Joiner of Middlesex	26 June 1817	10 July 1817
John Gravell	Labourer of Tipperary	27 June 1817	No record
John Hewitt	Farrier of Warwick	Died, 27 June 1817	
John Bogg	Weaver of Lanark	27th June 1817	7th July 1817
Thomas Carroll	Labourer of Limerick	28th June 1817	25 October 1817
James Lee	Labourer of King's County	28 June 1817	1 July 1817.
James Cahill	Ropemaker of Dublin	29 June 1817	1 July 1817
John Doby	Shoemaker of Ayr	30 June 1817	No record
John Martin	Papermaker of Taunton	30 June 1817	No record
Daniel Meades	Labourer of Cork	30 June 1817	No record
John Moales	Wheelwright of Somerset	30 June 1817	No record
Michael Cahill		1 July 1817	23 August 1817
Thomas Foley	Sailor of America	4 July 1817	No record
Edward Dunn	Labourer of Worcester	5 July 1817	10 July 1817
John Lynsky	Labourer of Galway	5 July 1817	21 July 1817
William Carlin	Weaver of Tyrone	5th July 1817	8 July 1817
James Savage	Labourer of Cork	5 July 1817	8 July 1817
Michael Shane	Labourer of Cork	5 July 1817	7 July 1817
Cornelius Mahoney	Labourer of Cork	10 July 1817	Next day.
Henry Potter	Labourer of York	11 July 1817	14 July 1817
Thomas Taylor	Labourer of Gloucester	11 July 1817	17 July 1817
Moses Edwards	Labourer of Carnarvon	Died, 12 July 1817	
John Frederic	Tailor of Hanover	13 July 1817	24 July 1817
Richard Dolton	Carpenter of Hereford	17 July 1817	No record
William Summers	Labourer of Berkshire	19 July 1817	1st August 1817
John Hutchinson	Labourer of Linton	21st July 1817	Same day
Michael Kelly	Labourer of Tipperary	23 July 1817	No Record
James Brien	Butcher of Cork	Died, 25 July 1817	
Michael Osbourne	Fisherman of Falmouth	Died, 27th July 1817	
John Quinn	Labourer of Tyrone	Died, 27 July 1817	

Table 20

Name	Occupation	Deserted	Rejoined 91
James Weir	Sawyer of Sterling	30 July 1817	3 August 1817
James Kelly	Carpenter of Cork	31 July 1817	Next day
Peter Scully	Labourer of Amargh	31 July 1817	2 August 1817
William Summers	Weaver of Lancashire	1 August 1817	5 August 1817.
Robert Dore	Labourer of Derry	Died, 3 August 1817.	
Sgt William Neal	Labourer of Kildare	Died 4 August 181.	
John Cook	Shoemaker of Chichester	4 August 1817	8 August 1817.
William Scott	Labourer of Boston	4 August 1817	8 August 1817
William Williams	Gardener of Bath	4 August 1817.	
	Recaptured and rejoined from England, 6 June 1818.		
Sgt Thomas McKibbon	Weaver of Derry	Died, 4 August 181.	
James Jervis	Labourer of Nottingham	7 August 1817	13 August 1817

courage Joseph Morris in his ambition to desert; when recaptured he had first been marched to Portchester Castle, then transferred to the West Indies, although not to the York Chasseurs. The indomitable John Martin (alias Vensmore), recaptured and returned to the York Chasseurs in Jamaica, successfully deserted again barely six months later, and William Williams, with the astuteness and cunning for escaping from Jamaica, not once but twice, seems to have possessed neither the intelligence nor the guile to evade further recapture.

Richard Haydon is something of an enigma: first a deserter from the 97th Regiment, then from York Chasseurs, who having deserted from Jamaica a month or so before his regiment's departure for Canada had then been released from London's Savoy Military Prison late 1819 to the 2nd (Queen's) Regiment, then still in the West Indies. Two years later, and presumably on his regiment's intended departure, he voluntarily enlisted for the 35th Regiment, from which he was eventually discharged with a pension in October 1834, suffering 'General Disability, Scars on the Skin from frequent Ulceration and Asthmatic Pulmonary Attacks'. Which begs the question: why desert, not once but twice, in the first place?

As all recaptured deserters required medical assessments before returning to overseas service, several York Chasseurs would acquire both a discharge and Certificate of Protection. For Thomas O'Reilly, it had been his 'Ulcerated Leg', and James West, a 'Diseased Ankle'. A poignant case is that of the Lanark weaver, John Bogg, with a history of 75 lashes for 'Making Away with his Greatcoat', 800 lashes for 'Absent without Leave' and 300 lashes for 'Theft,' who deserted a mere 13 days after his final punishment, only to be recaptured in Scotland, diagnosed a 'Consumptive' and discharged in February 1818. When Charles Waterman deserted the Jamaican planter capturing him had declined the bounty on offer, suggesting the deserter was not worthy. But amongst the list of regimental deserters, it is unquestionably the case of William Exton that provides the saddest of postscripts: 'Sentenced to be shot to death at St Vincent, 26th June 1815', while his three accomplices got 'Twelve Months Solitary Confinement in Irons aboard the Flag ship at Port Royal' commutations.

As the Regimental Casualty List in the West Indies so clearly illustrates, while consistently less than 50% of the complement (40% during 1818), the Irish, as a nation, were undeniably prominent as deserters (see Table 20, pages 58–59).

As for the punishment of flogging, the 1689 British Mutiny Act sanctioned it, the American Congress of April 1812 outlawed it and Napoleonic France derided it (although supporters argued that while the British Army might flog its deserters, the French Army often shot theirs).

If reputable line regiments employed the lash to instil discipline, it is hardly surprising that the York Chasseurs, a regiment of condemned soldiers, would use the cat-o'-nine-tails to excess, or as the Inspecting General commented:

> Courts-martial have been rather frequent and should be attributed to the composition, mostly Commuted Men. The courts-martial in a regiment of such material as the York Chasseurs is, will of course be numerous: There have been General and Regimental, 143. The Proceedings have been regular, the sentences generally severe, yet I am convinced necessary. It is painful to bring to notice the following circumstances. The Regiment of York Chasseurs since its arrival on the 26th day of September 1816 to the 1st May 1817, has inflicted 38, 995 lashes in consequence of the Proceedings and Sentences of 169 Courts-martial held during that period during.[92]

With general, garrison, detachment and regimental courts martial all passing judgements, it seems the regimental cat-o'-nine-tails had hardly rested, particularly with the number of offences that attracted flogging as a punishment. *A full list of men tried by Courts Martial is given in the Appendix, Tables 33–42*

Spread-eagled on a rigid tripod or triangle of sergeants' halberds, the offender would first be at the mercy of a drummer securing his ankles, legs and wrists. If the wrists were too loosely secured a prisoner, squirming in agony, would suffer unnecessary damage to neck, face, and possibly even to his eyes. Too tight and it would result in a circulation seriously restricted and numbness for days.

With wrists, thighs and ankles all efficiently secured, officers and men duly assembled, both charge and sentence would be read out. The officer commanding would instruct: 'Drum Major, see that the Drummers do their Duty', and the drum major counted out the strokes as the drummer, stripped to the waist, laid his cat-o'-nine tails to the unfortunate victim. When the drum major called out 'Stop twenty-five', the drummers changed over and punishment continued. At 50, as the adjutant or other delegated officer recorded each stroke as it landed, the drum major ordered: 'Stop fifty', and the drummers changed over again, and so on until completion of the punishment. Close by there was a pitcher of water, less it seems for humanitarian reasons than a means of restoring the unfortunate back to consciousness.

On the effects of corporal punishment, one contemporary observer recalled that on the first stroke, 'the diffusion of blood often created an immediate discolouration of the skin, with the back appearing as if sprinkled with strong coffee even before the second stroke could be struck'. Another remarked that, 'on occasions the blood copiously flowed by the fiftieth stroke', while claiming, rather dubiously, 'that at times, no blood would appear even after two hundred lashes'. Some witnesses also noted that at times the intensity of pain seemed to peak around the 150th to 200th stroke, then irrespective of the number apparently lessened as the punishment continued.

As for the debate on endurance of the horrors of the cat-o'-nine-tails, Sir Charles Napier's 1837 Treatise *On Military Law*, makes the comment that, on occasions offenders receiving 300 lashes or fewer apparently suffered more than those in receipt of 800. Alternatively, an offender would often endure 300 lashes with hardly a murmur, while another sentenced to 800 might barely withstand 25. Perhaps the inability to endure pain may explain the occasional notation, 'remittance of punishment'.

One contemporary eyewitness recalled that, while some offenders pleaded for the punishment to stop from almost the first cut, others withstood seven to eight hundred with hardly a murmur, and commented that there was often a rivalry as to who could withstand the most lashes, with the winner basking in the adulation of his peers.

In emphasising all the barbarity of military punishment, Henry Marshall's *Military Miscellany* (1846) recounts the vivid experience of a dutiful, though reluctant active participant:

> From the very first day I entered the service as drum-boy, and for eight years after, I can venture to assert, that, at the lowest calculation it was my disgusting duty to flog a man at least three times a week. From this painful task there was no possibility of shrinking, without the certainty of a rattan over my shoulders by a Drum-Major, or of me being sent to the blackhole. When the infliction is ordered to commence, each drum-boy, in rotation, is ordered to strip, for the purpose of administering twenty-five lashes (slowly counted by the Drum-Major) with freedom and vigour. After a poor fellow had received about 100 lashes the blood would pour down his back in streams, and fly about in all directions and every additional blow of the cat, so that by the time he had received 300, I have found my clothes all over blood from the knees to the crown of my head.

In the seventeenth century, the instrument of punishment had been a solid rod, which, over time, was to be modified, first to six cords or 'cats' and ultimately to nine, thrice knotted, sixteen-inch lengths of whipcord attached to either a drumstick or wooden handle. Drum majors were usually tasked with ensuring that the cords did not become entangled, too thick nor heavy with coagulated blood. Allegedly, to increase suffering, certain commanding officers, totally lacking in compassion, would encourage the use of matted cords. There were even rumours of commanding officers intentionally increasing the suffering by using cords soaked in brine.

As horrific as the ordeal must surely have been, the suffering had unquestionably been exacerbated with a left handed drummer replacing a right, allowing the cat-o'-nine-tails access to previously untouched parts of the back and there were allegations that, to increase the ordeal, the more brutal commanding officers routinely employed right- then left-handed drummers. If that was not sufficiently brutal, certain regiments increased the offender's anguish by striking only on the tenth drumbeat: Lash-beat-beat-beat-beat-beat-beat-beat-beat-Lash. These variations although not illegal were frowned on by Horse Guards.

With the skin of a repeat offender bloody and in a state of maceration, a painful and humiliating variation was the flogging of buttocks, or on rare occasions to the calves of the legs, which, in Marshall's opinion, invariably led to severe and crippling ulceration.

With the welfare of the offender more or less in the hands of the man wielding the lash, experienced regimental drummers were undoubtedly at a premium; if there was a consolation for the offender it was that the York Chasseurs drummers were undeniably experienced, and with the lash in the hands of well-versed experts it was unlikely they needed to cry out, 'For God's sake man, Strike Straight'.

Regarding the excessive punishment in the regiment, arguably this was the result not from an officered clique of sadistic floggers, but rather from the calibre of men they commanded. If the War Office had only released the funds necessary, in the opinion of both the commanding officer and inspecting major general more often than not the appropriate sentence might well have been solitary confinement.

> The blows of the Cat often struck to the bone and again on inspecting the aftermath a large poultice was taken off the wound. Oh what a sickening sight. The wound was perhaps eight inches by six inches, full of matter, in which were a number of black-headed maggots striving to hide themselves.

With his punishment over and in a state of bloody semi-consciousness, the unfortunate offender might now be escorted to hospital, where his mutilated shoulders and back would be soothed with 'sugar of lead' soaked cloths and protected with a 'saddle' or 'wrestling jacket' wide bandage. With a back mangled and bloody, convalescing from an ordeal in which, as with the talons of a hawk, each stroke of the cat cleaved 27 fresh lacerations to his skin, there had now existed the danger of infection; with an odour so foul it required immediate isolation, from which the more unlucky failed to return.

Yet, if a single visit to the punishment triangle had not caused enough suffering, what of the poor York Chasseur offender brought back to complete his full sentence? This question was referred to in Robert Hamilton's 1787 publication,

The Duties of a Regimental Surgeon Considered:

> Let us suppose that a man is taken down at the end of two hundred and fifty or three hundred lashes, and that his sentenced was one of a thousand, all of which he must receive, whether at two, three, or more times, before he is released from confinement. Let us suppose he is conveyed either to the guard-house or hospital, is daily dressed until the wounds are healed, and a new cuticle formed, which may be in a month or five weeks. He is now able to wear his clothes, yet perhaps scarcely able to suffer the weight and friction of his cross-belts, or the pressure of his haversack – the parts are as yet red and tender; notwithstanding, he is ordered a second time to the halberds, and at the end of two or three hundred more is a second time taken down, cured as before, a third time brought there, and so on till the whole judgment be inflicted ... the first few lashes tore open the newly cicatrized skin, so much that his back became instantly covered with blood, which flowed downwards under his clothes.

Of an offender awarded five hundred lashes, he wrote:

> He got four hundred before he was taken down; and in the space of six weeks was judged able to sustain the remainder of his punishment, as his back was entirely skinned over. The first twenty-five lashes of the second punishment tore the young flesh more than the former four hundred, the blood pouring at the same time in streams. By the time he got seventy-five his back was ten times more cut by the 'cats' than with the former four hundred – so that it was thought prudent to remit the remaining twenty-five, and take him down. With the prisoner declaring that his first punishment was trifling to what he suffered by the second.

As for the duties of the attending regimental surgeon, extraordinary as it may seem, it appears that not until 1838 was there any mandatory medical assessment before punishment commenced. Before that a surgeon's primary task was to ensure that in feigning excessive pain or distress no offender escaped his due punishment; although medical attendance did at least partially avoid the infliction of disabling or life-threatening injury. It appears that a surgeon would occasionally intervene and request a suspension of punishment, although it was likely that an offender would be returned to the triangle later. In some cases a surgeon might allow a flogging to continue, or as much as the offender could stand, in the knowledge that having endured at least two-thirds of the punishment, the remainder might be remitted.

Logic certainly dictates that repeated or excessive experience of the cat-o'-nine-tails would surely result in some degree of mental or physical deterioration for an offender, perhaps both: a surprisingly inaccurate hypothesis as it turns out, given that many York Chasseurs not only survived, but enthusiastically and repeatedly deserted.

Of these, the German-born, Mathew Schwartz, was a case in point. Despite accumulating 3,500 to 4,000 lashes, he went on to successfully desert on his thirteenth attempt. Edward Dunne, too, with his 1,000-lash parting gift from the 2nd

(Queen's) regiment and an estimated 2,700 as a Chasseur, still successfully deserted at his seventh attempt. Indeed, so resilient had serial deserters been that, of the eleven receiving sentences of 700 lashes or more, eight successfully deserted and two were later to be discharged at Quebec.

Unbelievable as it may seem, despite all the blood-splattered shredding of backs, during the entire existence of the regiment and taking an eight-week post-punishment period as a yardstick, flogging can only indirectly be attributed to eleven deaths. A remarkable statistic indeed, considering the possibility of post-traumatic shock, secondary infection, and constitutions perhaps weakened by prolonged dissipation and drunken debauchery. Another surprising revelation is that, while the more law-abiding of York Chasseurs died in their droves, their multi-flogged compatriots frequently survived. Perhaps the the single-minded and doggedly persistent deserter was better equipped to survive the harsh and dangerous environment.

Discussion raged between those for and against military flogging; in England, William Cobbett's *Weekly Register* described the process as 'that most heart rendering of all exhibitions this side of hell' and that 'even Bonaparte's soldiers did not have to listen to the piercing of a human creature so tortured'. So vehement was Cobbett in his opposition that in 1809, following the German Light Cavalry's suppression of a mutinying Ely Militia and the subsequent flogging of several militiamen, his *Political Register*'s editorial earned him a charge of sedition, two years in Newgate prison and a £1,000 fine.

Sir Francis Burdett, Cobbett's parliamentary ally, argued that the 1812 Mutiny Act, then under discussion, should deliberately exclude all references to flogging. In defence of the status quo, however, Burdett's parliamentary opponents argued that those against corporal punishment were merely pandering to the wishes of the mob, and sacrificing the honour of the British Army to their own petty ambitions.

Most unexpectedly, in 1812 the *Jamaica Pamphlet* had seemingly been in agreement with Burdett and Cobbett, 'while the law prohibited a slave from receiving more than 40 lashes at any one flogging, in contrast, the men who fought the nation's battles and protected its liberties could at times be sentenced to a 1000.' If civil opinion varied, so did that of the soldier. Sergeant Morris of the 75th Regiment considered flogging only turned a good man bad, and a bad man worse, while Benjamin Harris of the 95th Regiment, though detesting the sight of the lash, thought the British Army could not survive in its absence.

As the nineteenth century progressed and the statute book now protected horses and donkeys from excessive use of the whip, the nation's mariners and soldiers were still to suffer the cut of the cat-o'-nine-tails. Nonetheless, military punishment was gradually reforming. First, the 1808 legislation restricted sentencing to a maximum 1,000 lashes, followed by the 1812 limiting of regimental courts martial to 300 lashes and for all tribunals by 1829. By 1836, general courts martial would now be restricted 200-lash sentences, districts and regimentals to 150 and 100 respectively, and, by 1847, a universal ceiling of 50; and by 1879, 25.

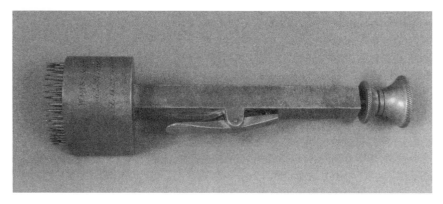

Spring-loaded machine for tattooing 'D' on deserters, 1840s
Courtesy of the Army Medical Services Museum

Flogging during peacetime would finally be abolished in 1870, and while campaigning, by 1881, although in military prisons the lash was still employed until 1907. Finally, after so many decades of pain, humiliation and bloodshed, the last flogging of a soldier on active service occurred in Afghanistan, July 1880, the offence, 'Sleeping on Duty', a somewhat perilous transgression when confronting fierce Afghan tribesmen.

An Act for Punishing Mutiny and Desertion Geo III 21st March, 1808

> And be it further enacted, that it shall be lawful for any Court-martial, before which any Non-commissioned officer and Soldier, who shall be tried for Desertion, to direct it, if it shall think fit, in addition to any other Punishment such court may award for any subsequent Desertion, that such Deserters be marked on the Left Side, Two inches below the Arm – pit with the letter D. Such Letter not be less than half an inch long, and be marked upon the Skin with some Ink or Gunpowder, or other preparation to as be visible, and conspicuous and not liable to be obliterated.

While the British Army may have discontinued the mediaeval practice of hot iron branding its deserters by 1779, stigmatisation would continue well into the nineteenth century, with men being marked with the letter 'D': first with bundled common sewing needles, the angular and serrated edge of a shark's tooth or, more effectively, bunched three-sided saddler's needles, which would both pierce and serrate, a process then followed by impregnating gunpowder into the wound as a marker. Though gunpowder proved effective in highlighting and preventing the D's obliteration, it perhaps even aided healing without festering. Technological modifications of the 1840s resulted in the introduction of the spring-loaded tattooing machine (see illustration above), and indigo or Indian ink as improved markers. For a regiment of serial deserters like the York Chasseurs, many already tattooed, the needles perhaps remained largely redundant.

As an alternative to a flogging, however, military offenders were also liable to solitary confinement; in the West Indies, despite the recommendations of a recent Military Act, the War Office had agreed funding for improved barrack spaces but not the facilities for additional solitary confinement. With little contemporary testimony to call upon, once again we turn to Henry Marshall, and specifically his 1830s observations on Coldstream Guards solitary confinement in England, a study that lacks exact parallels to the West Indies, but nevertheless illustrates the likely experience of a York Chasseur in solitary confinement.

> The prisoner is placed in a cell or black-hole, some black-holes are very dark, others might be light enough to read by. He is allowed plenty of straw, and 2 blankets, and more when required together with his great coat. He is made to wash and shave every morning, and he is to walk for an hour, under charge of a sentry in the morning and evening. Diet of bread, milk and water. His cell is carefully searched to ensure he had no tinder-box, pipes, spirits, tobacco or any other food concealed.

Once again, there were those who considered solitary confinement insufficiently punitive, and that the cell should be truly a black hole in which the prisoner should stay his entire sentence without release for exercise. An atrocious prospect most certainly, yet presumably less atrocious than the cat-o'-nine-tails.

As for the West Indies being the graveyard of the British Army, the *Hampshire Telegraph and Sussex Chronicle* left its readers in little doubt as to the perils waiting the nation's embarking soldiers.

> 19th April 1802. The 75th Regiment in the West Indies, is literally cut to pieces by the climate, 3 Captains, 7 Subalterns and about 150 Rank and File, being all they could muster at the last return.

> 7th May 1808. We are sorry to hear that the Battalion of Scots Royals, which is in Tobago, has of late lost many men by Yellow Fever. The 1st West India Regiment which is quartered alongside the Royals, is very healthy.

> 7th May 1808. The skeleton of the 85th Foot, which has been ten years in Jamaica, landed on Wednesday. They are come home about 120 strong, most of which are invalids.

> 4th July 1808. The skeleton of the 85th Regiment, which has been ten years in Jamaica, landed on Wednesday and marched into Hilsea Barracks; from whence the will march on Monday for Aylesbury. They are come home about 120 strong, most of which are invalids.

> 25th September 1809. The remains of the 37th Rank and File from the West Indies (scarcely 100 including Officers) were landed at Plymouth Docks on Sunday last.

> 5th January 1811. The skeletons of the 16th, 54th and 70th Regiments are

shortly expected home from the West Indies.

22nd July 1811. The 53rd Regiment is coming home from Jamaica a complete skeleton, having suffered so much from the climate.

29th July 1813. The 55th Regiment, or rather the skeleton of it, is under orders to return from Jamaica, after a service of nearly 13 years, during which it has been reduced to 40 men and a few Non-Commissioned Officers.

24th March 1817. The 18th Regiment has been 12 years on the West Indies service, during which its loss exceeds 70 Officers and 200 men but, being constantly recruited, it is now 1000 men strong.

25th October 1819. The accounts from Jamaica respecting the state of our troops there are extremely distressing. The 50th and 92nd Regiments have suffered severely and are reduced to mere skeletons.

22nd November 1819. 15 promotions of Officers in the 50th Regiment appear in Saturday's Gazette, in room of the others dead by fever in the West Indies.

With nineteenth-century medical opinion insisting on the 'theory of miasma' – disease-carrying 'mists' – as an explanation for the cause of malaria and yellow fever rather than the bite of the mosquito, survival in the West Indies was something of a lottery. As a consequence, with no immunity possible, in low-lying swamp areas malarial-infected Europeans at times died in droves; it was the same in urban areas, where the mosquito transmitted yellow fever. As for that other great killer, dysentery, many practitioners considered it simply a variant of the yellow fever miasma.

With the use of blood letting, purging and blistering as 'cures', it is interesting to note the treatments recorded in the *Practical observations of the diseases of the Army in Jamaica*.[93]

Treatment of Captain M'L.
1. Pills of Jalop and calomel and saline draughts and pendilivium in a nitre bath every hour during the night.
2. Blistering plaster between the shoulders.
3. Purgative enema.
4. Pills containing 30 grains of calomel with 1 of opium every 2 hours.
5. Blistering plasters to stomach and thighs.
6. Nitrous aether added to his drink.
7. 2 grains of opium every 2 hours washed down with 50 drops vitriolic aether in glass of peppermint.
8. CONVULSIONS CARRIED HIM OFF

When in 1838 two progressive reforming officers, Deputy Inspector Henry Marshall and Lieutenant Alexander Tullock, compared the sickness and mortality statistics of troops in the West Indies (including 45 York Chasseurs dead at Port Antonia and 13 out of the 57 that garrisoned Savannah-la-Mar, Jamaica, 1817), they concluded that immunity did not follow from acclimatisation. Endorsing Marshall and Tullock's conclusion that longevity of service in the West Indies was no guarantee of survival, records clearly demonstrate that a York Chasseur was more at risk during the ninth to twelfth and twenty-second to twenty-third

Table 21 Casualty Returns of the York Chasseurs (Dying Months)

Name	Origin	Occupation	
George Crossland	Beetson	Labourer	Died 1 October 1816
James Daulby	York	Carpenter	Died 1 October 1816
Thomas Redmond	Hereford	Labourer	Died 1 October 1816
Hugh Johnson	Ayr	Weaver	Deserted 1 October 1816
Edward O'Hara	Down	Labourer	Died 2 October 1816
John Chapman	Northampton	Labourer	Died 3 October 1816
Peter Brophy	King's County	Shoemaker	Died 4 October 1816
William McIndoe	Aberdeen	Glass Cutter	Deserted 6 October 1816
William Davis	Lancashire	Labourer	Died 6 October 1816
James Clancy	Dublin.	Labourer	Died 6 October 1816
John Barry	Limerick	Painter	Died 6 October 1816
Peter Dunning	Louth	Labourer	Died 6 October 1816
Peter Burns	Stratford	Glass Blower	Deserted 6 October 1816
John Higgins	Bath	Glass Grinder	Deserted 6 October 1816
Thomas Mason	York	Labourer	Died 7 October 181.
Joseph Wainwright	Salop	Labourer	Died 8 October 1816
Robert Duggatt	Wicklow	Weaver	Died 9 October 1816
John Donohoe	Galway	Shoemaker	Died 11 October 1816
Neil McMineiny	Carlow	Tinker	Died 11 October 1816
Thomas Corlett	Isle of Mann	Anchorsmith	Died 11 October 1816
Dennis Murphy	Belfast	Dry Salter	Died 11 October 1816
James Jackson	London	Brushmaker	Deserted 11 October 1816
Owen Leonard	Limerick	Labourer	Deserted 11 October 1816
Colour Sergeant James Simpson	Berwick	Labourer	Died 12 October 1816
James Edwards	Cardiff	Boat Builder	Died 12 October 1816
William Grey	London	Waiter	Died 12 October 1816
James BakeR	Middlesex	Butcher	Deserted 12 October 1816
Charles King	Devon	Wheelwright	Deserted 12 October 1816

Table 21 Continued

Name	Origin	Occupation	
Thomas Kyle	Roxburgh	Stocking Weaver	Died 12 October 1816
James Towland	Limerick	Tailor	Died 12 October 1816
George Spence	York	Labourer	Died 17 October 1816
Patrick Farrell	Devon	VictualleR	Died 17 October 1817
David Dellarmont	Ayr	Brasier	Died 18 October 1816
Robert Miller	London	Porter	Died 18 October 1816
Jacob Emery	York	Labourer	Died 19 October 1816
William Ormeroid	Aberdeen	Labourer	Died 19 October 1816
Richard Johnson	Cromarty	Fisherman	Died 19 October 1816
Richard Cully	Kipton	Horse Dealer	Died 21 October 1816
Robert Wyndwood	Worcestershire	Miner	Died 21 October 1816
John Kennair	Leeds	Labourer	Died 22 October 1816
James Mooney	Cork	Labourer	Died 22 October 1816
William Fletcher	Somerset	Labourer	Died 22 October 1816
Sergeant John Smith	York	Blacksmith	Died 22 October 1816
James Hennessy	Louth	Seaman	Died 22 October 1816
John Garrett	Nottingham	Frame Work Knitter	Died 22 October 1816
William Pearson	Lancasshire	Brass Founder	Died 23 October 1816
Corporal Thomas Fisher	Dublin	Brush Maker	Died 23 October 1816
William Brown	Edinburgh	Tailor	Died 24 October 1816
Corporal Richard Kenny	Sussex	Labourer	Died 25 October 1816
Daniel Shady	Limerick	Shoemaker	Died 28 October 1816

months following his arrival; periods that coincided with the more unhealthy months of October to December. It seems clear, therefore, that determined York Chasseurs had exploited the spring and summer 'deserting' months, while endeavouring to survive the wet and 'dying' months of autumn and winter (see Table 21, above).

Marshall and Tullock also concluded that, in general, military mortality in the West Indies was at least four to five times as great as among troops in Britain, and in the more unhealthy years, nearly sixteen times greater. With such statistics, it seems hardly surprising, therefore, that the York Chasseurs should suffer a thirty percent death rate.

According to Captain Joseph Anderson, his contentment with his new West

Indies billet had changed after his men began dying daily of yellow fever. Losing so many men to the fever was bad enough – the regimental paymaster died almost immediately on arrival – Anderson, with the prospect of a long life in the balance, concluded that yellow fever ignored neither officer nor soldier.

In revealing that Jamaica's hospital admissions had been twice as numerous as on any other station, two thirds of which having proved fatal, Marshall and Tullock had described the island as being

> Much more subject to disease in endemic form than any other West India Station: and on such occasions it is often of an extremely fatal description, scarcely yielding to any mode of treatment. They appeared without warning and often suddenly, at periods when the troops have for sometimes previously enjoyed a comparative immunity from disease, and in some corps raged with such severity that nearly one half died of those attacked – sparing neither age, sex or condition, the temperate or intemperate and with the prudent and thoughtless falling victim in nearly equal degrees.[94]

Table 22 Deaths by Yellow Fever in the 92nd and 50th of Foot, June/July 1819

	92nd Foot			*50th Foot*		
	Strength	*Died*	*Ratio*	*Strength*	*Died*	*Ratio*
Commissioned Officers	27	10	37%	30	11	36.7%
Officer's Wives	5	4	80%			
Soldiers	769	231	30%	650	275	42.3%
Soldier's Wives	90	30	33.3.%	60	29	48.3%
Soldier's Children	50	30	66%.	70	38	54.3%

As fearful as the experience of the York Chasseurs had been, the regiment seems to have been spared the suffering of the 92nd and 50th Foot in Jamaica in June and July 1819.

In spite of the yellow fever, malaria and dysentery, the Inspecting General considered many of the deaths self inflicted. 'There has been much sickness and mortality since the arrival of the Corps in Jamaica; much of which is to be attributed to excessive drinking'.[95] In fairness to all drunken soldiery, not just the York Chasseurs, rum was an important and traditional soldier's prophylactic in the fight against yellow fever; and as lead was used widely in the process of distilling raw rum it is a matter of speculation how many died of fever or as the result of adulteration of their rum. In defence of the York Chasseurs and their blatant lack of sobriety, when visiting Jamaica a full twenty years after the disbandment of the regiment, Marshall and Tullock observed 'that men were frequently seen in the streets in the highest state of intoxication, if exposure to a meridian sun without a hat to shelter their heads was not dangerous enough'.[96]

Chapter Five

Officers

At the head of a regiment was its colonel, usually a general officer, for whom a colonelcy would embody recognition and reward, the chance to dispense patronage, with rights to the clothing supply paid with a lump sum from the government (apart from greatcoats supplied by the Ordnance), an opportunity to make money. From the *Hampshire Telegraph and Sussex Chronicle*:

> Monday, 22nd November 1813. 'Major General Andrew Hay has got his Regiment, as a reward for his service.'

Andrew Hay's York Chasseurs tenancy lasted only until April 1814 when, as general officer of the night outside Bayonne, he was killed staving off an unexpected and sudden sortie by the French garrison, a death made even more tragic, not just for Hay but also for the two hundred or so dead and wounded alongside him, as Napoleon Bonaparte had already abdicated several days earlier.

> British blood has been shed through the treachery of the Governor of Bayonne, a warm disciple of the Bonapartian School who had been acquainted with the changes of Government.[97]

While Andrew Hay's death may have been that of a hero, it seems doubtful that Major General Robinson was amongst the chief mourners, bearing in mind his vitriol against Hay for the lack of recognition and gratitude shown towards him and his brigade during the Battle of San Sebastian.

> As a fool and I verily believe, with many others on my side, an arrant coward. That he is a paltry, plundering old wretch is established beyond doubt. That he is no Officer is clear, and that he wants spirit is firmly believed, ergo, he ought not to be a General. The man who has been the principle occasion of this want of candour is General Hay, my Compeer'. Yet these jealous pated rascals, conscious of want of prowess, think to snatch our Laurels from us.[98]

In support of Andrew Hay, however, it might help to look more closely at his out-spoken detractor. Why, for example, was he not given a command until five months after arrival; and what truth in the rumour that Wellington had actually doubted his quality as a leader? As for the events at San Sebastian, what explains the discrepancy between Robinson's version and that of the official report? 'With Sir James Leith wounded, Major General Hay succeeded to the command and ably conducted the attack along the ramparts himself with the judgement and gal-lantry that so often has marked his conduct'.[99] Finally, quoting Wellington him-self, 'I sincerely lament the loss of Major-General Hay, whose services and merits I have had frequent occasion to bring under your Lordship's notice'.[100]

With her husband dead, Hay's widow made her return from France to Peckham House, Fordingbridge, Hampshire, where she began lobbying 'people of influence' in support of some formal recognition of her late husband and his services to the nation. Parliament responded by erecting monuments in St Paul's Cathedral to Hay and four other major generals 'Who fell gloriously in the service of their Country'.[101] In light of such posthumous accolades, history fails to record the comments of Major General Sir F P Robinson.

The author knows little of Andrew Hay's successor, Major General Hugh Mackay Gordon, with the exception that he succeeded to the colonelcy while on 16th Regiment half pay, and later, disputed with his predecessor's representatives over rights to the clothing assignment.

With Major General Sir Dennis Pack as colonel, the third within three years, the York Chasseurs now had as its colonel an officer of considerable distinction. Gazetted as cornet of the 14th Light Dragoons in 1791, Pack had first seen action in Flanders and later, as an 8th Light Dragoon, would witness at first hand the dis-aster of Quiberon. As lieutenant colonel commanding the 71st Regiment, Pack had received the first of his war wounds during the 1806 capture of Cape of Good Hope and, a year later in South America, was first a prisoner-of-war, an escapee and then wounded for a second time during General Whitelocke's disastrous attack on Buenos Aires.

Commanding the 71st Regiment in the Peninsular war where, after the battles of Rolica and Vimeiro, Pack's ability to inspire won him promotion to 'local colonel', and detached duties with the Portuguese Army, with whom he com-manded a brigade at Busaco, Almeida and, as brigadier-general, had stormed Ciudad Rodrigo. Promoted major general and given command of Wellington's 9th British brigade at Vitoria, Pyrenees, Nivelle, Nive, Orthez, Toulouse, Pack, having being wounded on at least eight different occasions during his service career, suffered his ninth during the conflict at Waterloo.

As regimental agent and the colonel's personal appointee, Mr John Kirkland's absence of uniform in no way disguised his importance to the regiment. Without him no regimental bill was settled, nor any officer or man paid. Although com-paring John Kirkland with his responsibilities to the 1st (Royal Scots) Regiment, 21st (North British Fusiliers) Regiment, Nova Scotia Fencible Infantry and York Chasseurs, with that of Greenwood, Cox and Co, whose client list included the

Royal Artillery, Engineers, nineteen cavalry regiments, 163 battalions of infantry, 21 militia regiments and the Royal Wagon Train, it seems in 1813 Kirkland was extremely small fry.

Small fry or not, Kirkland's role as regimental agent was identical to that of his rivals. The receipt of funds from the Paymaster General's Office, a deduction to cover unexpected contingencies and personal expenses (2d in the £ from each regiment), and forwarding the residue on to the regimental paymaster for troop payment and various other expenses.

With each company captain allocated direct responsibility for his men's payment, captain's would then account back to the regimental paymaster, the paymaster back to the Agent, and the Agent to the Secretary at War, who then certificated the final account between Agent and Paymaster-General.

From little acorns, however, great oaks grow, and following his 1824 appointment as General Agent for the War Department so grew the career of John Kirkland. Knighted in 1838 and rewarded further several years later when the Prince Consort, colonel of various British regiments, appointed him his agent. Of his initial appointment in 1824, it might be wondered how much his success depended on the influence of illustrious uncle, the renowned Canadian explorer Sir Alexander Mackenzie. As General Agent of the York Chasseurs, it seems Kirkland, at the behest of the War Office and from 8 Bennett Street, St James, spent much of his time chivvying reluctant Chasseurs officers out to their regiment in the West Indies.

> Captain Phillips – Reference the length of time you have already been permitted to be absent from the York Chasseurs since the date of your promotion to the regiment, HRH cannot comply with your request for further leave.[102]

> Lieutenant MacBean – As the opportunity is likely soon to offer for you to embark to join your regiment in Jamaica HRH cannot accede to your request for further leave of absence.[103]

As for the York Chasseurs Regiment of Infantry, while its colonel served Wellington in France and Agent John Kirkland forwarded payments from London on to the Isle of Wight, moulding the conversion of military prison ship miscreants into disciplined soldiers was the responsibility of their new commanding officer, Lieutenant Colonel Andrew Coghlan. Coghlan was described by Captain Joseph Anderson as 'a smart, experienced officer, very kind but a strict disciplinarian; as there were no end to our parades, we soon became a most efficient regiment, and the most united and happy corps of officers I ever knew'.[104] A year later, with the regiment under readiness to depart the Isle of Wight for Guernsey, thence to the West Indies, Coghlan handed command to Major Joseph Paterson, the senior field officer, and retired to half pay – although a few months later he took command of the 8th Royal Veteran Battalion at Portsmouth.

With Andrew Coghlan retired, Major Paterson, veteran of Egypt, Ciudad Rodrigo and Badajoz, took temporary command at Barbados in February 1815 until the arrival of his new commanding officer, Lieutenant Colonel John Ewart. An officer unscathed at Copenhagen, Fuentes d' Onor, Salamanca and the storming of Ciudad Rodrigo, wounded at both Vimeiro and Badajoz, who later risked French shot and shell and the deadly bite of the mosquito in the West Indies, earned a Royal York Ranger's majority without purchase, and finally the York Chasseurs lieutenant-colonelcy.

A year or so later, having commanded his regiment at Guadeloupe with distinction, Ewart left the West Indies on health grounds, and with Major Paterson also absent in England, the command fell to Major Peter Dumas. This period might be described as that of 'the missing or reluctant lieutenant-colonel'. Lieutenant Colonel George Francis Waldo Flucker, promoted out of the Bourbon Regiment without purchase in September 1815, remained in England for over a year despite repeated instructions from Horse Guards, when the Commander-in-Chief finally intervened, and he applied for half pay. Thereupon, in line with the common practice of single battalion regiments possessing dual lieutenant colonels (although generally with only one serving at any one time) in May 1817 the post was assigned to Joseph Twigg and George Arthur. Twigg, with no intention of leaving England for the West Indies, swiftly applied for half pay, while Arthur, recorded as 'Absent without Leave' until February 1819, was already serving as military commandant at British Honduras. A reluctance to embark for the West Indies was not merely the prerogative of lieutenant colonels. Lieutenant Bowker Walsham, promoted out of the 18th (Royal Irish) Regiment, would prolong his 'certificated illness' for as long as possible before exchanging with Lieutenant Le Court, currently on Chasseurs Britanniques half pay.

Horse Guards. 7th December 1814.[105]

It appears by a Medical Report, dated 3rd December 1814, which has been made in your Case, that you are recovered from your late illness as to be fit for Embarkation for the West Indies, the Commander in Chief expects that you will be present at the Army Depot in the Isle of Wight on the 24th December, and in readiness to embark to join the York Chasseurs, with which your Services are much required.

Lieutenant Bowker Walsham   Harry Calvert Adjutant-General

The Adjutant General even encountered officers' intransigence when he attempted to return Major Joseph Paterson to his regiment in the West Indies. On leave of absence for health grounds, this disciplined war veteran successfully stretched six months into almost two years before returning and to resume command from Major Dumas.

For his own personal survival, however, it might have been expedient of Lieutenant William Humble to have taken half pay. Left sick at Guernsey and not arriving in the West Indies until thirteen months later, Humble was dead in Tobago within seven months.

On the other hand, Ensign Walter Ashe's persistent refusal to take passage for

Table 23 Officers Absent Without Leave

Major Joseph Paterson	5 September 1815–16 March 1816 (ill health) – Rejoined
Surgeon Augustus Stromeyer	10 November 1815–10 May 1816 (ill health) – h.p. March 1816
Assistant Surgeon James Sproule	6 December 1815–6 June 1816 (ill health) – h.p. 1818
Captain Stewart	embarked for Europe 10 April 1816. (ill health) – h.p. December 1817
Lieutenant McBean	embarked for Europe 25 April 1816 (private affairs) – query – resigned.
Lieutenant Colonel Ewart	embarked for Europe, 14 July 1816. (Leave of Absence) – March 1819 – Lt-Col 61st
Lieutenant Simeon Farrar	embarked for Europe, 26th June 1816 (ill health) – h.p December 1816
Lieutenant Joseph Jones	5th October 1816 – 4 October 1817 (ill health) – Query – h.p.
Assistant Surgeon George Brien	to proceed to sea on a cruiser. January 1817 (ill health) – Died June 1817
Quartermaster Lourie	7 February 1817 – 7 February 1818 (ill health) – h.p. 1820
Captain Holland Daniell	7 February 1817 (private affairs) – h.p. December 1818
Capt Anderson	sailed in H.M.S. Salisbury on 11 January 1818 (sick leave) – h.p. January 1819
Pay Master John McIntyre	sailed for England 9 May 1818 (ill health) – Ret full pay. 1819
Captain Jonathan Parker	sailed for Europe 1 June 1818 (ill health) – h.p. December 1818
Surgeon Lewis	sailed for Europe, 22 June 1818
Lieutenant William Bell	Leave of Absence in the Island, June 1818 (ill health) – Rejoined.
Adjutant John Tennant	Leave of Absence in the Island, June 1818 (ill health) – Rejoined
Surgeon John Lewis	13 March 1818–24 September 1818 (ill health)
Lieutenant B Gaynor	Sailed for Europe on Sick Leave from Port Antonia, 1 August 1818. – h.p. December 1818
Lieutenant Thomas Sutherland	On Leave, 10 January 1819. Rejoined
Adjutant John Tennent (Lieutenant)	On Leave, 10 January 1819 (ill health) – h.p. March 1819
Captain Edward Stehelin	embarked for Europe, 19 April 1819 September 1819 – Capt 41st Regt.

the West Indies would cost him dear socially.

> MEMORANDUM. – His Royal highness, the Prince Regent has been
> pleased, in the name and on the behalf of his Majesty, to approve of
> Ensign Walter. L. Ashe, of the York Chasseurs, to be dismissed the serv-
> ice.[106]

Ensign Baylis, receiving the Adjutant-General's curt demand 'to explain through
your commanding officer, on joining the regiment, the circumstances which
occasioned the delay in your joining',[107] had simply resigned.

In a pestilential West Indies, the division was clear – ailing officers departed on
lengthy convalescences to England and then often to half pay (see Table 23, page
75), while their men stayed, became sick, recovered or died. Yet, in spite of all
such advantages, officers would still die (see Table 24, below).

Table 24 Officers Dying in the West Indies

Paymaster Thomas Thompson	Died at St Anns, Barbados, 22 March, 1815
Captain Edward Brien Brutus Balguy	Died at St Ann's, Barbados, 16 May, 1815
Lieutenant W.R. Humble	Died at Tobago, 3 June 1816
Lieutenant Charles Le Court	Died at Tobago, 18 August 1816
Captain Charles Vallency	Died at Kingston, 19 October, 1817
Assistant Surgeon Charles Whyte	Appointed from Medical Staff vice Brien deceased
Ensign Daniel McCarthy	Died at Jamaica, 28 October, 1818
Lieutenant Francis McMurran	Died Stony Hill, Jamaica, 20 January, 1819
Lieutenant Robert Maxwell	Died Port Maria, Jamaica, 18 January, 1819

Even the most distinguished of regiments possessed one dissolute officer or
more, and for the York Chasseurs this mantle fell to Captain Edward Brian
Balguy. Charged at Barbados with 'Drunk as Regimental Captain of the Day,
repeatedly quitting his quarters while under close arrest, and drinking to such an
excess in the mess-room as to require a sergeant and a file of men to carry him out
still sitting on a chair',[108] Bulgay's defence was that, celebrating 'the glorious
Achievements on the Peninsula', his enthusiasm unwisely overcame him. His
defending officer nevertheless argued his innocence through extenuating circumstances, citing Bulgay's previous war wounds and a shattered and enfeebled
constitution, prone to even the smallest amount of alcohol and – possibly a
clincher – his epilepsy. Even before the Court's recommendation of 'Dismissal
from the Service' reached London for its Royal Ratification, Bulgay was dead and
never discovered 'That his disgraceful habit made him unfit for Service although,
in consideration of his former good Conduct, His Wounds, and the Court's recommendation, his Commission could be sold at its regulated value'.[109]

For the long-serving Lieutenant John Heath, former Sicilian Regiment quartermaster and 6th Garrison Battalion ensign, his problem may well have been

that, being commissioned from the ranks, he was socially speaking 'not a gentleman'. Charged and found guilty of 'Scandalous and Infamous Conduct, such as is unbecoming the Character of an Officer and Gentleman in Striking Lieutenant James Richards',[110] the Court recommended cashiering. In consideration of his long service, and the fact that his pay as a serving officer was the only support for a wife and five children, the Court urged clemency and recommended that Heath should retire on half pay, with which the Prince Regent later concurred. On a second charge of 'Highly unofficerlike conduct in writing several very improper and very disrespectful Letters to Lieutenant Colonel John Ewart', [111] Heath was totally exonerated due to his lack of any formal education, a judgement that seemingly confirmed Heath's status as a 'temporary gentleman'. Unlike Bulgay, Heath lived long enough to learn of his fate – but only just.

Unlike Heath, Captain John Montgomery may have justifiably claimed to be both an officer and gentleman, yet the Adjutant General still had to jog his memory over debt.

> The Revd Gervas Finlay, late Master of the School at Dundalk having preferred a complaint against you to the Commander in Chief for having neglected to pay the sum of £319. 2s Irish, in which you stand indebted to him, since the year 1811, for the Education of your Sons'.[112]

As for a young Ensign James Robert Disney, he was in trouble before even joining, but after four years or so of trouble-free service to his credit, Lieutenant Disney, as with the vast majority of fellow junior officers, went permanently to half pay.

> I have the honor to transmit to you herewith the Copy of a Minute of the Collegiate Board held at the Royal Military College representing the very improper conduct of Ensign Disney of the York Chasseurs who was a Gentleman Cadet pursuing his Studies at that Establishment. I am directed to add, that in consequence of the Report of the Collegiate Board, it is the Commander in Chief's Pleasure, that Ensign Disney shall not be indulged with any Leave of Absence, but forwarded to the Regiment by the first opportunity.[113]

While the vast majority of junior officers would go to half pay following disbandment, there were exceptions: George Mainwaring, a lieutenant during the 1820s Burmese War, and a captain in the Scinde Campaign of the 1840s, who, in 1850, and as a major with 35 years of continuous service, retired with the full pay of a captain. William Bell, another officer presumably lacking the necessary funds for advancement, commissioned lieutenant of the 58th Regiment, January 1823, and yet not promoted to captain until February 1838, sadly died two years later. Edward Sutherland, a lieutenant of the 77th Regiment, April 1825, who in 1838 was still a lieutenant retired on a captain's half pay to be employed first as the Royal Hospital Chelsea's storekeeper, and later, Barrack Master at Woolwich. Major Peter Dumas, who temporarily commanded, spent almost four years on half pay before his promotion into the 65th Regiment as lieutenant colonel. Dumas finally retired, July 1832, to become Lieutenant Governor at Gravesend and Tilbury Fort, on £173. 7s. 6d per annum.

In the memoirs of Joseph Anderson there can be found only the briefest of insights into officering with the York Chasseurs. Anderson, barely sixteen and an ensign of the 8th Regiment at the Battle of Maida, a twenty-year-old 24th Regiment lieutenant, Egyptian Campaign veteran, partially blind in one eye from Egyptian ophthalmia, wounded at Talavera, a survivor of Busaco and Fuentes D'Onora who, suffering from fever and ague, had later departed for England on six months leave of absence. With his convalescence over and restored to full health, apart from his defective eyesight, Anderson began making serious preparations for the long sea passage to India and the 24th's Regiment's 1st Battalion, when through the patronage of his district commander, he had been unexpectedly gazetted as captain to the York Chasseurs Regiment of Infantry. 'Had I never seen General Ackland, I would not have been a captain for ten years or more'.[114] It was the captaincy of a regiment that in spite of its status as a regiment of incorrigibles appears to have elicited neither social embarrassment nor military condemnation; in fact, according to Anderson, the exact opposite seems to have been the case. 'On joining the York Chasseurs at Sandown barracks I was pleased at finding the officers a fine set of young fellows, all promoted from other regiments for their services or strong family interests'.[115]

Later, at Barbados, Anderson recalled that all went well at first, the garrison fit and healthy, the quarters good and the climate not as bad as previously had been expected. Then, with his men dying of yellow fever, the York Chasseurs seemingly began to suffer more than most of the other regiments.

After spending the best part of 1814 converting military reprobates into disciplined soldiers in Barbados, Anderson soon exchanged his duties as a company captain for the responsibilities of a deputy-judge-advocate-general with, his first trial being that of the previously mentioned Captain Edward Brian Brutus Balguy. Several months later however, with a sea-borne assault of Guadeloupe now imminent, and being one of just a handful of York Chasseurs officers experienced in battle, Ewart understandably recalled him to the regiment. In compensation, Ewart later obtained Anderson his appointment as Guadeloupe's deputy-assistant-quartermaster-general.

Eighteen months into his appointment, with the York Chasseurs about to depart St Vincent for Jamaica, Anderson faced a dilemma. Should he exchange into another regiment and retain his position on Guadeloupe but go to the bottom of the captain's seniority list, or forfeit his lucrative appointment to retain his seniority as the York Chasseurs second captain? After much thought and consideration, Anderson rejoined his old regiment, amongst whom he enjoyed 'considerable satisfaction in the company of Major Dumas, his new commanding officer, and his gay and happy brother officers'.

With Major Dumas temporarily in command, Anderson now experienced two enjoyable years travelling to Falmouth, Montego Bay, Maroon Town and

Savannah-la-mar, inspecting the four companies he commanded until, with Major Paterson's return, Major Dumas relieved him. With four years in the West Indies, Anderson began giving serious thought to returning to England on health grounds. This was a far easier proposition might be envisaged; appearing before the Medical Board, not a single serious question was asked of him and he received twelve months leave of absence in England. There, with the York Chasseurs now disbanded, after two years on half pay, he returned to Jamaica as captain of the 50th Regiment to spend the next four years as deputy-judge-advocate before 'with very little fuss' he returned once more to England on health grounds.

In November 1833, now major of the 50th Regiment, Anderson arrived on Norfolk Island's penal colony where almost on arrival and with very little cere-mony he neutralised an imminent threat of mutiny, obtained depositions regard-ing a previous and serious general mutiny and hanged thirteen of its ringleaders. Of his time of Norfolk Island, Anderson later claimed that under his five-year tenure as commandant he seldom had need of the lash, an assertion others most strongly disputed. 'A stern master who gave two convicts three-hundred lashes apiece for neglecting to sow corn properly', or, as the charge sheet read, 'Robbing the Earth of its seed'.[116] Without a single plough on the island and with agricul-tural labour viewed as a punishment, it seems that under Anderson convicts may have hoed until exhaustion.

Despite his return to the regiment, Anderson's deteriorating health eventually resulted in a return to his family in Australia and two years of convalescence. Returning to India in time to accompany his 50th Regiment back to England, from where in 1848 after 43 years of military service and £6,000 from the sale of his commission safely pocketed, Anderson finally returned to Australia with his family, where in partnership with his retired lieutenant-general elder brother he obtained squatter's rights to 80,000 acres of land along Australia's Goulburn river. Joseph Anderson, Victoria State legislator, landowner, military veteran and cap-tain of York Chasseurs died at Fairlee House, South Yarra (nowadays a suburb of Melbourne), 18 July 1877.

With the facts scanty, it is virtually impossible to explain the enlistment of Charles Willis and Henry Gurley as 'Gentleman Volunteers'. What was the rela-tionship between Willis and Gurley? Why were they both in Jamaica and above all why did they select the York Chasseurs in preference to one of the more reputable regiments? Regarding Willis's eventual commission as ensign, what was his social status and under whose influence was he elevated from common soldier to com-missioned officer? An elevation made even more incomprehensible by the fact that he had married only a few months earlier when still a private. Perhaps his newly acquired in-laws were his inspiration.

Notwithstanding all the imponderables, with the York Chasseurs departing for Canada, Willis remained in Jamaica with the 50th Regiment, in which he served, first as ensign, lieutenant and then quartermaster, and in January 1831 a 38th Regiment lieutenancy without purchase. After seventeen years of continuous service, Charles Willis, youthful civilian in Jamaica, gentleman volunteer and

York Chasseurs private, finally sold his lieutenant's commission and returned to life as a civilian, perhaps to his native village of Headcorn, Kent.

With the regiment requiring both a surgeon and assistant, Augustus Stromeyer, formerly assistant surgeon, Foreign Regiment of Infantry, joined on the Isle of Wight as regimental surgeon in February 1814, followed a month later by Assistant Surgeon James Sproule, and a year later in Barbados, George Brien as additional assistant surgeon. A most fortunate addition indeed as it turned out, as by November of that year Stromeyer had left on health grounds, followed a month later by Sproule, leaving the regiment's medical well being in the hands of one solitary assistant surgeon until August the next year, and the arrival of Surgeon John Lewis.

Once back in England Stromeyer would progress from leave of absence to half pay, then to a medical doctorate. Following this, diploma in hand, Stromeyer returned to Hamburg and died there in January 1828. Sproule, on the other hand, with his convalescence leave over, served a further two years as surgeon assistant to the 2nd Royal Veteran Battalion, before also going to half pay.

Although both Stromeyer and Sproule managed to survive the West Indies, Assistant Surgeon Brien, sick and on passage from Port Royal, died aboard *H.M.S. Cherub* on 29 June 1817. With Brien dead and Assistant Surgeon Thomas Young, a recent arrival from England now tending the sick, Surgeon John Lewis also left for England on health grounds and of course to eventual half pay.

In April 1818, with Thomas Young now aided by Assistant Surgeon Charles Whyte (seconded locally for the dead Brien) and five hospital assistants, its seems preparations may have been under way for the soon to be expected onset of fever, sickness and death. A confrontation for which Assistant Surgeon Thomas Young's experience cutting and sawing in Badajoz, Vitoria, Pyrenees, Nivelle, Nive, Orthes and Toulouse would scarcely have equipped him when dealing with the deadly effects of the mosquito (see Table 25, below).

Table 25 Regimental Deaths in Jamaica (October 1817–October 1818)[117]

1817			1818									
Oct	Nov	Dec	Jan	Feb	Mar	Apr	May	June	July	Aug	Sept	Oct
6	8	6	5	9	11	16	21	24	29	31	38	44

As for their post-York Chasseur careers, Young became surgeon to the 50th Regiment (1826) and 95th Regiment (1834); in contrast, Charles Whyte, six years his junior, had become surgeon to the 69th Regiment (1826), staff surgeon (1836) and then, after forty-two years service, Bombay's deputy inspector general. He retired December 1860.

While the fate of condemned soldiers was discharge in a far away Canada, officers obviously had greater choices (see Table 26, opposite).

Table 26 Officers Absent or Departing

Officers returning directly to England
Major Joseph Paterson
Lieutenant William Rothwell
Lieutenant Charles Dellamaine
Lieutenant John Hodges
Lieutenant William Bell
Lieutenant Thomas Sutherland
Ensign George Laye
Ensign Thomas Richardson
Assistant Surgeon Thomas Young.
Officers already in England on private affairs
Major Peter Dumas
Lieutenant William Souper
Officers departing the regiment in Canada.
Captain John Stewart
Captain Robert Nolan
Lieutenant William Hay
Lieutenant Joseph Stainton
Lieutenant Benjamin Warton
Lieutenant Corry (Carey)
Lieutenant James Mackay
Lieutenant George Mainwaring
Lieutenant Cornel Jessop
Ensign Richard Sparkes
Ensign Edward Sutherland
Ensign Charles Dormer
Assistant Surgeon Charles Whyte

A full list of officers serving with the York Chasseurs is given in the Appendix, Table 43

Chapter Six

Men

The York Chasseurs, a conglomeration of misfits, deserters, thieves, battle hardened veterans, greenhorns and regimental drummers with their cat-o'-nine-tails often working overtime; a pot-pourri of military malefactors and the occasional trustworthy volunteer, such as the 87th and 95th Regiment veteran, Colour Sergeant William Perry, who, with the regiment disbanded, went on to serve three months with the 10th Royal Veteran Battalion, eighteen with the 61st Regiment, and further seven with the 50th Regiment before enlisting in May 1826 as company sergeant major to the 2nd West India Regiment at New Providence. A regiment from which, barely two years later, with 'His health much impaired and his constitution worn out by repeated attacks of Intermittent Fever and long service in a tropical climate', he left for a well-deserved pension.

Perry's career is a stark contrast to that of the silver-tongued miscreant, John Longworth, 2nd Dragoon Guard deserter who, despite his record of twice being flogged for desertion and once for theft, was sent to the Bourbon Regiment at Barbados as sergeant, then to the 1st West India Regiment as colour sergeant.

True to form, however, Longworth's 'Willful Disobedience of Orders' soon had him reduced and dispatched from Barbados and the 1st West India Regiment to the 15th Regiment at Grenada. There, with the regiment now stationed at Halifax, Nova Scotia, he deserted fifteen months later. Eighteen months later, having made his way back to the regiment's Isle of Wight depot, he inexplicably surrendered. Reunited with a returning 15th Regiment in July 1821, Longworth's lack of military commitment again emerged just eleven months later when with the 15th Regiment at Hull waiting embarkation for Ireland he deserted for a second time.

For all further narrative on John Longworth, the author remains deeply indebted to Dr Hamish Maxwell-Stewart, University of Tasmania.[118] Commencing with the revelation that Longworth, the deserter, can be next found at the 1826 Derby Assizes being 'transported for life to Van Dieman's Land for stealing two saddles'.[119] Dr Hamish Maxwell-Stewart suggests that, during his passage out aboard the *Andromeda*, during a possible post-sentencing interview, Longworth may have impressed Gunn, superintendent of the prison barracks, by regaling him with his service with the Dragoon Guard, York Chasseurs, Bourbon and 1st West India Regiments – though presumably omitting his experiences in the 15th Foot. While no actual evidence exists, the fact is that, despite his reputation as an 'insolent fighter and thief', Longworth wassufficiently impressive to be installed in the choice billet of prison barracks gatekeeper almost immediately on arriving in Van Dieman's Land. There, shortly afterwards, the former chimney sweep and stone throwing convict, Peter Kirkham, won a month on the chain gang for disrespecting Longworth's position and dignity.

Even so and despite all attempts at restraint, Longworth's days in his choice billet were numbered. Failing to pay his due respect to a much-affronted Lieutenant Miller, he was promptly transferred to the service of Samuel Grant, settler, only to cross swords with the overseer and receive a three month stay on the chain gang. All the same, if Lazarus could arise, so could John Longworth. Temporarily avoiding the sweat and toil of the chain gang from his rapidly acquired position as sub-overseer, three months later, for possessing a 'far too insolent attitude' and for knocking several teeth out of a fellow convict, Longworth was back on the chain gang again.

Implausible as it may seem when he was released Longworth soon became incorporated into the convict field police force. This tenure was rapidly terminated when he was charged with 'willful neglect of duty in not apprehending Samuel Shone a runaway convict and presumptuously refusing to obey the orders of the police chief and magistrate'.[120] He returned to the chain gang once more. Working his way up to overseer once again his obduracy 'in refusing to obey the orders of Constable Williamson when employed in the pursuit of plundering natives',[121] resulted in yet another stint on the chain gang.

Following this his behaviour may even have worsened: charged with 'Refusing to Obey Orders and Slandering a Military Officer',[122] he spent the following six months at Hobart in irons where he was charged with 'Repeatedly Striking the Overseer as well as Throwing Stones at Him',[123] for which he suffered a 25-stroke lashing. Even with his sentence served and assigned to settler John Cole, 'Disobedience and Insolence' would once again see Longworth back at Hobart in irons.

Released from the chain gang at the personal intervention of the lieutenant governor he was sent to the newly established penal settlement at Port Arthur where within a month and despite 'this man's violent disposition appears to render him quite uncontrollable',[124] Longworth was appointed a constable; a surprising decision, indeed, considering his proven predilection for violence.

In December 1833, accused of 'embezzling slop clothing and obtaining a set of government bedding under false pretences',[125] Longworth was removed from Port Arthur back to Hobart Town, where he was once again sentenced. Finally, after eight years as a transported felon, Longworth received his 'Ticket-of-Leave' and a year later married 'free-woman' Mary Ann Bailey. After four years of married life he was caught 'Embezzling Twenty Shillings of Wheat from his Employer',[126] and faced a further three years of transportation. Served oppor-

tunely in his new homeland of Van Dieman's Land, and not in New South Wales
as the court recommended. With the 2nd Dragoon Guards, York Chasseurs,
Bourbon, 1st West India and 15th Regiment, as well as years as a transported convict, now all behind him, 1854, drunk and free, Longworth died of crushed lungs
while falling under the wheels of the brewer's dray he was driving. Dead drunk
and now dead, at least he enjoyed the last laugh, in never admitting that he had
been an undetected 15th Regiment deserter since June 1822.

Just as interesting as John Longworth's, however, is the tale of Patrick Fanning
and John Glossop, men who early 1816 while at Guadeloupe, confessed to murders allegedly committed back in Britain. With their confessions accepted, as they
were both were at sea, chained and under armed guard, the facts were already
being forwarded for further investigation, Fanning's to Dublin Castle and
Glossop's to the Chief Magistrate of Suffolk.

> Horse Guards. 29 March 1816.[127]
>
> The Commander in Chief desires you take measures for sending John
> Glossop & Patrick Fanning of the York Chasseurs to this Country in order
> that the necessary enquiries may be initiated respecting the Murders
> which they state themselves to have committed
>
> Lt Gen Sir J Leith. Guadeloupe   Harry Calvert. Adjutant General.

Beyond doubt, an extraordinary and bizarre set of circumstances. First Patrick
Fanning's confession to the murder of Tobias Roc, Roscrae, Ireland in 1806, and
the Chief Clerk of Tipperary County's decisive conclusion: 'It appears that
Fanning's confession does not agree with the circumstances attending that murder he alluded to, and that his Testimony is at variance with the Evidence.'[128]
Secondly, the official reaction to John Glossop's alleged 1812 Suffolk murder of
some yet unidentified individual. 'The Chief Magistrate at Bow Street, who was
directed by his Lordship to make enquiries into the above Circumstances, by
which you will perceive that the Story is considered as a fabrication.'[129]

With the investigations concluded by May of the same year, in July, with both
self-confessed murderers landing at Portsmouth, August, the Commander-in-
Chief pronounced his decision:

> That the accounts given by Patrick Fanning and John Glossop of Murders
> committed by them are fabrications, most probably contrived with a view
> to their getting removed from the West Indies. To counteract this object it
> is the C in C's desire that they be sent back as Prisoners to the Regiment
> to which they belong by the very first opportunity.[130]

It seems inconceivable that Fanning and Glossop should risk the noose of the
hangman for murders they were apparently both innocent of. Were conditions in
the regiment and the West Indies really that so horrendous? Nonetheless, arriving back in Jamaica as ordered and with their confessions dismissed as fabrication,

in December 1816, both were in trouble again.

Patrick Fanning
4 July 1817. 'Theft.' 200 lashes reduced to One Months Drill.
10 January 1818. 'For having a pair of trowsers not his own possession'.
Sentenced to 250 lashes, 225 received, 25 lashes remitted.
2 September 1818. 'Selling his Necessaries.' Sentenced to 250 lashes, 225
received, 25 lashes remitted.
Deserted 4 October 1818. Rejoined 13 October 1818. (No punishment records
held.)
Deserted 2 March 1819. (No record of rejoining.)

John Glossop
Deserted 4 January 1818 and 7 January 1818. Tried by CM & punished for both
offences.'
Deserted 9 March 1818. No date of rejoining. (No punishment records held.)
Deserted 18 April 1818. Rejoined 27 April 1818. (No punishment records held.)
Deserted 29 August 1818. Rejoined 23 October 1818. (No punishment records
held.)
Deserted 27 January 1819.

Unfortunately for Glossop, having successfully escaped from Jamaica back to
England, he then suffered the misfortune of recapture. After which, it seems
Glossop's resolve must have prevailed once more, for, despite unearthing orders
for his march from Dartford to Portchester Castle, no record exists of his arrival.
Is it possible, therefore, that Glossop had escaped his captors yet again?

Undoubtedly more affecting is the saga of James Howieson, Edinburgh
Militia Volunteers and 91st Regiment deserter, a companion of Ecklin, Fountain
and Longworth in both the Bourbon and 1st West India Regiments. Whereas they
were soon reduced and moved on from the 1st West India Regiment, Howieson
served ten years as its sergeant major until demoted to private. Hospitalised once
during fourteen years of service in the West Indies, within four months of his
demotion and following a decade of seemingly unblemished service as sergeant
major, Howieson was dead. Perhaps humiliation had been too heavy a burden.

With 1,540 or so York Chasseurs sharing a multiplicity of experiences, regret-
tably time and space allows for the inclusion of but a few. Men like Gunner
William Maxwell, 7th Battalion Royal Artillery, sentenced at Woolwich Arsenal to
500 lashes for 'Absence, Insolence and Riotous Conduct',[131] who, after commutation and despite receiving a 999 stroke lashing for 'Quitting the Barracks with his
Bayonet fixed and resisting the Officer,' managed to die a York Chasseurs sergeant.

Gunner Thomas Devlin, despite his 1,000 lashes for 'Firing a musket loaded
with ball while a prisoner in the Guard Room and Maliciously saying he would
complete the purpose for which he fired the musket at a future period', would

still successfully desert. As did James McClure, 36th Regiment deserter and persistent York Chasseurs offender, despite 250 lashes for 'Absent from Parade,' 300 for 'Refusing to go on Guard Duty' and a 1,000 lashes for 'Stabbing Private William Price and Making Use of Mutinous and Threatening words to Captain Anderson'.

Resolute individuals such as William Ralph who received 1,000 lashes for being 'Drunk and Absenting from his Guard and Refusing to become a Prisoner, and, Using Mutinous and Insolent Expressions to Captain Parker in the Execution of his Duty and Attempting to Strike the said Officer', yet survived to be discharged later at Quebec. Thomas Webster, with his 100 lashes for 'Refusing to go on Drill when Ordered,' 200 lashes for being 'Drunk in Barracks' and finally 1,000 lashes for 'Desertion and Threatening Behaviour and Mutinous Conduct to Captain Anderson and Colour Sergeant Sewell', paid exorbitantly for his errors by dying six months later.

While service with the York Chasseurs often led to desertion or death, for Private Angus McDonald, late of the 79th (Cameron Highlanders) Regiment of Foot, it proved something of a lifeline. Sentenced to be shot 'For Desertion to the Enemy on or about the 23rd October 1813 near the Advance Post from the Camp above Urdache, and for Disobedience of Orders in Going Beyond the Piquets on the Same Day',[132] after commutation McDonald survived to be discharged at Quebec.

Amongst the ranks of the York Chasseurs were also the Snoxalls, brothers James, William, and Cousin Thomas, marched from Huntingdon, Cambridgeshire, to the Isle of Wight prison ships as deserters from the 5th Regiment. For them fortunes varied: William 'Left behind on Detachment', James discharged at Quebec and Thomas dead at Jamaica. Less certain, however, is the relationship between Isaac and Thomas Trimby who as deserters from the 10th Regiment marched from Fisherton Anger, Wiltshire. As with the Snoxalls, their fate with the York Chasseurs were different, with Isaac discharged at Quebec and Thomas dying in the West Indies.

Exiled to the West Indies and perhaps with an obvious lack of immortality in minds, a small number made the effort of bequeathing their possessions, no matter how little, to their loved ones.

Willed to the Next of Kin[133]
Drum Major William Bailey. Eight pounds and ten shillings to his father, George Bailey, Newbury, Berkshire.
Sergeant John Carter. All his Effects to wife Elizabeth, 'The Artichoke', George Street, Richmond, London.
Corporal Samuel Glasse. Two pounds, seventeen shillings, to his mother, Sarah Glasse, Armagh, Co Tyrone.
Corporal William Lewis. One pound, five shillings to his mother, Ann Lewis, Merthyr Tydfil.
Private Ralph Allen. Ten shillings, ten pence to wife Mary, Stockton on Tees.

Private William Babbington. Five shillings and a penny to wife, 24 James Street, Manchester.

Private Thomas Bromley. One pound, seven shillings and a penny to his brother, Sergeant Bromley, Arundal Street, Sheffield.

Private John Butler. Seventeen shillings and sixpence to wife Mary.

Private Patrick Carroll. Nine shillings and thrupence to his wife.

Private Thomas Field. One shilling and sevenpence ha'penny to mother Catherine, resident of Whitechapel Workhouse.

Private Andrew Fitzgerald. Six shillings and sevenpence ha'penny to brother Thomas, 28 Edge Street, Manchester.

Private William Grey/Gray. Eleven shillings and ten pence to wife Mary, King's Arms, Horsley Downs.

Private John Mackay/McKay. One pound and ten pence to wife Mary of Ballyclare.

Private James Menzies. Seventeen shillings and thru'pence to mother, Mary Menzies, Rainsford, Falkirk.

Private John Pegler, Four pounds, ten shillings and sixpence to Samuel Pegler, Wotten-under-Edge.

Private Charles Redding/Reading. One pound, nineteen shillings and a penny to father Benjamin, Birmingham.

Private Aaron Sandwich. Three shillings and eight pence to father Richard, Kirkland, Kendal.

Private David Smith. Eleven shillings and eleven pence to wife Esther, 5 Nicholson Road, Edinburgh.

In the pages of *Hamilton's Campaign with Moore and Wellington during the Peninsular War*,[134] published in New York in 1847 (see illustration on page 88), readers might read of the exploits of Sergeant Anthony Hamilton, an 'Old Soldier', who as a youth exchanged life in Donegal County, Ireland, for the British Army and active service with the 43rd regiment (Light Infantry) and later as a 'volunteer sergeant' with the York Chasseurs in the West Indies.

With the 2nd Battalion of the 43rd Regiment at Vimeiro in Portugal in August 1808, Hamilton witnessed 'The enemy advanced upon us with determination and valour, but after a desperate struggle on our part, were driven back with great slaughter'.[135] Hamilton survived but 119 regimental comrades were killed, wounded or missing, a casualty list approximately one sixth of the army's entire losses that day.

Four months later, with the 2nd Battalion part of the rear guard of Sir John Moore's army as it retreated towards Corunna, embarkation and safety, Hamilton recalled such scenes of horror as 'Roads bestrewed by the bodies of men dying and the agonies of women still more dreadful to behold'.[136]

A year or so later, with Corunna and all its appalling tragedies behind him, Hamilton's writes of 'charging up the streets of Oporto, making many prison-

HAMILTON'S CAMPAIGN

WITH

MOORE AND WELLINGTON

DURING

THE PENINSULAR WAR.

ORIGINAL AND COMPILED.

PUBLISHED FOR THE AUTHOR.

TROY, N. Y.:

PRESS OF PRESCOTT & WILSON, CCXXV RIVER-STREET.

1847.

Title page from the book Hamilton's Campaign with Moore and Wellington

ers'[137] (12 May 1809), and of 'being severely wounded at Talavera by the explosion of a bomb-shell, and ... left upon the field, till the engagement was over. My skull was fractured, in consequence of which, I have suffered severely from the wound'[138] (July 27/28 July 1809). Graphic yet rather confusing, as both battalions of the 43rd Regiment were in England at that time.

At the battle of Busaco (27 September 1810) Hamilton was now somehow with with 43rd Regiment's 1st battalion, a resolute French column marching towards them under a withering fire of musket and cannon. The 43rd received the order to advance and 'a charge of bayonets followed: the whole column was routed, and driven down the hill with prodigious slaughter'.[139] At Sabugal the following year (3 April 1811), it seems Hamilton escaped death once again while '27 men of my own company were cut down, 13 of whom were killed, and others, myself amongst the number, wounded'.[140]

Of the blood-stained storming of Ciudad Rodrigo (19 January 1812), where each of the regimental companies provided ten men for the 'Forlorn Hope' (a spearhead of of volunteers to be first into the breach), Hamilton writes:

> Our division consisting of the brigades of Major-General Vandeleur and Colonel Barnard, was directed to assault the smaller breach, headed by a storming party of forlorn hope of 300 men, led by Major Napier of the 52nd. This party, to which I belonged were volunteers.[141]

Again, at the even more blood-stained storming of Badajoz (6 April 1812), as one of ten company volunteers for the forlorn hope, Hamilton waxes even more graphic:

> On reaching the glacis we were discovered by the garrison, and instantly a tremendous fire opened. Though the carnage in our ranks were very great, we continued our advance, and entered the covered way at the points where the palisades had been destroyed by the batteries. Owing to the darkness of the night and our attention being fixed to the fire of the enemy we came unexpectedly upon the counterscarp, and nearly half our party, myself among the number, were precipitated into the ditch below. Much bruised by the fall I lay a few minutes insensible, till on the arrival of the main body, the ladders were fixed down the counterscarp, and the descent into the ditch was quickly effected.[142]
>
> At the foot of the main breach landing of his troops, fell Sir Charles McLeod the colonel of our Regiment, as brave a soldier as ever drew a sword. 21 officers of the regiment were either killed or wounded, and of the 10 men of our company who volunteered for the forlorn hope, only myself and man by the name of Cummings came back alive, both wounded.[143]

Even in the aftermath of such a battle, few could argue that Hamilton's behaviour appeared completely unimpeachable.

The men of our regiment were so intoxicated and given up to excess, that

it was difficult to find sober men to bury the dead. At the request of our
Major, I, with the assistance of another soldier, dug our Colonel's grave.
We buried him on the top of the Powder-mill hill, outside the town'.[144]

Of Salamanca (22 July 1812), despite the direct involvement of the 43rd
Regiment, Hamilton writes primarily in the third person; and regarding Vitoria
(21 June 1813) he was surprisingly brief.

> This was the last battle in which I was engaged. We drove the French from
> Vittoria to the confines of their own country. On the day they crossed the
> lines, we had a sharp skirmish with the enemy. We then took up our posi-
> tion on the heights of Bara or Vera, where we encamped and remained
> until the latter part of August.[145]

For Hamilton, disaster struck 30 August 1813, when on a foggy advanced picket
guard he and his companions were suddenly surrounded by the French army, and
'having fired all our ammunition away, we were over powered and taken prisoner'.[146] Marched into Holland and then on to France, guarded only by French
invalids, Hamilton, along with fourteen other prisoners managed to escape,
although not without danger. 'For no sooner had we got into the woods than a
smart volley came whizzing round our ears, the effect of which we avoided by
covering ourselves on the retreat by the trees'.[147]

Reaching the safety of the advancing Prussians, Hamilton remained in Paris
until the official conclusion of peace. Following which, he boarded a King's cutter
for England, and rejoined the 2nd Battalion at Hythe Barracks, Kent.

Where, almost immediately

> An order came from the War Office, for ten sergeants to join the Duke of
> York Chasseurs, a regiment then forming on the Isle of Wight. As one of
> those ten, I volunteered, and joined that regiment, and shortly we were
> ordered to the island of St Vincent, in the West Indies.[148]

After a year or so at St Vincent with the York Chasseurs dispatched to Jamaica,
Hamilton spent time garrisoning at Fort George, Port Antonia, where 'During
our stay in this Fort we were much afflicted with disease, especially with the vom-
ito and yellow fever. Sixty-two of our company died. Here I was confined to the
hospital for three months'.[149]

Discharged at Quebec, August 1819, Hamilton wrote of

> Each private receiving from the British government a grant of land in
> Upper Canada of one hundred acres and a years provisions. Being a
> Sergeant my grant was two hundred acres, but I never saw the land nor
> availed myself of the Royal bounty. These grants were forfeited in 1843. A
> year ago, while at the Crown office in Montreal, an offer was made to me
> of one hundred acres in the consideration of my former services as a sol-
> dier in the British army.[150]

Discharged and employed as a Grand River navvy, Hamilton, the Peninsular veteran and York Chasseur sergeant suddenly developed an appetite for strong liquor! 'Here I was shorn of my strength, or more properly speaking, of my money'.[151] A failing apparently exacerbated by working the following winter in Potsdam, New York, as a waiter. 'Here I studied the drunkard's system of navigation, and had many a hard cruise in the sea of intemperance, in which my frail bark was well nigh foundered'.[152]

Hamilton spent the summer of 1820 as a canal navvy on a seven-gill-a-day grog allowance, followed by a disastrous entrepreneurial venture as a peddler when both his goods and pack were stolen in Vermont. This veteran soldier, navvy, failed peddler and perhaps near alcoholic, settled in Franklin County, where he worked on the farm of Francis Rublee and became acquainted with the Gray family, eventually marrying their daughter.

In his narrative, curiously, Hamilton makes no further reference to his wife but instead concentrates on the kindhearted piousness of his mother-in-law, particularly on her taking every opportunity to make him a Christian.

> I sought the Lord and he heard the voice of my supplication, and restored once more to me the joys of his supplication, and I again found pleasure in his service. Upon reflection, I can now see, that had I never been persuaded to read the bible, I should, in a probability have found a drunkards grave. But I thank God that he ever snatched me as a brand from the burning, and from the fires which the cursed bowl kindles on the drunkard's vitals while on earth.[153]

By 1841, however, with his father-in-law dead, his wife allegedly fleeced out of her true property rights, and a New York State resident, Hamilton, the reformed alcoholic and born-again Christian, was describing himself as a travelling lecturer of the 'Great Temperance Reformation Movement', and as such 'at the request of a large circle of acquaintances and friends, as well as from my own choice, I offer to my numerous readers (as I hope they may be) a brief and unvarnished account of my humble life and adventures'.[154]

Hamilton's Campaign with Moore and Wellington is, beyond doubt, a tale of martial dedication and duty, although unfortunately with one small but significant shortcoming. To be exact: neither the muster rolls of the 1st or 2nd Battalion of the 43rd Regiment nor of the York Chasseurs Regiment of Infantry record the presence of an Anthony Hamilton. So, is this a work of complete fiction? If not, and clearly not the work of Sergeant Anthony Hamilton, whose autobiographical narrative is it? This author believes that it is the somewhat embellished history of the 43rd regimental deserter Patrick Maher/Meagher, who took the name Anthony Hamilton after his discharge in Canada and his involvement in the American Temperance movement.

'Hamilton', an Irishman, writes of enlisting in the 43rd Regiment and setting out from 'Hive' Barracks for the 1807 Copenhagen campaign; the corresponding pay and muster roll for the 2nd Battalion 43rd Regiment at Hythe Barracks, Kent, records 'Boy Patrick Maher', a volunteer from Ireland, being promoted to private,

June 1807. There is no mention of a Hamilton, of course.

The following year at Vimeiro, Portugal, with the 43rd Regiment, 'Hamilton' writes: 'In this battle I was actively involved'; while no Hamilton is mentioned in the 43rd's regimental pay and muster roll (September–December 1808), there is a Drummer Patrick Maher, 'Stationed Abroad'.[155] Of the horrific 'Retreat from Corunna' in January 1809, 'Hamilton' writes of 'The road bestrewed by the bodies of men dying'; regimental records show Drummer Patrick Magher 'Missing in Spain', just one of the many detached stragglers during the retreat.

Following Corunna, with both 43rd battalions returned safely to England, 'Hamilton' writes of charging up the streets of Oporto taking many prisoners (May 1809), and at Talavera (July 1809) being severely wounded by the explosion of a bomb-shell. But 'Hamilton' could hardly be in two places at once, with his regiment in England at the time he claimed to be fighting in Portugal and Spain. Maher, however, is recorded on the pay and muster lists of the 1st Battalion Embodied Detachment.[156] This force was two battalions strong, made up of the convalesced sick, wounded and stragglers from the retreat to Corunna, with companies made up of men from the same regiment to encourage *esprit de corps*. The 43rd company was made up of the remnants of the 43rd Regiment and fought alongside their 52nd and 95th Light Infantry comrades in the Embodied Battalion with considerable merit at Talavera.

> Although as a regiment the 43rd were not present at Talavera, their company of detachments under Lieutenants Brown and Brockman, formed on a hill to the extreme left of the position, greatly distinguished itself by repulsing at the point of the bayonet a formidable attack. This company, consisting of 4 sergeants and 100 rank and file, lost 10 privates; Lieutenant Brown was wounded, and Captain Gardiner of the regiment, brigade-major to General Stewart, killed.[157]

At Busaco, September 1810, the 1st Battalion rejoined the conflict and the 43rd Company of the Embodied Battalion rejoined the 43rd Regiment, and with the 52nd and 95th Regiments, fused into a new and innovative Light Brigade. 'Hamilton' writes of 'a charge of bayonets ... the whole column was routed, and driven down the hill with prodigious slaughter'. The following year at Sabugal (3 April 1811), 'Hamilton' escapes death: '27 men of my own company were cut down, 13 of whom were killed, and others, myself amongst the number, wounded'; regimental records show Patrick Maher escaping unscathed.

At the storming of Ciudad Rodrigo (January 1812), 'Hamilton' claims to have volunteered for the 'forlorn hope' (first through the breach), and again in April at the even more bloody storming of Badajoz, where 300 officers and 5,000 attackers fell and where 43rd Regiment lost 20 officers and 355 killed or wounded, exceeding any other regiment. Maher was reported as sick in March and again in June, after the engagements took place. Records indeed show that James Fergusson, Maher's company captain, commanded the 43rd Regiment's volunteers storming Ciudad Rodrigo, and later, in spite of unhealed wounds, led a 300-strong party of

43rd, 52nd and 95th regimental volunteers at Badajoz. With no records obtainable on the men who accompanied him into the breach, it remains inconclusive as to Maher's participation. Maybe Hamilton/Maher volunteered at Ciudad Rodrigo and Badajoz; yet if Drummer Patrick Maher had been so heroic as his alter ego 'Hamilton' claimed, why was there no regimental recommendation for promotion to, for example, the newly introduced rank of colour sergeant?

The following list identifies the regimental recommendations for colour sergeant at the introduction of the rank in 1813. No mention of Patrick Maher – or Anthony Hamilton.

William Fitzpatrick, volunteered at the storming of St. Sebastian; lost an arm.

Richard Griffiths, volunteered at the storming of St. Sebastian.

Aaron Loveman, stormer at Badajoz.

Moses Loveman, stormer at Badajoz.

Samuel Rand, stormer at Badajoz; afterwards Quarter-Master of the regiment and Knight of Windsor.

Morgan Jones, distinguished at Badajoz.

Ewan Cameron, received a commission in 1815.

Thomas Blood, stormer at St. Sebastian, wounded severely. Received a commission in the 6th Regiment, 10 of November, 1813; his Lieutenancy on the 8th of September, 1814.

Samuel Armitage, stormer at St. Sebastian.

William Paroe, stormer at St. Sebastian.[158]

Having survived Vitoria in June 1813, 'Hamilton's' last battle was on the 30 August where, surrounded by the French on a fog-bound piquet line and having valiantly fired off all their ammunition, he and his comrades reluctantly surrendered; coincidentally, the 43rd Regiment's casualty returns record the desertion of 'Private Patrick Maher. Labourer of Ardfinnan, Tipperary'[159] three days later on 2 September.

Returning eventually to England, 'Hamilton' writes of departing for St Vincent as one of ten York Chasseurs volunteer sergeants, although the pay and muster records of the York Chasseurs fail to record such additions to the regiment. However, among this list of new arrivals at St Vincent was Private Patrick Maher, 43rd regimental deserter. Maher or Meagher's career in the York Chasseurs can be summarised thus: appointed drummer, made two unsuccessful desertion attempts in Jamaica with two likely floggings, discharged at Quebec.

The table overleaf records those men who joined the York Chasseurs from the 43rd Regiment which 'Hamilton' claims to have been part of. Only four men were subsequently discharged at Quebec as Hamilton claims to have been: Brown, Cahill, Kenyon and Meagher. These have been marked with asterisks. Brown did not join the 43rd Regiment until after the retreat from Corunna, where Hamilton claims to have been present; Cahill and Kenyon joined the York Chasseurs in 1814, when Hamilton claimed to have been in Europe; while

Table 27 York Chasseurs Sentenced from the 43rd Regiment

Name	Joined York Chasseurs	
Ahern, John	29 June 1815	Volunteered into the 58th while still at Jamaica, March 1819
Brown/Browne, Edward*	29 June 1815	Discharged Quebec
Brown, John	18 October 1816	Deserted – 31 May 1819
Bull, William	29 June 1815	Deserted – 8 May 1819
Cahill, Michael*	5 February 1814	Discharged Quebec
Crossland, George	29 June 1815	Died – 1 October 1816
Dougherty, John	29 June 1815	Died – 1 November 1817
Kenyon, John*	1 February 1814	Discharged Quebec
Land, Edward	29 June 1815	Died – 10 December 1817
Maher/ Meagher, Patrick*	29 June 1815	Discharged Quebec
Murphy, Dennis	1 February 1814	Died – 11 October 1816
Pearce, John	25 March 1814	Deserted – 2 June 1814
Truesdale, John	29 June 1815	Deserted – 30 May 1819
Wainwright, Joseph	29 June 1815	Died – 8 October 1816
Winwood, Richard	7 March 1814	Died – 21 October 1816

Maher/Meagher arrived in St Vincent in November 1815 at the very time Hamilton claimed to have arrived there.

In Canada land offers were made to discharged servicemen, but neither the names of Maher nor Hamilton appear in the records; under which name would he have claimed it? Likewise, while Sergeant Thomas Leonard, late of the 50th Regiment of Foot and colour sergeant of the York Chasseurs, claimed his 1793–1814 Military General Service medal, significantly 'Sergeant Anthony Hamilton', survivor of Corunna, Oporto, Talavera, Ciudad Rodrigo, Badajoz, Salamanca and Vitoria, and self-aggrandising author, did not.

Hamilton's narrative is a mixture of fact and fiction; who can be sure of what happened in Canada and America after his discharge; and what reasons lay behind his change of identity and the motivation for writing his book. Perhaps Maher wanted to conceal his disgrace as a deserter. 'Hamilton' became a stalwart of the 'Great Temperance Reformation Movement' and his fictional service record may have played well to Temperance audiences; whatever the case it managed to fool readers and military academics for over a century.

A full list of men serving with the Yoork Chasseurs is given in the Appendix, Table 44

Chapter Seven

Canada and Disbandment

By late 1818, with Louis XVIII safely settled at Versailles, Napoleon banished to St Helena and a British Army reduction of 35,000 officers and men under way, York Chasseur officers currently in England, on leave, convalescing or waiting embarkation had all immediately gone to half pay. Even the recaptured Private Thomas Covell, a deserter from Jamaica, unexpectedly benefited.

> Horse Guards. 23rd November, 1818
>
> As the York Chasseurs have been ordered to be disbanded, His Royal Highness approves of Thomas Covell, who has been committed to confinement at Louth, as a Deserter from that regiment, being discharged and furnished with the usual protecting Certificate of Discharge.
>
> John Macdonald. Deputy Adjutant General[160]

Nevertheless, with officers in Britain placed on half pay and Private Thomas Covell happily in receipt of a Certificate of Discharge, it was not until January 1819 that Major Paterson, acting commanding officer at Jamaica, learnt of the regiment's planned deployment to Quebec and intended disbandment. For officers still in Jamaica, however, the choices were simple: proceed to Canada and receive two months full pay on disbandment or lose no time in returning to England and receive two months full pay on arrival.

The vast majority of men took passage for Canada and disbandment, based perhaps on the recommendation of company officers or even the commanding officer in person; a minority had two further options, discharge at Jamaica (see Table 28, on page 96) or a transfer into a regular line regiment currently stationed in the West Indies.

Inconsistency almost certainly describes the behaviour of the 22-year-old former 23rd regimental deserter, Michael Leader, who, having volunteered for the 58th Regiment, promptly deserted 67 days later. After which and possibly more inexplicably, a recaptured Leader gave 17 further years of apparently unblemished service in both the East and West Indies, which was only terminated when in

Table 28 Regimental Transfers in Jamaica

From	Name	Date	To
Volunteer	Colour Sergeant Hector Mackay	June 1819	50th Foot
? General Service Deserter	Sergeant Evan Davies	March 1819	2nd West India Regiment
? 62nd Volunteer 3rd Foot Guards Deserter	Sergeant Thomas Forrester	March 1819	2nd West India Regiment
Volunteer	Corporal James Darby	June 1819	58th Foot
23rd Deserter	Drummer Michael Leader	March 1819	58th Foot
43rd Deserter	Drummer John Ahern	March 1819	58th Foot
48th Deserter	Private William Haswell	March 1819	58th Foot
14th or 98th Deserter	Drummer James Brown	June 1819	92nd Foot

1836, having suffered two severe bouts of dysentery and with a diagnosis of 'Chronic Dysentery and a Debilitated Constitution' he was invalided to England and a pension.

As bizarre was the behaviour of the former 43rd deserter, John Ahern, a volunteer for the 58th Regiment and later the 21st Regiment, who, when discharged five years later in England, would volunteer for the Royal African Corps. Despite all his volunteering, it seems Ahern was hardly God's gift to the military, for he was discharged to a pension with general conduct described as merely 'tolerable'.

Far easier to explain are the actions of Colour Sergeant Hector Mackay and Corporal James Darby who as volunteers and with post-war unemployment widespread amongst discharged soldiers perhaps looked to the regular pay, victuals and added security of the military.

For those taking their discharge in Jamaica (see Table 29 opposite), a gunsmith, schoolmaster, jeweller and blacksmith, even a potter, baker, blacksmith or shoemaker might just compete in a slave-based economy; but for the others the West Indies was teeming with impoverished, unskilled and unemployed Europeans. Newcomers such as Private John Richards, unskilled with a wife to support, and a sentence of solitary confinement for attempted stabbing of his wife behind him, had no guarantee of employment.

Horse Guards instructions apparently reached Jamaica by early January 1819, and it seems Paterson may well have decided to delay its general circulation as long as was possible, an extremely far-sighted decision as it turned out. With the news breaking through official channels or barrack-room rumour the reaction was just as Paterson had anticipated, namely a dramatic rise in desertion, perhaps because men desperate to return to their loved ones considered Jamaica a more expedient embarkation point for Europe than Canada (see Table 31, on page 98).

With the Regimental Headquarters embarking aboard *Chapman* and those companies garrisoning San la Mar (sic), Port Antonia, Lucea, Falmouth and Maroon Town, aboard the transport vessels *Ocean* and *Nautilus*, the York Chasseurs departed Montego Bay, Jamaica, on 24 June 1819, leaving behind four sergeants, five corporals, five drummers and 91 private soldiers as recent successful deserters.

After 49 days at sea and four York Chasseurs dead, 28 sergeants, nine drummers and 533 private soldiers all stepped ashore at Quebec, and were finally discharged on 24 August 1819, with the exception of three sergeants, two corporals and six privates, all volunteers, discharged a month later to return aboard the *Nautilus* to Portsmouth on Saturday 23 October 1819.

In light of the regiment's record of ill discipline and desertion, no one could ques-

Table 29 Men Discharged at Stony Hill, Jamaica, June, 1819

Colour Sergeant William Browning	Labourer of St Martins, Kent
Armourer Sergeant Francis O'Brien	Gunsmith of Cork
Corporal James Wilcox	Weaver of Westleigh, Lancashire
Drummer James Binder	Labourer of Woodham, Essex
Private Dennis Curran	Labourer of Fermanagh
Private Joseph Daniels	Potter of Staffordshire
Private John Dugan	Labourer of Galway
Private Robert Goulding	Labourer of Antrim
Private Henry Gwilliams	Blacksmith of Gloucestershire
Private John Hartshorn	Schoolmaster of Warwickshire
Private Samuel Jones	Labourer of Worcestershire
Private Thomas Lambeth	Jeweller of Warwick
Private Henry Lovell	Baker of Halifax
Private John Monaghan	Labourer of Fermanagh
Private John Murphy	Shoemaker of Wexford
Private John Richards	Labourer of Leeds
Private Francis Rossean	Shoemaker of Dublin
Private John Sellard	Weaver of Gloucestershire
Private John Shea	Labourer of Tipperary

tion the resident Deputy Adjutant General's sense of trepidation at the thought of hordes of condemned and dissolute ex-soldiers descending on the good people of Quebec (see Appendix, Table 45, pages 298–315). His anxieties were entirely misplaced, however, 'In that their conduct both previous to and since the reduction has been much more quite and orderly than was expected from the Report which had been received of their general character and composition'.[161]

Why were condemned regiments like the Royal West Indies Rangers, Royal

York Rangers and York Chasseurs all disbanded in Canada? Could it be that their criminality, ill reputation and seriousness of sentencing made them too undesirable to return to Britain?

Significantly, following the American War of 1812–1814 and invasion of Upper

Table 30 Desertion Attempts in Jamaica (1819)

January	February	March	April	May	June
3	12	49	90	58	19

24 June: Regiment embarked aboard transport vessels

Canada, the colony's militia now had a pressing need for experienced discharged soldiers, irrespective of reputation, to offset the expense of additional regular regiments needed from Britain. Consequently, with Europe now at peace but with Ontario rife with republican sympathisers, settling 'loyal' British immigrants and discharged soldiers along the inland military waterway between the Ottawa River and Lake Ontario, would likely dilute any existing republicanism.

With discharged soldiers settling Perth Military Settlement's surrounding regions, with all men aged between 16 and 60 liable for duty, any future incursion into Lanark County would now meet a militia with more than just a smattering of experienced former soldiers.

Later events demonstrated, however, that a scheme offering free land to discharged soldiers would only be as effective as the quality of those actually participating, a point clearly highlighted when comparing the experience of the 99th Regiment against that of condemned regiments. When men of the 99th were offered the choice between the £10 discharge bounty or waste land, almost 300 of the regiment chose land, a year's full rations and two months full pay. In stark contrast, the vast majority of Royal York Rangers discharged at Nova Scotia selected the bounty; of the 540 Royal West India Rangers discharged at Quebec, only 40 preferred homesteading; and, from 567 discharged York Chasseurs, only 53 would opt for waste land.

There is some doubt as to how many of those Royal York Rangers, Royal West India Rangers or York Chasseurs choosing land actually became homesteaders, or indeed even took up their option. It is scarcely surprising that few condemned soldiers, many more used to the loom, industrial factory or the urban rookeries than the plough or the milking shed, should elect for the hardships of farming in preference to £10 (40 dollars frontier) in ready money, when in front of them lay the long, tedious and sometimes hazardous passage from Quebec to Lanark County. 'He lands at Quebec, where he goes to Montreal (180 miles) in a steamboat, thence in carriage, or he walks, 9 miles, to where they embark in the great boats for Upper Canada; these boats are forced against the stream by long poles, and gain twenty-twenty-five miles per day'.[162]

For those York Chasseurs who made the passage, they arrived at a settlement first established in 1815 by 700 men, women and children from Greenock, Scotland, following the promise of free land, implements and rations, on the banks of the River Tay, Lanark County. Tough and resourceful Scottish immigrants, well used to all the hardships expected in settling the newly surveyed townships of Bathurst, Beckwith, Russell and Drummond.

> Arrived at his land, he has no shelter till he builds his house, except at the habitation of some neighbour, and this rarely happens, as they stand very distant from each other; he must then immediately cut down trees and build his house with the trunks, clear his land of brushwood etc by fire, and then plant between the trunks, as it is difficult to root them up, and by degree ameliorate his land, till he has got a comfortable dwelling place for his cattle etc.[163]

With a number preferring Perth's urban environment, by 1816 both immigrant and discharged soldiers now set about clearing land, building log cabins and preparing for the onset of their first Canadian winter. Sadly, as with many such ventures, progress was slow in the presence of extreme hardship; and thus it was in the case in Lanark County where in 1818 and the following two years of partial crop failures, many of the neediest survived only as a result of the government's half ration free handouts. By 1821, however, as cleared land became more productive and with essential commodity prices moderating, Perth Military Settlement not only survived, but was now prospering.

Each military claimant pledged to clear a minimum seven acres of scrubland in five years, so life was still one of hard toil. On the other hand, with each discharged soldier-cum-settler in receipt of a free shovel, axe, hoe, scythe, knife, hammer, kettle and handsaw, and for some the makings of a log cabin – twelve panes of glass, a pound of putty and twelve pounds of nails – there was the backup of government assistance.

Predictably, while 53 York Chasseurs may have chosen land over bounty, only

Table 31 Free Land Allowances for Discharged Soldiers

Half-pay Colonels	1200 acres
Half-pay Majors	1000 acres
Half-pay Captains	800 acres
Half-pay Subalterns	500 acres
Discharged Sergeants	200 acres
Discharged Corporals	150 acres
Discharged Privates	100 acres

seventeen seem to have bothered to travel and take up residence (see Table 32, pages 100–101) and emulate the sturdy, hardworking, farming Scottish immigrants.

As the 1816–1822 *Upper Canada Land Records* clearly indicates, about 1,000 discharged soldiers from regiments as diverse as DeMeuron's, DeWatterville's, regular infantry and cavalry regiments, as well as former sailors, all received free land

Table 32 York Chasseurs Allocated Land Grants in Upper Canada, 12 February to 18 September 1819[164]

Name	Country	Date	Township	Conc.	Lot	Remarks
Sergeant John Taylor	England	18 Sept 1819	Beckwith	8	SW6	No record
John Pollard	England	ditto	ditto	8	SW9	No record
John Mosley	England	ditto	ditto	8	NE9	No record
William Allan	England	ditto	ditto	9	SW4	No record
Jonas Alberton	England	ditto	ditto	9	NE4	No record
William Mills	England	ditto	ditto	9	SW5	No record
William Philpot	England	ditto	ditto	9	NE5	No record
Michael McConnell	Ireland	22 Sept 1819	ditto	10	NE13	Wife & son*
Thomas Riley	Ireland	ditto	ditto	10	SW13	No record
Sergeant John Cocker	England	ditto	ditto	9	10	No record
George Cliff	England	ditto	ditto	9	SW11	Wife, son & daughter*
Dennis Gingley	England	ditto	ditto	10	SW11	Unaccompanied*
Thomas Connor	Ireland	ditto	ditto	10	NE11	Wife, son & daughter*
Cpl Patrick Fitzgerald	Ireland	ditto	ditto	10	SW9	No record
Cpl Thomas Quirk	Ireland	ditto	ditto	10	NE12	No record
Dennis O'Laughlin	Ireland	ditto	ditto	10	SW12	No record
John McDonald	Ireland	ditto	ditto	10	8	Unaccompanied*
William Melson	Ireland	ditto	ditto	11	8	Unaccompanied*
Bernard McStravock	Ireland	ditto	ditto	11	NE11	Unaccompanied*
James Carson	Ireland	ditto	ditto	11	SW12	Unaccompanied*
Roderick McKenzie	Scotland	ditto	ditto	11	NE12	No record
Edward Garry	Ireland	ditto	ditto	11	SW13	No record
James Nash	England	ditto	ditto	11	NE13	Wife and son*
John Millage	England	ditto	ditto	9	NE11	Unaccompanied*
William Richardson	England	ditto	ditto	6	SW6	No record
John Kelly	England	ditto	ditto	6	NE6	No record
Sgt David Oram	Ireland	1 Oct 1819	Drummond	2	SW25	No later record
Richard Allan	England	3 Oct 1819	ditto	4	NE25	No later record
Andrew Murphy	Ireland	ditto	ditto	4	SW22	No later record
William Wilson	England	ditto	ditto	3	NE25	Unaccompanied*
Sgt Maj William Hyland	Ireland	ditto	Bathurst	4	SW13	No later record

Upper Canada, Located Settlers. Continued

Name	Country	Date	Township	Conc.	Lot	Remarks
SgtThomas Leonard	Spain	ditto	ditto	10	15	Wife, 2 sons and daughter★
Michael Grady	Ireland	7 Oct 1819	ditto	10	SW16	No later record
James Ramsey	Scotland	ditto	ditto	10	NE14	No later record
William Rippon	England	ditto	ditto	10	SW14	No later record
Richard Beasley	England	ditto	ditto	10	SW13	No later record
Joseph Hazledine	England	ditto	ditto	10	NE13	No later record
John Brogan	Ireland	ditto	ditto	10	NE12	No later record
John Horan	Ireland	ditto	ditto	10	SW12	No later record
Joseph Holly	England	ditto	ditto	9	NE 8	No later record
Timothy Grindrick	England	ditto	ditto	9	SW 8	No later record
Cpl Robert Clarke	Ireland	ditto	ditto	6	NE 6	Unaccompanied★
William Bygrove	Ireland	ditto	ditto	7	SW 6	Unaccompanied★
Angus Cameron	Scotland	12 Oct 1819	ditto	7	NE5	No later record
James Trueman	England	15th Oct 1819	ditto	7	SW11	No later record
William Thorp Exchanged to 9 SW15	England	ditto	ditto	11	NE14	Unaccompanied★
Thomas Hays 10 October, 1820 exchanged to Beckwith Concession 10, Lot NE9★	Ireland	19 Oct 1819	Beckwith	11	SW10	Wife
Stephen Smith	Ireland	21 Oc 1819	Bathurst	8	NE13	No later record
James Robinson	Ireland	27 Oct 1819	Bathurst	8	SW13	No later record
Cpl Richard Crone	Ireland	8 Jul 1820	Drummond	4	NE23	Unaccompanied★

★ *denotes proof of settlement*

grants. Some of whom persevered and indeed prospered, while others it seems, with their free supply of rations exhausted, simply melted away. (Legend has it that one former sergeant exchanged his 200 acres for a single bottle of rum.) Disbanded and dispersed, if not to Lanark County, then where? Upper and Lower Canada, to Britain or to the more 'civilised' United States of America?

Of all Lanark County's York Chasseurs, arguably it is Thomas Leonard who proves of most interest. Born in Gibraltar (1778–1780), son of Private Patrick Leonard of the 50th (Royal West Kent) Regiment who in September 1790, as a ten-year-old still in Gibraltar, followed his father into the regiment. Possibly for the first time in his life, with a guinea and a half bounty clutched in his young palm and his experienced father fending off predators, the twelve-year-old Thomas would have felt quite affluent.

In February 1794, with just three years of service, rumours of revolt in Corsica gave the teenage drummer his first experience of real soldiering when the 50th

Sergeant Thomas Leonard dressed in 1854 militia-style uniform

Courtesy of Dr Therald (Ted) Leonard

Regiment, alongside a regiment of cavalry and four regiments of infantry, landed to preserve the island from the menace of revolution. The expedition ended in failure, however, when two years later the united French and Spanish fleets commanding the Mediterranean directed their attentions towards Corsica where the majority of inhabitants supported the revolutionary cause, and the British army prudently withdrew to the security of Elba.

Returning to Gibraltar early 1797, by June the 50th Regiment were in Portugal garrisoning Fort St Julian, where Private Thomas Leonard embarked as part of the Egyptian Expeditionary Force. Landing under intense cannon fire at Aboukir Bay, the regiment next advanced towards Alexandria where in March 1801 with 1,100 British soldiers dead or wounded, over 50 of them from his own regiment, the young private survived his first bloody battle.

Thomas Leonard's Military General Service medal with campaign clasps showing Egypt, Vimeira, Corunna, Vitoria, Nivelle, Orthes and Toulouse

Courtesy of Dr Therald (Ted) Leonard

Less than a month later with the French having made two courageous but desperate charges against an exposed 50th, and with 1,700 French and 1,500 British soldiers lying wounded and dead 'Tyr the God of Battle and Victory' once again spared the life of the twenty-year-old private, though not that of the British Commander, General Ralph Abercrombie, who died of a gangrenous thigh wound a week later.

In fact, Leonard's good fortune would even extend to the battle's aftermath where, in temperatures often 120 degrees fahrenheit in the shade, he not only avoided the plague and dysentery destroying friend and foe alike, but the scourge of 'Egyptian ophthalmia' that so afflicted the 50th Regiment that it acquired the epithet, 'Blind Half-Hundred'.

With victory achieved and leaving Egypt's blood-sodden sands, flies and diseases behind it in May 1802 the 50th landed in Ireland where five years later Sergeant Thomas Leonard would embark for Copenhagen. A year after that, having defeated Denmark, the regiment, nearly 1,000 men strong, took passage from Portsmouth to Portugal as part of Lieutenant-General Sir Arthur Wellesley's army.

In Portugal, having first protected Wellesley's disembarking reinforcements from the withering fire of General Junot's skirmishing *tirailleurs* from Vimeira Hill, the 50th Regiment with combined disciplined musket fire and the bayonet, would now disperse the rapidly advancing massed columns of the enemy.

The 50th were next to me as we went, and I recollect the firmness with which they rushed on that charge, appearing like a wall of iron. The enemy could not stand the sight, and before we encountered they turned and ran for it.[165]

Defeated and in full flight back to Lisbon, the French had now left the battlefield strewn with hastily flung muskets, side arms, well-filled knapsacks and about 1,000 dead. The regiment's legacy of the battle was the soubriquet acquired by the fact that their faces were grimed from powder, smoke, sweat and black dye of their shako's – 'The Dirty Half-Hundred'.

Hampshire Telegraph and Sussex Chronicle. Monday January 2nd, 1809

SPIRITED CONDUCT OF THE 50th REGIMENT AT THE BAT-TLE OF VIMIERA – The gallant conduct of this Regiment, which is common with the rest of our troops engaged in the memorable battle of Vimiera – eminently distinguished themselves.
    During the hottest part of the action, the 50th was stationed in a valley, on the brow of which Sir A Wellesley had placed himself, looking on with anxious expectation to the result of a charge made upon them by a strong and superior body of the enemy. The 50th stood with arms ordered while the French were coming down on them with great fury, until they had arrived within twenty yards. They then immediately shouldered arms, and fired with the utmost steadfastness; then rushed with fixed bayonets upon the enemy. Having made a difficult conversion movement they completely routed them and drove them back. The gallant Sir A Wellesley exclaimed with exultation of joy at their heroic conduct; and instantly gal-loped off to the left wing, declaring himself assured of victory.

After Vimeiro, Leonard and his regiment marched along the Tagus until crossing the Zezere River to join Sir John Moore's main army at Salamanca, and later to take part in the heartrending 'Retreat from Corunna'. During which, closely pur-sued by a vastly superior French army and with the 50th Regiment frequently forming part of the rearguard, their fearful forced marches hampered by deep December snow, chilled by wintry blasts, through continuous winter rains and across ice-cold fast running rivers, men, women and children of Moore's tragic army made a gradual and piteous passage towards Corunna and sanctuary. 'At intervals rain poured down with such tremendous force, that our open and strag-gling columns were compelled to halt, and close up in a solid body; in order that only the exterior of the mass might be exposed to the pelting fury of the storm'.[166]
    Harassed by the enemy and with the British Army's much-vaunted discipline at times crumbling, drunken soldiers, pitifully exhausted women and children, many completely barefooted, lay abandoned and at the mercy of their pursuers. Scenes of such tragedy that the 50th Regiment, replenished with both clothing and footwear from an abandoned store, through mind-numbing continuous wind, rain, sleet and snow, but with discipline intact, would have to fight through

as rearguard.

Finally, 16 January 1809, a pursued British army, numbering less than 15,000 men and just nine cannons, now turned to confront the 20,000 men and massed cannon of Marshall Soult. With Sergeant Leonard and his regiment positioned nearest the enemy and as French cannon round shot landed, the 50th, alongside the 42nd Regiment, now turned on their enemy with a savage bayonet charge. In the following hours of vicious and often hand-to-hand fighting and before embarking to safety, the British army lost its commander, Lieutenant General Sir John Moore, and the 50th Regiment approximately 180 wounded and dead.

With the British army back in England with '700 wounded and sick soldiers being landed at Royal Hospital, Haslar, where more were being carried hourly',[167] a bedraggled but safe 50th Regiment, and a still unscathed Thomas Leonard, could now make their slow, and, for many of the veterans, exhausting march, out from the Gosport peninsula towards the peaceful tranquility of a Kent barrack-room.

During the Walcheren Expedition that followed, the 50th Regiment once again flirted with danger and death, although not so much from French shot and shell but rather from 'the fever', a pestilence so deadly as to force an eventual British withdrawal, and so ubiquitous as to affect even a sturdy Thomas Leonard.

> The poisonous exhalations and marsh miasmata from the loathsome waters of the canal, Combined with the fervid and contaminated air, generated and extended the deadly endemic. Men and officers were attacked in the most sudden and violent manner while on parade, and were led away under the fatal illness, from which they were soon released by the hand of death. The hospitals were filled, and the convalescents reduced to so low a state, that it was a considerable time before they were fit for any service.[168]

Ostensibly sufficiently recovered to accompany his regiment to Lisbon, like many veterans of Walcheren, he soon re-convalesced in Abrantes General Hospital. Restored to sufficient health, Leonard participated in and survived Vitoria, and in the battle's aftermath escorted the regimental wounded to hospital. Presumably, not before acquiring a share of the 'King's Ransom' strewn and abandoned by Marshall Jourdan's stricken army.

A month later, with or without battlefield booty, Leonard was once again facing danger when the 50th Regiment defended a pass in the Pyrenees against the rejuvenated army of Marshall Soult.

They surprised part of D'Armagnac's Division just as they had gained the summit of the Lessessa Pass in the centre, and, immediately charging, drove them clean out of the pass. They joined the 34th Regiment, and these regiments poured a destructive fire on the advancing foe. But Abbe's Division having arrived, they were again compelled to fall back, and the 50th Regiment now retired to the position taken up by the 92nd Regiment.

Miltary chest belonging to Thomas Leonard
Courtesy of Dr Therald (Ted) Leonard

Here they formed in line in front of about 5,000 of the enemy, who advanced in contiguous columns. The Regiment, undaunted by numbers, charged, and crossing bayonets with the confident foe, threw them into confusion. The loss of the regiment was so severe, that it was obliged to retire a short distance, when it again charged, crossing bayonets a second time with the imposing columns, who, confident in their great numerical superiority, rallied after each charge, and kept up such a destructive fire as reduced the regiment in a short time to about half the number it brought into action.

The regiment again retired in the steadiest manner about 200 paces, and it was again preparing to charge when an order was received to retire to a rocky ridge a little in the rear, where it was followed by the 92nd Regiment, who had lost two-thirds of their numbers, in this gallant struggle.[169]

With Wellington and the allied cause in ascendancy and Soult in retreat, in fording the Vive River and with the battles of Pyrenees and Nivelle behind them, the 50th Regiment and Thomas Leonard were now heading the British advance. Musket and powder held aloft, wading through cold, breast-high rapid running water, under covering fire of British cannon against heavy musketry, the regiment routed their opponents with bayonet.withstanding a fierce counter-attack, the bayonets of the 50th Regiment once again flashed dispersing the strong column of French infantry barely fifteen paces away.

Now, with the British Army on French soil, and despite two battles still to come and death stalking even the most minor skirmishes, the odds began lengthening on Leonard's survival. Toulouse, Leonard's last battle, was also the most pointless, as Bonaparte had abdicated four days earlier. Afterwards, in June 1814, with death and destruction finally concluded, the 1st Battalion of the 50th Regiment took passage from Bordeaux for duty in Ireland, but leaving Sergeant Leonard behind as Acting Assistant Provost Marshall until the October.

At that moment, with his years of hazardous campaigning safely negotiated, logic might have it that Leonard, accompanied by his Irish born wife and two young children, would continue peacetime soldiering in Ireland. On the contrary, for Leonard, a sergeant of ten years seniority with twenty-six years of unblemished service with the regiment deserted in July 1816.

Instead of the prestige due to a time-honoured sergeant, Leonard faced a reduction to private, a passage across the Irish Sea and Severn Estuary to Gloucester and a cold prison cell, followed by an eight-day march to Portsmouth, a crossing to the Isle of Wight, and finally along with 63 other drafts, a passage to the West Indies. Leonard might well have reflected on his ignominious position and the uncertain future that lay ahead for him and his family.

While Leonard's decision to desert may seem incomprehensible, the glowing testimonial accompanying him into confinement makes the entire episode even more unfathomable:

> Thomas Leonard served from the 1st September 1790 until the 24th of July 1816, being born in the Army and enlisted in Gibraltar, at the age of ten years, of which time he was above twelve years a non commissioned officer, viz. ten years a sergeant and two a corporal, the former rank he held at leaving the Regiment, that he was present with the corps at the capture of the Island of Corsica: and the different operations of the campaign in Egypt; at the expedition to Copenhagen, the battle of Vimeiro; the taking of the Island of Walcheren and South Beolin; the battle of Vittoria and every other action in which they were engaged during the Spanish War. That he was a noble soldier and was always a worthy good man.[170]
> Signed this 17th day October 1816. C. Hill. Colonel Commanding. 50th Regiment

Why would a sergeant of such obvious quality be so carelessly dismissed from the regiment and not simply reduced to private? It is possible that at some point he had openly fallen out with a commissioned officer, the consequence of which would have been his removal from the regiment, and the testimonial compensation for a blatant injustice.

Landing in Jamaica as a private in November 1816, by April Leonard was a ser-

Above: Concession allocated to Sergeant Thomas Leonard, Bathurst, Canada

Courtesey of Mr and Mrs Willows

Above: Scrubland in Bathurst, Canada, similar to that cleared by Thomas Leonard

geant again and by February 1819 colour sergeant, restoring in some slight measure his professional self respect. Discharged at Quebec, the six foot one inch, 40-
year-old, totally inexperienced in civilian life, with a wife and three young
children, now made the long passage to Upper Canada, Concession 10, Lot 15,
Bathurst, Lanark County, to their 200 acres of Waste Land. Two years later and
possibly as a true measure of the man, having cleared the requisite area of scrubland demanded, Leonard graduated to fully-fledged rate-paying landholder.

In November 1821, in possession of a Discharge Certificate confirming 'he
was not incapacitated by a sentence of a General Courts Martial from receiving a
Pension,'[171] Leonard began to receive his 'one shilling and eleven pence per diem'
army pension, and in 1824 he purchased Pierre Lavaynt's Concession 6, Lot 24
for £112. He did not sell his original 200 acres for a further five years, and then for
a mere £25, which begs the question of how he had accumulated his capital – 'battlefield booty' perhaps.

In January 1830 a number of Lanark County's increasingly ageing pensioners
all assembled at the inn of Thomas Wickharing, Perth, and there discussed peti-
tioning the Governor in Chief with regards to the difficulties of reporting in person at Bytown (modern day Ottawa).

> To – His Excellency Sir James Kempt. K.C.B. Governor in Chief and
> Commander of the Forces.[172]
> The Petition of his Majesty's Out Pensioners residing in the county of
> Lanark and its vicinity,
> Humbly Herewith.
> That your petitioners in consequence of an order issued by the
> Commissionary General, directing all pensioners to attend annually at
> Bytown.
> Your Excellencies Petitioners most respectfully beg leave to state that
> last years fatiguing journey, was attended with more expense than many
> petitioners quarterly allowances came to; likewise the extreme hardships
> to all, owing to the distance being from S Sherbrooke 180 miles there and
> returning meant travelling 180 miles in the depth of winter on bad roads.
> This to men debilitated by wounds, age and other diseases contracted in
> the services, has occasioned many deaths or sickness since last year.
> Which induces us most humbly to solicit tour Excellency's protection,
> and humbly hope that your Excellency will be graciously pleased to take
> our case into your serious consideration and direct that a Commissioned
> Officer be directed to attend at Perth for the purpose of identifying and
> paying Pensioners residing in the County of Lanark and its vicinity.
> Which indulgence will add to the many memorable Acts of your
> Excellency of the Old Soldiers, save life and much unnecessary expense to
> the loss of poor families.
>
> By order of the meeting.

Quarter Master Sergeant Alex Matheson	Late Glengary Fencibles.
	Chairman.
Sergeant Alexander McDonald	Late Canadian Fencibles

Quarter Master Sergeant Edward Collings	?
Sergeant Thomas Leonard	Late York Chasseurs
Charles McManus	Late 103rd Foot
James Robinson	Late 104th Foot.
John Charles.	Late Canadian Fencibles.
James McMaster	Late 27th Inniskillings
Denis Noonan	Late 41st Foot.
Michael Cullan	Late 8th Foot
Joseph Kernel	?
Robert Fitzsimmons	9th Dragoons.
William Sullivan	7th Royal Veteran Battalion.
Sergeant John Rice	?

Secretary
Perth. 8th January 1830

It may well have taken in excess of six years, but eventually persistence and logic did overcome the bureaucratic mindset.

Bathurst Courier and Ottawa General Advertiser. Friday September 2nd 1836.

NOTICE TO CHELSEA & GREENWICH PENSIONERS Pensions will be paid at the Office of the Commissariat, nearest to the place at which they reside.

After ten years of hard toil on the land, and both well in their fifties, £100 changed hands and Thomas and Elizabeth took retirement at Perth, the farm passing to their eldest son James. Ten years after that, in December 1840, two days before James's marriage to Jane Cooper Caldwell, with £100 changing hands again, the sixty-year-old Leonards returned to the homestead. By the time of the 1851 census, the farmstead was producing peas, oats, wheat, Indian corn and potatoes in abundance, and had as livestock a bull, three milk cows, four calves, two horses, two sheep and five pigs.[173] Finally, in March 1854, now in their seventies, they accepted from Duncan McIntyre's the sum of £350, and once again retired to Perth, where Thomas Leonard, survivor of Egypt, Corunna, Walcheran, Spain, Portugal and the West Indies, and sometime deserter, died. His widow survived him.

The Perth Courier. Friday, October 9th, 1868.

'Leonard – On Saturday last, the 3rd inst, at his residence and in the 93rd year of his age, Sergeant Thomas Leonard.'

Born the son of a private soldier in eighteenth-century Gibraltar, Leonard became a respected ratepayer of Lanark County and witnessed the taming of Lanark

NOTICE.

WHEREAS, it has been the practice for the Chelsea and Kilmainham Pensioners to give up their Instruction Papers to Agents, and receive their Pensions through that channel, instead of appearing personally for the purpose of being identified as His Majesty's instructions require. The Commissary General hereby gives notice, that all Pensions must be claimed in person, at least once in each year.—The Pensioners resident at Richmond, Perth and vicinity will in future receive their Pensions, on and after the 25th December 1828 at By-Town instead of Montreal, and they must claim their first payment at that Post in person, so that their existence and identity may be proved, as no other person or persons are (pursuant to Act of Parliament) entitled to receive the same, under any pretence whatsoever if the Pensioner is living. Any Pensioner wishing to change his place of residence must notify the same through the Commissariat Officer from whom he received his last payment.

COMMISSARIAT, HEAD QUARTERS,
Quebec, 18th September 1828.

Notice for Lanark County military pensioners, 1828

County and the trappings of nineteenth-century society and innovation – the advent of the railway, public library, mechanics institute and debating society, macadamised and plank roads, even the formation of a local cricket club.

Of their progeny, the author is extremely grateful for both the contribution and encouragement of Dr Therald L (Ted) Leonard DDS, a direct descendent of Thomas Leonard, who now resides in Auburn, near Seattle, Washington.

Of their eldest son James, it seems that after seven years of marriage, his wife had chosen to leave, taking her children with her, accompanying her parents to Salt Lake City with the Church of Jesus Christ of Latter-day Saints, perhaps in flight from her husband's alleged appetite for strong liquor.

At Monroe, Michigan, death struck James's wife and her father, although James did manage to see his wife before she died. He left his children in the care of his surviving in-laws and travelled on to Detroit where he joined the 15th Infantry, and fought in the Mexican War. Eventually he returned to Bathurst and died there on 29 March 1882, aged 74.

Thomas, the Leonards' youngest son, also migrated to America, where he joined the New Hampshire Volunteers and fought for the Union. The Civil War over, Thomas settled in Haverhill, New Hampshire, and set up a harness shop. He died there in 1905. Nothing is known of Mary Ann Leonard and John, the Leonards' second eldest child.

With old York Chasseurs comrades like Corporal William Bygrove to the south-west and Corporal Robert Clarke to the northeast, Leonard had the company of those who had endured the European wars and the oppressive heat, hurricanes, mosquitoes of the West Indies. In the long Canadian winter no doubt they talked of long dead comrades and the warmer Caribbean climes with wistful nostalgia.

William Bygrove first appears on the 16th Regiment's Regimental Roll in December 1811 to March 1812, and as the regiment left Cork for Quebec in March 1814, was recorded as a 'Prisoner – Sent to the Army Depot to Serve Abroad'.[174] Whether a convict or deserter, Bygrove arrived at the prison-ship on 1 May 1815. Released to the regiment in June 1815, Bygrove arrived at St Vincent in November and settled Bathurst's Concession 7, Lot SW 6 after his discharge at Quebec.

Land records reveal that in April 1847, with his wife Mary (née Paget) dead, and three young children to support, Bygrove sold out to the former York Chasseurs corporal, Robert Clarke, for £37. By the 1851 census, Bygrove, along with thirteen-year-old Elizabeth, Edward, aged eleven, and the nine-year-old Isabella, now occupied Concession 8, Lot 12 at Bathurst.

Elizabeth is known to have married Robert McClary and Edward, Elizabeth Gamble, but Isabella's marital status is still something of a mystery. The *Perth Courier* of 19 February 1864 records a letter at Perth's post office giving Isabella Bygrove as addressee, so it clear that at that date she was still a spinster. William Bygrove, himself, like Thomas Leonard, lived a long life, dying in his ninetieth year at Bollingbrooke, Lanark County.

John Millage, a nineteen-year-old Bath labourer, enlisted at Bath for the 55th (Westmoreland) Regiment in 29 November 1816, and having pouched his £5 bounty, deserted just six days later, for which he was imprisoned at Portchester Castle in January 1817, released in April to the York Chasseurs and a posting to Jamaica in May.

Discharged to settle Beckwith's Concession 9, Lot 11 north-east, Millage married Christianna Kennedy and in the 1830s accepted £40 for his homestead, somewhat less than the going rate if one considers the price Richard Crone received for his homestead in 1839.

Of those men discharged at Quebec, perhaps the most unfathomable is William Hyland, a former clerk of Queen's County, who in January 1812, while at the East India Company's Isle of Wight depot, volunteered for the 2nd Battalion, 12th Foot, where he was promoted colour sergeant in September 1814 and transferred into the 1st battalion bound for India, from which in December 1814 he deserted.

Received from the prison ship in June 1815 it appears Hyland's military experience and higher level of learning marked him out for early promotion; already a sergeant on arriving at St Vincent in November 1815, following the death of Thomas Henshaw he was promoted sergeant major in November 1817. As a former deserter, now a senior non-commissioned officer, one wonders how Hyland's elevation might have resonated amongst his fellow sergeants let alone among subordinate volunteers.

In Canada, Hyland, accompanied by his wife, initially opted for Bathurst's 'Waste Land', but at Kingston, Ontario, he apparently experienced a change of mind and enlisted in the 70th Regiment, aged twenty-seven. He joined the regiment in January 1820; by February he was already its pay master sergeant, a post he held until returned to England as corporal in August 1825. Hospitalised on arrival, Hyland rejoined his regiment in October and was discharged as a civilian the following January.

The question remains: what qualities did Hyland possess that merited promotion to York Chasseurs sergeant major in preference to those experienced volunteers who served alongside him?

Maybe it was the fear unemployment in Quebec that motivated Thomas Curtis and John Croker to enlist for the 60th, a regiment from which Curtis's 'Injured knee while on Duty' would result in his departure to a pension in December 1824, and 'Disease of the Head and Melancholic Affliction' for Croker in October 1825.

It is unclear whether York Chasseurs private and former 32nd Regiment deserter, Edward Hoffer, was still in Canada when in October 1820 he enlisted for the 19th 1st Yorkshire (N. Riding) Regiment, where he served for a further 18 years until he was discharged with a pension aged 47 – a 'Good and Efficient Soldier suffering from "Muscular Debility, Varicose Veins of the Legs, Chronic Cough and a Weakened Constitution from the Effect of his Long Service"'.

During 1833, using Mathew Lawson as his intermediary, Edward Duffy, 1st

Foot regimental deserter and York Chasseurs condemned private, applied to the
War Office for his 'Guadeloupe Bounty'.

> Murray, Northumberland County.[175]
>
> (Un-dated, but recorded by the War Office, 28th August 1833).
> To the War Office.
> Edward Duffy, formerly of the county of Londonderry, Ireland, a private
> if the York Cheshire Regiment, 2nd Company, enlisted in the year of
> 1814, then aged thirteen years, having served five years and being present
> at the taking of the Island of Guadeloupe on the 11th day of August 1815
> under the command of Colonel John Ewitt, does humbly seek from the
> War Office the prize money to which he is entitled as a Soldier in that
> engagement, and which he has never yet received.
> An answer to this is humbly requested, and any additional information
> required shall be obtained by writing to Edward Duffy, directed to the
> Care of Mr Mathew Lawson.
>
> Murray, Near Brighton, Upper Canada.
> A former application was not answered for what cause is not known to the
> writer.

Unfortunately for Duffy, even if such a bounty had existed, to the bureaucratic
mind his cause was probably already lost: for the regimental muster roll of 1818
had inadvertently recorded his death, and not that of the Monaghan Militia
deserter and York Chasseurs private, John Duffy.

Of the two McCarthy's discharged at Quebec, it is almost certainly Private
John McCarthy of the 2nd battalion, 44th Regiment, 'Sentenced at Ostende for
Desertion, November 1814', who arrived at St Vincent in November 1815.
Decades later, old and destitute, he made a desperate plea for assistance.

> 23rd January 1865. Low County of Ottawa[176]
>
> Lieut General Sir W. F. Williams. Bart. Commanding the Forces in B.N.
> America
> Sir
> Some months since I petitioned the Rt Hon the Secretary at War,
> London, for relief in consideration of my services as Drummer from 1809
> to 1819 in the "York Chasseurs" commanded by Colonel Hewitt, the sub-
> ordinate Officers of my company being Captain Fisher and Lieut
> Chesney – And also of my services in Canada from 1837 to 1840 as
> Drummer in the Glengary Volunteers Commanded by Col McDonnell –
> and my Company under the command of his son Capt McDonnell.
> The Hon John Hamilton (Inkerman) having kindly undertaken to
> forward my petition, addressed it by mistake (as he lately told me) "to Sir
> William W.F. Williams" And being in a most destitute condition. I take the
> liberty of requesting you to forward the said petition to the proper
> Authorities at the War Office. And refer them to the Muster Roll of 1818
> or 1819, as regards the York Chasseurs – and to that of 1837 to 1840 with

regards to the Glengary Volunteers.
And thereby ensure the lasting gratitude of
Sir
Your most obedient Servant
John McCarthy
Drummer
P.S. Please address in reply to John McCarthy. Drummer. Low County of
Ottawa. Canada East.

It can only be hoped his plea met with approval.

It is fitting that we conclude this saga of military felons deposited in Canada with Thomas Plymouth, the archetypal York Chasseur. He was man who volunteered as a corporal of the 6th of Foot, and despite arriving at St Vincent a private, was a corporal again within weeks and a sergeant within the year.

'Disobedience of Orders and saying he did not give a damn for the Adjutant', soon had him reduced to private, but with the accompanying 300 lash mercifully remitted. Three months later, accused of 'Drunk on Guard and Playing Cards', Plymouth had once again escaped the cat-o'-nine-tails with a 300 lash sentence commuted to solitary confinement. Discharged at Quebec and in spite of there being no evidence of any land application in his name, like numerous sons throughout history he attempted to impress his mother with his successes. The truth is that Thomas Plymouth may have been many things, but a Canadian landowner he was not.

War Office[177]
My Lord
Application having been made to this Office by a poor woman named Mary Plymouth relative to her son Thomas Plymouth, who was discharged at Quebec on the 24th August 1819 from the York Chasseurs when that Corps was disbanded, and who she states received a quantity of land in North America in lieu of the Out-Pension. I have the honor to request that you will acquaint me whether there is any record of this man's destination at the Station under your Command and if so, that you will state whether he appears to be now living.
I have the honor to be My Lord Your Lordships most obedient Servant.
To Lt General The Earl of Dalhousie, Canada, Palmerston, 20th June 1827.

Finally, with no battle honours, no monuments and bones scattered throughout the West Indies, what might one say was the York Chasseurs' legacy? A resolute opposition to authority, perhaps, combined with a capability to withstand punishment.

The grave of Sergeant Thomas Leonard , Craig Street Cemetery, Perth, Lanark County, Ontario, Canada

Appendix

Tabel 33 Nominal List of Men Tried by General Courts Martial from 25 March 1815 to 24 September 1815[178]

Name	Date	Nature of Offence	Sentence
William Rippon	29 March 1815	Absent from Evening Parade	300 lashes (100 remitted)
James Doolan	1 April 1815	Drunk on Guard	300 lashes (remitted to 16 days Solitary Confinement)
John Driscoll	ditto	Drunk on Guard	300 lashes (150 remitted)
William Exton	ditto	Absent without leave	300 lashes (250 remitted)
Cpl Robert Graham	ditto	Drunk on passage at Bridgetown, Barbados	Reduced
Joseph Walker	3 April 1815	Absent without leave	300 lashes (150 remitted)
Robert Tunnage	ditto	Absent without leave	300 lashes (200 remitted)
John Bogg	ditto	Making away with his Greatcoat	150 lashes (75 remitted)
William Hart	10 April 1815	Absenting himself from his piquet and remaining out of barracks all night	300 lashes (150 remitted)
Robert Graham	ditto	Drunk on Piquet	14 days Solitary Confinement (8 days remitted)
Thomas Wilson	ditto	Drunk on Guard.	14 days Solitary Confinement (8 days remitted)
John Stewart	ditto	Absent without leave	300 lashes (150 remitted)
Thomas Hutchinson	12 April 1815	Drunk and Absent from Parade	200 lashes (100 remitted)
Cpl James Simpson	13 April 1815	Theft	Sentenced to be reduced, awarded 200 lashes (lashes remitted)
John Cascallian	ditto	Absent without leave	300 lashes

Continued

Name	Date	Nature of Offence	Sentence
Cpl William Brown	20 April 1815	Unsoldierlike conduct in being drunk	Reduced
Thomas Field	ditto	Highly disrespectful language	100 lashes
John Raybold	ditto	Refusing to drill	150 lashes Received 25 lashes, the remainder commuted to Solitary Confinement
Daniel Thomas	24 April 1815	Insubordinate Conduct at drill	300 lashes (100 remitted)
Thomas Webster	ditto	Refusing to go to drill when ordered	200 lashes (100 remitted)
Cpl David Jones	27 April 1815	Drunk on Guard Duty	Reduced
Cpl George Palmer	ditto	Drunk on Piquet	Reduced
John Pollett	9 May 1815	Making away with his Necessaries.	150 lashes (50 remitted)
Patrick Cunningham	ditto	Making away with his Necessaries	150 lashes (50 remitted)
Edward Tarling	15 May 1815	Making away with his Necessaries	150 lashes (Commuted to 20 days Solitary Confinement)
James Glenn	ditto	Making away with his Necessaries	14 days Solitary Confinement (11 days remitted)
James McClure	16 May 1815	Absent from morning parade and making away with his Necessaries	Awarded 300 lashes (50 lashes received, remainder commuted to 20 days Solitary Confinement)
Dmr Thomas Roberts	22 May 1815	Drunk and absence from his practice	150 lashes (50 remitted)

Continued

Name	Date	Nature of Offence	Sentence
Christopher Armstrong	ditto	Having Necessaries in his possession not his own property	200 lashes
Charles Field	25 May 1815	Absent from Parade and making away with his Blanket	200 lashes (50 remitted)
John Campbell	ditto	Making away with his Shirt	150 lashes (Commuted to 30 days Solitary Confinement)
James Ahern	27 May 1815	Drunk on Guard	300 lashes (150 remitted)
James McGovern	31 May 1815	Absent without leave	300 lashes (100 remitted)
Sgt Thos Jones	ditto	Exchanging his Regimental Trowsers	Reduced
William Steel	ditto	Insubordinate Language to Commanding Officer	200 lashes (Commuted to 20 days Solitary Confinement)
David McLeod	3 June 1815	Drunk on Guard	300 lashes
Michael Maloney	ditto	Destroying a Fowle belonging to Captain Anderson	150 lashes (50 remitted)
Dennis Gingley	7 June 1815	Having in his possession a knife belonging to the Officer's Mess	200 lashes (Commuted to 10 days Solitary Confinement)
Edward Donally	9 June 1815	Contempt to Captain Daniell	200 lashes (50 remitted)
Sgt Francis Taylor	ditto	Neglect of Duty	Reduced
James Kane	12 June 1815	Insolent Language	150 lashes
Thomas Webster	ditto	Drunk in Barracks	200 lashes
Robert Copping	ditto	Theft	300 lashes
Edward Donally	27 June 1815	Making away with his Necessaries	200 lashes

Continued

Name	Date	Nature of Offence	Sentence
Christopher Armstrong	ditto	Absent without leave	200 lashes
John Longworth	4 July 1815	Having in his possession a Shirt not his Own	200 lashes
Henry McNamee	6 July 1815	Insubordinate Conduct	300 lashes
William Folkett	10 July 1815	Absent from Tattoo	200 lashes
James McLure	ditto	Refusing to go to Guard Duty	300 lashes
James Cooley	ditto	Insolent Language	200 lashes
John McNally	11 July 1815	Drunk and Absent from Parade	200 lashes
John Donohoe	ditto	Drunk and Absent from Parade	200 lashes
Daniel Thomas	ditto	Repeatedly Dirty	150 lashes
Michael Maloney	ditto	Absent from Parade	200 lashes
John Driscoll	14 July 1815	Insolence	200 lashes
Michael Maloney	ditto	Drunk	200 lashes
John Cocking	24 July 1815	Drunk on Guard	300 lashes
Edward Wynn	ditto	Drunk on Guard	300 lashes
Thomas West	28 July 1815	Insolent Language	150 lashes
Cpl George Wilkinson	ditto	Abusive Language	Reduced
Sgt Chas Reddings	3 August 1815	Absent from Morning Parade	Reduced
Thomas Counsell	17 August 1815	For having in his Possession a French Coin	300 lashes (150 remitted)
James Stewart	ditto	For having in his Possession a French Coin	300 lashes (200 remitted)
Samuel Stevens	29 August 1815	Losing Greatcoat	200 lashes (150 remitted)

Continued

Name	Date	Nature of Offence	Sentence
Edward Lloyd	ditto	Losing Greatcoat	200 lashes (150 remitted)
James Savage	22 September 1815	Drunk on Guard	200 lashes (100 remitted)
William Braddock	ditto	Unsoldierlike Conduct	150 lashes (75 remitted) FORGIVEN
Charles Field	22 May 1815	Making away with a Pair of Trowsers	14 days Solitary Confinement
Samuel Redding	31 May 1815	Drunk on Guard	300 lashes
Miles Whitaker	27 June 1815	Absent from Parade	300 lashes
Cpl John Whitehead	10 July 1815	Absent from Parade	Reduced
James Ferguson	11 July 1815	Drunk on Guard	300 lashes
Sgt John Cummings	14 July 1815	Unbecoming Conduct	Reduced
Robert Miller	6 September 1815	Refusing to be Confined	100 lashes

Table 34 Nominal List of Men Tried by Garrison Courts Martial from 25 March 1815 to 24 September 1815

Name	Date	Nature of Offence	Sentence
Joseph Hazledine	17 April 1815	Taking Rum into the Naval Arsenal Guard Barracks	30 days Solitary Confinement (commuted to 10 days)
Nicholas Quirk	28 April 1815	Drunk on Barrier Beach Guard	300 lashes
Daniel Weaver	ditto	Drunk on Barrier Beach Guard	300 lashes
John Richards	ditto	Drunk on Barrier Beach Guard	300 lashes
John Ratcliffe	ditto	Drunk on Barrier Beach Guard	300 lashes
James Jervis	ditto	Drunk on Barrier Beach Guard	300 lashes.
Stephen Smith	ditto	Drunk on Barrier Beach Guard	300 lashes
Benjamin Shaw	14 September 1815	Drunk on Parade	200 lashes
William Folkett	ditto	Drunk and Insolent to Corporal Smith	200 lashes
James Clarke	ditto	Absent from Evening Parade and out of Barracks all Night	300 lashes (200 remitted)
John Taylor	16 September 1815	Drunk on Evening Parade	300 lashes
Dmr Thos Roberts	ditto	Drunk and Insolent on Evening Parade	300 lashes
Jeremiah Coakley	19 September 1815	Drunk on Town Guard	300 lashes (150 remitted)
James Clarke	25 September 1815	Loosing or Making Away with Greatcoat and Blue Trowsers	300 lashes

Table 35 Nominal List of Men Tried by General Courts Martial from 25 September 1816 to 24 March 1817, Stony Hill, Jamaica[179]

Name	Date	Nature of Offence	Sentence
George Kender	22 November 1816	Desertion from 29 Sept–Oct 1816	400 lashes (remitted)
William Ralph	ditto	Drunk & Absenting from his Guard Refusing to become a Prisoner. Using Mutinous & Insolent Expressions to Capt Parker in the Execution of his Duty & Striking or Attempting to Strike the said Officer	1000 lashes
John Weaver	4 December 1816	Desertion 17 Aug 1816	200 lashes (remitted
George Ridley	ditto	Desertion 16th Aug 1816	The court considers the Long confinement these Prisoners to have been of Sufficient Punishment. (500 lashes of each individual remitted)
John Kearney	ditto	Desertion 19 Aug 1816}	
Charles Joyce	ditto	Desertion 18 Aug 1816}	
Thomas Gould	ditto	Desertion 16 Aug 1816}	
Thomas Webster	ditto	Desertion 20 June 1816 & Threatening Behaviour & Mutinous Conduct to Capt Anderson & Color Serg Sewell, at Fort Augusta 25 November 1816	1000 lashes
James McLure	10 December 1816	Stabbing Pte Wm Price Making use of mutinous and threatening words to Capt Anderson	1000 lashes
Ed Dunningham	9 January 1817	Desertion when on Main Guard on 22 Dec 1816 & Not Returning till 7th January 1817	700 lashes
John Lynsky	13 January 1817	Desertion when on Main Guard at Stony Hill. 28 December 1816, and not returning until brought back by an escort 10 January 1817	800 lashes

Table 36 Nominal List of Men Tried by General Regimental Courts Martial from 25 September 1816 to 24 March 1817

Name	Date	Nature of Offence	Sentence
Thomas Carroll	8 October 1816	Desertion 22 Sept 1816	200 lashes
? Wilson	21 October 1816	Desertion 22 Sept 1816	200 lashes
John Richardson	ditto	Deserting 22nd September and not returning till brought back a Prisoner on 14th October 1816	800 lashes (400 remitted)
Pat Rock	ditto	Deserting 1 September & not returning till returning till brought back 14th October 1816	800 lashes
Richard Stephenson	ditto	Desertion 10 July–9 October 1816	800 lashes (400 remitted)
Hugh Johnston	ditto	Desertion 30 September–11 October 1816	800 lashes
William McIndoe	ditto	Desertion 30 September–11 October 1816	800 lashes
Michael Boyle	ditto	Desertion 10 October–12 October 1816	800 lashes
Joseph Haywood	ditto	Desertion 10 October–12 October 1816	800 lashes

Table 37 Nominal List of Men Tried by Regimental Courts Martial from 25 September 1816 to 24 March 1817

Name	Date	Nature of Offence	Sentence
Cpl Dennis	26 September 1816	Absent from Evening Parade	150 lashes & reduced (lashes remitted)
Cpl Moore	ditto	Absent from Evening Parade	150 lashes & reduced (lashes remitted)
Edward McGeary	ditto	Absenting himself 5 months without leave	300 lashes
James Mooney	ditto	Absenting himself 5 months without leave	300 lashes
John Fleming	ditto	Absenting himself 5 months without leave	300 lashes
William Beatson	ditto	Absent from Evening Parade	200 lashes (75 remitted)
Joseph Kirby	2 October 1816	Quitting the Garrison without Leave	200 lashes (remitted)
James Mitchell	ditto	Quitting the Garrison without Leave	200 lashes (remitted)
? Smith	ditto	Quitting the Garrison without leave	200 lashes (remitted)
Richard Finch	17 October 1816	Loosing or making away with a pair of Shoes	200 lashes (Died in the Regimental Hospital while under sentence)
? Dawson	ditto	Absenting himself one night without leave200 lashes	(Remitted due to his previous Good Character)
Thomas Bowden	ditto	Selling a Blanket not his Property	200 lashes (Remitted due to his previous Good Character)
? Materson	18 October 1816	Making away with Regimental Necessities	200 lashes (remitted)
John Callaghan	ditto	Breaking his Firelock	200 lashes

Continued

Name	Date	Nature of Offence	Sentence
Cpl Goulding	25 October 1816	Drunk on Guard	200 lashes & to be reduced (lashes remitted due to his previous Good Character)
Cpl Fidler	ditto	Contemptuously taking off his Badge as Corporal	200 lashes and to be reduced. (lashes remitted due to his previous Good Character)
Henry Ingram	ditto	Absent from his Guard	300 lashes
Edward Croston	ditto	Drunk on Guard.	300 lashes
John Truesdale	ditto	Drunk on Parade	200 lashes (remitted)
James Long	ditto	Absenting himself one month without leave	300 lashes (175 remitted)
Cpl Lowe	4 November 1816	Drunk on Guard	200 lashes and to be reduced (lashes remitted)
Thomas Cavall	ditto	Making away with part of his Regimental Necessities	300 lashes
John McCabe	ditto	Theft	200 lashes
Cpl Watts	2 December 181	Forgery on Lt Watson	300 lashes & reduced
? King	ditto	Presenting a Forged Order knowing it to be so	300 lashes
Thomas Higgins	ditto	Forgery	300 lashes
Sgt Plymouth	10 December 1816	Disobedience of Orders and saying he did not give a damn for the Adjutant	300 lashes and to be reduced. (Lashes remitted due to his previous Good Character)
Peter Lanaghan	ditto	Absent from his Barracks Overnight	100 lashes (Remitted due to his Former Good Character)

Continued

Name	Date	Nature of Offence	Sentence
Thomas McCabe	ditto	Telling Cpl Brooks to Kiss His Arse	150 lashes (Commuted to Solitary Confinement)
? Burns	ditto	Having in his Possession 2 Hospital Shirts not his own	300 lashes
James Donaldson	ditto	Offering a pair of shoes for Sale at Port Maria	300 lashes
Thomas Chamberlain	21 December 1816	Attempting to Strike Ensign Mainwaring	300 lashes (Remitted due to his Former Good Character)
William Thompson	ditto	Calling Sergeant Anderson a Damned Little Rascal	100 lashes
? Gould	ditto	Making or attempting to strike Sergeant Wm Anderson	200 lashes
Abraham Usill	ditto	Drunk on Guard	300 lashes
John Whitehead	23 December 1816	Preferring Erroneous Charges against Ensign Maxwell	300 lashes
William Crooks	ditto	Passing Rum to the Prisoner	150 lashes
Thomas Roberts	24 December 1816	Striking Sergeant Alwright	300 lashes
Daniel Cremer	ditto	Absenting from His Guard without Leave	300 lashes
James Dochety	ditto	Theft & Striking Sergeant Alwright	300 lashes
John. Jordon	ditto	Drunk on Guard	300 lashes
Cpl Gleeson	ditto	Drunk on Guard	200 lashes and reduced
Thomas Plymouth	ditto	Drunk on Guard	300 lashes (remitted)
Thomas Noonan	ditto	Passing Rum to Prisoner	100 lashes
John Campbell	ditto	Drunk on Guard	300 lashes (100 remitted)

Continued

Name	Date	Nature of Offence	Sentence
William Rocklidge	ditto	Drunk on Guard	300 lashes
Patrick Rooney	ditto	Loosing or Making Off with a Shirt	200 lashes
John Fleming	ditto	Loosing or Making Off with a Shirt	200 lashes
J Mitchell	26 December 1816	Drunk and Absenting himself from Parade	150 lashes
? Johnston	ditto	Drunk and Absenting himself from Parade	150 lashes
William Clements	ditto	Drunk and Absenting himself from Parade	150 lashes
Pat Donohoe	ditto	Drunk and Absenting himself from Parade	150 lashes
Thomas Higgins	ditto	Theft	300 lashes
William Aldridge	ditto	Making away with his Necessaries	Solitary Confinement
John McCabe	ditto	Drunk on Guard	300 lashes
Dennis Mahoney	ditto	Loosing or Making away with his Necessaries.	Solitary Confinement.
Bernard Martin	ditto	Absenting himself without leave from Evening Parade	150 lashes
Silas Green	ditto	Drunk and Absent from Evening Parade	150 lashes
John Kelly	ditto	Drunk on Evening Parade	150 lashes
Michael Murray	7 January 1817	Absenting himself without leave 1 Night	250 lashes
Thomas Carroll	ditto	Absenting himself from his Guard & not returning until brought back a prisoner	300 lashes
Silas Green	ditto	Making away with Articles of his Necessaries	200 lashes
Owen Leonard	ditto	Absenting himself 6 Weeks without leave Leave	300 lashes

Continued

Name	Date	Nature of Offence	Sentence
William Bull	ditto	Drunken and riotous after hours and abusing Sergeant James	300 lashes
Charles Rogers	14 January 1817	Selling a shirt not his Own	200 lashes
James Gettis	ditto	Purchasing the Above shirt	200 lashes
Daniel Crennor	ditto	Drunk on Guard	300 lashes
William Dennis	ditto	Out of Barracks after hours & Striking a Sentinel	300 lashes (100 remitted)
Patrick Rock	ditto	Theft	200 lashes
Jason Fidler	ditto	Refusing to Drill when Ordered	100 lashes (remitted)
John Travell	21 January 1817	Absenting himself 2 weeks without leave	300 lashes
Charles Waterman	ditto	Absenting himself 2 weeks without leave	300 lashes
John Campbell	ditto	Absenting himself 2 weeks without leave	300 lashes
James Kelly	ditto	Absenting himself 2 weeks without leave	300 lashes
William Wilson	ditto	Striking Sergeant Hartshorn & Cpl Davies	300 lashes
William Conroy	ditto	Drunk on Parade	200 lashes
Charles Quinn	ditto	Theft	300 lashes
Thomas Chamberlain	ditto	Selling his Necessaries	200 lashes
Michael Galvin	ditto	Selling his Necessaries	150 lashes
William Gladden	29 January 1817	Absenting himself 6 months without leave	300 lashes
Sgt Jordon	10 February 1817	Striking Capt Byrne and Challenging to fight a Private	Reduced and Solitary Confinement
William Conroy	ditto	Drunk on Guard	300 lashes.
Francis Davey	ditto	Drunk on Guard	300 lashes
James Brogan.	ditto	Drunk on Guard	300 lashes

Continued

Name	Date	Nature of Offence	Sentence
John Davies	ditto	Drunk on Guard	Solitary Confinement
William Brigham	ditto	Drunk on Guard.	Solitary Confinement
John Dunning	ditto	Drunk on Guard	Solitary Confinement
? McMahon	ditto	Drunk & Absent from his Guard	300 lashes (100 remitted)
George Stokes	ditto	Sleeping on his Post while Sentinel	300 lashes (25 remitted)
John Slade	ditto	Forgery	300 lashes
Michael Dudley	ditto	Forgery	300 lashes
Joseph Holly	ditto	Drunk & Absent from Evening Parade	150 lashes (remitted)
John Power	ditto	Drunk & Absent from Evening Parade	150 lashes (remitted)
? Fleming	17 February 1817	Drunk on Guard.	300 lashes
Charles Rogers	ditto	Selling part of his Regimental Necessaries	200 lashes
John Gravell	ditto	Offering a pair of Shoes for Sale	300 lashes
? Cummings	ditto	Selling a Shirt	300 lashes (remitted)
? Griffiths	ditto	Drunk on Guard	300 lashes
? Burns	26 February 1817	Drunk when Sentinel on his post	300 lashes
Joseph Bergler	ditto	Absenting himself without leave for 2 months	300 lashes
John Briers	ditto	Making away with his Regimental Necessaries	300 lashes
Cpl Sweeny	1 March 1817	Drunk on Guard & Playing Cards	Reduced
James Reed	ditto	Drunk on Guard & Playing Cards	300 lashes (remitted)

Continued

Name	Date	Nature of Offence	Sentence
George Ridley	ditto	Drunk on Guard & Playing Cards	300 lashes
Thomas Plymouth	ditto	Drunk on Guard & Playing Cards	300 lashes (remitted)
Cpl Asquith	ditto	Striking Sergeant Cummings & Resisting a File of the Guard	175 lashes and to be reduced (lashes remitted due to Former Good Character)
William Summers	6 March 1817	Absenting himself 3 weeks without leave	300 lashes
John Doby	ditto	Drunk on Guard.	300 lashes.
Norman McKinna	ditto	Theft	300 lashes
James Lee	ditto	Absenting himself 1 week without Leave	300 lashes
James Cahill	ditto	Absenting himself 1 week without Leave	300 lashes
Edward Garratty	ditto	Absent from Tattoo & Striking Sergeant Dyson	300 lashes
William Dodd	ditto	Drunk & Absent from Parade & found on their way to Stony Hill Taverns	300 lashes
Thomas Dodd	ditto		
Dmr Roberts	ditto	Drunk & Absent from Ev Parade & Leaving Limits of the Garrison	200 lashes and reduced
John McCristy	11 March 1817	Absent from morning & Evening Parade	150 lashes
Thomas Noonan	ditto	Theft	300 lashes
William Crooks	ditto	Loading a Firelock at 3-0-clock in the morning & making use of Threatening Language	300 lashes
Cpl Henderson	19 March 1817	Drunk on Guard	Reduced

Continued

Name	Date	Nature of Offence	Sentence
James Mitchell	ditto	Leaving Limits of Garrison without Leave & being	150 lashes
John Davies	ditto	found close to Stony Hill Taverns	

Table 38 Nominal List of Men Tried by Detachment Courts Martial from April 5 1817 to 17 February 1818, Stony Hill, Jamaica[180]

Name	Date	Nature of Offence	Sentence
Samuel Thornton	10 December 1817	Absenting himself without leave	300 lashes
Thomas Noonan	ditto	Breaking into Taylors Shop	300 lashes.
Robert Byrne	ditto	Absent without Leave	300 lashes
John Bull	ditto	Absent without Leave	300 lashes
Richard Hughes	ditto	Making away with Regimental Necessities	200 lashes plus stoppage
Thomas Walsh	15 December 1817	Making away with Regimental Necessities	300 lashes
John Bachelor	ditto	Making away with Regimental Necessities	300 lashes
George Hamilton	ditto	Making away with Regimental Necessities	300 lashes
Sampson Meigh	27 December 1817	Making away with Regimental Necessities	300 lashes (Remitted in consequence of his former Good Character and being strongly recommended by the Court)
Morris Hackett	ditto	Having pair of trowsers not his own and resisting Corporal and File of the Guard in the execution of their Duty	200 lashes
George Robinson	ditto	Absenting himself without Leave	300 lashes
Alexander McLaren	ditto	Absenting himself without leave	300 lashes
Joseph Chamberlain	ditto	Absenting himself without leave	300 lashes
George McMahon	ditto	Making away with Regimental Necessities	200 lashes
William Thorn	ditto	Making away with Regimental Necessities	300 lashes

Continued

Name	Date	Nature of Offence	Sentence
Thomas Cummins	29 December 1817	Drunk on Duty	200 lashes
James Elliott	ditto	Unsoldierlike Conduct in Threatening the Life of a Sergeant	300 lashes
Thomas Carroll	10 January 1818	Making away or losing 10lbs of Ammunition	150 lashes
Patrick Tanning	ditto	Having a pair of trousers not his own property	250 lashes (225 remitted)
Peter Sutherland	ditto	Absent without Leave	300 lashes (175 remitted)

Table 39 Nominal List of Men Tried by Garrison Courts Martial from 5 April 1817 to 17 February 1818

Name	Date	Nature of Offence	Sentence
Richard Hughes	31 July 1817	Making away with Regimental Necessities	200 lashes (125 remitted)
Thomas McCabe	ditto	Making away with Regimental Necessities	200 lashes (150 remitted)
John Frederic	ditto	Absent without Leave	300 lashes

Table 40 Nominal List of Men Tried by Detachment Courts Martial from 5 April 1817 to 17 February 1818.

Name	Date	Nature of Offence	Sentence
George Hamilton	23 August 1817	Absent without Leave	300 lashes
William Aldridge	ditto	Absenting himself from his Guard	150 lashes (100 remitted)
William Thorpe	ditto	Absenting himself from his Escort Duty and returning Drunk	200 lashes (remitted to solitary confinement)
Cpl Dunnett	ditto	Unsoldierlike Conduct. Drunk on Escort Duty	200 lashes and to be reduced (lashes remitted)
Thomas Cummins	8 September 1817	Having a Shirt not his Property	300 lashes (200 remitted)
William Marcott	ditto	Drunk and Riotous in Barracks	250 lashes (150 remitted)
Cornelius Mahoney	2 October 1817	Drunk on Duty	300 lashes
Cpl James Stewart	ditto	Theft	200 lashes and to be reduced. (Reduced and Solitary confinement)
George Hamilton	ditto	Theft	300 lashes
Thomas Walsh	ditto	Drunk on Duty	300 lashes (150 remitted)
Thomas Till Lloyd	ditto	Absent without Leave	300 lashes
John Foster	30 October 1817	Drunk on Duty	300 lashes (150 remitted)
William Scott	ditto	Persuading Patrick Tanning to Desert and Steal Blanket	300 lashes (50 remitted)
Charles Waterman	ditto	Making Away with Regimental Necessities	200 lashes
John Frederic	ditto	Absenting Himself without Leave	300 lashes

Continued

Name	Date	Nature of Offence	Sentence
John Rudd	ditto	Making Away with Regimental Necessities	200 lashes (150 remitted)
Thomas Carroll	ditto	Absent without Leave	300 lashes
Charles Nowland	ditto	Absent without Leave	300 lashes
George Cooper	ditto	Absent without Leave	300 lashes

Table 41 Nominal List of Men Tried by Regimental Courts Martial from 5 April 1817 to 17 February 1818

Name	Date	Nature of Offence	Sentence
Daniel Gleeson	12 April 1817	Absenting himself without Leave	300 lashes
John Burns	ditto	Absenting himself without Leave	300 lashes
William Kindler	ditto	Absenting himself without Leave	300 lashes
Thomas Quirk	ditto	Drunk and absenting himself from his Guard	300 lashes (100 remitted)
Sgt Hartshorn	16 April 1817	For Unsoldierlike conduct	To be Reduced (remitted)
Thomas Noonan	28 April 1917	Theft	300 lashes
Thomas Higgins	ditto	On Suspicion of Theft	300 lashes
Daniel Gleeson	ditto	On Suspicion of Theft	300 lashes
Sgt Hartshorn	ditto	Drunk and absent from parade	Reduced
Patrick Dunaghan	ditto	Buying Regimental Necessaries	Solitary Confinement
Thomas Quirk	ditto	Selling his Necessaries	150 lashes (remitted to solitary confinement)
Sgt William Brown	ditto	Drunk & Absent from Parade	Reduced
Thomas Mulveany	ditto	Drunk & Absent from Parade	150 lashes
Michael Galvin	ditto	Drunk & Absent from Parade	150 lashes
James Kelly	ditto	Drunk on Duty	300 lashes
Michael Flynn	ditto	Neglect of Duty on his Post	300 lashes
Charles Joyce	ditto	Neglect of Duty on his Post	300 lashes
Cpl James Ferguson	ditto	Drunk & absent from Parade	Reduced

Continued

Name	Date	Nature of Offence	Sentence
Charles Hodge	ditto	Theft	200 lashes (reduced to Solitary Confinement)
George Spence	ditto	Drunk & Absent from Parade	150 lashes
Thomas Carroll	9 May 1817	Absent without Leave	300 lashes
John Kearny	ditto	Absent without Leave	300 lashes
John Lynsky	ditto	Absent without Leave	300 lashes
Cpl John Smith	17 June 1817	Unsoldierlike Conduct, Drunk & Riotous in Barracks.	To be reduced and Solitary Confinement (Solitary Confinement remitted)
James Weir	19 June 1817	Absent without Leave	300 lashes
Michael Dalton	ditto	Absent without Leave	300 lashes
George Hamilton	ditto	Absent without Leave	300 lashes
William Scott	ditto	Absent without Leave	300 lashes
Sgt F Rosser	24 June 1817	Unsoldierlike conduct stating a falsehood to Maj Gen Conran	Reduced
Thomas Quirk	ditto	Theft	300 lashes
Francis Rosser	27 June 1817	Unsoldierlike Conduct	Solitary Confinement
John Bogg	ditto	Theft	300 lashes
Patrick Mayer	ditto	Theft	300 lashes
Alexander McLaren	ditto	Absent without Leave	300 lashes.
Francis Rosser	3 July 1817	Unsoldierlike Conduct	300 lashes
James Lee	4 July 1817	Absent without Leave	300 lashes
James Cahill	ditto	Absent without Leave	300 lashes
George Morrow	ditto	Drunk on Duty	300 lashes

Continued

Name	Date	Nature of Offence	Sentence
Thomas McCabe	ditto	Drunk on Duty	300 lashes
Patrick Fanning	ditto	Theft	200 lashes. (Reduced to 1 months drill)
Michael Shane	ditto	Absent without Leave	300 lashes
Peter Sutherland	ditto	Absent without Leave	300 lashes
Edward Dunn	16 July 1817	Absent without Leave	300 lashes
Thomas Ford	25 July 1817	Absent without Leave	300 lashes
Thomas Mulveany	ditto	Theft	150 lashes. (reduced to Solitary Confinement)
John Hutchinson	ditto	Absent without Leave	300 lashes
Charles Joyce	ditto	Making away with his Regimental Necessaries	300 lashes
George McMahon	ditto	Drunk on Duty & Theft	300 lashes
John Boggins	ditto	Making away with his Regimental Necessaries	300 lashes
Sgt John Spencer	2 August 1817	Absent from Evening Parade	Reduced
Sgt John Skilling	ditto	Absent from Evening Parade	Reduced
John Kelly	ditto	Absent without Leave	300 lashes
George Hamilton	ditto	Absent without Leave	300 lashes
Patrick Nulty	ditto	Making away with his Regimental Necessaries	200 lashes (75 remitted)
Thomas Walsh	ditto	Making away with his Regimental Necessaries	200 lashes (50 remitted)
James Weir	5 August 1817	Absent without Leave	300 lashes
Joseph Hoddell	ditto	Selling his Regimental Necessaries	Acquitted

Continued

Name	Date	Nature of Offence	Sentence
Robert Taylor	ditto	Attempting to Desert	300 lashes (100 remitted)
William Bull	ditto	Selling his Regimental Necessaries	300 lashes (100 remitted)
William Summers	ditto	Absent without Leave	300 lashes
John Cook	ditto	Absent without Leave	300 lashes
William Scott	ditto	Absent without Leave	300 lashes
Edward Crosston	ditto	Unsoldierlike Conduct in Striking a Sergeant	100 lashes
James Jarvis	15 August 1817	Absent without Leave	300 lashes
George Hill	18 August 1817	Selling his Regimental Necessaries	Not Guilty
William Wilson	ditto	Absent without Leave	300 lashes
John Hughes	ditto	Theft	Not Guilty
Thomas Vennor	1 September 1817	Thef	300 lashes
William Marlott	ditto	Absent without Leave	300 lashes
Cornelius Quinn	ditto	Absent without Leave	300 lashes
Thomas Cummings	ditto	Theft	300 lashes
Michael Shane	ditto	Neglect of Duty	150 lashes
B McCormick	ditto	Drunk on Duty	300 lashes
John B. Marshall	ditto	Unsoldierlike Conduct in firing at a negro woman	300 lashes
Stephen Nully	ditto	Drunk on Duty	300 lashes
John Boggins	2 September 1817	Absent without Leave	300 lashes
Charles Nowland	ditto	Absent without Leave	300 lashes
John Hutchinson	ditto	Absent without Leave	300 lashes

Continued

Name	Date	Nature of Offence	Sentence
John Burgess	ditto	Absent without Leave	300 lashes
John Johnson	ditto	Absent without Leave	300 lashes
Mathew Schwartz	ditto	Absent without Leave	300 lashes
William Strethers	ditto	Selling his Necessaries	250 lashes (50 remitted)
Patrick Fanning	ditto	Selling his Necessaries	250 lashes (25 remitted)
Bernard Flannaghan	ditto	Selling his Necessaries	90 lashes (40 remitted)
Thomas Costello	ditto	Unsoldierlike Conduct. Repeated Drunkeness	200 lashes. (Reduced to Solitary Confinement)
Mathew Schwartz	10 October 1817	Absent without Leave	300 lashes.
John Richards	ditto	Unsoldierlike conduct Attempting to stab his wife	300 lashes (Reduced to Solitary confinement)
Charles Joyce	17 November 1817	Unsoldierlike conduct in forging a Sergeant's name.	300 lashes (25 remitted)
Robert Morris	ditto	Coming to Parade improperly dressed. Insolence to an Officer	Solitary Confinement
William Marcott	ditto	Drunk on Parade	Solitary Confinement
Jeremiah Hughes	ditto	Drunk on Parade	Solitary Confinement
Charles Nowland	22 November 1817	Absent without Leave	300 lashes
George Cooper	26 November 1817	Making away with his Necessaries	300 lashes
Sgt William Anderson	ditto	Unsoldierlike Conduct. Drunk on Escort Duty	300 lashes and to be reduced (300 lashes remitted)

Continued

Name	Date	Nature of Offence	Sentence
Cpl John Hartshorn	10 December 1817	Unsoldierlike conduct. Repeatedly drunk whilst Hospital Steward.	300 lashes and to be reduced. (Lashes remitted)
Richard Hughes	15 January 1818	Absent without Leave	Solitary Confinement.
George McGee	ditto	Loosing or making away with his Great Coat	Solitary Confinement
Michael Shan	20 January 1818	Drunk on Parade. Making away with 10lbs of his ammunition	200 lashes
Walter Robinson	22 January 1818	Sleeping on his Post	300 lashes remitted to one month Solitary Confinement.
Thomas Rieley	ditto	Sleeping on his Post	300 lashes remitted to one month Solitary Confinement
Michael Murray	26 January 1818	Making away with his Regimental Necessaries	220 lashes (50 remitted)
James Kelly	30 January 1818	Theft	200 lashes
William Griffiths	ditto	Drunk & Riotous in Barracks	14 Days Solitary Confinement.
Silus Green	ditto	Selling his Regimental Necessaries	14 Days Solitary Confinement
James Campbell	2 February 1818	Drunk on Guard	300 lashes
Patrick Loughman	ditto	Unsoldierlike conduct in threatening to make a false report of the Commanding Officer and Adjutant	300 lashes
Joseph Ellison	ditto	For giving False Evidence at a Courts-martial	300 lashes
Charles Waterman	ditto	Absent without Leave	300 lashes
James Elliott	9 February 1818	Unsoldierlike conduct in refusing to go to drill & striking an N.C.O.	21 days Solitary Confinement

Table 42 Nominal List of Men Tried by General Courts Martial from 5 April 1817 to 17 February 1818

Name	Date	Nature of Offence	Sentence
Edward Dunn	23 April 1817	Absent without Leave	900 lashes
John Heals	ditto	Absent without Leave	800 lashes
John Bogg	ditto	Absent without Leave	800 lashes
John Doby	ditto	Absent without Leav	900 lashes.
Joseph Hoddell	ditto	Absent without Leave	900 lashes
Thomas Devlin.	21 July 1817	1. For firing a musket loaded with ball while a prisoner in the Guard Room. 2. For maliciously saying he would complete the purpose for which he fired the musket at a future period.	1000 lashes

Table 43 Officers Serving with the York Chasseurs (Regimental Rank Only)

Lieutenant Colonel Andrew Coghlan
23 May 1792. Ensign. 72nd (Highland).
14 September 1792. Lieutenant.
24 September 1795. Lieutenant. Regiment raised for Service in the West Indies.
1 May 1796. Captain. 45th (Nottinghamshire)
19 October 1809. Major. 2nd Garrison Battalion.
13 September 1810. Major. 21st (Royal North British Fuzileers)
11 November 1813. Lieutenant-Colonel. York Chasseurs.
31 August 1815. Lieutenant-Colonel. 8th Royal Veteran Battalion.
1819. Lieutenant-Colonel. Retired on full-pay.
25 October 1822. Lieutenant-Colonel. 3rd Royal Veteran Battalion.
1827. Lieutenant-Colonel. Retired on full-pay.
Died 1837–1838.

Lieutenant Colonel John Ewart
1 November 1803. Ensign. 52nd (Oxfordshire) Foot.
10 March 1804. Lieutenant.
8 May 1806. Captain.
October 1812. Major. Royal York Rangers.
15 September 1814. Lieutenant Colonel. York Chasseurs.
March 1819 – February 1823. Lieutenant Colonel 67th (South Hampshire) Foot.
1827. Lieutenant Colonel of a Recruiting District.
1837. Colonel Inspecting Field Officer.
9 November 1846. Major General.
30 October 1852. Colonel 67th (South Hampshire) Foot.
24 October 1854. Died.

Major Peter Dumas
1 June 1797. Cornet. 20th (East Devonshire) Foot.
5 November 1797. Lieutenant and Adjutant.
19 March 1812. Captain. 99th (Prince of Wales's Tipperary) Foot.
22 June 1815. Major. York Chasseurs.
22 November 1819. Major half-pay.
1 May 1823. Lieutenant-Colonel. 65th (2nd North Yorkshire) Foot.
17 August 1832. Lieutenat-Colonel half-pay.
23 July 1832. Appointed Lieutenant-Governor. Gravesend and Tilbury Fort. At one hundred and seventy pounds, seven shillings and sixpence per annum.
1848. Died.
Served at the 1799 Blockade of Malta, 1801 Egyptian Campaign and at the Battle of Maida.

Major Joseph Paterson
17 May 1799. Ensign. 28th (North Gloucestershire) Foot.
2 September 1802. Lieutenant. 55th (Westmoreland) Foot.
7 May 1807. Captain. 77th (East Middlesex) Foot.
8 October 1814. Major. York Chasseurs.
14 December 1819. Major half-pay.
31 December 1825. Lieutenant Colonel on half-pay.
28 June 1838. Colonel.
11 November 1855. Major-General.

Captain Joseph Anderson
27 June 1805. Ensign. 78th Highland or (Rothshire Buffs)
6 October 1808. Lieutenant. 24th (Warwickshire) Foot.
27 January 1814. Captain. York Chasseurs.
1 January 1819. Captain half-pay.
3 May 1821. Captain. 50th (West Kents) Foot.
16 February 1826. Major.
1 April 1841. Lieutenant-Colonel.

Capt Edward Balguy
14 August 1800. Ensign. 4th West India Regiment.
25 October 1803. Ensign. 53rd (Shropshire) Foot.
28 August 1804. Lieutenant. 36th (Herefordshire) Foot.
15 December 1808. Captain.
25 March 1814. Captain. York Chasseurs.
14 March 1815. Court-martialled. Guilty 'Allowed to receive the regulated value of his Commission'.
16 May 1815. Died at Barbados.

Captain William Dallas
1 September 1808. Ensign. 9th (East Suffolk) Foot.
13 October 1811. Lieutenant.
15 March 1815. Captain. York Chasseurs.
21 May 1818. Captain half-pay.

Captain Charles Harris
29 August 1811. Lieutenant. 3rd (King's Own) Dragoons.
10 November 1813. Captain. York Chasseurs.
Possibly as Lieutenant to the 60th – 12 June 1816.

Captain Holland Daniel
23 June 1807. Lieutenant. 61st (South Gloucestershire) Foot.
7 November 1813. Captain. York Chasseurs.
25 December 1818. Captain half-pay.
3 August 1820. Captain. 38th (1st Staffordshire)
25 August 1821. Captain half-pay.
25 March 1824. Captain 98th Foot.
18 November 1831. Captain half-pay.

Captain Charles Fisher
18 June 1812. Lieutenant. 85th (Oxfordshire and Buckinghamshire) Light Infantry.
11 April 1816. Captain. York Chasseurs.
1820 to half-pay.

Captain John Augustine Ingram
1803. Ensign. 11th Battalion of Reserve.
25 November 1806. Ensign. 1st (Royal Scots) Foot.
18 October 1808. Lieutenant. 15th (Yorkshire East Riding) Foot.
3 October 1811. Captain. 24th (Warwickshire) Foot.
20 April 1815. Captain. York Chasseurs.
1816. Retired on half-pay.
21 June 1827. Captain. 69th (South Lincolnshire) Foot.
1829. Resigned.

Captain Richard Lundin
23 June 1808. Ensign. 73rd (Highland) Foot.
10 May 1810. Lieutenant.
27 January 1814. Captain. York Chasseurs.
12 March 1815. Captain half-pay.
1833. Died.

Captain Hector Mackay
30 April 1812. Ensign. Royal African Corps.
5 November 1813. Lieutenant. York Chasseurs.
5 July 1815. Captain.
7 May 1818. Captain half-pay (ill-health).

Captain John Montgomery
5 November 1807. Lieutenant. 67th (South Hampshire) Foot.
16 June 1808. Captain. 21st (Royal North British Fuzileers) Foot.
2 March 1815. Captain. York Chasseurs.
4 November 1819. 58th (Rutlandshire) Foot.
1823. Resigned or retired.

Captain Robert Nolan.
31 August 1806. Lieutenant. Duke of York's Royal Irish.
4 May 1815. Captain.
26 February 1816. Captain York Chasseurs.
29 December 1819. Captain half-pay.

Capt Jonathan Parker
6 June 1809. Ensign. 1st (Royal Scots) Foot.
1 June 1812. Lieutenant.
31 March 1814. Captain. York Chasseurs.
25 December 1818. Captain half-pay.
4 May 1820. Captain 68th (Durham) Foot.
1830. No record.

Captain Joseph Stainton
24 January 1811. Ensign. 94th Foot.
8 November 1813. Lieutenant. York Chasseurs.
2 December 1819. Captain – half-pay.
29 March 1821. Captain. 37th (North Hampshire) Foot.
4 August 1825 – half-pay.

Captain Edward Benjamin Stehelin
22 August 1806. Lieutenant. 16th (Bedfordshire) Foot.
6 July 1815. Captain. York Chasseurs.
23 September 1819. Captain. 41st Foot.
1828–29. Died.

Captain James Stewart
25 May 1808. 2nd Lieutenant. (Adjutant) 21st (Royal North British Fuzileers).
2 January 1810. 1st Lieutenant. (Adjutant)
5 November 1813. Lieutenant. (Adjutant) York Chasseurs.
2 March 1815. Captain.
10 April 1816. Embarked for Europe (ill health)

Lieutenant William Fleming Bell
7 April 1814. Ensign. York Chasseurs.
2 May 1815. Lieutenant.
7 December 1819. Lieutenant half- pay.
16 January 1823. Lieutenant. 58th (Rutlandshire) Foot.
4 February 1838. Captain.
1840. No record.

Lieutenant William Lucius Carey
14 May 1812. Ensign. 101st (Duke of York's Irish).
30 September 1813. Lieutenant.
3 May 1815. Lieutenant. York Chasseurs.
23 December 1819. Lieutenant half-pay.
30 December 1819. Lieutenant. 17th (Leicestershire) Foot.
1 December 1823. Lieutenant half-pay.
26 May 1825. Captain. 96th Foot.
20 January 1832. Captain half-pay.

Lieutenant Charles Dellamaine
12 August 1813. Ensign. 7th Battalion 60th (Royal American) Foot.
16 June 1814. Lieutenant. York Chasseurs.
11 December 1819. Lieutenant half-pay.

Lieutenant James Robert Disney
10 November 1814. Ensign. York Chasseurs.
20 July 1815. Lieutenant.
1819. Lieutenant half-pay.

Lieutenant William Henry Douglas
3 December 1812. Ensign. 90th (Perthshire Volunteers)
9 November 1813. Lieutenant. York Chasseurs.
23 March 1815. Lieutenant 26th (Cameronians) Foot.
25 March 1817 – half-pay.

Lieutenant Simeon Farrar
26th November 1813. Lieutenant. York Chasseurs.
19th February 1819. Lieutenant – half-pay.

Lieutenant Brian Gaynor
2 March 1815. Ensign. 99th Foot.
20 April 1815. Lieutenant. York Chasseurs.
25 December 1818. Lieutenant half-pay.
25 March 1824. Lieutenant. 99th Foot.
1830. Captain 99th Foot.
1835. No record.

Lieutenant Adolphus Leighton Gray
8 November 1813. Ensign. York Chasseurs.
10 November 1814. Lieutenant.
11 December 1819. Lieutenant – half-pay.
13 February 1823. Lieutenant. 46th (South Devonshire) Foot.
1828. No further record.

Lieutenant William Hay
Ensign. 4th Ceylon Regiment.

6 November 1813. Lieutenant York Chasseurs.
23 December 1819. Lieutenant half-pay.
8 April 1825. Lieutenant. 65th (2nd North Yorkshire N Riding) Foot.
10 November 1837. Captain half-pay.

Lieutenant William Heath
1808. Quartermaster. Sicilian Regiment of Foot.
3 November 1808. Ensign. Sicilain Regiment of Foot.
1813. Ensign. 6th Garrison Battalion. (North Britain).
5 November 1813. Lieutenant. York Chassuers.
18 December 1815. Court-martialled – permitted to retire on half-pay.

Lieutenant John Hodges
11 November 1813. Ensign. York Chasseurs.
14 March 1815. Lieutenant.
11 December 1819. Lieutenant – half-pay.

Lieutenant William Humble.
4 March 1813. Lieutenant. 5th West Indian Regiment.
16 December 1813. Lieutenant. York Chasseurs.
Died at Tobago, 3 June 1816.

Lieutenant Connell Vereker Jessop
3 August 1815. Ensign. York Chasseurs.
26 December 1818. Lieutenant half-pay.
30 December 1824. Lieutenant 2nd West India Regiment.
No further trace.

Lieutenant Joseph Jones
20 May 1813. Lieutenant. 6th West India Regiment.
29 February 1816. Lieutenant. York Chasseurs.
1819. Query Lieutenant half-pay.

Lieutenant William John Williams Jones
27 November 1816. Lieutenant. York Chasseurs.
22 May 1817. Lieutenant half-pay.

Lieutenant George Laye
14 September 1815. Ensign. York Chasseurs.
29 April 1819. Lieutenant half-pay.
9 December 1824. Lieutenant. Royal African Corps.
24 March 1825. Lieutenant half-pay.

Lieutenant Charles Le Court
13 May 1813. Ensign. Chasseurs Brittaniques.
26 Janaury 1815. Lieutenant. York Chasseurs.
25 November 1815. Known to be at Tobago.
1817. No record.

Lieutenant James Mackay
14 September 1815. Lieutenant. York Chasseurs.
1820. Lieutenant half-pay.
13 July 1821. Paymaster. 1st West India Regiment.
3 November 1825. Paymaster half-pay.

Lieutenant George Mainwaring
3 May 1815. Ensign. York Chasseurs.
17 September 1817. Lieutenant.
23 December 1819. Lieutenant half-pay.
10 October 1821. Lieutenant. 87th (Prince of Wales Own Irish).
1840. 1st Lieutenant. 87th now (Royal Irish Fusileers)
1842. Captain. 22nd (Cheshire) Foot.
1850. Major 22nd Foot. Retired Captain's full-pay.

Lieutenant Robert Maxwell
15 March 1815. Ensign. York Chasseurs.
28 November 1816. Lieutenant.
18 January, 1819. Died Port Maria, Jamaica,

Lieutenant James McBean
13 January 1814. Exchanged as Ensign into the York Chasseurs from the 46th Foot.
15 March 1816. Lieutenant.
25 April 1816. Embarked for Europe (private affairs).
Being refused an extension to his Leave of Absence, 15 March 1817, probably resigned his commission as not to half-pay.

Lieutenant Francis McMurran
14 January 1814. Ensign. York Chasseurs.
16 March 1815. Lieutenant.

Lieutenant James Richards
10 November 1813. Lieutenant. York Chasseurs.
1819. Half-pay.

Lieutenant William Ross
31 October 1811. Ensign. 26th (Cameronian)
9 November 1815. Lieutenant.
8 May 1817. Lieutenant. York Chasseurs.
November 1819. Lieutenant. 50th (West Kent)

Lieutenant William Rothwell
10 July 1811. Ensign. 85th (Bucks Volunteers Light Infantry) Foot.
25 November 1813. Lieutenant. York Chasseurs.
11 December 1819, half-pay.
7 April 1825. Lieutenant. 62nd (Wiltshire) Foot.
12 October 1826. Lieutenant – half-pay.
Died 1840–1842.

Lieutenant William Henry Souper
9 September 1795. Ensign 1st (Royal Scots) Foot.
28 September 1797. Lieutenant. 2nd West India Regiment.
1 May 1801. Paymaster. Chasseurs Brittaniques.
10 June 1813. Paymaster – Lymington.
4 May 1815. Ensign. York Chasseurs.
25 December 1817. Lieutenant.
25 July 1817. Lieutenant half-pay.
1821. Paymaster of Recruiting Districts.
1834. No record.

Lieutenant Edward Sutherland
27 November 1817. Ensign. York Chasseurs.
30 December 1819. Ensign. 87th (Prince of Wales Own Irish).
5 October 1820. Ensign. 46th (South Devonshire) Foot.
14 April 1825. Lieutenant. 77th (Middlesex) Foot.
25 December 1838. Captain half-pay.
1848. Captain half-pay. Storekeeper Royal Hospital, Chelsea.
1856. Barrack Master at Woolwich.
1857. Gentleman at Arms. Barrack Master at Woolwich.
No further record.

Lieutenant John Tennant
23 March 1815. Ensign (Adjutant) York Chasseurs.
17 September 1817. Lieutenant. (Adjutant)
16 March 1819. Lieutenant half-pay.
Died, 1829–1830.

Lieutenant Benjamin Wharton
24 December 1812. 46th (South Devonshire) Foot.
9 December 1813. Lieutenant. York Chasseurs.
23 December 1819. Lieutenant – half-pay.
25 March 1824. Lieutenant. 99th Foot.
Died 1831.

Ensign Charles Baillie Brisbane
21 March 1816. Ensign. York Chasseurs.
6 March 1817. Ensign. 9th (East Norfolk) Foot.
20 May 1819. Lieutenant.
9 June 1825. Captain half-pay.
19 October 1826. Captain. 34th (Cumberland) Foot.
20 August 1841. Major.
13 December 1842. Major half-pay.
1844–45. Died.

Ensign Charles Dorner
28 November 1816. Ensign.
2 December 1819. Lieutenant half-pay.

Ensign Daniel McCarthy
20 July 1815. Ensign. York Chasseurs.
29 October 1818. Died.

Ensign Henry Paxton Williams
9 June 1814. Ensign. 7th West India Regiment.
5 September 1816. Ensign. 6th West India Regiment.
6 March 1817. Ensign. York Chasseurs.
1 April 1819. Ensign. 2nd West India Regiment.
22 November 1821. Lieutenant.
6 September 1822. Lieutenant half-pay.
17 September 1827. Captain. 2nd West India Regiment.
1840. No record.

Ensign Thomas Richardson
25 December 1817. Ensign. York Chasseurs.
25 December 1818. Ensign – half-pay.

Ensign Skellern
Resigned 30 May 1814.

Ensign Baylis
Resigned 30 May 1814.

Ensign Richard Annesley Sparkes
8 February 1816. Ensign. York Chasseurs.
17 December 1819. Ensign half-pay.

Quartermaster James Lowrie
2 December 1813. Quartermaster. York Chasseurs.
1820 – half-pay.
24 February 1820. Ensign. 9th Royal Veteran Battalion.
26 September 1822. Adjutant. 2nd Royal Veteran Battalion.
1827. Retired on full-pay.

Paymaster James Thompson
Died at St Ann's, Barbados. 22 March 1815.

Paymaster John McIntyre
28 May 1811. Lieutenant. 71st Foot.
25 November 1813. Adjutant.
2 May 1816. Paymaster York Chasseurs.
1819. Retired on full-pay.

Surgeon Augustus Stromeyer
28 January 1808. Assistant Surgeon. Watteville's Regiment.
25 December 1812. Staff.
1813. Awarded Peninsular Medal.
16 December 1813. Surgeon. York Chasseurs.
28 March 1816. Retired half- pay.
1823. Acquired Medical Doctrate. (MD)
12 January 1828. Died Hamburg.

Surgeon John Lewis
28 March 1816. Surgeon. York Chasseurs.
1819 Half-pay.

Assistant Surgeon Sproule
17 March 1814. Assistant Surgeon. York Chasseurs.
7 November 1816. 2nd Royal Veteran Battalion.
1818. Assistant Surgeon half-pay.

Assistant Surgeon George Brien
29 June 1817. Died aboard the Cherub, on passage from Port Royal, Jamaica.

Assistant Surgeon Charles Whyte
14 May 1818. Assistant Surgeon. York Chasseurs.
17 December 1819. Assistant Surgeon half-pay.
2 November 1820. Assistant Surgeon. 61st (South Gloucestershire) Foot.
15 November 1826. Surgeon. 69th (South Lincolnshire) Foot.
30 December 1836. Staff Surgeon.
1848. Staff Surgeon. Barbados.
1849. Staff Surgeon. Portsmouth.

6 January 1854. Deputy Inspector General. Bombay.
21 December 1860. Half-pay Honourary Inspector General.
1881–1882. Died.

Assistant Surgeon Thomas Young.
10 December 1812. Hospital Assistant. 71st (Highland) Foot.
9 September 1813. Assistant Surgeon.
7 November 1816. Assistant Surgeon. York Chasseurs.
10 August 1820. Assistant Surgeon. 50th (West Kent) Foot.
4 May 1826. Surgeon.
24 February 1834. 95th (Derbyshire) Foot.

Table 44 Men of the York Chasseurs Regiment of Infantry.
Bn – Battalion. PS – Prison-ship. WIs – West Indies. YCs – York Chasseurs

Sergeants

Allwright, Francis. Coldstream Guards. Marched from Romsey and confined aboard PS, 16 September 1813. Joined YCs as sergeant 1 February 1814. Promoted colour sergeant 25 February 1814. Arrived in the WIs 14 December 1814. 'Private Roberts received 300 lashes for Striking Sergeant Alwright and Private James Dochety 300 lashes for Theft and Striking Sgt Alwright, 24th December 1816'. Discharged Quebec 24 August 1819.

Annis, Charles. 70th Foot. Marched from Stafford and confined aboard PS, 17 September 1813. Joined YCs 5 February 1814 and arrived in the WIs 14 December 1814. Promoted corporal 9 October 1817, and sergeant 25 May 1818. Discharged Quebec, 24 August 1819.

Bailey, William. Labourer of Newbury. Berkshire Militia. Marched from Liverpool and confined aboard PS, 3 March 1815. Joined YCs 29 June 1815, and arrived in the WIs as sergeant 5 November 1815. Appointed Drum-Major. Died Jamaica 27 August 1817. Effects, eight pounds and ten shillings, willed to his father, George Bailey of Newbury, Berkshire'.

Benfield/Binfield, Richard. Labourer of Kent. Marched from Windsor as 'Volunteer' from the 2nd Bn 5th Foot, 1 April 1815. Arrived in the WIs as sergeant 5 November 1815. Died Grenada as colour sergeant, 19 February 1816.

Boyes, Henry. Clerk of Lancaster. 7th Foot. Marched from Devizes and confined aboard PS, 8 June 1813. Joined YCs as sergeant paymaster clerk 5 February 1814. Arrived in the WIs 14 December 1814. Died 10 November 1816.

Brickle/Brittle, Samuel. Labourer of Nottinghamshire. 1st Bn 3rd Foot Guards. Marched from St Albans and confined aboard PS as Samuel Brickle, 10 January 1815. Joined YCs as Samuel Brittle, 29 June 1815. Arrived in the WIs 5 November 1815. Promoted corporal 13 July 1816, and Sergeant 3 August 1817. Deserted in Jamaica 17 April 1819. No record of rejoining.

Brown, George. Royal Horse Artillery. Marched from Aberdeen and confined aboard PS, 15 August 1813. Joined YCs 5 February 1814, and arrived in the WIs 14 December 1814. Employed as orderly in the General Hospital before being promoted to corporal, 3 October 1815, sergeant 10 November 1815, and colour sergeant 25 April 1818. Discharged Quebec 24 August 1819.

Browning, William. Labourer of St Martins, Kent. 4th Dragoons. Marched from

Warwick and confined aboard PS, 15 December 1814. Joined YCs 29 June 1815, and arrived in the WIs 5 November 1815. Promoted corporal, 27 December 1816, sergeant, 29 November 1817, and colour sergeant 1 March 1818. Discharged Stony Hill, Jamaica, 10 June 1819.

Burns/Byrnes/Barnes, Nicholas. Optician of Liverpool. East India Company. Marched from Liverpool and confined aboard PS as Nicholas Burns 16 April 1815. Joined YCs 29 June 1815, and arrived in the WIs as Nicholas Byrnes, 5 November 1815. Promoted corporal 27 September 1816, and sergeant 13 February 1817. Died Jamaica as Nicholas Byrnes or Barnes, 10 September 1818.

Buyss/Buijss, Cornelius. Shoemaker of Amsterdam. 26-year-old Buyss, along with Laurence Roovers, enlisted into the Barbados Volunteer Emigrant Regiment, 25 September 1803. (1804 – York Light Infantry Volunteers). Promoted corporal on enlistment and sergeant 24 November 1806. Reduced 4 June 1809. After serving primarily at Prince Rupert, Dominica and Antigua, Buyss was discharged during 1812 and, along with Lauwrence Roovers and 26 of the regiment, arrived in England seemingly at public expense. Enlisting for the 1st Battalion Tower Hamlets Militia 11 December 1812, Buyss and Roovers then volunteered for the York Chasseurs 18 December 1813. (Eight Guinea Bounty). Promoted corporal 2 February 1814, Buyss arrived in the WIs 14 December 1814. Promoted sergeant 1 May 1817, and colour sergeant 10 February 1819. Discharged Quebec 24 September 1819, Buyss, as a volunteer, returned to England at public expense and a pension, 'Conduct on discharge Extremely Good'.

Carlow, Anthony. Shoemaker of Dorset. 1st Battalion Tower Hamlets Militia volunteer, 6 December 1813. (Eight Guinea Bounty). Promoted sergeant 27 December 1813, and colour sergeant 13 February 1817. Arrived in WIs 14 December 1814. Died Jamaica, 27 December 1818.

Carter, John. 22nd Light Dragoons. Marched from Savoy Military Prison and confined aboard PS, 23 December 1813. Joined 7 March 1814, and arrived in the WIs 14 December 1814. Promoted corporal 3 September 1814, and sergeant 6 August 1816. Died 25 October 1816. Effects willed to his wife, Elizabeth Carter, The Artichoke, George Street, Richmond, London.

Carter, John. Labourer of Cottingham. 39th Foot. Marched from Winchester and confined aboard PS, 19 March 1815. Joined YCs 29 June 1815, and arrived in WIs as sergeant, 5 November 1815. Died Jamaica, 8 October 1817.

Cocker, John. Royal Artillery Driver. Marched from Chesterfield and confined aboard PS, 17 September 1813. Joined YCs 1 February 1814, and arrived in the WIs 14 December 1814. Promoted corporal 29 August 1816, and sergeant 20 April 1818. Discharged Quebec, 24 August 1819. Allocated Concession 9. Lot 10, Beckwith township. No evidence found of him settling there.

Cummings, John. Labourer of Midlothian. 94th Foot. Marched from Dunbarton and confined aboard PS, 10 September 1813. Joined YCs 5 February 1814, and arrived in the WIs 14 December 1814. Promoted corporal 25 August 1814, and sergeant 25 December 1814. Sentenced to be reduced for 'Unbecoming Conduct', 14 July 1815, 'but FORGIVEN'. Died St Vincent 10 November 1815.

Davis/Davies, Evan. Labourer of Cardigan. Deserter, General Service or 62nd Foot. Transferred from Albany Barracks to Portchester Castle. Joined YCs 2 May 1817, and arrived in the WIs 25 January 1818. Promoted corporal March 1818, sergeant 25 June 1818, and colour sergeant 24 November 1818. Transferred to 2nd West India Regiment 25 March 1819.

Denny, Robert. 2nd Bn 84th Foot. Transported from Portsmouth and confined aboard PS, 1 November 1813. Joined YCs 5 February 1814, and arrived in the WIs 14 December 1814. Promoted corporal 25 March 1814, sergeant 25 April 1814, and colour sergeant 18 October 1816. Discharged Quebec.

Dougherty/Dogherty, Richard. Labourer of Armagh. 52nd Foot. Marched from Chatham and confined aboard PS, 19 November 1814. Joined YCs 29 June 1815, and arrived in the WIs as corporal 5 November 1815. Reduced 29 January 1816. Promoted corporal 25 August 1817, and sergeant 9 October 1817. Died Jamaica 29 October 1817.

Dowd/Dowds/Dows, Patrick. Carpenter of Carlow. Royal Artillery. Marched from Chester and confined aboard PS, 29 January 1815. Joined 29 June 1815, and arrived in the WIs as sergeant 5 November 1815. Died Kingston, Jamaica, 28 August 1816.

Dyson, Richard. 2nd Bn 84th Foot. Marched from Wakefield and confined aboard PS, 20 March 1814. Joined YCs 29 June 1815, and arrived in the WIs 5 November 1815. Promoted corporal 25 December 1815, and sergeant 9 August 1816. 'Private Garratty received 300 lashes for being Absent from Tattoo and Striking Sergeant Dyson, 6 March 1817'. Discharged Quebec.

Ecklin/Echlin, Christopher. Shoemaker of Fermoy. Enlisted for the 2nd Bn 5th Foot, 1807 or 1808. Promoted corporal 24 January 1808. Campaigned in both Portugal and Spain. 'Sick in Spain', rejoining his regiment as sergeant 9 December 1812. Returned to England March 1813. Marched from Windsor to Portsmouth as sergeant volunteer 6 May 1815. Deserted at Portsmouth while waiting passage for St Vincent 13 July 1815.

Adjutant General's Instructions. 25 July 1815.

Ecklin should be sent with other Deserters on board the Prison-ship at the Isle of Wight, where it is conceived they can be kept in better security than at Fort Cumberland, and until an opportunity offers for their being embarked for Foreign Service.

Arrived in the WIs as corporal 5 November 1815. Promoted sergeant 2 January 1816. Transferred to Bourbon Regiment as colour sergeant 24 February 1816. With the Bourbon Regiment under Orders of Disbandment, transferred as colour sergeant to the 1st West Regiment, 25 April 1816. Reduced for 'Unsoldierlike Conduct and Irregularities on the 17th and 18th Days of August'. Transferred to the 25th Foot as Private 22 August 1816. Left West Indies with his regiment 25 June 1817. Arrived Deptford, Kent, 25 July 1817, and marched to Weedon Barracks, Buckinghamshire. From November 1817, employed on 'Recruiting Duties within the Huntington District.' 'Qualified for 14 years service Additional Pay, 24 September 1819'. Deserted 12 October 1819. No record of rejoining.

Edwards, Eneas. Labourer of Portsmouth. Royal Horse Guards. Confined aboard PS, 9 March 1814. Joined YCs 25 March 1814. Promoted corporal 6 April 1814, and sergeant 25 April 1814. Arrived in the WIs 14 December 1814. Reduced March 1815. Promoted corporal 11 June 1815, and sergeant 25 December. Reduced 7 June 1817. Promoted sergeant 21 February 1818. Died Jamaica 14 October 1818.

Edwards, William. 2nd Bn 87th Foot. Marched from Kingston and confined aboard PS, 13 January 1814. Joined YCs 1 February 1814, and arrived in the WIs 14 December 1814. Promoted corporal 2 September 1815, and sergeant March 1815. Reduced 16 October 1815. Promoted corporal 13 February 1817, and sergeant 25 August 1817. Discharged Quebec.

Edwards, William Henry. Painter of Deptford. General Service. Marched from Savoy Military Prison and confined at Portchester Castle 16 October 1816. Joined YCs 3 April 1817, and arrived in the WIs 25 May 1817. Promoted corporal, then pay master sergeant, 25 August 1817. Died Jamaica 22 October 1817.

Elliot/Elliott, James. Either 28th Foot marched from Bristol, 4 February 1815, or 84th, marched from Chester and confined aboard PS, 18 May 1815. Joined YCs 29 June 1815, and arrived in the WIs 5 November 1815. Promoted corporal 25 January 1816, and sergeant 24 February 1816. Discharged Quebec.

Farlie/Fairlie/Fairlee, Mathew. 70th Foot. Marched from Perth and confined aboard PS, 3 September 1813. Joined YCs as corporal 1 February 1814. Promoted sergeant 25 February 1814. Arrived in the WIs 14 December 1814. Promoted colour sergeant (date unknown). Discharged Quebec.

Ford, Patrick. 28th Foot. Marched from Horsham and confined aboard PS (date unknown). Joined YCs 5 February 1814, and arrived in the WIs 14 December 1814. Promoted corporal 25 July 1816, and sergeant 10 May 1818. Discharged Quebec.

Forrester, Thomas. Labourer of Liverpool. 1st Bn 3rd Foot Guards. Marched from Shepton Mallet and confined aboard PS, 7 March 1813. Joined YCs 29 June 1815, and arrived in the WIs as corporal, 5 November 1815. Promoted sergeant 4 February 1816, reduced 17 August 1816. Promoted corporal 25 November 1816, and sergeant 4 March 1818. Transferred to 2nd West India Regiment 25 March, 1819.

Fountain, John. 3rd Bn 95th Foot. Marched from Savoy Military Prison and confined aboard PS, 29 October 1813. Joined YCs 5 February 1814. Promoted corporal 24 February 1814, and sergeant 10 April 1814. Arrived in the WIs 14 December 1814. Transferred to the Bourbon Regiment as sergeant 25 February 1816. With the regiment under orders of disbandment, transferred as colour sergeant to the 1st West India Regiment, 25 April 1816. Sentenced to 200 lashes and ordered to be reduced for 'Repeatedly Absenting Himself from Parade and Refusing to go on Parade when Ordered', 3 August 1816. Corporal punishment remitted and reinstated to colour sergeant. Reduced at St Lucia 20 January 1818, and transferred to the Royal York Rangers. Disbanded Halifax, Nova Scotia, 19 June 1819.

Frazer, William. Labourer of Antrim. 48th Foot. Marched from Glasgow and confined aboard PS, 5 February 1815. Joined YCs 29 June 1815, and arrived in WIs as corporal, 5 November 1815. Promoted sergeant 4 February 1816. Died Jamaica 23 February 1817.

Gallagher, Terrence. School teacher of Innishclose. Volunteered from the Donegal Militia volunteers for the 1st Bn 45th Foot, 12 May 1805. 1806–1807 at Monte Video, South America. September 1813, in Portugal/Spain, and November 1813, France. Returned with the regiment to England and promoted to corporal September 1814. Deserted 9 December 1814. Marched from Winchester and confined aboard PS, 4 March 1815. Joined YCs 29 June 1815, and arrived in the WIs 5 November 1815. Promoted corporal December 1815, sergeant June 1816, and school master sergeant the next day. Alternated between pay and school master sergeant. Discharged Quebec as schoolmaster sergeant.

Gilmore, Thomas. Labourer of Tyrone. Corporal, 2nd Bn 18th Foot. Sentenced at Jersey to 'General Service for Life for Desertion', 11 February 1814. Transported from Jersey and confined aboard PS, 30 April 1815. Joined YCs 29 June 1815, and arrived in the WIs as sergeant 5 November 1815. Deserted in Jamaica 16 April 1819. No record of rejoining.

Glass/Glasse, Samuel. Weaver of Derry. 21st Foot. Marched from Chester and confined aboard PS, 2 August 1813. Joined YCs as corporal 5 February 1814, and promoted sergeant 25 February 1814. Arrived in the WIs 14 December 1814. 'Killed in Action at Guadeloupe', 9 August 1815. Willed his effects, two pounds seventeen shillings and ten pence to his mother, Sarah Glasse of Armagh, County Tyrone.

Halleran, Malcolm. 12th Foot. Marched from Chester and confined aboard PS, 16 April 1815. Joined YCs 5 July 1815, vice William Whiteham. Arrived in the WIs 5 November 1815. Promoted corporal 9 August 1816, and sergeant 13 March 1818. Discharged Quebec.

Harris, William. Either 7th Bn Royal Veteran Battalion marched from Savoy Military Prison, 16 March 1813, or 2nd Bn Royals from Savoy Military Prison and confined aboard PS, 19 August 1813. Joined YCs 1 February 1814, and arrived in the WIs 14 December 1814. Promoted corporal 25 August 1815, and sergeant 31 August 1817. Discharged Quebec.

Healey/Healy, Nicholas. Labourer of Galway. 101st Foot. Marched from Savoy Military Prison and confined aboard PS, 11 December 1814. Joined YCs 29 June 1815, and arrived in the WIs 5 November 1815. Promoted corporal 25 January 1816, and sergeant 25 October 1816. Died 9 November 1816.

Henshaw, Thomas. Sawyer of Chester. Joined 2nd Bn 21st (Royal North British Fusiliers), October 1804. Promoted corporal January 1805, and sergeant September 1805. Served in Scotland and 'Recruiting Duties in Ireland'. Volunteered as sergeant major, 25 December 1813. Arrived in the WIs 14 December 1814. Died Jamaica 10 November 1817.

Hickling, John. Bricklayer of Leicestershire. Royal Artillery. Marched from Leicester and confined aboard PS, 27 July 1813. Joined YCs February 1814. Promoted corporal 14 April 1814, and sergeant 24 April 1914. Arrived in the WIs 14 December 1814. Died 14 November 1816.

Howieson, James. Joined 91st Foot from the Edinbugh Militia Volunteers, 28 May 1812. Deserted 30 May 1813. Marched from Edinburgh and confined aboard PS, 18 January 1814. Joined YCs 31 March 1814. Promoted corporal 6 April 1814, and sergeant 24 April 1814. Arrived in the WIs 14 December 1814. Transferred to the Bourbon Regiment 24 February 1816. With the Bourbon Regiment under Orders of disbandment, transferred to the 1st West India Regiment as colour sergeant, April 1816. Promoted sergeant major 25 October 1818, but reduced to private 1 June 1828. Despite only one instance of 'hospitalisation' during his entire 14 years in the WIs, died 27 September 1828, less than four months after demotion.

Hyland, William. Clerk of Mountrath, Queen's County. Volunteered from the East India Company's, Isle of Wight Depot, for the 2nd Bn 12th Foot, 8 January 1812. Promoted sergeant 22 May 1812, and colour sergeant, date unknown. Transferred to an India bound 1st Bn, 19 September 1814, but deserted 31 December 1814. Marched from Exeter and confined aboard PS, 20 January 1815. Joined YCs 29 June 1815, and arrived in the WIs as sergeant, 5 November 1815. Promoted colour sergeant, 2 January 1816, and sergeant major, 11 January 1817. Discharged at Quebec. Accompanied by his wife, Hyland first opted for Concession 4. Lot SW 13. Bathurst township, but, 4 January 1820 at Kingston, Ontario, instead had enlisted as private to the 70th. Promoted pay master sergeant, 24 January 1820. Hyland had then remained as pay master sergeant until June 1825, when, reduced to corporal, 9 August 1825, he arrived back in England the month following, but only to be hospitalised. Rejoining his regiment, 8 October 1825, Hyland had finally been discharged, 26 January 1826.

James, George. Joined the 2nd Bn 79th Foot at Greenock, 9 July 1813 (Eleven Guinea Bounty). Deserted 15 June 1814. Marched from Greenock and confined aboard PS, 14 August 1814. Joined YCs 29 June 1815, and arrived in the WIs as sergeant 5 November 1815. Promoted colour sergeant 24 February 1816. Discharge by purchase – 'Paid by Edward Johnston Esq for the Discharge of Colour Sergeant George James, 28th March 1818'.

James, Thomas. Spinner of Wicklow. Royal Artillery. Marched from Nottingham and confined aboard PS, 1 August 1813. Joined YCs as sergeant 1 February 1814, and arrived in the WIs 14 December 1814. Died at the Regimental Hospital, St Vincent, 8 November 1815.

Jones, Thomas. Labourer of Limerick. 23rd Foot. Confined aboard PS, 22 April 1815. Joined YCs 29 June 1815, and arrived in the WIs as sergeant 5 November 1815. Died Jamaica 12 July 1816.

Kane/Cane, Austin. Labourer of Mayo. 1st Foot. Marched from Bristol and confined aboard PS, 18 May 1815. Joined YCs 29 June 1815 and arrived in WIs 5 November 1815. Promoted corporal 14 April 1816, sergeant 10 November 1816, and drum-major December 1817. Died Jamaica 10 January 1819.

Lawton, Charles. 3rd Bn 56th Foot. Marched from Savoy Military Prison and confined aboard PS, 6 January 1815. Joined YCs 29 June 1815. Promoted sergeant and 'Left on Detachment' at the Isle of Wight as regiment departed for St Vincent. Providing two substitutes, Lawton gained his discharged (December 1815–March 1816).

Leonard, Thomas. Born Gibraltar 1779/1780. Leonard followed his father, Private Patrick Leonard, into the 1st Battalion 50th (West Kent) Foot at Gibraltar 1 September 1790, aged 10 years. Promoted sergeant October 1806; years of campaigning with the regiment eventually gained Leonard his General Service Medal and Campaign Clasps – Egypt, Vimiera, Corunna, Vittoria, Nivelle, Nive, Orthes and Toulouse. Even so, with 26 years of service and while on detached duty at Cardonagh, Ireland, Leonard deserted, 24 July 1816. Joining the York Chasseurs 17 October 1816, Leonard arrived in the West Indies 21 December 1816, to be promoted corporal March 1817, sergeant April 1817, and colour sergeant February 1819. Discharged Quebec and allocated 200 acres, Concession 10. Lot 15. Bathurst, Lanark County, Ontario. Several years later Leonard purchased an additional 100 acres, Concession 6. Lot 24, while retaining his original allocation for several years afterwards. Awarded Chelsea Hospital Out Pension, 14 November.1821, 'one shilling, and eleven pence per diem'. Died 3 October 1868 in his 93rd year; buried in Craig Street Cemetery, Perth, Lanark County, Ontario.

Mackay, Hector. Labourer of Sutherland. Volunteered at the Isle of Wight, 19 January 1814 (Eleven Guineas Bounty). Arrived in the WIs 14 December 1814. Promoted sergeant 25 February 1814, and colour sergeant 27 April 1817. Volunteered into the 50th Foot while still in Jamaica, 7 June 1819, but invalided to England a few months later.

Mann, William. Joined YCs at Jamaica as sergeant from the 1st European Garrison, May 1817. Discharged Quebec.

Martine/Martyn/Meutiqu, Francis. Labourer of Valencia, Spain. De Meuron's Corps. Transported from Malta and confined aboard PS, 4 August 1812. Left the Isle of Wight for Jamaica and the 6th Bn 60th Regiment, November 1812. Arrived in the WIs January 1813. Promoted corporal 7 May 1815, and sergeant 14 February 1817. Transferred into the York Chasseurs in Jamaica as private 25 May 1817. Promoted sergeant 17 November 1817. Deserted in Jamaica 27 April 1819. No record of rejoining.

Marwick, William. 2nd Bn 36th Foot. Marched from Chichester and confined aboard PS, 21 April 1815. Joined YCs 29 June 1815, and arrived in the WIs 5 November 1815. Promoted corporal 25 November 1816, and sergeant 4 August 1817. Discharged Quebec.

Maxwell, William. Labourer of Tyrone. Joined the 7th Bn Royal Artillery, 2 June 1808. Sentenced at Woolwich to 500 lashes for 'Absence, Insolence and Riotous Conduct', 8 June 1814. Presumably commuted corporal punishment for 'Unlimited General Service'. Marched from Woolwich and confined aboard PS, 7 July 1814. Joined YCs 29 June 1815, and arrived in the WIs as sergeant 5 November 1815. Sentenced at St Vincent to 999 lashes and ordered to be reduced for 'Quitting the Barracks with his Bayonet fixed and Resisting the Officer', 23 December 1815. Promoted corporal 3 December 1816, and sergeant 25 December 1816. Died Jamaica 28 November 1817.

McCamus, James. Servant of Neath County. Volunteered directly into the regiment while at Dublin, recorded on the regimental strength as from 24 September 1814. Arrived in the WIs 14 December 1814. Promoted corporal 13 May 1815, and sergeant 3 October 1815. Reduced 17 January 1816. Promoted corporal 8 August 1816, and sergeant 25 November 1816. Discharged Quebec. Joined the 85th Foot 13 March 1821, and served as private until 20 August 1835, when discharged to a pension. Reason for discharge 'Disability contracted on duty and aggravated by Dissipation'.

McEwan, Daniel. Labourer of Perth. Royal Artillery. Marched from Preston and confined aboard PS, 14 November 1813. Joined YCs 7 March 1814, and arrived in the WIs 14 December 1814. Promoted corporal 6 July 1815, and sergeant 1 May 1815. Died St Vincent 10 September 1815.

McKibbon/McKibben, Thomas. Weaver of Derry. 91st Foot. Marched from Chester and confined aboard PS, 8 December 1813. Joined YCs 5 February 1814, and arrived in the WIs 14 December 1814. Promoted corporal 25 September 1814, and sergeant 3 January 1815. Died Jamaica 6 August 1817.

McLacklan/McLachlin/McLoughlin, Alexander. Weaver of Paisley. Volunteered as sergeant of the 21st Foot and, December 1813, immediately promoted colour sergeant. Arrived in the WIs 14 December 1814. Died Jamaica 19 January 1817.

McMullen/McMillan, Alexander. Labourer of Tyrone. 26th Foot. Transported from Hilsea, Portsmouth, and confined aboard PS, 1 November 1814. Joined YCs 29 June 1815, and arrived in the WIs as sergeant 5 November 1815. Died Jamaica 20 April 1819.

Murphy, James. Labourer of Roscommon. Marched from Petworth and confined aboard PS, 8 September 1813. Joined YCs 5 February 1814, and arrived in the WIs 14 December 1814. Promoted corporal 2 May 1815, and sergeant 3 October 1816. Died Jamaica 27 May 1818.

Neal/Neale, William. Labourer of Kildare. 2nd Bn 7th Foot. Transported from Portsmouth and confined aboard PS, 21 August 1814. Joined YCs 29 June 1815, and arrived in the WIs 5 November 1815. Promoted corporal 23 May 1816, and sergeant 27 September 1816. Died Jamaica 4 August 1817.

Newall, John. 19th Dragoons. Marched from Bedford and confined at Portchester Castle, 2 October 1816. Joined YCs 3 April 1817, and arrived in the WIs 25 May 1817. Promoted corporal 28 October 1817, and sergeant 27 May 1818. Discharged Quebec.

Norris, John. Brass Founder of Dudley. 23rd Light Dragoons. Marched from Bristol and confined aboard PS, 31 July 1813. Joined YCs February 1814, and arrived in the WIs 14

December 1814. Promoted corporal 25 February 1814, and sergeant 21 July 1814. Died Grenada 3 September 1815.

O'Brien, Francis. Gunsmith of Cork. 28th Foot. Marched from Plymouth and confined aboard PS, 30 October 1813. Joined YCs as sergeant 1 February 1814, and arrived in the WIs 14 December 1814. Appointed armourer sergeant 25 February 1814, reduced 19 May 1816. Following Armourer Sergeant William Wilson's unsuccessful attempt at desertion, re-appointed armourer sergeant 21 January 1818. Discharged Jamaica 10 June 1819.

Oram, David. 7th Dragoon Guards. Marched from Pershall and confined aboard PS, 27 April 1815. Joined YCs 29 June 1815, and arrived in the WIs as sergeant 5 November 1815. Discharged Quebec. Allocated Concession 2. Lot SW 25. Drummond. No evidence of him settling there.

Perry, William. County Tyrone. Volunteered from the Albany Barracks Staff, 2 April 1815, previous service with 87th and 95th Foot. Arrived in the WIs 5 November 1815, and immediately promoted colour sergeant. Discharged Quebec. Subsequently served with the 10th Royal Veteran Battalion, 61st, 50th and the last two years of his service, as company sergeant major, 2nd West India Regiment, after enlisting at New Providence. Medically discharged to a pension 24 September 1828. 'His health has been much impaired and his constitution worn out by repeated attacks of Intermittent Fever and long service in a tropical climate'.

Roberts, Thomas. Labourer of County Down. 19th Light Dragoons. Marched from Harwich and confined aboard PS, 8 August 1813. Joined YCs as sergeant 1 February 1814, and promoted colour sergeant the next day. Arrived in the WIs 14 December 1814. Reduced 18 August 1815. Promoted corporal 3 October 1815, and sergeant 15 October 1815. Deserted while in Jamaica 2 March 1819. No record of rejoining.

Roovers, Laurence. Labourer from Holland. 20 year old Laurence Roovers, alongside an older Cornelius Buyss, volunteered for the Barbados Volunteer Emigrant Regiment, 25 September 1803. (1804 – York Light Infantry Volunteers). Promoted corporal 18 January 1811, reduced 15 August 1811. Served primarily at Prince Rupert, Dominica, and Antigua, Roovers, along with other members of the York Light Infantry Volunteers including Buyss, discharged and sent to Europe at public expense. (March–December 1812). Joining the 1st Battalion Tower Hamlets Militia 11 December 1812, Laurence Roovers and Cornelius Buyss later volunteered for the York Chasseurs, 18 December 1813 (Eight Guinea Bounty). Promoted corporal, 1 March 1814, and sergeant, 3 September. Arrived in the WIs 14 December 1814. Died Tobago August 1816.

Ross, Donald. Ross, Scotland. Private of the 42nd Foot, (10 May 1807–27 November 1814), who volunteered while serving on the Isle of Wight with the 1st Garrison Staff Company. Joined YCs as corporal 19 April 1814, and arrived in the WIs 14 December 1814. Promoted sergeant 25 November 1815. 'Discharged from the Regimental Books and granted a Chelsea Out-Pension, 1st February 1820. Conduct – 'Extremely Good'.

Seaman, Robert. 3rd Foot Guards. Marched from London and confined at Portchester Castle, 21 January 1817. Joined YCs 3 April 1817, and arrived in the WIs 25 May 1817. Promoted from private to pay master sergeant on the death of Pay Master Sergeant Edwards 23 October 1817. Discharged Quebec. Possibly returned to England at public expense.

Sewell, John. Framework knitter of Nottingham. Volunteered from the 2nd Battalion Tower Hamlets Militia (Six Guinea Bounty). Joined YCs as corporal 6 December 1813, promoted sergeant 2 February 1814, and colour sergeant 14 April 1814. Arrived in the WIs 14 December 1814. Died Jamaica 6 November 1818.

Simpson, James. Labourer of Berwick. Joined at the Isle of Wight as a volunteer colour sergeant April 1814. Arrived in the WIs 14 December 1814. Died 12 October 1816.

Sitch Voysey, James. Cutler of Middlesex. Corporal volunteer from the 2nd Bn Royal Scots, 13 March 1814. Promoted sergeant immediately on joining. Deserted from the Isle of Wight, 27 July 1814. No record of rejoining regiment.

Skilling, William. Labourer of Cheshire. 1st Dragoon Guards. Marched from Bristol and confined aboard PS, 22 October 1814. Joined YCs 29 June 1815, and arrived in the WIs as corporal 5 November 1815. Promoted sergeant 9 May 1816. Died Jamaica 19 April 1818.

Smith, Charles. Clerk of the East Indies. 11th Dragoons. Marched from Hounslow and confined aboard PS, 1 May 1815. Joined YCs 29 June 1815, and arrived in the WIs as corporal 5 November 1815. Promoted sergeant 25 February 1816. Died Jamaica 5 July 1818.

Smith, John. Blacksmith of Dore, South Yorkshire. Joined YCs 29 June 1815, and arrived in the WIs 5 November 1815. Promoted corporal 7 January 1816, and sergeant 30 May 1816. Died 22 October 1816.

Smith, John. Labourer of Waterford. 13th Foot. Marched from Chester and confined aboard PS, 2 October 1813. Joined YCs as drummer 5 February 1814. Promoted drum-major March 1814. Deserted from the Isle of Wight,13 July 1814. No record of rejoining.

Spencer, John. Royal Artillery. Marched from Leicester and confined aboard PS, 3 March 1815. Joined YCs 29 June 1815, and arrived in the WIs 5 November 1815. Promoted corporal 25 December 1815, sergeant 31 May 1816, and colour sergeant 7 November 1818. Deserted in Jamaica 9 March 1819. No record of rejoining.

Sweeting, William. Clerk of Somerset. 18th Light Dragoons. Marched from Dorchester and confined aboard PS, 19 February 1814. Joined YCs as corporal 7 March 1814. Promoted sergeant 25 March 1814, reduced 25 June 1814. Arrived in the WIs 14 December 1814. Promoted corporal 28 April 1815, and sergeant,4 September 1815. Died Grenada 16 December 1815.

Taylor, John. 2nd Bn 4th Foot. Marched from St Edmondsbury and confined aboard PS, 27 July 1813. Joined YCs as corporal 5 February 1814. Promoted sergeant 25 April 1814, reduced 11 December 1814. Arrived in the WIs 14 December 1814. 200 lashes for being 'Drunk at Evening Parade', 16 September 1815. Promoted corporal 14 December 1816, and sergeant 25 January 1817. Discharged Quebec. Allocated Concession 8. Lot SW 6, Beckwith. No evidence of him settling there.

Temple, Abraham. 85th Foot. Marched from Newark and confined aboard PS, 1 August 1813. Joined YCs as corporal 5 February 1814. Arrived in the WIs 14 December 1814. Reduced, 25 December 1814. Promoted corporal 1 April 1815, reduced 26 September 1815. Promoted corporal 25 February 1817, sergeant 25 June 1817, and colour sergeant 11 June 1819. Discharged Quebec.

Till, William. 76th Foot. Marched from Hexham and confined aboard PS, 26 March 1814. Joined YCs 29 June 1815, and arrived in the WIs as corporal 5 November 1815. Promoted sergeant 27 December 1816. Discharged Quebec.

Toole, Patrick. 3rd Foot Guards. Marched from Bristol and confined aboard PS, 27 September 1813. Joined YCs 5 February 1814, and arrived in the WIs 14 December 1814. Promoted corporal 10 August 1815, and sergeant 19 June 1816. Discharged Quebec.

Upcroft/Upcross, John. Dyer of Middlesex. Volunteer from the 2nd Bn Tower Hamlets Militia (Six Guinea Bounty). Joined YCs as corporal 6 December 1813, and promoted sergeant 2 February 1814. Arrived in the WIs 14 December 1814. Died Jamaica 23 June 1817.

Wilson, Andrew. Labourer of Ayr. Volunteered as sergeant of the 21st Foot, joined as quarter master sergeant, 25 December 1813. Arrived in the WIs 14 December 1814. Invalided from Jamaica to Chatham 3 February 1819.

Wilson, William. Blacksmith of Northampton. Either West Kent Militia marched from Windsor, 6 April 1814, 42nd from Edindurgh, 16 April 1814, 2nd Bn 64th Foot from Colchester, 21 October 1814, or Royal Horse Artillery marched from Nottingham and confined aboard PS, 2 May 1815. Arrived in the WIs 14 December 1814. Deserted in Jamaica 16 January 1818. No record of rejoining.

Wyman/Weyman, John. Volunteer from the 2nd Battalion Tower Hamlets Militia. (Six Guinea Bounty). Joined YCs as corporal 10 December 1813, and promoted sergeant 1 February 1814. Arrived in the WIs14 December 1814. Died 21 July 1815.

Yeoman, William. Labourer of Manchester. 38th Foot. Marched from Southampton and confined aboard PS, 14 February 1814. Joined YCs 25 March 1814. Promoted corporal 25 May 1814, and sergeant,15 July 1814. Arrived in the WIs 14 December 1814. Died Barbados 12 May 1815.

Corporals

Angus, John. Royal Artillery. Marched from Aberdeen and confined aboard PS, 5 September 1813. Joined YCs 5 February 1814, and arrived in the WIs 14 December 1814. Promoted corporal 24 September 1817. Discharged Quebec.

Arnold, Robert. Joined the 61st Foot, 25 April 1803. Marched from Liverpool and confined aboard PS, 28 September 1815. Joined YCs 19 October 1816, and arrived in the WIs 21 December 1816. Promoted corporal 29 November 1817. Discharged Quebec.

Barry, Thomas. Arrived in the WIs 24 January 1818. Promoted corporal 27 November 1818. Discharged Quebec.

Bell, John. Blacksmith of Antrim. Royal Artillery. Marched from Chester and confined aboard PS, 8 December 1813. Joined YCs 7 March 1814, and left behind sick when the regiment departed for the WIs. Arrived in the WIs 5 November 1815. Promoted corporal 26 October 1816. Died Jamaica 16 September 1817.

Blackie, John. Butcher of Roxborough. 1st Bn 26th Foot. Marched from Edinburgh and confined aboard PS, 18 January 1814. Joined YCs 25 March 1814. Deserted on the Isle of Wight 17 April 1814. Rejoined 28 April 1814. (No punishment records held.) Promoted corporal 1 February 1816. Discharged Quebec.

Bloom, Paul. 23rd Light Dragoons. Marched from Chester and confined aboard PS, 14 November 1813. Joined YCs 5 February 1814, and arrived in the WIs 14 December 1814. Promoted corporal 28 September 1814, and sergeant 10 June 1815. Reduced 1 January 1816. Promoted corporal 28 May 1818. Discharged Quebec.

Bragg, Richard. Ropemaker of Blackburn. 85th Foot. Marched from Savoy Military Prison and confined aboard PS, 8 June 1815. Joined YCs 29 June 1815, and arrived in the WIs 5 November 1815. Promoted corporal 25 December 1815. Died Grenada 30 January 1816.

Bridge, William. Miner of Bury, Lancashire. Royal Artillery. Marched from Chester and confined aboard PS, 21 September 1813. Joined YCs as corporal 1 February 1814. Deserted from the Isle of Wight 25 June 1814. No record of rejoining.

Bygrove, William. Joined the 16th Foot early 1812. Transported from Cork to be 'Sent to the Army Depot to Serve Abroad.' Marched from Bristol and confined aboard PS, 1 May 1815. Joined YCs 29 June 1815, and arrived in the WIs 5 November 1815. Promoted corporal 16 February 1817. Discharged Quebec. Settled on Concession 7. Lot SW 6. Bathurst. Sold part to ex-Corporal Robert Clarke, York Chasseurs, for £37, 3 April 1847. 1851 census, widower William Bygrove, daughters Eliza, Isabella and son Edward all settled on Concession 8. Lot 12, Bathurst. Served in Captain Kinnear's Company of the 1st Regiment, Lanark Militia, (Bathurst, Dalhousie & Sherbrooke).

Carroll, William. Labourer of Kerry. 71st Foot. Marched from Bristol and confined aboard PS, 26 February 1815. Joined YCs 29 June 1815, and arrived in the WIs 5 November 1815. Promoted corporal 25 December 1815. Deserted from Tobago 4 May 1816. No record of rejoining.

Clarke, Robert. Weaver of St Lukes, Dublin. New recruit from England joining the 2nd Bn 44th Foot in Spain, 18 October 1812. Returned to England, 13 July 1813, and deserted at Steyning 13 August 1813. Marched from Horsham and confined aboard PS, 8 September 1813. Joined YCs 5 February 1814, and arrived in the WIs 14 December 1814. Promoted corporal 24 April 1814, and sergeant 14 September 1815. Reduced 2 October 1815. Promoted corporal 27 December 1816. Discharged Quebec. Settled Concession 7. Lot NE 6. Bathurst. Served in Captain Kinnear's Company of the 1st Regiment, Lanark Militia (Bathurst, Dalhousie & Sherbrooke).

Crone/Croughan, Richard. Either 3rd Bn 1st Foot or 3rd Bn 1st Foot Guards. Transported from Portsmouth and confined aboard PS as Richard Crone, 27 December 1814. Joined YCs 29 June 1815, and arrived in the WIs as Richard Croughan 5 November 1815. Promoted corporal 20 December 1817. Discharged Quebec as Richard Crone. Settled Concession 4. Lot NE 23. Drummond. Sold to John Sheals for £100, 23 July 1839.

Daley/Dailey/Dally/Davey, John. Weaver of Tyrone. 71st Foot. Marched from Glasgow and confined aboard PS, 11 March 1815. Joined YCs 29 June 1815, and arrived in the WIs 5 November 1815. Promoted corporal 4 April 1817. Deserted from Jamaica 31 August 1818. No record of rejoining.

Darby, James. From Handsworth. Joined 90th Foot, 15 April 1805, and served until 6 March 1817. Volunteered at Albany Barracks, 19 March 1817. Arrived in the WIs 25 May 1817. Promoted corporal 25 September 1817. Transferred voluntarily to the 58th Foot at Spanish Town, Jamaica, 25 March 1819. Discharged as sergeant to a pension 26 November 1828.

Davies/Davis, James. 56th Foot. Marched from Shepton Mallet and confined aboard PS, 29 May 1815. Joined YCs 29 June 1815, and arrived in the WIs 5 November 1815. Promoted corporal 19 August 1816. 'Reduced and awarded Solitary Confinement for Drunk on Guard, 10 February 1817'. Promoted corporal 5 April 1817. Discharged Quebec.

Deagan/Deegan/Degan/Deigan, William. 23rd Light Dragoons. Marched from Maidstone and confined aboard PS as William Degan, 1 July 1814. Joined YCs 29 June 1815, and arrived in the WIs as Deagan or Deegan, 5 November 1815. Promoted corporal 3 August 1817. Discharged Quebec as Deigan.

Devlin/Develin, Charles. 103rd Foot. Marched from Wilton and confined aboard PS, 4 November 1814. Joined YCs 29 June 1815, and arrived in the WIs 5 November 1815. Promoted corporal 3 January 1816. Discharged Quebec.

Duggan, William. Papermaker from Cork. 100th Foot. Marched from Maidstone and confined aboard PS, 30 January 1814. Promoted corporal 7 April 1814. Deserted from the Cove of Cork 8 October 1814. No record of rejoining.

Edwards, Henry. Watchmaker of Hereford. 1st Bn 26th Foot. Transferred from the Newport Gaol, Isle of Wight, and confined aboard PS, 6 January 1815. Joined YCs 29 June 1815, and arrived in the WIs as corporal, 5 November 1815. Died Grenada 1 January 1816.

Eve, Charles. 44th Foot. Marched from Chelmsford and confined aboard PS, 29 May 1815. Joined YCs 29 June 1815, and 'Left on Detachment' at Guernsey as the regiment departed for St Vincent. Arrived in the WIs 19 December 1816. Promoted corporal 15 January 1819. Discharged Quebec.

Fewkes, John. Volunteer of the 2nd Bn Tower Hamlet Militia who joined as corporal 9 December 1813 (Six Guinea Bounty). Reduced 14 June 1814. Promoted corporal 10 August 1814. Arrived in the WIs 14 December 1814. Discharged Quebec. Probably returned to England at public expense.

Fisher, Thomas. Brush maker of Dublin. 52nd Foot. Marched from Maidstone and confined aboard PS, 15 March 1815. Joined YCs 29 June 1815, and arrived in the WIs 5 November 1815. Promoted corporal 17 March 1816. Died 23 October 1816.

Fitzgerald, Patrick. Either 22nd or 46th Foot. Confined aboard PS, 10 April 1815. Joined YCs 29 June 1815, and arrived in the WIs 5 November 1815. Promoted corporal 2 October 1817. Discharged Quebec. Accompanied by wife and daughter under seven, allocated Concession 10. Lot SW 9. Beckwith. No evidence found of settling there. Concession transferred from the Crown to George Brooks, 24 May 1824.

Fletcher, William. Volunteer from the 2nd Bn Tower Hamlets Militia. Joined YCs 10 December 1813 (Six Guinea Bounty). Promoted corporal 1 February 1814, and sergeant 25 September 1814. Reduced 13 January 1815. Promoted corporal 16 March 1816. Arrived in the WIs 12 December 1814. Discharged at Quebec 24 September 1819. Probably returned to England at public expense.

Freed, Edward. Sailor of Kent. 70th Foot. Marched from Maidstone and confined aboard PS, 10 September 1813. Joined YCs 7 March 1814, and arrived in the WIs 14 December 1814. Promoted corporal 25 November 1816. Deserted from Jamaica 22 August 1818. No record of rejoining.

Gleeson, John. Labourer of Lancashire. 44th Foot. Marched from Chester and confined aboard PS, 27 April 1815. Joined YCs 29 June 1815, and arrived in the WIs as corporal 5 November 1815. Deserted from Tobago 5 May 1816. No record of rejoining.

Hughes, Richard. Man Milliner of Liverpool. 2nd Dragoon Guards. Marched from Wakefield and confined aboard PS, 23 January 1814. Joined YCs 25 March 1814. Left sick at Cork General Hospital as regiment departed for the WIs. Arrived in the WIs 5 November 1815. Promoted corporal 17 March 1816. Died Jamaica 21 August 1817.

Humphries/Humphreys, Richard. Labourer of Sussex. 50th Foot. Marched from Petworth and confined aboard PS as Richard Humphries or Humphreys, 6 March 1814. Joined YCs as Richards Humphries 7 March 1814. Arrived in the WIs 14 December 1814.

Promoted corporal 12 August 1816. Deserted from Jamaica 26 May 1819. No record of rejoining.

James, William. Bricklayer of Cornwall. 2nd Bn 53rd Foot. Marched from Wilton and confined aboard PS, 4 November 1814. Joined YCs 29 June 1815, and arrived in the WIs as corporal 5 November 1815. Reduced 30 November 1815. Promoted corporal 4 February 1817. Died Jamaica 3 February 1819.

Jeffries/Jeffry, William. 32nd Foot. Marched from Truro and confined aboard PS, 12 October 1813. Joined YCs 5 February 1814, and arrived in the WIs 14 December 1814. Promoted corporal 7 February 1819. Discharged Quebec.

Kenny, Richard. Labourer of Sussex. 55th Foot. Marched from Ely and confined aboard PS, 27 July 1813. Joined YCs 1 February 1814, and arrived in the WIs as corporal 14 December 1814. Died 25 October 1816.

Lewis, John. 9th Light Dragoons. Marched from Nottingham and confined aboard PS, 26 November 1813. Joined YCs 1 February 1814, and arrived in the WIs 14 December 1814. Promoted corporal 12 January 1815, and sergeant 17 March 1816. Reduced 17 March 1816. Promoted corporal 11 September 1817. Discharged Quebec.

Lewis, William. Labourer of Yealand. 2nd Bn 5th Foot. Marched from Chelmsford and confined aboard PS, 27 April 1815. Joined YCs 29 June 1815, and arrived in the WIs 5 November 1815. Promoted corporal 3 September 1817. Died Jamaica 20 September 1817. Willed his effects, one pound and five shillings to mother, Ann Davis of Merthyr Tydfil.

Lowe/Low, John. Stationer of Lancashire. Joined the 84th Foot, 8 January 1809. Marched from Bristol and confined aboard PS, 2 February 1815. Joined YCs 29 June 1815, and arrived in the WIs 5 November 1815. Promoted corporal 25 February 1816. Died 5 September 1816.

Lowe, Samuel. Royal Horse Artillery. Marched from Dartford and confined aboard PS, 24 October 1813. Joined YCs 1 February 1814, and promoted corporal 6 June 1814. Left sick at Cork and died, December 1815.

Lynch, John. Labourer of Cork. 97th Foot. Marched from Bristol and confined aboard PS, 14 March 1814. Joined YCs 29 June 1815, and arrived in the WIs 5 November 1815. Promoted corporal 30 July 1815. Died 21 May 1816.

Marlow, John. Labourer of Leicestershire. 2nd Foot Guards. Marched from Dover and confined aboard PS, 25 March 1816. Joined YCs 19 October 1816, and arrived in the WIs 21 December 1816. Promoted corporal 5 March 1817. Died Jamaica 5 November 1817.

Martin, Richard. Labourer of Middlesex. 2nd Bn Tower Hamlets Militia volunteer joining as corporal 6 December 1813 (Six Guinea Bounty). Promoted sergeant 2 February 1814. Arrived in the WIs 14 December 1814. Reduced 4 November 1815. Promoted corporal 8 December 1816. Died Jamaica 2 September 1817.

McConnell, Charles. Clerk of Dublin. 1st Life Guards. Marched from Hyde Park and confined aboard PS, 3 July 1815. Joined YCs 19 October 1816, and arrived in the WIs 21 December 1816. Promoted corporal 14 March 1818. Deserted in Jamaica 15 May 1819. No record of rejoining.

McGenniss/McGinness, Thomas. 54th Foot. Marched from Chester and confined aboard PS, 16 April 1815. Joined YCs 29 June 1815, and arrived in the West Indies 5

November 1815. Promoted corporal 25 February 1816. Discharged Quebec.

McNally, Andrew. Labourer of Carlow. Kilkenny Militia. Marched from Harwich and confined aboard PS, 21 September 1813. Joined YCs 5 February 1814. Promoted corporal 9 April 1814. Deserted from the Isle of Wight 29 June 1814. No record of rejoining.

Moore, John. Weaver of Derby. 70th Foot. Marched from Dumfries and confined PS, 10 September 1813. Joined YCs 1 February 1814, and arrived in the WIs 14 December 1814. Promoted corporal 20 March 1818. Died Jamaica 23 June 1818.

Morris, John. Tinker of Biddle. Either 1st Foot Guards marched from St Albans, 12 January 1814, or 11 Royal Veteran Battalion marched from Winchester and confined aboard PS, 18 January 1814. Joined YCs 29 June 1815, and arrived in the WIs as corporal 5 November 1815. Died Grenada 23 February 1816.

Mulhearn, Anthony. 2nd Bn 93rd Foot. Marched from Plymouth and confined aboard PS, 2 October 1814. Joined YCs 29 June 1815, and arrived in the WIs 5 November 1815. Promoted corporal 10 September 1816. Discharged Quebec.

Norris, Thomas. Cutler of Sheffield. Royal Artillery. Marched from Chester and confined aboard PS, 1 November 1813. Joined YCs 1 February 1814. Promoted corporal 25 March 1814 and sergeant 7 June 1814. Reduced 11 July 1814. Arrived in the WIs 14 December 1814. Promoted corporal,6 August 1815. 'Killed in Action at Guadeloupe, 9 August 1815'.

Palmer, George. Labourer of Speen, Berkshire. Joined the 6th Foot, 7 November 1806. Marched from Deal and confined aboard PS, 6 March 1814. Joined YCs 25 March 1814. Promoted corporal 1 July 1814, and arrived in the WIs 14 December 1814. 'Reduced for Drunk on Piquet, 27th April 1815'. Promoted corporal 4 August 1815, and sergeant 1 February 1816. Reduced 30 May 1816. Promoted corporal 20 October 1816. Died Jamaica 4 January 1817.

Peckham, Richard. 2nd Bn 73rd Foot. Marched from Savoy Military Prison and confined aboard PS, 3 March 1815. Joined YCs 29 June 1815, and arrived in the WIs 5 November 1815. Promoted corporal 12 November 1818. Discharged Quebec.

Perry, Jeremiah or **Nehemiah.** 1st Bn 87th Foot. Marched from Dorchester and confined aboard PS, 8 December 1814. Joined YCs 29 June 1815, and arrived in the WIs 5 November 1815. Deserted 14 November 1815. Rejoined 19 December 1815 (No punishment records held.) Promoted corporal 17 August 1816. Discharged Quebec.

Powell, Samuel. Labourer of Kilkenny. 19th Dragoons. Marched from Chester and confined aboard PS, 26 October 1814. Joined YCs 29 June 1815, and arrived in the WIs 5 November 1815. Promoted corporal 25 March 1816. Died 5 December 1816.

Quinlon/Quinlan, Timothy. Labourer of Galway. 1st Life Guards. Marched from Savoy Military Prison and confined aboard PS, 10 January 1815. Joined YCs 29 June 1815, and arrived in the WIs 5 November 1815. Promoted corporal 25 October 1816. Died Jamaica 15 November 1817.

Quirk, Thomas. 22nd Bn 55th Foot. Marched from Bristol and confined aboard PS, 23 October 1814. Joined YCs 29 June 1815, and arrived in the WIs 5 November 1815. Promoted corporal 21 March.1817. Discharged Quebec. Accompanied by wife, allocated Concession 10. Lot 12. Beckwith. No evidence found of them settling there. Concession granted to Thomas Hatton, 11 April 1827.

Reilly/Rieley, James. 92nd Foot. Marched from Bristol and confined aboard PS, 26 February 1815. Joined YCs 29 June 1815, and arrived in the WIs 5 November 1815. Promoted corporal 4 January 1816, and sergeant 7 January 1816. Reduced 7 July 1816. Promoted corporal 2 May 1818. Discharged Quebec.

Russell, James. Labourer of Queen's County. 2nd Bn Coldstream Guards. Marched from Savoy Military Prison and confined aboard PS, 21 August 1814. Joined YCs 29 June 1815, and arrived in the WIs 5 November 1815. Promoted corporal 25 November 1816. Died Jamaica 19 January 1817.

Ryan, Daniel. Labourer of Tipperary. 16th Dragoons. Marched from Bristol and confined aboard PS, 15 January 1815. Joined YCs 29 June 1815, and arrived in the WIs 5 November 1815. Promoted corporal 26 October 1816. Died 16 November 1816.

Smith, Henry. 3rd Dragoon Guards. Marched from Canterbury and confined aboard PS, 13 March 1814. Joined YCs 25 March 1814, and arrived in the WIs 14 December 1814. Promoted corporal March 1815. Discharged Quebec.

Strong, James. Weaver of Renfrew. 70th Foot. Marched from Edinburgh and confined aboard PS, 1 March 1814. Joined YCs 25 March 1814, and arrived in the WIs 14 December 1814. Promoted corporal 1 June 1816 and sergeant 11 November 1816. Reduced 19 May 1817. Promoted corporal 25 May 1818. Died Jamaica 28 December 1818.

Symes/Symms, James or **Alexander.** Weaver of Paisley. Volunteer from the 56th Foot. Joined YCs at Albany Barracks as Corporal James Symes, 25 June 1815. Arrived in the WIs as Alexander Symms, 5 November 1815. Died Grenada 21 December 1815.

Taylor, Benjamin. Blacksmith of Yorkshire. Royal Artillery. Marched from Savoy Military Prison and confined aboard PS, 11 March 1815. Joined YCs 29 June 1815, and arrived in the WIs 5 November 1815. Promoted corporal 18 June 1817. Deserted from Jamaica 27 April 1819. No record of rejoining.

Taylor, Francis. Labourer of Yorkshire. 1st Bn 34th Foot. Marched from Haddington and confined aboard PS, 25 August 1813. Joined YCs 25 March 1814, and arrived in the WIs as sergeant 14 December 1814. 'Reduced for Neglect of Duty, 10th June 1815'. Promoted corporal 3 July 1816. Died Jamaica 29 November 1817.

Taylor, Joseph. 2nd Foot Guards. Marched from Kingston on Hull and confined aboard PS, 3 November 1814. Joined YCs 29 June 1815, and arrived in the WIs 5 November 1815. Promoted corporal 17 December 1817. Discharged Quebec.

Turner, James. Dyer of Bury. 25th Light Dragoons. Marched from Savoy Military Prison and confined aboard PS, 29 September 1813. Joined YCs 25 March 1814. Promoted corporal 6 June 1814. Reduced 4 September 1814. Promoted corporal 21 September 1814 and arrived in the WIs 14 December 1814. Discharged Quebec.

Turrell, Thomas. 3rd Foot Guards. Marched from Hitchin and confined aboard PS, 4 February 1814. Joined YCs 25 March 1814. Promoted corporal 8 September 1814. Left sick Cork General Hospital as the regiment departed for the WIs. Regiment informed of Turrell's desertion, August 1817. No further record.

Vaughan, Sampson. Coldstream Guards. Marched from Oxford and confined aboard PS, 14 September 1813. Joined YCs 1 February 1814, and arrived in the WIs 14 December 1814. Promoted corporal 25 January 1818. Discharged Quebec.

Wilcox, James. Weaver of Westleigh, Lancashire. 1st Bn Royals. Marched from Maidstone and confined aboard PS, 25 August 1813. Joined YCs 5 February 1814, and arrived in the WIs 14 December 1814. Promoted corporal 27 April 1817. Discharged at Stony Hill, Jamaica, 10 June 1819.

Wilson, Thomas. Labourer of Bow. 52nd Foot. Marched from Maidstone and confined aboard PS, 18 December 1814. Joined YCs 29 June 1815, and arrived in the WIs 5 November 1815. Promoted corporal 24 February 1816. Deserted from Jamaica 29 September 1816. No record of rejoining.

Wood/Woods, Robert. Weaver of Monaghan. 55th Foot. Transported from Portsmouth and confined aboard PS, 14 February 1813. Joined YCs 5 February 1814. Promoted corporal 25 April 1814. Deserted at Falmouth 27 September 1814. No record of rejoining.

Drummers and Privates

Aaron, Robert. Labourer of Westminster. West Middlesex Militia. Marched from Nottingham and confined aboard PS, 7 January 1814. Joined YCs 7 March 1814, and arrived in the WIs 14 December 1814. Deserted from Jamaica, 29 March 1818. No record of rejoining.

Alberton/Abberton, Jonas. 38th Foot. Marched from Bristol and confined aboard PS, 18 May 1815. Joined YCs 29 June 1815, and arrived in the WIs 5 November 1815. Discharged Quebec. May have settled Concession 9. Lot 4 NE, Beckwith.

Abbott, John. Labourer of Rowner, Hampshire. Royal Wagon Train. Marched from Croydon and confined aboard PS, 24 December 1813. Deserted from the Isle of Wight 22 May 1814. No record of rejoining.

Abbott, Thomas. Pte. 4th Dragoon Guards. Marched from Newcastle and confined aboard PS, 14 August 1814. Joined YCs 29 June 1814, and arrived in the WIs 5 November 1815. Discharged Quebec.

Ablett, Manby or Manly. Butcher of Suffolk. 2nd Bn 63rd Foot. Marched from Canterbury and confined aboard PS, 8 August 1813. Joined YCs 5 February 1814, and arrived in the WIs 14 December 1814. Promoted corporal 29 May 1815, and sergeant 14 April 1816. Reduced 9 August 1816. Died 14 November 1816.

Adams, John. Labourer of Banff. Artillery Driver. Marched from Chester and confined aboard PS, 16 April 1815. Joined YCs 29 June 1815, and arrived in the WIs 5 November 1815. Died Jamaica 24 June 1819.

Adams/Adam, William. Labourer of Queens County. 2nd Bn 62nd Foot. Marched from Bristol and confined aboard PS, 20 November 1813. Joined YCs 25 March 1814. Deserted from the Cove of Cork 30 September 1814. No record of rejoining.

Addingley, Robert. Weaver of Antrim. 55th Foot. Marched from Preston and confined aboard PS, 14 March 1814. Joined YCs 25 March 1814, and arrived in the WIs 14 December 1814. 'Died of wounds received in action at Guadeloupe, 9th August 1815'.

Addsetts/Adsetts, William or **John.** 19th Foot. Confined aboard PS, 14 October 1815. Joined YCs 19 October 1816, and arrived in the WIs 21 December 1816. Discharged Quebec.

Ahern, James. Labourer of Kerry. 2nd Bn 30th Foot. Confined aboard PS, 18 December 1813. Joined YCs 25 March 1814, and arrived in the WIs 14 December 1814. 300 lashes for being 'Drunk on Guard', 27 May 1815, 150 lashed remitted. Died 27 November 1816.

Ahern, John. Lisburn, County Antrim. 2nd Bn 43rd Foot. Marched from Plymouth and confined aboard PS, date unknown. Joined YCs 29 June 1815, and arrived in the WIs as drummer 5 November 1815. Reduced 2 December 1815. Promoted drummer 18 November 1817. Transferred as drummer to the 58th Foot in Jamaica, March 1819. Joined the 21st Foot as trumpeter/bugler 25 May 1822. Discharged in England and re-enlisted for the Royal African Corps at Dorchester, 31 August 1824. 'Discharged with General Conduct – Tolerable'. Granted Out-Pension, 12 December 1826.

Alcock/Alcocks, John. Labourer of Kent. 1st Foot Guards. Marched from Monmouth and confined at Portchester Castle, 19 December 1816. Joined YCs 3 April 1817, and arrived in the WIs 25 May 1817. Deserted from Jamaica 29 April 1819. No record of rejoining.

Aldridge, William. 3rd Foot Guards. Marched from London and confined aboard PS, 20 February 1816. Joined YCs 19 October 1816, and arrived in the WIs 21 December 1816. Solitary confinement for 'Making away with his Necessaries', 26 December 1816; 150 lashes for 'Absenting himself from his Guard', 23 August 1817, 50 lashes remitted. Discharged Quebec.

Aley/Hay, John. 2nd Bn 69th Foot. Marched from Colchester and confined aboard PS as John Aley, 3 October 1813. Joined YCs as John Hay 5 February 1814, and arrived in the WIs 14 December 1814. Discharged Quebec as John Aley.

Allen, James. 16th Light Dragoons. Marched from St Augustine's and confined aboard PS, 13 October 1814. Joined YCs 29 June 1815, and arrived in the WIs 5 November 1815. Deserted Jamaica 22 February 1818. Rejoined 13 January 1819. (No punishment record held.) Discharged Quebec.

Allen, Joseph. Framework knitter of Derby. 1st Bn 95th Foot. Marched from Derby and confined aboard PS, 12 January 1814. Joined YCs 5 February 1814, and arrived in the WIs 12 December 1814. Deserted in Jamaica 11 October 1818. No record of rejoining.

Allen, Ralph. Labourer of Long Newton. 16th Foot. Marched from Savoy Military Prison and confined aboard PS, 17 January 1815. Joined YCs 29 June 1815, and 'Left on Detachment' as the regiment departed for the WIs. Arrived Jamaica 25 May 1817. Died Jamaica 30 September 1817. Willed his effects, ten shillings and ten pence, to wife Mary at Stockton on Tees.

Allen, Richard. 48th Foot. Marched from Bristol and confined aboard PS, 3 February 1815. Joined YCs 29 June 1815, and arrived in the WIs 5 November 1815. Discharged Quebec. Allocated Concession 4. Lot 25 NE. Drummond. No evidence found of him settling there.

Allen, William. 23rd Light Dragoons. Marched from Chester and confined aboard PS, 3 March 1814. Joined YCs 29 June 1815, and arrived in the WIs 5 November 1815. Discharged Quebec. Allocated Concession 9. Lot SW4, Beckwith. No evidence found of him settling there.

Allsop/Alsop, Alexander. 2nd Bn 24th Foot. Marched from Savoy Military Prison and confined aboard PS, 9 January 1814. Joined YCs 1 February 1814, and arrived in the WIs 14 December 1814. Discharged Quebec.

Anderson, David. 100th Foot. Transferred from Albany Barracks and confined aboard PS, 12 March 1816. Arrived in the WIs 16 June 1816. Deserted 5 August 1816. No record of rejoining.

Anderson, John. Labourer of Lanark. 2nd Bn 53rd Foot. Marched from Oxford and confined aboard PS, 12 September 1813. Joined YCs 23 March 1814. Deserted from the Isle of Wight, 2 July 1814. No record of rejoining.

Anderson, William. Labourer of Limerick. 27th Foot. Confined aboard PS, 23 January 1814. Joined YCs 25 March 1814, and arrived in the WIs 14 December 1814. Promoted corporal 4 June 1815. Reduced 7 March 1816. Promoted corporal 30 September 1816, and sergeant 13 October 1816. Private Thompson awarded 100 lashes for 'Calling Sergeant Anderson a Damned Little Rascal' and Private Gould awarded 200 lashes for 'Making or attempting to Strike Sergeant William Anderson', 21 December 1816. Sergeant Anderson: '300 lashes and Ordered to be reduced for Unsoldierlike Conduct, 26th November 1817'. Reduced but corporal punishment remitted. Deserted 5 July 1818. Rejoined 7 July 1818. (No punishment records held.) Deserted 9 March 1819. Returned to England, recaptured and confined Savoy Military Prison 2 July 1819. Transferred to Isle of Wight for transportation to a regiment in the West Indies.

Apsland, William. Labourer of Devizes. 55th Foot. Marched from Savoy Military Prison and confined aboard PS, 13 October 1814. Joined YCs 29 June 1815, and arrived in the WIs 5 November 1815. Died St Vincent 19 March 1816.

Armstrong, Christopher. Labourer of Fermanagh. 18th Foot. Marched from Chester and confined aboard PS, 1 November 1813. Joined YCs 5 February 1814, and arrived in the WIs 14 December 1814. 200 lashes for 'Having Necessaries possibly not his Own, 22nd May 1815'; '200 for Absent without Leave, 27th June 1815'. Died Jamaica 5 February 1817.

Armstrong/Anderson, Joseph. Labourer of Yorkshire. Either 75th Foot marched from Salford, 19 March 1813, or 2nd Dragoons marched from Preston and confined aboard PS, 8 December 1813. Joined YCs as Joseph Armstrong 1 February 1814. Deserted from the Isle of Wight as Joseph Anderson, 19 June 1814. No record of rejoining.

Arnold, John. 11th Veteran Battalion. Marched from Chichester and confined aboard PS, 10 October 1813. Joined YCs 5 February 1814, and arrived in the WIs 14 December 1814. Discharged Quebec.

Arnold Joseph. Royal Artillery. Marched from Barnstable and confined aboard PS, 2 August 1814. Joined YCs 29 June 1815, and arrived in the WIs 5 November 1815. Discharged Quebec.

Arthur, David. Tailor of Ayr. Enlisted for the 2nd Light Dragoons, 9 December 1797. Marched from Cambridge and confined aboard PS, February 1815. Joined YCs 29 June 1815, and arrived in the WIs 5 November 1815. Died Jamaica 19 November 1818.

Ashboult/Ashbolt, James. Labourer of Hampton. 7th Light Dragoons. Marched from Savoy Military Prison and confined PS, 17 April 1813. Joined YCs 29 June 1815, and arrived in the WIs 5 November 1815. Deserted in Jamaica 2 June 1819; rejoined 5 June 1819. (No punishment records held.) Discharged Quebec.

Aspill/Aspell, Michael. Labourer of Longford. 5th Foot. Marched from Dover and confined aboard PS, 15 May 1816. Joined YCs 19 October 1816, and arrived in the WIs 21 December 1816. Deserted from Jamaica 22 December 1818. Returned to England, recaptured by Daniel Fulland at Gosport, Hampshire, 15 July 1819 (Twenty Shillings Bounty). Sent to Portchester Castle for disposal.

Asquith, Christopher. Labourer of Lewes. 1st Bn 52nd Foot. Marched from Maidstone and confined aboard PS, February 1815. Joined YCs 29 June 1815, and arrived in the WIs 5 November 1915. Promoted corporal 25 November 1816. 175 lashes and ordered to be reduced for 'Striking Sergeant Cummings & Resisting a File of the Guard', 1 March 1817. Corporal punishment remitted due to 'Previous Good Conduct'. Deserted in Jamaica 23 June 1818. Returned to England, recaptured and confined in Savoy Military Prison. 'Unfit for Military Service in Consequence of a Diseased Liver'. Furnished with 'Protective Certificate' and discharged, 3 November 1818.

Babington, William. Whitesmith of Lancashire. 11th Dragoons. Marched from Salford and confined aboard PS, 26 December 1813. Joined YCs 1 February 1814, and arrived in the WIs 14 December 1814. Died Jamaica 28 November 1817. Willed his Effects, five shillings and a penny, to his wife Elizabeth Babbington, 24 St James Street, Manchester.

Bachelor/Batchelor, John. Weaver of Gloucestershire. 38th Foot. Marched from Wigan and confined at Portchester Castle, 3 March 1817. Joined YCs 3 May 1817, and arrived in the WIs 25 May 1817. Deserted in Jamaica 15 November 1817; rejoined 12 December 1817. 300 lashes for 'Making Away with his Regimental Necessities', 15 December 1817. Deserted in Jamaica 3 March 1819; rejoined 12 March 1819. (No punishment records held.) Discharged Quebec.

Bailey, John. Wheelwright of Hereford. 12th Foot. Marched from Plymouth and confined aboard PS, 26 March 1815. Joined YCs 29 June 1815, and arrived in the WIs 5 November 1815. Died, 30 September 1816.

Baker, James. Butcher of Middlesex. 4th Foot. Marched from Norwich and confined aboard PS, 14 November 1813. Joined YCs 5 February 1814. Deserted while still on the Isle of Wight, June 1814. Recaptured and re-confined aboard PS until regiment left for the WIs (No punishment records held.) Arrived in the WIs 14 December 1814. Deserted 12 October 1816. No record of rejoining.

Ball, Thomas. Labourer of St Mary's, Nottinghamshire. 73rd Foot. Marched from Savoy Military Prison and confined aboard PS, 11 November 1813. Joined YCs as corporal, 1 February 1814 Reduced 6 June 1814. 'Cut his own throat in the Guard Room, 22nd September 1814'.

Balston. William. 1st Dragoon Guards. Marched from Bristol and confined aboard PS, 23 January 1814. Joined YCs 25 March 1814, and arrived in the WIs 12 December 1814. Promoted corporal 20 June 1814, sergeant 25 September 1814. Reduced 2 January 1815. Discharged Quebec.

Banks, James. 22nd Foot. Marched from Glasgow and confined aboard PS, 5 September 1813. Joined YCs 7 March 1814, and arrived in the WIs 14 December 1814. Discharged Quebec.

Barber, Amos. Baker of North Yanworth. 1st Bn 6th Foot. Marched from Dorchester and confined aboard PS, 19 February 1814. Joined YCs 7 March 1814, and arrived in the WIs 14 December 1814. Died, 15 March 1815.

Barber, Robert. 2nd Bn 63rd Foot. Marched from Walshingham and confined aboard PS, 19 August 1813. Joined YCs 5 February 1814, and arrived in the WIs 14 December 1814. Discharged Quebec.

Barker, William. 25th Foot. Marched from Winchester and confined aboard PS, 13 July 1816. Joined YCs 9 October 1816, and arrived in the WIs 21 December 1816. Died Jamaica 15 May 1819.

Barlow, James. Cooper of Fermanagh. Warwick Militia. Marched from Bristol and confined aboard PS, 13 January 1814. Joined YCs 25 March 1814, and arrived in the WIs 14 December 1814. 'Attempted to desert from Barbados "By Slaten"(a type of boat)', 30 March 1815. (No punishment records held.) Discharged Quebec.

Barrett, John. Labourer of Berkshire. 99th Foot. Transported from Portsmouth and confined aboard PS, 2 June 1815. 'Received Twenty Shilling Bounty for the capture at Portsea of James Patching 99th Foot, 15th September 1815'. Arrived in the WIs 5 November 1815. Died St Vincent 9 June 1816.

Barry, George. Fustian cutter of Manchester. 69th Foot. Transported from Belem, Portugal, and confined aboard PS, 7 November 1813. Joined YCs 5 February 1814. Deserted in Falmouth, 27 September 1814. No record of rejoining.

Barry, James. Painter of Limerick. 25th Foot. Marched from Bristol and confined aboard PS, 16 September 1813. Joined YCs as corporal 1 February 1814. Reduced 18 March 1814. Deserted at Cove of Cork, 30 September 1814. No record of rejoining.

Barry, John. 8th Foot. Transported from Portsmouth and confined aboard PS, 8 July 1815. Joined YCs 29 June 1815, and arrived in the WIs 5 November 1815. Died 7 October 1816.

Barry, William. Weaver of Middlesex. 1st Bn 1st Foot Guards. Marched from Savoy Military Prison and confined aboard PS, 12 February 1815. Joined YCs 29 June 1815, and arrived in the WIs 5 November 1815. Died Jamaica 9 May 1817.

Batchelor, Thomas. Labourer of Gloucestershire. 2nd Bn 24th Foot. March from Savoy Military Prison and confined aboard PS, 22 August 1813. Joined YCs as corporal, February 1814; reduced a month later. Arrived in the WIs 14 December 1814. Died General Hospital, Barbados, 15 April 1815.

Bates, Thomas. Royal Artillery Driver. Sentenced to 'General Service for Desertion', 29 January 1814. Marched from Woolwich and confined aboard PS, 20 February 1814. Joined YCs 25 March 1814, and arrived in the WIs 14 December 1814. Discharged Quebec.

Batkin/Badkin, William. Labourer of Newcastle. Coldstream Guards. Marched from Wakefield and confined aboard PS, 18 February 1815. Joined YCs 29 June 1815, and arrived in the WIs 5 November 1815. Died Granada, 23 December 1815.

Baylis/Bayless/Boyles, William. 2nd Bn 63rd Foot. Marched from Huttingdon and confined aboard PS, 19 May 1815. Joined YCs as William Baylis, 29 June 1815. Arrived in the WIs 5 November 1815. Discharged Quebec as William Boyles.

Beasley/Baseley, Richard. Coldstream Guards. Marched from Savoy Military Prison and confined aboard PS, 22 January 1815. Joined YCs 29 June 1815, and arrived in the WIs 5 November 1815. Discharged Quebec. Allocated Concession 10. Lot SW 13. Bathurst. No evidence of him settling there.

Beatson, William. Weaver of Lanark. 2nd Bn 79th Foot. Marched from Greenock and confined aboard PS, 28 December 1813. Joined YCs as drummer 5 February 1814. Arrived in the WIs 14 December 1814. Reduced 13 August 1816. 200 lashes for being 'Absent from

Evening Parade', 26 September 1816, 75 lashes remitted. Promoted drummer 17 February 1817. Died Jamaica, 26 March 1818.

Beby/Bealey, Samuel. Labourer of Hereford. 12th Foot. Marched from Bristol and confined aboard PS as Samuel Bealey, 24 August 1814. Joined YCs as Samuel Beby, 29 June 1815. Arrived in the WIs 5 November 1815. Died Jamaica, 21 September 1816.

Beck, William. Sailor or labourer of Gloucestershire. 48th Foot. Marched from Haddington and confined aboard PS, 1 December 1813. Joined YCs 5 February 1814. Deserted while still at the Isle of Wight, 7 July 1814. Rejoined 27 July 1814 (No punishment record held.) Arrived in the WIs 14 December 1814. Deserted in Jamaica 14 August 1818. Rejoined the next day. Deserted in Jamaica 5 October 1818. Rejoined 8 October 1818 (No punishment records held.) Discharged Quebec.

Belton, James. Weaver of Cambridge. 30th Foot. Marched from Savoy Military Prison and confined aboard PS, 12 December 1815. Joined YCs 29 June 1815. Deserted off Stokes Bay, Gosport, 1 July 1815. No record of rejoining.

Bennett, John. 36th Foot. Marched from Chester and confined aboard PS, 3 March 1815. Joined YCs 29 June 1815, and arrived in the WIs 5 November 1815. Discharged Quebec.

Bennett, Michael. Labourer of Cork. 97th Foot. Marched from Bristol and confined aboard PS, 16 April 1815. Joined YCs 29 June 1815, and arrived in the WIs 5 November 1815. Died Jamaica, 29 June 1816.

Bennett, Patrick. 44th Foot. Marched from Bath and confined aboard PS, 30 May 1815. Joined YCs 29 June 1815, and arrived in the WIs 5 November 1815. Discharged Quebec.

Bergler, Joseph. Labourer of Waterford. De Roll's Regiment. Marched from York Hospital and confined aboard PS, 21 October 1814. Joined YCs 29 June 1815, and arrived in the WIs 5 November 1815. Deserted 17 January 1816. Rejoined 21 March 1816 (No punishment record held.) Deserted 29 December 1816. Rejoined,16 February 1817. 300 lashes for 'Absenting himself without Leave for 2 months', 27 February 1817. Deserted from Jamaica 17 October 1817. No record of rejoining.

Berry, Michael. 27th Foot. Marched from Bristol and confined aboard PS, 15 January 1815. Joined YCs 29 June 1815 and arrived in the WIs 5 November 1815. Deserted 23 August 1818. Rejoined 25 August 1818 (No punishment record held.) Discharged Quebec.

Berr, Samuel. 16th Light Dragoons. Marched from Southampton and confined aboard PS, 10 November 1813. Joined YCs 5 February 1814, and arrived in the WIs 14 December 1814. Died, 1 September 1815.

Bew, Thomas. Labourer of Berkshire. Royals. Marched from Musselborough and confined aboard PS, 9 January 1814. Joined YCs 7 March 1814, and arrived in the WIs 14 December 1814. Died, 23 November 1816.

Biffen, Charles. Shoemaker of Chichester. 2nd Foot. Marched from Chester and confined aboard PS, 8 December 1813. Joined YCs as corporal 7 March 1814. Promoted sergeant 28 April 1814. Reduced 13 September 1814. Deserted in Guernsey 22 September 1814. No record of rejoining.

Billingsley, Thomas. Enlisted to YCs as volunteer from King George's Stafford Militia,

13 April 1814. On Furlough, 25 April 1814–24 June 1814. Remained in Europe and discharged from the regiment 'on providing two substitutes, 8th April 1815'.

Binder, James. Labourer of Woodham, Essex. 55th Foot. Marched from Congleton and confined aboard PS, 12 December 1813. Joined YCs 1 February 1814, and arrived in the WIs 14 December 1814. Promoted drummer, January 1815. Discharged at Stony Hill Barracks, Jamaica, 10 June 1819.

Bird, Henry. Labourer of Stroud. 36th Foot. Marched from East Grinstead and confined aboard PS, 24 October 1813. Joined YCs 7 March 1814, and arrived in the WIs 14 December 1814. Died, 18 December 1816.

Bird, Phillip. Labourer of Monaghan. 4th Foot. Marched from Horsemongers Jail and confined aboard PS, 1 September 1813. Joined YCs 5 May 1814, and arrived in the WIs 14 December 1814. Deserted from Jamaica, 31 May 1819. No record of rejoining.

Bird, Samuel. East Middlesex Militia. Marched from Fisherton and confined aboard PS, 18 February 1814. Joined YCs 25 March 1814. Deserted while still at the Isle of Wight. Recaptured and confined aboard PS until the regiment sailed for the WIs (date of desertion and punishment not known). Arrived in the WIs 14 December 1814. Promoted drummer 22 November 1817. Discharged Quebec.

Berkinshaw/Birkinshaw, John. Royal Artillery. Marched from Chester and confined aboard PS, 1 November 1813. Joined YCs 7 March 1814, and arrived in the WIs 14 December 1814. Discharged Quebec.

Bishop, James. Labourer of Hampshire. 39th Foot. Marched from Bridport and confined aboard PS, 11 September 1813. Joined YCs as drummer 5 February 1814. Arrived in the WIs 14 December 1914. Deserted in Jamaica 1 April 1819. Rejoined as private 4 April 1819 (No punishment record held.) Discharged Quebec, died six days later at the General Hospital.

Black/Blake, Robert. Weaver of Antrim. Royals. Marched from Chester and confined aboard PS, 1 November 1813. Joined YCs 7 March 1814. Deserted from the Isle of Wight 24 June 1814. No record of rejoining.

Blair, Andrew. Labourer of Tyrone. 22nd Foot. Marched from Chester and confined aboard PS, 15 October 1813. Joined YCs 5 February 1814. Deserted while still at the Isle of Wight, 27 July. Recaptured 4 August 1814 (No punishment record held.) Confined aboard PS until transferred to the Royal African Corps, 5 September 1814.

Blake, John. 2nd Bn 37th Foot. Marched from Maidstone and confined aboard PS, 12 September 1813. Joined YCs 1 February 1814, and arrived in the WIs 14 December 1814. Discharged Quebec.

Boddy, Joseph. 19th Foot. Marched from Hull and confined aboard PS, 19 November 1813. Joined YCs 29 June 1815, and arrived in the WIs 5 November 1815. Discharged Quebec.

Bogg, John. Weaver of Lanark. Joined the 2nd Bn 79th Foot at Dundee, 4 February 1813. (Eleven Guinea Bounty). Marched from Glasgow and confined aboard PS, 15 December 1813. Joined YCs 7 March 1814, and arrived in the WIs 14 December 1814. 150 lashes for 'Making away with his Greatcoat', 3 April 1815, 75 lashes remitted; 800 lashes for being 'Absent without Leave', 23 April 1817; 300 lashes for 'Theft', 26 June 1817. Deserted from Jamaica 9 July.1817, 13 days after previous 300 lash flogging. Returned to Scotland and recaptured. 'Surgically examined and discharged', 19 February 1818, in consequence of appearing consumptive.

Boggins, James. Shoemaker of Taunton. 73rd Foot. Marched from Oakham and confined at Portchester Castle, 22 December 1816. Joined YCs 3 April 1817, and arrived in the WIs 25 May 1817. 300 lashes for 'Making away with his Regimental Necessaries', 25 July 1817. Deserted in Jamaica 20 August 1817. Rejoined 24th August 1817. 300 lashes for being 'Absent without Leave', 2 September 1817. Deserted from Jamaica 8 October 1817. No record of rejoining.

Bolton, John. Cordwainer of County Down. 44th Foot. Marched from Chester and confined aboard PS, 28 January 1815. Joined YCs 29 June 1815, and arrived in the WIs 5 November 1815. Deserted from Jamaica, 31 May 1817. No record of rejoining.

Booth, Joseph. Carpenter of Chester. 23rd Dragoons. Marched from Chester and confined aboard PS, 31 December 1813. Joined YCs 7 March 1814. Deserted while still at the Isle of Wight, 7 July 1814. Hospitalised and rejoined 15 July 1814 (no punishment record held.) Arrived in the WIs 14 December 1814. Died Jamaica, 31 March 1819.

Boram/Boran, James. Labourer of Essex. 44th Foot. Marched from Chelmsford and confined aboard PS, 29 May 1815. Joined YCs 29 June 1815, and remained 'On Detachment' as the regiment left for St Vincent. Arrived in the WIs 19 December 1816. Deserted in Jamaica 23 August 1818. Rejoined 27 August 1818 (No punishment record held.) Discharged Quebec.

Bottoms/Battams, Benjamin. Labourer of Hertfordshire. 7th Hussars. Marched from Savoy Military Prison and confined aboard PS, 14 November 1813. Joined YCs 7 March 1814, and arrived in the WIs 14 December 1814. Died St Vincent, 31 July 1815.

Bouchier, Arthur (alias **Charleton/Chaldron, Andrew**). Shoemaker of Dublin. 17th Light Dragoons. Marched from Dartford and confined aboard PS, 10 October 1813. Joined YCs, alias Andrew Chaldron or Charleton, 1 February 1814. Arrived in the WIs 14 December 1814. Promoted corporal as Arthur Bouchier, January 1815. Sergeant, 24 August 1816. Reduced 28 January 1819. Deserted from Jamaica 8 April 1819. No record of rejoining.

Bourdman/Boarman/Boardman, Richard. Coldstream Guards. Marched from Cambridge and confined aboard PS as Richard Bourdman or Boardman, 12 November 1814. Joined YCs 29 June 1815, and arrived in the WIs as Richard Boadman, 5 November 1815. Discharged at Quebec as Richard Boarman.

Bowden, Thomas. 26th Foot. Marched from Chester and confined aboard PS, 10 May 1815. Joined YCs 29 June 1815, and arrived in WIs 5 November 1815. 200 lashes for 'Selling a Blanket not his Property', 17 October 1816. Remitted 'due to His Previous Good Character'. Discharged Quebec.

Bowen/Bowan/Bowden, John. Royal West India Rangers. Marched from Exeter and confined aboard PS as John Bowden, 8 October 1813. Joined YCs 25 March 1814 as John Bowen. Arrived in the WIs 14 December 1814. Promoted corporal September 1814, sergeant 25 December 1815, and colour sergeant 25 November 1818. Reduced 5 February 1819. Discharged as John Bowen at Quebec. Possibly allocated Concession 9. Lot 11NE. Burgess. No evidence of him settling there.

Bowen/Bowden, George. 3rd Bn 95th Foot. Marched from Savoy Military Prison and confined aboard PS, 29 October 1813. Joined YCs as George Bowen 5 February 1814.

Arrived in the WIs 14 December 1814. Discharged as George Bowden at Quebec.

Bowes/Bowse, Martin. Served three and half years with the Royal Wagon Train before joining the 32nd Foot, 30 November 1802. Marched from Bristol and confined aboard PS as Martin Bowse, 26 March 1815. Joined YCs as Martin Bowes, 29 June 1815. Arrived in the WIs 5 November 1815. Discharged Quebec.

Bowles, John. Framework knitter of Leicestershire. Royal Artillery. Marched from Savoy Military Prison and confined aboard PS, 5 January 1814. Joined YCs 25 March 1814. Deserted while still at the Isle of Wight, 2 July 1814. No record of rejoining.

Boyle/Boyles, Michael. 73rd Foot. Marched from Chelmsford and confined aboard PS, 31 January 1814. Joined YCs 29 June 1815, and arrived in the WIs 5 November 1815. Deserted 10 October 1816. Rejoined 12 October 1816. 800 lashes for 'desertion 10th October–12th October 1816', 21 October 1816. Discharged Quebec.

Brackley, Bartholemew. Weaver of Cork. 2nd Bn 11th Foot. Marched from Maidstone and confined aboard PS, 1 February 1815. Joined YCs 29 June 1815, and arrived in the WIs 5 November 1815. Deserted at St Vincent, 4 June 1816. No record of rejoining.

Braddock, William. Sweep of Middlesex. 52nd Foot. Marched from Maidstone and confined aboard PS, 9 January 1814. Joined YCs 1 February 1814, and arrived in the WIs 14 December 1814. 150 lashes for 'Unsoldierlike Conduct, 25 September 1815, 75 lashes remitted. Deserted in Jamaica 22 December 1818. No record of rejoining.

Bradshaw, William. Transferred from the 49th's Depot, Portsmouth, and confined aboard PS, 21 March 1815. Joined YCs 29 June 1815, and 'Left on Detachment (sick) at Fort Cumberland, Portsmouth'. Deserted at Guernsey 14 October 1815. No record of rejoining.

Bradwell, John. Silk weaver of Macclesfield. 2nd Bn Foot Guards. Marched from Aylesbury and confined aboard PS, 1 August 1813. Joined YCs 5 February 1814, and arrived in the WIs 14 December 1814. Died Garrison Hospital, Grenada, 5 September 1815.

Brady, Thomas. Bricklayer of Louth. 2nd Bn 11th Foot. Marched from Liverpool and confined aboard PS, 20 May 1815. Joined YCs 29 June 1815, and arrived in the WIs 5 November 1815. Died, 18 November 1816.

Brady, Thomas. Labourer of Neath. New Brunswick Fencible Infantry. 'Sentenced at Frederickton, Canada, to General Service for Desertion, 11th October 1815'. Transferred to the York Chasseurs in the WIs 24 February 1816. Died, 17 November 1816.

Brien/Brian/Bryan, James. Labourer of Kilkenny. 44th Foot. Tranported from Portsmouth and confined aboard PS, 3 May 1815. Joined YCs 29 June 1815, and arrived in the WIs 5 November 1815. Deserted in Jamaica 29 March 1817. Rejoined 26 April 1817 (No punishment record held.) Died Jamaica, 25 July 1817.

Brierley/Briley, William. Sweep of Stockport. 22nd Foot. Marched from Savoy Military Prison and confined aboard PS as William Briley, 8 August 1813. Joined YCs as William Brierley, 1 February 1814. Deserted while still at the Isle of Wight, 30 April 1814. Rejoined 1 May 1814 (No punishment record held.) Arrived in the WIs 14 December 1814. Died Jamaica, 21 September 1818.

Briers/Bryers, John. Labourer of Huntington. 2nd Bn 83rd Foot. Marched from

Huntington and confined aboard PS, 25 August 1813. Joined YCs 5 February 1814, and arrived in the WIs 14 December 1814. 300 lashes for 'Making Away with his Regimental Necessities', 26 February 1817. Died Jamaica, 25 September 1817.

Brigham, William. Of Doncaster. 68th Foot. Marched from Chester and confined aboard PS, 22 December 1815. Joined YCs 19 October 1816, and arrived in the WIs 21 December 1816. Sentenced to solitary confinement for 'Drunk on Guard', 10 February 1817. Died Jamaica, 25 June 1819, the day prior to the regiment departing for Canada.

Broadman/Boardman, John. Labourer of Norfolk. 77th Foot. Marched from Bristol and confined aboard PS as John Broadman, 7 February 1816. Joined YCs as John Boardman, 16 May 1816. Arrived in the WIs 25 June 1816. Died Jamaica, 14 February 1817.

Brogan, John. Mountrath, Queen's County. Joined the 28th Foot, 10 May 1808. Confined aboard PS, 19 December 1815. Joined YCs 19 October 1816, and arrived in the WIs 21 December 1816. 300 lashes for being 'Drunk on Guard', 10 February 1817. Discharged Quebec. 'Awarded seven pence per diem out-pension, 9 June 1821. General Conduct on discharge, Good'. Allocated Concession 10. Lot NE 12. Bathurst. Deeds in possession of Sheriff John Powell and concession passed to Samuel Clandiman for two pounds fourteen shillings and a penny, 28 March 1840.

Bromley, Thomas. Wood turner of Derby. 76th Foot. Marched from Bristol and confined aboard PS, 24 August 1813. Joined YCs 5 February 1814, and arrived in the WIs 14 December 1814. Died Stony Hill, Jamaica, 12 September 1816. Willed Effects of one pound seven shillings and a penny to brother, Sergeant Bromley of Arundal Street, Sheffield.

Bromley, William. Weaver of Lanark. 2nd Bn 71st Foot. Marched from Edinburgh and confined aboard PS, 10 September 1813. Joined YCs 1 February 1814, and arrived in the WIs 14 December 1814. Deserted in Jamaica, 28 April 1819. No record of rejoining.

Brooks, Isaac. Painter of Gloucestershire. 1st Bn 3rd Foot Guards. Marched from Savoy Military Prison and confined aboard PS, 24 February 1815. Joined YCs 29 June 1815, and arrived in the WIs 5 November 1815. Died Jamaica, 24 April 1818.

Brookes/Brooks, Lewis. Roper of Chatham. 25th Light Dragoons. Marched from Savoy Military Prison and confined aboard PS, 29 September 1813. Joined YCs 1 February 1814, and arrived in the WIs 14 December 1814. Died St Vincent Regimental Hospital, 4 September 1815.

Brookes/Brooks, Thomas. Labourer of Middlesex. 7th Foot. Marched from Derby and confined aboard PS, 7 October 1813. Joined YCs 1 February 1814. Deserted while still at the Isle of Wight, 2 July 1814. No record of rejoining.

Brophy/Brensey, Peter. Shoemaker of King's County. 2nd Bn 45th Foot. Marched from Bristol and confined aboard PS as Peter Brophy or Brensey, 23 October 1814. Joined YCs as Peter Brophy, 29 June 1815. Arrived in the WIs 5 November 1815. Died, 4 October 1816.

Brough, George. Labourer of Yorkshire. 2nd Bn 82nd Foot. Marched from Scarborough and confined aboard PS, 13 March 1814. Joined YCs 25 March 1814 and arrived in the WIs 14 December 1814. Died, 30 September 1816.

Brown/Browne, Edward. 43rd Foot. Marched from Andover and confined aboard PS, 2

June 1815. Joined YCs 29 June 1815, and arrived in the WIs 5 November 1815. Discharged Quebec.

Brown/Browne, Hugh. Royal Scots. Marched from Glasgow and confined aboard PS, 25 February 1815. Joined YCs 29 June 1815, and arrived in the WIs 5 November 1815. Discharged Quebec.

Brown, James. Labourer of Dublin. Joined 10th Hussars, 26 December 1805. Sergeant when 'Sentenced to General Service for Desertion'. Marched from Romford and confined aboard PS, 21 October 1814. Joined YCs 29 June 1815, and arrived in the WIs 5 November 1815. Promoted corporal 4 February 1816, sergeant 24 September 1816. 'Reduced and placed in the hand of the Civil Powers at Spanish Town, Jamaica, 24th October 1816'. Promoted corporal 1 May 1817, sergeant 7 August 1817. Reduced 9 May 1818. Deserted in Jamaica, 28 July 1818. No record of rejoining.

Brown, James. Tailor of Aberdeen. Either 2nd Bn 14th Foot marched from Salford, 7 May 1816, and confined aboard PS, or 98th Foot marched from Winchester and confined at Portchester Castle, 20 October 1816. Joined YCs 3 April 1817, and arrived in the WIs 25 May 1817. Promoted drummer 2 March 1819. Voluntarily joined the 92nd Foot in Jamaica, 11 June 1819.

Brown, John. Labourer of Shropshire. 2nd Bn 43rd Foot. Marched from Plymouth and confined aboard PS, 1 January 1816. Joined YCs 18 October 1816, and arrived in the WIs 21 December 1816. Deserted in Jamaica, 31 May 1819. No record of rejoining.

Brown, Joseph. Labourer of Leeds. Either 91st Foot marched from Durham, 10 January 1815, or 1st Bn 51st Foot transferred from Portsmouth and confined aboard PS, 25 October 1814. Joined YCs 29 June 1815. Deserted off Stokes Bay, Gosport 1 July 1815. No record of rejoining.

Brown, Thomas. Labourer from Middlesex. General Service Recruit confined aboard PS, 27 February 1816. Joined YCs 17 May 1816, and arrived in the WIs 25 June 1816. Deserted in Jamaica 28 August 1816. No record of rejoining. (Not known which Thomas Brown was 'detained in the Savoy Military Prison, 25 November 1816, and marched to Portchester Castle to await disposal, 25 October 1817').

Brown, Thomas. Weaver of Huddersfield. 95th Foot. Marched from Chester and confined aboard PS, 27 April 1815. Joined YCs 29 June 1815, and arrived in the WIs 5 November 1815. Deserted at Grenada, 27 December 1815. No record of rejoining. (Not known which Thomas Brown 'detained in the Savoy Military Prison, 25 November 1816, and marched to Portchester Castle to await disposal, 25 October 1817').

Browne/Brown, Uriah. Labourer of Yorkshire. Joined the 1st Foot Guards 2 April 1805. Marched from Savoy Military Prison and confined aboard PS, 26 February 1815. Joined YCs 29 June 1815, and arrived in the WIs 5 November 1815. Died Jamaica, 3 April 1817.

Brown, William. 95th Foot. Marched from Savoy Military Prison and confined at Portchester Castle, 12 October 1816. Joined YCs 3 April 1817, and arrived in the WIs 25 May 1817. Discharged Quebec.

Brown, William. Labourer of Lancaster. Either Royal Artillery marched from Chester, 2 October 1813, 10th Light Dragoons marched from Horsham, 6 August 1813, or 2nd Foot Guards transferred from Newport Gaol and confined aboard PS, 27 October 1813. Joined YCs 1 February 1814. Deserted while still at the Isle of Wight, 31 August 1814. Rejoined 4 September 1814 (No punishment record held.) Arrived in the WIs 14 December 1814.

Deserted at Barbados, 10 March 1815. No record of rejoining.

Brown/Browne, William. Tailor of York. Either 3rd Guards marched from London, 25 September 1814, 2nd Bn 7th Foot marched from Leicester, 10 August 1814, 48th Foot from Bristol, 28 May 1815, 50th Foot from Portsmouth, 11 April 1815, or 6th Bn 60th Foot marched from Savoy Military Prison and confined aboard PS, 14 August 1814. Joined YCs 29 June 1815, and arrived in the WIs 5 November 1815. Discharged Quebec.

Brown, William. Weaver of Fife. Either Royal Artillery marched from Chester, 2 October 1813, 10th Light Dragoons marched from Horsham, 6 August 1813, or 2nd Foot transferred from Newport Gaol and confined aboard PS, 27 October 1813. Joined YCs 5 February 1814, and arrived in the WIs 14 December 1814. Promoted corporal 28 April 1814. Reduced for 'Unsoldierlike Conduct in being Drunk', 21 April 181'. Promoted corporal 27 September 1815, sergeant 18 November 1815. Reduced for 'Drunk & Absent from Parade', 28 April 1817. Promoted corporal 25 August 1817. Reduced 1 January 1819. Discharged Quebec.

Brown/Browne, William. Labourer of Wooley, Warwickshire. Either 3rd Guards marched from London, 25 September 1814, 2nd Bn 7th Foot marched from Leicester, 10 August 1814, 48th Foot marched from Bristol, 28 May 1815, 50th Foot from Portsmouth, 11 April 1815, or 6th Battalion 60th Foot marched from Savoy Military Prison and confined aboard PS, 14 August 1814. Joined YCs 29 June 1815, and arrived in the WIs as corporal, 5 November 1815. Reduced, date unknown. Died, 14 September 1816.

Brown, William. Painter of Manchester. Royal Wagon Train. Marched from Dartford and confined aboard PS, 6 March 1814. Joined YCs 25 March 1814, and arrived in the WIs 14 December 1814. 'Killed in Action' at Guadeloupe, 9 August 1815.

Browne, William. Tailor from Edinburgh. Either 3rd Guards marched from London, 25 September 1814, 2nd Bn 7th Foot marched from Leicester, 10 August 1814, 48th Foot marched from Bristol, 28 May 1815, 50th Foot from Portsmouth 11 April 1815, or 6th Battalion 60th Foot marched from Savoy Military Prison and confined aboard PS, 14 August 1814. Joined YCs 29 June 1815, and arrived in the WIs 5 November 1815. Died, 24 October 1816.

Bruce, William. Labourer of Mearns. Royal Horse Artillery. Marched from Lewes and confined aboard PS, 17 September 1813. Joined YCs 5 February 1815, and arrived in the WIs 14 December 1814. Died St Vincent, 24 July 1815.

Brunkhurst, Augustus. Labourer of Prussia. 3rd Hussars, King's German Legion. Marched from Savoy Military Prison and confined aboard PS, 12 February 1815. Joined 6th Bn 60th Foot in Jamaica, 7 February 1816. Transferred into the York Chasseurs, 25th May 1817. Deserted in Jamaica, 27 April 1819. No record of rejoining.

Bryan/Brien, John. Sailmaker of Tipperary. 4th Foot. Marched from Dover and confined aboard PS, 14 April 1816. Joined YCs 19 October 1816, and arrived in the WIs 21 December 1816. Deserted in Jamaica, 12 December 1818. No record of rejoining.

Bryan/Brien, Michael. Servant of Wexford. Wessex Militia. Marched from Bristol and confined aboard PS, 26 February 1815. Joined YCs 29 June 1815, and arrived in the WIs 5 November 1815. Drowned St Vincent, 7 September 1816.

Bull, John. Labourer of Tipperary. 1st Bn 3rd Foot. Marched from Fisherton and confined aboard PS, 3rd August 1815. Joined YCs 29 June 1815, and arrived in the WIs 5 November 1815. Deserted in Jamaica, 25 November 1817. Returned the same day. 300

lashes for being 'Absent without Leave', 10 December. Died Jamaica, 3 June 1819.

Bull, Thomas. Joined the Royal Marines, 7 December 1807. Discharged, 18 September 1815. Volunteered for York Chasseurs, 9 October 1816. Arrived in the WIs 21 December 1816. Discharged Quebec.

Bull, William. Labourer of Salop. Joined the 43rd Foot, 25 April 1805. Marched from Plymouth and confined aboard PS, 19 December 1814. Joined YCs 29 June 1815, and arrived in the WIs 5 November 1815. 300 lashes for 'Drunken and Riotous after Hours and Abusing Sgt James', 7 January 1817; 300 lashes for 'Selling his Regimental Necessaries', 5 August 1817, 100 lashes remitted. Deserted in Jamaica, 1 April 1819. Rejoined the next day (No punishment record held.) Deserted in Jamaica, 1 May 1819 (Date of rejoining and punishment unknown). Deserted in Jamaica, 8 May 1819. No record of rejoining.

Bunn, Robert. Cork cutter of Liverpool. 3rd Foot. Marched from Warwick and confined at Portchester Castle, 17 January 1817. Joined YCs 3 April 1817, and arrived in the WIs 25 May 1817. Died Jamaica, 27 September 1817.

Burgess, James. Labourer of Mayo. 32nd Foot. Marched from Chester and confined aboard PS, 26 May 1815. Joined YCs 2 June 1815, and remained at Guernsey as the regiment left for St Vincent. Arrived in the WIs 21 December 1816. Died Jamaica, 18 October 1818.

Burgess, John. Labourer of Mayo. 1st Bn 83rd Foot. Marched from Plymouth Docks and confined aboard PS, 24 September 1814. Joined YCs June 29 1815, and arrived in the WIs 5 November 1815. Deserted in Jamaica, 28 April 1817. Rejoined 10 May 1817. (No punishment record held.) Deserted in Jamaica, 26 August 1817. Rejoined 28 August 1817. 300 lashes for being 'Absent without Leave', 2 September 1817. Deserted in Jamaica, 8 November 1817, Rejoined 3 May 1818 (No punishment records held.) Deserted in Jamaica, 23 August 1818. Rejoined the next day. (No punishment records held.) Deserted in Jamaica, 27 August 1818. Rejoined, 20 September 1818. (No punishment records held.) Deserted in Jamaica, 10 November 1818. No record of rejoining.

Burke, William. 46th Foot. Joined 10 April 1815, possibly a 'Volunteer'. Arrived in the WIs 5 November 1815. Discharged Quebec.

Burns, James. Labourer of Dublin. 8th Foot. Marched from Tilbury Fort and confined aboard PS, 6 May 1815. Joined YCs 29 June 1815, and arrived in the WIs 5 November 1815. Deserted 11 March 1816. Rejoined 19 March 1816. (No punishment records held.) Deserted in Jamaica, 31 August 1818. Rejoined, 18th October 1818. (No punishment record held.) Deserted in Jamaica, 3 March 1819. (No record of rejoining). Not known which Burns received 300 lashes for being 'Drunk on Guard', 26 February 1817.

Burns/Byrne, John. Either 1st or 40th Foot. Marched from Chester and confined aboard PS, 27 April 1815 . Joined YCs 29 June 1815, and arrived in the WIs 5 November 1815. Deserted in Jamaica 23 March 1817. Rejoined 1 April 1817. 300 lashes for 'Absenting himself without Leave',12 April 1817. Discharged Quebec. Not known which Burns received 300 lashes for being 'Drunk on Guard', 26 February 1817.

Burns/Byrne, John. Embarked Spithead, one of 300 'Unattached Deserters' joining the 2nd Foot, 25 April 1816. Arrived in the WIs 5 June 1816. Deserted 18 July 1816. Rejoined 21 July 1816. 1,000 lashes, 23 July 1816. Transferred into the York Chasseurs, 25 August 1816. Discharged Quebec. Not known which Burns received 300 lashes for being 'Drunk on Guard', 26 February 1817.

Burns, Peter. Glassblower of Stratford. 2nd Bn 59th Foot. Marched from Andover and confined aboard PS, 10 September 1815. Embarked Spithead, one of 300 'Unattached Deserters' joining the 2nd Foot, 25 April 1816. Arrived in the WIs 5 June 1816. Deserted 24 July 1816. Rejoined same day. 600 lashes 25 July 1816. Transferred into the York Chasseurs, 25 August 1816. Deserted 6 October 1816. No record of rejoining.

Burns, William. Labourer of Wicklow. 45th Foot. Marched from Chester and confined aboard PS, 10 September 1815. Embarked Spithead, one of 300 'Unattached Deserters' joining the 2nd Foot, 25 April 1816. Arrived in the WIs 5 June 1816. Deserted 18 July 1816. Rejoined, 21 July 1816. 1,000 lashes, 23 July. Transferred into the York Chasseurs, 25 August 1816. Deserted in Jamaica, March 1818. Returned the same day. (No punishment records held.) Deserted in Jamaica, 29 June 1818. Rejoined the next day. (No punishment records held.) Deserted in Jamaica, 3 January 1819. Rejoined the next day. (No punishment records held.) Deserted in Jamaica, 4 April 1819. No record of rejoining. Not known which Burns received 300 lashes for being 'Drunk on Guard', 26 February 1817.

Burt/Birt, Abraham. Carpenter of Pimlico. 10th Hussars. Marched from Kingston, Surrey and confined aboard PS, 15 November 1814. Joined YCs 29 June 1815, and arrived in the WIs 5 November 1815. Deserted in Jamaica, 30 March 1819. No record of rejoining.

Butcher, John. Labourer of Sussex. 76th Foot. Marched from Maidstone and confined aboard PS, 29 September 1813. Joined YCs 7 March 1813, and arrived in the WIs 14 December 1814. Died Tobago, 6 September 1816.

Butler, John. Tailor of Fermanagh. 97th Foot. Marched from Bristol and confined aboard PS, 14 March 1814. Joined YCs 25 March 1814, and arrived in the WIs 14 December 1815. Died St Vincent, 29 January 1816. Willed his effects, seventeen shillings and sixpence, to wife Mary.

Butler, William. Labourer of Taunton. 6th Dragoons. Marched from Wilton, near Taunton, and confined at Portchester Castle, 3 April 1817. Arrived in the WIs 25 May 1817. Deserted in Jamaica, 8 June 1817. No record of rejoining.

Butterfield, Edward. Possibly civil convict condemned to the York Chasseurs. Marched from Bristol and confined aboard, PS 15 January 1815. Joined YCs 29 June 1815, and 'Left on Detachment' as the regiment departed for St Vincent. Arrived in the WIs 25 May 1817. Discharged Quebec.

Byers, John. Royal Scots. Marched from Tilbury Fort and confined aboard PS, 27 January 1816. Joined YCs 16 May 1816, and arrived in the WIs 25 June 1816. 'In the hands of the Civil Power at Montego Bay, Jamaica, for a Criminal Offence from 23rd November 1817 until March 1819'. Discharged Quebec.

Byford/Bayford, Thomas. 2nd Bn 7th Foot. Marched from Newport, Essex and confined aboard PS, 17 September 1813. Joined YCs 7 March 1814. Deserted while still on the Isle of Wight, 10 June 1814. No record of rejoining.

Byrne, Laughlin. 30th Foot. Marched from Chester and confined aboard PS, 2 October 1813. Joined YCs 7 March 1814. Sick at Cork General Hospital as the regiment left for Barbados. Regiment notified by Agent of Byrne's desertion, June 1817.

Byrne/Bearn/Beam, Robert. Weaver of Lancashire. 91st Foot. Marched from Canterbury and confined aboard PS, 23 October 1814. Joined YCs 29 June 1814, and arrived in the WIs 5 November 1815. Deserted in Jamaica, 4 December 1817. Rejoined 6

December 1817. 300 lashes for being 'Absent without Leave', 10 December. Died Jamaica, 15 May 1819.

Byworth, Thomas. 1st Foot Guards. Marched from Bury and confined aboard PS, 17 April 1815. Joined YCs 29 June 1815, and arrived in the WIs 5 November 1815. Deserted in Jamaica, March 1819. Rejoined April 1819. (No punishment records held.) Discharged Quebec.

Cahill, James. Rope maker of Dublin. 11th Foot. Marched from Bristol and confined aboard PS, 12 September 1815. Embarked Spithead, one of 300 'Unattached Deserters' joining the 2nd Foot, 25 April 1816. Arrived in the WIs 5 June 1816. Deserted 5 July 1816. 1,000 lashes and marked with 'D', 25 July 1816. Transferred into the York Chasseurs, 25 August 1816. Deserted in Jamaica, 28 February 1817. Rejoined, 5 March 1817. 300 lashes for absenting himself without leave, 6 March 1817. Deserted in Jamaica 29 June 1817. Rejoined 1 July 1817. 300 lashes for being absent without leave, 4 July 1817. Died Jamaica, 28 August 1817. Having received 1,600 lashes over a 14 month period, Cahill died approximately seven weeks after his last flogging.

Cahill, Michael. 2nd Bn 43rd Foot. Marched from Canterbury and confined aboard PS, 10 August 1813. Joined YCs 5 February 1814, and arrived in the WIs 14 December 1814. Deserted in Jamaica 1 July 1817. Rejoined 23 August 1817. (No punishment records held.) Discharged Quebec.

Callaghan, John. Labourer of Tipperary. Either 2nd Bn 37th marched from Maidstone, 19 May 1815, or 7th Dragoon enlisting, 26 December 1812. Joined YCs 29 June 1815, and arrived in the WIs 5 November 1815. Discharged Quebec. Not known which John Callaghan 'awarded 200 lashes for Breaking his Firelock, 18th October 1816'.

Callaghan, John. Shoemaker of Cavan. Either 2nd Bn 37th marched from Maidstone, 19 May 1815, or 7th Dragoon enlisting 26 December 1812. Joined YCs 29th June 1815, and arrived in the WIs 5th November 1815. Deserted in Jamaica 31 March 1819. Rejoined. (No date of rejoining or punishment received). Discharged Quebec. Not known which John Callaghan 'awarded 200 lashes for Breaking his Firelock, 18th October 1816'.

Cambell/Campbell, James. 1st Bn 21st Foot. Marched from Ayr and confined aboard PS, 28 December 1813. Joined YCs 7 March 1814, and arrived in the WIs 14 December 1814. 300 lashes for being 'Drunk on Guard', 2 February 1818. Discharged Quebec.

Cameron, Angus. 2nd Bn 26th Foot. Marched from Carlisle and confined aboard PS, 22 August 1813. Joined YCs 7 March 1814, and arrived in the WIs 14 December 1814. Discharged Quebec. Allocated Concession 7. Lot NE 5 Barthurst. No evidence found of him settling there, concession reallocated to Pierre Klein, 30 October 1821.

Camfield/Campfield, John. Labourer of Hatfield. 49th Foot. Marched from Tilbury Fort and confined aboard PS as John Goldsmith, 7 May 1815. Joined YCs as John Camfield, 29 June 1815, and arrived in the WIs 5 November 1815. Died as John Campfield, 10 December 1816.

Campbell, Archibald. 2nd Foot Guards. Marched from Maidstone and confined aboard PS, 13 February 1813. Joined YCs 7 March 1814, and arrived in the WIs 14 December 1814. Discharged Quebec.

Campbell, Daniel. Joined YCs 29 June 1815, and arrived in the WIs 5 November 1815. Discharged Quebec.

Campbell, Dennis. Labourer of Armagh. 1st Bn 52nd Foot. Marched from Maidstone and confined aboard PS, 6 December 1814. Joined YCs 29 June 1815, and arrived in the WIs 5 November 1815. Deserted in Jamaica, 28 April 1817. No record of rejoining.

Campbell, John. Umbrella maker of Lisburn. 2nd Bn 91st Foot. Marched from Glasgow and confined aboard PS, 19 September 1813. Joined YCs 5 February 1814, and arrived in the WIs 14 December 1814. 150 lashes for 'Making away with his Shirt', 25 May 1815. Commuted to 30 days solitary confinement; 300 lashes for being 'Drunk on Guard', 24 December 1816, 100 lashes remitted. Deserted, 28 December 1816. Rejoined, 12 January 1817. 300 lashes for 'Absenting himself two weeks without Leave', 12 January 1817. Deserted in Jamaica, 10 July 1818. Rejoined, 20 July 1818. (No punishment records held.) Deserted in Jamaica, 3 March 1819. Rejoined, 12 March 1819. (No punishment records held.) Deserted in Jamaica, 1 May 1819. No record of rejoining.

Campbell, Martin. 2nd Bn 51st Foot. From Portsmouth and confined aboard PS, 1 November 1814. Joined YCs 29 June 1815, and arrived in the WIs 5 November 1815. Discharged Quebec.

Cannavan/Kannavan, James. 27th Foot. Marched from Bristol and confined aboard PS, date unknown. Joined YCs 29 June 1815, and arrived in the WIs 5 November 1815. Discharged Quebec.

Cantrell, Charles. 86th Foot. Marched from Bristol and confined aboard PS, 26 February 1815. Joined YCs 29 June 1815, and arrived in the WIs 5 November 1815. Discharged Quebec.

Capell, Alexander. Shoemaker of Dunkirk. Transferred from the 6th Bn 60th Foot in Jamaica, 25 May 1817. Deserted in Jamaica,19 May 1819. No record of rejoining.

Carmody/Carmoody, Patrick. Labourer of Limerick. From the 46th's Isle of Wight Depot and confined aboard PS, 4 February 1816. Joined YCs 20 March 1816, and arrived in the WIs 21 December 1816. Died Jamaica, 12 February 1817.

Carney, John. Labourer of Monaghan. Either Royal Wagon Train marched from Maidstone, 24 June 1813, or 90th marched from Chester and confined aboard PS, 15 October 1813. Joined YCs 7 March 1814, and arrived in the WIs 14 December 1814. Died, 26 November 1816.

Carroll, Daniel. 3rd Foot. Marched from Dover and confined aboard PS, 16 July 1816. Joined YCs 19 October 1816, and arrived in the WIs 21 December 1816. Discharged Quebec.

Carroll, James. Labourer of Leicestershire. 8th Light Dragoon. Marched from Chester and confined aboard PS, 25 June 1815. Joined YCs 29 June 1815, and arrived in the WIs 5 November 1815. Died Grenada, 8 December 1815.

Carroll, James. Labourer of Tralee. Joined the 28th Foot, 13 May 1805. Marched from Chester and confined aboard PS, 18 May 1815. Joined YCs 29 June 1815, and arrived in the WIs 5 November 1815. Discharged Quebec.

Carroll, Patrick. Labourer of Roscommon. 51st Foot. Marched from Monmouth and confined aboard PS, 20 September 1813. Joined YCs 7 March 1814, and arrived in WIs 14 December 1814. 'Died Guadeloupe, 10th August 1815. One of Seven rank and file supposed to have been poisoned'. Willed his effects – nine shillings and threepence, to his wife.

Carroll, Thomas. Labourer of Limerick. 1st Bn 44th Foot. Transferred from Newport Gaol, Isle of Wight, and confined aboard PS, 2 January 1815. Joined YCs 29 June 1815, and arrived in the WIs 5 November 1815. Deserted, 22 September 1816. Rejoined, 28 September 1816. 200 lashes for 'Desertion', 8 October 1816. Deserted in Jamaica, 25 January 1817. Rejoined, 26 January 1817. 300 lashes for 'Absenting himself from his Guard & not returning until brought back a Prisoner', 27 January 1817. Joined from desertion, 2 May 1817. 300 lashes for being 'Absent without leave', 9 May 1817. Deserted in Jamaica, 28 June 1817. Rejoined from desertion, 25 October 1817. 300 lashes for being 'Absent without leave', 30 October 1817; 150 lashes for 'Making away or losing 10lbs of Ammunition', 10 January 1818. Deserted in Jamaica, 2 April 1818. Returned the same day. (No punishment records held.) Deserted in Jamaica, 30 August 1818. No record of rejoining.

Carson, James. Joined YCs 1 February 1814, and arrived in the WIs 14 December 1814. Discharged Quebec. Settled Concession 11. Lot 12, Beckwith. Sold to William Murphy for £50, 8th August 1825.

Carter, George. 1st Bn 13th Foot. Marched from Andover and confined aboard PS, 27 November 1814. Joined YCs 29 June 1815, and arrived in the WIs November 1815. Died, 7 November 1816.

Carver, James. Card maker of Halifax. 2nd Bn 15th Foot. Transported from Guernsey and confined aboard PS, 9 September 1815. Joined YCs 19 October 1816, and arrived in the WIs 21 December 1816. Died Jamaica, 29 October 1818.

Cascallian, John. Framework knitter of Armagh. 25th Foot. Marched from Tilbury Fort and confined aboard PS, 10 December 1813. Joined YCs as drummer 1 February 1814. Deserted while still on the Isle of Wight, 9 July 1814. Rejoined 24 July 1814. (No punishment records held.) Arrived in the WIs 14 December 1814. Deserted 21 February 1815. Rejoined 8 March 1815. (No punishment records held.) Deserted 4 April 1815. Rejoined 8 April 1815. 300 lashes for being 'Absent without Leave', 13 April 1815. Deserted 31 May 1815. No record of rejoining.

Casey, Michael. 97th Foot. Marched from Bristol and confined aboard PS, 14 March 1814. Joined YCs 23 March 1814, and arrived in the WIs 14 December 1814. Discharged Quebec.

Cassiday/Cassidy, Thomas. Weaver of Mayo. 56th Foot. Marched from Chester and confined aboard PS, 1 November 1813. Joined YCs 1 February 1814, and arrived in the WIs 14 December 1814. Died St Vincent, 10 August 1815.

Cathcart, James. Labourer of Tipperary. 2nd Bn 18th Foot. Marched from Glasgow and confined aboard PS, 18 September 1814. Joined YCs 29 June 1815, and arrived in the WIs 5 November 1815. Promoted drummer 25 December 1815. Reduced 11 May 1816. Promoted drummer 4 December 1816. Deserted in Jamaica 25 July 1818. Rejoined 28 July 1818. (No punishment records held.) Reduced 5 October 1818. Promoted drummer 25 October 1818. Deserted in Jamaica 2 May 1819. Rejoined as private 6 May 1819. (No punishment records held.) Deserted in Jamaica 16 May 1819 (Date of rejoining and punishment unknown). Deserted in Jamaica, 30 May 1819. No record of rejoining.

Caulfield/Caufield/Coffield, Brien or **Bryan.** Labourer of Wexford. 2nd Bn 9th Foot. Marched from Daventry and confined aboard PS, 25 December 1814. Joined YCs 29 June 1815, and arrived in the WIs 5 November 1815. Deserted in Jamaica 31 May 1817. No record of rejoining.

Chamberlain, Joseph. Labourer of Shilton, Leicestershire. 19th Foot. Marched from Leicester and confined aboard PS, 12 December 1813. Joined YCs 7 March 1814. Deserted while still at the Isle of Wight 7 July 1814. Rejoined 15 July 1814. (No punishment records held.) Arrived in the WIs 14 December 1814. Deserted in Jamaica 20 November 1817. Rejoined 18 December 1817. 300 lashes, 27 December 1817. Deserted in Jamaica 19 June 1818. Rejoined 28 June 1818 (No punishment records held.) Deserted in Jamaica 27 April 1819. No record of rejoining.

Chamberlain, Thomas. 9th Foot. Marched from the Savoy Military Prison and confined aboard PS, 11 January 1816. Joined YCs 19 October 1816, and arrived in the WI 21 December 1816. On the day of his arrival, sentenced to 300 lashes for 'Attempting to Strike Ensign Mainwaring', remitted due to his 'Former Good Character'. 200 lashes for 'Selling his Necessaries', 21 January 1817. Discharged Quebec.

Chambers, Charles. 24th Foot. Marched from Savoy Military Prison and confined aboard PS, 10 May 1815. Joined YCs 29 June 1815, and arrived in the WIs 5 November 1815. Died, 4 November 1816.

Chambers, Joseph. 2nd Bn 5th Foot. Marched from St Albans and confined aboard PS, 7 July 1814. Joined YCs 29 June 1815, and arrived in the WIs 5 November 1815. Discharged Quebec.

Channon, William. Cooper of Norfolk. 94th Foot. Marched from Bristol and confined aboard PS, 18 May 1815. Joined YCs 29 June 1815, and arrived in the WIs 5 November 1815. Promoted drummer 29 September 1816. Died Jamaica, 13 February 1817.

Chapman, James. Wheelwright of Spadhurst, Kent. West Kent Milita. Sentenced 'General Service for Desertion,' and marched from Norman Cross to be confined aboard PS, 19 October 1813. Joined YCs 1 February 1814. Deserted while still at the Isle of Wight 3 June 1814. Date of rejoining and punishment unknown. Arrived in the WIs 5 November 1814. Deserted in Jamaica, 31 July 1817. No record of rejoining.

Chapman, John. Labourer of Northampton. 33rd Foot. Marched from Worcester and confined aboard PS, 26 February 1814. Joined YCs 25 March 1814, and arrived in the WIs 14 December 1814. Died, 3 October 1816.

Chapman, William. Wool spinner of Somerset. 3rd Bn Royal Artillery. Marched from Rye and confined aboard PS, 20 March 1814. Joined YCs 29 June 1815, and arrived in the WIs 5 November 1815. Died, 10 November 1816.

Chapman, William. Cooper of Norfolk. 2nd Bn 4th Foot. Marched from Colchester and confined aboard PS, 6 February 1816. Joined YCs 17 May 1816, and arrived in the WIs 25 June 1816. Died Jamaica, 25 October 1817.

Charles, Peter. Labourer of Tipperary. Joined YCs 3 April 1817, and arrived in the WIs 25 May 1817. Deserted, 16 August 1817. No record of rejoining.

Clamp, William. Labourer of Leicestershire. 17th Foot. Marched from Leicester and confined aboard PS, 24 March 1815. Joined YCs 29 June 1815, and arrived in the WIs 5 November 1815. Died Jamaica, 21 January 1819.

Clancey/Clancy, James. Labourer of Dublin. 16th Light Dragoons. Marched from Maidstone and confined aboard PS, 1814 (date unknown) Joined YCs 29 June 1815, and arrived in the WIs 5 November 1815. Died, 6 October 1816.

Clarey, James. Labourer of Leicestershire. 4th Dragoons. Marched from Bristol and confined aboard PS, 26 December 1813. Joined YCs 7 March 1814, and remained on the Isle of Wight as the regiment left for Barbados. Died, 25 November 1814.

Claridge, William. Labourer of Gloucestershire. 85th Foot. March from St Austine and confined aboard PS, 12 January 1814. Joined YCs 5 February 1814. Left sick and died at Cork General Hospital, 4 February 1815.

Clarke, James. Labourer of Cavan. 2nd Bn 9th Foot. Marched from Glasgow and confined aboard PS, 14 November 1813. Joined YCs 5 February 1814, and arrived in the WIs 14 December 1814. 300 lashes for being 'Absent from Parade & out of Barracks all Night', 14 September 1815, 200 lashes remitted. 300 lashes for 'Loosing or making away with Greatcoat and Blue Trowsers', 28 September 1815. Discharged Quebec.

Clarke, James. Coalminer of Dudley. Joined YCs 29 June 1815, and arrived in the WIs 5 November 1815. Discharged Quebec.

Cleaver, William. Transferred to YCs from Royal York Rangers at Barbados, 3 July 1815, and, on Lieutenant Colonel Ewart's recommendation, transferred to the 18th Foot in Jamaica, 24 January 1817. With a proviso that Cleaver be permitted to return to England when his new regiment embarked the West Indies.

Clement/Clements/Clemments, William. Stone cutter of Bath. 1st Bn Coldstream Guards. Marched from Savoy Military Prison and confined aboard PS, 26 January 1815. Joined YCs 29 June 1815, and arrived in the WIs 5 November 1815. 150 lashes for being 'Drunk and Absenting himself from Parade', 26 December 1816. Deserted in Jamaica 29 April 1819. Rejoined 1 May 1819. (No punishment records held.) Discharged Quebec.

Clemmings/Cleming/Clenning, John. Seaman of Banff. 12th Foot. Marched from Bristol and confined aboard PS, 26 May 1815. Joined YCs 29 June 1815, and arrived in the WIs 5 November 1815. Died, 27 September 1816.

Cliff, George. Life Guards. Transported from Foveaux, marched from Dover and confined aboard PS, 24 September 1815. Joined YCs 16 May 1816, and arrived in the WIs 25 June 1816. Promoted corporal 8 November 1816. Reduced 24 October 1818. Discharged Quebec. Cliff, with wife and children, settled Concession 9. Lot 11 SW. Beckwith. Sold to Henry James, 1825. Served in the Lanark Militia commanded by Colonel Josias Taylor.

Coakley, Jeremiah. 97th Foot. Marched from Bristol and confined aboard PS, 19 September 1813. Joined YCs 1 February 1814, and arrived in the WIs 14 December 1814. Discharged Quebec.

Coccoran/Corcoran, Alexander. Labourer of Tipperary. General Service Recruit. Marched from Southampton District and confined aboard PS, 19 September 1813. Joined YCs 5 February 1814. Deserted at Sandown, Isle of Wight, 10 February 1814. Retaken next day. No record of rejoining regiment.

Cockerell/Cockerill, William. 46th Foot. Confined at Portchester Castle, 3 April 1817. Arrived in WIs 25 May 1817. Discharged Quebec.

Cocking/Cockings, John. 16th Foot. Marched from Chester and confined aboard PS, 3 March 1813. Joined YCs 23 March 1814, and arrived in the WIs 14 December 1814. Promoted corporal 28 April 1814. Reduced September 1815. 300 lashes for being 'Drunk on Guard', 24 July 1815. Discharged Quebec.

Coddy/McCoody, Patrick. Labourer of Galway. 11th Foot. Marched from Bristol as Patrick McCoody or Bernard Brady, and confined aboard PS, 15 January 1815. Joined YCs as Patrick McCoody, 29 June 1815. Arrived in the WIs as Patrick Coddy, 5 November 1815. Died Jamaica as Patrick Coddy, 8 January 1819.

Coffey/Coffee, Dennis. 16th Foot. Confined aboard PS, 23 January 1813. Joined YCs 25 March 1814, and arrived in WIs 14 December 1814. Discharged Quebec.

Coffey, Edward. Shoemaker of Cork. 37th Foot. Marched from Bristol and confined aboard PS, 20 November 1813. Joined YCs 7 March 1814. Deserted at Cove of Cork, 30 September 1814. No record of rejoining.

Cole, Thomas. 57th Foot. Marched from Maidstone and confined aboard PS, 22 October 1813. Joined YCs 7 March 1814, and arrived in the WIs 14 December 1814. Discharged Quebec.

Coleman, John. Baker of Sevenoaks. 24th Foot. Marched from Maidstone and confined aboard PS, 2 June 1815. Joined YCs 29 June 1815, and arrived in the WIs 5 November 1815. Deserted in Jamaica 3 May 1818. Rejoined 9 May 1818. (No punishment records held.) Discharged Quebec.

Coleman, Michael. 2nd Bn 44th Foot. Marched from Maidstone and confined aboard PS, 19 October 1813. Joined YCs 1 February 1814, and arrived in the WIs 14 December 1814. Died Jamaica, 4 October 1817.

Collingwood. Samuel. 83rd Foot. Marched from Chester and confined aboard PS, 22 December 1815. Joined YCs 19 October 1816, and arrived in the WIs 21 December 1816. Discharged Quebec.

Collins/Collin, Benjamin. Shoemaker of York. 95th Foot. Marched from Savoy Military Prison and confined at Portchester Castle, 21 December 1816. Joined YCs 3 April 1817, and arrived in the WIs 25 May 1817. Deserted in Jamaica, 28 October 1818. Rejoined March 1819. (No date of return or record of punishment received). Discharged Quebec.

Collins, James. Labourer of Oxford. 3rd Foot. Marched from Reading and confined aboard PS, 7 May 1815. Joined YCs 29 June 1815, and arrived in the WIs 5 November 1815. Died Jamaica, 10 June 1819.

Collins/Cullan, John. Blacksmith of Kent. 2nd Dragoons. Marched from St Austin's and confined aboard PS, 1 December 1813. Joined YCs as Cullan, 7 March 1814, but changed to Collins on the pay and muster list. Deserted while still at the Isle of Wight, 27 July 1814. No record of rejoining.

Collins, Thomas. Labourer of Hilsea, Hampshire. 18th Hussars. Marched from Lewes and confined aboard PS, 23 January 1814. Joined YCs 25 March 1814. Deserted while still on the Isle of Wight, 2 April 1814. No record of rejoining.

Collins, William. 66th Foot. Transported from Portsmouth and confined aboard PS, 30 May 1815. Joined YCs 29 June 1815, and arrived in the WIs 5 November 1815. Promoted corporal 25 February 1816. Reduced 4 February 1817. Discharged Quebec.

Collis, Stephen. Baker of Bethnal Green. 1st Bn 95th Foot. Confined aboard PS, 8 September 1813. Joined YCs 1 February 1814. Deserted while still on the Isle of Wight, 10 June 1814. No record of rejoining.

Colly/Colley/Cully, Richard. Horse dealer of Kipton. Royal Artillery. Marched from Durham and confined aboard PS as Colley, 21 May 1815. Joined YCs 29 June 1815, and arrived in the WIs as Colly, 5 November 1815. Died as Cully, 21 October 1816.

Common, John. Miner of Cornwall. Royal Wagon Train. Marched from Savoy Military Prison and confined aboard PS, 25 December 1813. Joined YCs 7 March 1814, and arrived in the WIs 14 December 1814. Died, 20 September 1815.

Connell, Andrew. Labourer of Cavan. 36th Foot. Marched from Chester and confined aboard PS, 8 December 1813. Joined YCs 1 February 1814. Deserted while still on the Isle of Wight, 10 February 1814. Retaken the next day. Rejoined 20 February 1814, hospitalised and re-confined aboard PS until regiment left for the WIs. (No punishment records held.) Arrived in the WIs 14 December 1814. Died, 9 May 1815.

Connell, John. Labourer of Cork. Marched from Battle and confined aboard PS, 19 November 1813. Joined YCs 1 February 1814, and arrived in the WIs 14 December 1814. Died St Vincent, 11 September 1815.

Connell, Marcus. 2nd Bn 50th Foot. Marched from Hastings and confined aboard PS, 6 December .1814. Joined YCs 29 June 1815, and 'Left on Detachment'. No further record.

Connell, Timothy. 54th Foot. Marched from Chester and confined aboard PS, 15 August 1813. Joined YCs 1 February 1814, and arrived in the WIs 14 December 1814. Discharged Quebec.

Connelly, Peter. Labourer of Mayo. Joined the 32nd Foot, 2 March 1807. Marched from Bristol and confined aboard PS, 4 February 1815. Joined YCs 29 June 1815, and arrived in the WIs 5 November 1815. Died Jamaica, 11 December 1817.

Connery/Conroy, Edward. Labourer of Locklau. Royal Artillery. Marched from Savoy Military Prison and confined aboard PS, 19 September 1813. Joined YCs 1 February 1814. Deserted Sandown, Isle of Wight, 10 February 1814. Retaken next day. No further record.

Connery/Conroy, William. 76th Foot. Marched from Horsham and confined aboard PS, 13 September 1813. Joined YCs as William Connery, 5 February 1814. Arrived in the WIs 14 December 1814. 300 lashes for being 'Drunk on Guard', 10 February 1817.' Discharged at Quebec as William Conroy.

Connor, John. Shoemaker of Port Arlington. Transferred to YCs from the 6th Bn 60th Foot in Jamaica, 25 May 1817. Deserted in Jamaica, 12 June 1817. No record of rejoining.

Connor, Thomas. 87th Foot. Transported from Portsmouth and confined aboard PS, 8 February 1814. Joined YCs 7 March 1814, and arrived in the WIs 14 December 1814. Discharged Quebec. Accompanied by wife and two daughters settled on Concession 10. Lot NE 11, Beckwith. Sold to Daniel McAra for thirty-one pounds and five shillings, 6 April 1827.

Conroy, John. Weaver of Galway. 2nd Bn 49th Foot. Marched from Savoy Military Prison and confined aboard PS, 30 October 1814. Joined YCs 29 June 1815, and arrived in the WIs 5 November 1815. Deserted in Jamaica, 25 November 1817. No record of rejoining.

Cook/Cooke, John. Shoemaker of Chichester. Either 1st Bn 50th marched from Fisherton, 3 August 1814, or 2nd Bn 87th marched from Plymouth Docks and confined aboard PS, 20 December 1814. Joined YCs 29 June 1814, and arrived in the WIs 5 November 1815. Deserted in Jamaica 4 August 1817. Rejoined next day. 300 lashes for being 'Absent without leave', 8 August 1817. Died Jamaica, 14 December 1817.

Cooke, Daniel. Button maker of Aston. 29th Foot. Marched from Worcester and confined aboard PS as Samuel or Daniel Cooke, 25 December 1815. Embarked Spithead as Daniel Cooke, one of 300 'Unattached Deserters' joining the 2nd Foot, 24 April 1816. Arrived in the WIs 5 June 1816. Transferred into York Chasseurs, 25 August 1816. Deserted, 16 September 1816. No record of rejoining.

Cooley, James. 23rd Light Dragoons. Marched from Bristol and confined aboard PS, 21 August 1813. Joined YCs 5 February 1814, and arrived in the WIs 14 December 1814. 200 lashes for 'Insolent Language', 10 July 1815. Discharged Quebec.

Cooney, Michael. Labourer of Queens County. Wagon Artillery. Marched from Derby and confined aboard PS, 5 February 1814. Deserted while still at the Isle of Wight, 5 July 1814. No record of rejoining.

Cooper, George. Labourer of Clare. 77th Foot. Marched from Bristol and confined at Portchester Castle, date unknown. Joined YCs 3 April 1817, and arrived in the WIs 25 May 1817. Deserted in Jamaica, 10 October 1817. Returned the next day. 300 lashes for being 'Absent without leave', 30 October 1817. 300 lashes for 'Making away with his Necessaries', 26 November 1817. Deserted in Jamaica 3 April 1819. Rejoined the next day. Deserted in Jamaica 28 April 1819. Rejoined 9 May 1819. Deserted in Jamaica 2 June 1819. Rejoined 5 June 1819. (No punishment records held.) Discharged Quebec.

Copestake/Copesteak, Joseph. Labourer of Derby. 79th Foot. Marched from Warwick and confined aboard PS, 2 June 1816. Joined YCs 19 October 1816, and arrived in the WIs 21 December 1816. Deserted in Jamaica 29 April 1819. Rejoined 11 May 1819. (No punishment records held.) Discharged Quebec.

Copping, Robert. Sweep of Suffolk. Transferred from the 63rd Recruit Depot, Isle of Wight, to be confined aboard PS, 6 November 1813. Joined YCs 7 March 1814, and arrived in the WIs 14 December 1814. 300 lashes for 'Theft', 12 June 1815. Deserted in Jamaica, 3 March 1819. No record of rejoining.

Corlett, Thomas. Anchorsmith of the Isle of Man. 36th Foot. Transferred from Portsmouth and confined aboard PS, 1 July 1814. Joined YCs 29 June 1815, and arrived in the WIs 5 November 1815. Died, 11 October 1816.

Costello, Thomas. Watchmaker of Fermanagh. 6th Dragoons. Marched from Chester and confined aboard PS, 15 October 1813. Joined YCs 1 February 1814, and arrived in the WIs 14 December 1814. Promoted drummer 25 February 1814. Reduced 20 May 1816. Promoted drummer 13 August 1816. Reduced December 1816. Promoted drummer 26 February 1818. Deserted in Jamaica 29 April 1819. Rejoined as private soldier. (No date of rejoining and punishment). Discharged Quebec. Not known if this was the Thomas Costello sentenced to 200 lashes for 'Unsoldierlike Conduct and Repeated Drunkeness', but commuted to solitary confinement, 2 September 1817.

Costello, Thomas. Joined the 2nd Bn 87th Foot 12th August 1806. Marched from Plymouth Docks and confined aboard PS, 20 December 1814. Joined YCs 29 June 1815, and arrived in the WIs 5 November 1815. Discharged Quebec. Not known if this was the Thomas Costello sentenced to 200 lashes for 'Unsoldierlike Conduct and Repeated Drunkeness', but commuted to solitary confinement, 2 September 1817.

Cottle, William. 2nd Bn 3rd Foot. Marched from Marlborough and confined aboard PS, 3 August 1813. Joined YCs 5 February 1814, and arrived in the WIs 14 December 1814. Discharged Quebec.

Cottrell/Cotterell, George. Brushmaker of Chorley, Lancashire. 2nd Bn 84th Foot. Marched from Maidstone and confined aboard PS, 15 December 1813. Joined YCs 1 February 1814. Deserted while still at the Isle of Wight, 13 June 1814. No record of rejoining.

Cottrell/Cotterell, Robert. 52nd Foot. Marched from Winchester and confined aboard PS, 16 August 1813. Joined YCs 7 March 1814. During June 1814 and while still on the Isle of Wight, Cotterell had been first hospitalised and then re-confined aboard PS (reason unknown). Left sick at Guernsey as the regiment left for WIs. Deserted, recaptured and marched from Truro to PS, 24 June 1815. Agent informed regiment of Cottrell's repeat desertion, June 1817.

Coughlan/Coughlin, Patrick. 2nd Bn 50th Foot. Marched from Bristol and confined aboard PS, 22 October 1814. Joined YCs 29 June 1815, and arrived in the WIs 5 November 1815. Discharged Quebec.

Couldridge/Coldridge, Thomas. East London Militia. 'Sentenced to General Service for Desertion' at Sunhill Row, 30 March 1815. Marched from London and confined aboard PS, 9 April 1815. Joined YCs 29 June 1815, and arrived in the WIs 5 November 1815. Discharged Quebec.

Counsell, Thomas. Labourer of Wicklow. 17th Light Dragoons. Marched from Savoy Military Prison and confined aboard PS, 19 September 1813. Joined YCs 5 February 1814. Deserted while still at the Isle of Wight, 10 February 1814. Retaken the next day by William Brading (Twenty Shillings Bounty). Hospitalised and re-confined aboard PS until the regiment left for the WIs. (No punishment records held.) Arrived in the WIs 14 December 1814. 300 lashes at Guadeloupe for 'having in his Possession a French Coin', 17 August 1815, 150 lashes remitted. 300 lashes for being 'Drunk on Parade', 21 November 1817. Died Quebec, 20 August 1819, four days prior to regiment's disbandment.

Covell, Thomas. Labourer of Lincolnshire. 3rd Dragoons. Marched from Louth and confined aboard PS, 25 February 1815. Joined YCs 29 June 1815, and arrived in the WIs 5 November 1815. Deserted 2 November 1816. Rejoined 4 November 1816. 300 lashes for 'Making Away with part of his Regimental Necessities', 4 November 1816. Deserted in Jamaica, 16 April 1818. Returned to England, recaptured and confined at Louth, Lincolnshire, and where. 'As the York Chasseurs have been orded to be disbanded, HRH approves of Thomas Covell, who has been committed to confinement at Louth as a Deserter from that regiment, being discharged and furnished with the usual protecting Certificate of Discharge'.

Cowan, John. Labourer of Cavan. 2nd Bn 9th Foot. Marched from Glasgow and confined aboard PS, 14 November 1813. Joined YCs as drummer 5 February 1814 and arrived in the WIs 14 December 1814. Reduced December 1814. Promoted drummer 25 May 1816. Reduced 21 November 1817. Promoted drummer 26 March 1818. Deserted in Jamaica 2 June 1819. Rejoined as private 5 June 1819. (No punishment records held.) Died Quebec, 24 August 1819, the day of regiment's disbandment.

Cowan, Thomas. Butcher of Cork. 55th Foot. Marched from Woodbridge and confined aboard PS, 3 August 1813. Joined YCs 1 February 1814. Deserted while still at the Isle of Wight, 7 July 1814. Rejoined 15 July 1814. (No punishment records held.) Deserted at Bear Haven, Cork, 10 October 1814. No record of rejoining.

Cowen/Cowan, William. Miner of Sterling. Joined YCs 19 October 1816, and arrived in the WIs 21 December 1816. Deserted 29 April 1819. Rejoined 6 May 1819. Deserted 21 May 1819. Rejoined the same day. (No punishment records held.) Discharged Quebec.

Cox, Bryan or **Brian.** Sailor of Yorkshire. 31st Foot. Marched from Savoy Military Prison and confined at Portchester Castle, 18 January 1817. Joined YCs 3 April 1817, and arrived in the WIs 25 May 1817. Deserted in Jamaica, 6 June 1817. No record of rejoining

Craig, Andrew. Joined 6th Dragoon Guards, 23 February 1813. Marched from York and confined aboard PS, 31 July 1814. Joined YCs 29 June 1815, and arrived in the WIs 5 November 1815. Discharged Quebec.

Craig, John. Shoemaker of Berwick. 7th Bn Royal Artillery. Marched from Savoy Military Prison and confined aboard PS, 13 March 1814. Joined YCs 25 March 1814, and arrived in the WIs 14 December 1814. Died Jamaica, 9 January 1817.

Craig, William. 22nd Dragoons. Marched from Savoy Military Prison and confined aboard PS, 31 December 1813. Joined YCs 1 February 1814, and arrived in the WIs 14 December 1814. Discharged Quebec.

Crandon, David. 2nd Bn 45th Foot. Marched from Gloucester and confined aboard PS, 6 November 1814. Joined YCs 29 June 1815, and arrived in the WIs 5 November 1815. Deserted 12 May 1815. Rejoined 17 May 1815. (No punishment records held.) Discharged Quebec.

Crane, John. Labourer of Kent. 1st Bn 70th Foot. Marched from St Augustine and confined aboard PS, 30 January 1814. Joined YCs 25 March 1814, and arrived in the WIs 14 December 1814. Died, 27 September 1816.

Crawford, Thomas. Labourer of Dublin. 29th Foot. Marched from Chester and confined at Portchester Castle, 27 December 1816. Joined YCs 3 April 1817, and arrived in the WIs 25 May 1817. Deserted in Jamaica, 3 June 1817, nine days after arrival. No record of rejoining.

Creemer/Creamer/Cremer/Crennor/Cramer, Daniel. Labourer of Kilkenny. 31st Foot. Marched from Bristol and confined aboard PS as Daniel Cremer or Creemer, 28 May 1815. Joined YCs 29 June 1815, and arrived in the WIs as Daniel Creemer, 5 November 1815. As Daniel Cremer: 300 lashes for 'Absenting from His Guard without Leave', 24 December 1816. As Daniel Crennor: 300 lashes for being 'Drunk on Guard',14 January 1817. Deserted in Jamaica as Daniel Cramer 26 June 1818. Rejoined 13 July 1818. (No punishment records held.) Deserted in Jamaica 20 June 1819, just days prior to the regiment leaving Jamaica. Rejoined, date unknown. Discharged as Daniel Creamer at Quebec.

Croker, John. From Dawby, Gloucestershire. Joined 2nd Bn 53rd Foot, 1 May 1811. Transported from Hilsea, Portsmouth and confined aboard PS, 7 January 1815. Joined YCs 29 June 1815, and arrived in the WIs 5 November 1815. Discharged Quebec. At Quebec, 11 October 1820, the twenty-six-year-old John Croker enlisted for the 60th Foot. Granted pension and discharged, 11 October 1825. Reason for discharge, 'Disease of the Head and Melancholic Affliction'.

Crooks, William. Royal Artillery. Marched from Chester and confined aboard PS, 24 March 1815. Joined YCs 29 June 1815, and arrived in the WIs 5 November 1815. 150 lashes for 'Passing Rum to the Prisoner', 23 December 1816. 300 lashes for 'Loading a Firelock at 3-o-clock in the morning and making use of Threatening Language', 11 March 1817. Discharged Quebec.

Crosby, John. Sailor of Carlow. 65th Foot. Marched from Dartford and confined aboard PS, 5 February 1815. Joined YCs 29 June 1815, and arrived in the WIs 5 November 1815.

Deserted at Grenada, 11 March 1816. No record of rejoining.

Cross, Richard. Butcher of York. 4th Dragoons. Marched from Chester and confined aboard PS, 28 January 1815. Joined YCs 29 June 1815 and arrived in the WIs 5 November 1815. Died, 6 November 1816.

Crossland/Crossman, George. Labourer of Beetson. Possible 'Bounty Jumper', having enlisted for both 43rd and 52nd Regiments. Transported from Hilsea, Portsmouth, and confined aboard PS as George Crossland, 18 February 1815. Joined YCs 29 June 1815, and arrived in the WIs as George Crossman, 5 November 1815. Died as George Crossland, 1 October 1816.

Croston, Edward. Royals. Marched from Liverpool and confined aboard PS, 11 August 1813. Joined YCs 1 February 1814, and arrived in the WIs 14 December 1814. 300 lashes for being 'Drunk on Guard', 25 October 1816; 100 lashes for 'Unsoldierlike Conduct in Striking a Sergeant', 5 August 1817. Promoted corporal 25 October 1818. Reduced 3 February 1819. Discharged Quebec.

Croughan/Croghan, Hugh. 2nd Bn 38th Foot. Marched from Fisherton and confined aboard PS, 12 October 1813. Joined YCs as corporal 1 February 1814. Promoted sergeant 25 March 1814. Reduced 6 June 1814. Arrived in the WIs 14 December 1814. Promoted corporal (date unknown), sergeant 17 January 1816. Reduced 27 September 1816. Discharged Quebec.

Crump, John. Cordwainer of St Mary's, Nottinghamshire. 2nd Bn Royal Artillery Drivers. Marched from Savoy Military Prison and confined aboard PS, 23 January 1813. Joined YCs 25 March 1814. Deserted while still at the Isle of Wight 4 May 1814. No record of rejoining.

Cubis/Cubiss, John. 3rd Bn 95th Foot. Marched from Savoy Military Prison and confined aboard PS, 5 February 1815. Joined YCs 29 June 1815, and arrived in the WIs 5 November 1815. Discharged Quebec.

Cullen, Peter. Labourer of Carlow. 13th Dragoons. Marched from Chester and confined aboard PS, 26 October 1815. Joined YCs 29 June 1815, and arrived in the WIs 5 November 1815. Deserted at Tobago 4 May 1816. No record of rejoining.

Cullen, William. Arrived in Jamaica as 99th transfer from England, 6 June 1818. Discharged Quebec.

Cummings, Charles. Coachman of Ewell, Surrey. 56th Foot. Marched from Savoy Military Prison and confined aboard PS, 11 November 1813. Joined YCs 5 February 1814. Deserted at Sandown, Isle of Wight, 22 February 1814. Retaken two days later, hospitalised and rejoined, 6 March 1814. (No punishment records held.) Arrived in the WIs 14 December 1814. Promoted corporal 28 April 1815, sergeant 25 September 1815. Reduced 2 December 1819. Deserted in Jamaica 17 April 1819. No record of rejoining. It is unclear whether Charles or Thomas Cummings was sentenced to 300 lashes for 'Selling his shirt', 17 February 1817, punishment remitted.

Cummings/Cummins, Thomas. Cotton spinner of Tyrone. Either 87th marched from Bristol, 7 February 1816, or 36th Foot marched from Chester and confined aboard PS, 28 April 1816. Joined YCs 19 October 1816, and arrived in the WIs 21 December 1816. Deserted in Jamaica 31 May 1817. Rejoined 8 June 1817. (No punishment records held.) 300 lashes for 'Theft', 1 September 1817; 300 for 'Having a Shirt in his Possession not his own Property', 10 September, 100 lashes remitted. Deserted in Jamaica 27 July 1818.

Rejoined 19 October 1818. (No punishment records held.) Died Jamaica, 8 June 1819. It is unclear whether Charles or Thomas Cummings was sentenced to 300 lashes for 'Selling his shirt', 17 February 1817, punishment remitted.

Cummings, William. Labourer of Cumberland. 91st Foot. Marched from Woolwich and confined aboard PS, 12 September 1813. Joined YCs 1 February 1814, but remained sick at Cork General Hospital as the regiment left for the WIs. Arrived in the WIs 5 November 1815. Promoted corporal 29 December 1815, sergeant 8 August 1816. Reduced 6 October 1818. Deserted in Jamaica, 18 May 1819. No record of rejoining.

Cummings, William. Volunteer from 2nd Garrison Staff Corps 8 January 1817. Remained at the Isle of Wight Depot. Discharged 1817, date unknown.

Cunningham, Patrick. Labourer of Tipperary. 97th Foot. Marched from Bristol and confined aboard PS, 29 September 1813. Joined YCs 1 February 1814, and arrived in the WIs 14 December 1814. 150 lashes for 'Making away with his Necessaries', 9 May 1815, 50 lashes remitted. Died Jamaica, 19 November 1818.

Cunningham, William. Labourer of Monaghan. Royal Horse Artillery. Marched from Chester and confined aboard PS, 2 October 1813. Joined YCs 7 March 1814, and arrived in the WIs 14 December 1814. Deserted in Jamaica 25 August 1818. No record of rejoining.

Curley, Peter. 2nd Bn 3rd Foot. Marched from Gloucestershire and confined aboard PS, 17 January 1816. Embarked Spithead, one of a 300 'Unattached Deserters' joining the 2nd Foot, 25 April 1816. Arrived in the WIs 5 June 1816. Transferred into the York Chasseurs 25 August 1816. Discharged Quebec.

Curran, Dennis. Labourer of Armagh. 27th Foot. Marched from Chester and confined aboard PS, 15 October 1813. Joined YCs 5 February 1814. Deserted while still on the Isle of Wight, 22 September 1814. Rejoined 27 September. (No punishment records held.) Arrived in the WIs 14 December 1814. Discharged from Stony Hill Barracks, Jamaica, 10 June 1819.

Curran, Patrick. Weaver of Forthill. 18th Foot. Marched from Chester and confined aboard PS, 31 December 1813. Joined YCs 7 March 1814, and arrived in the WIs 14 December 1814. Died Jamaica, 16 October 1817.

Curtis/Curtiss, Thomas. From London. 48th Foot. Marched from Bristol and confined aboard PS, 17 June 1815. Joined YCs 29 June 1815, and arrived in the WIs 5 November 1815. Discharged Quebec. At Quebec, 4 November 1820, enlisted into the 60th. Discharged to a pension 21 December 1824. Reason: 'Injuring his Knee whilst on Duty'. Character on discharge – 'Good'.

Dalamont/Dellamont/Dellarmont, David. Brazier of Ayr. 2nd Dragoons. Marched from Newcastle and confined aboard PS, 7 October 1813. Joined YCs 1 February 1814, and arrived in the WIs 14 December 1814. Died, 18 October 1816.

Dale, Thomas. Labourer of Warwick. Joined YCs 29 June 1815, and arrived in the WIs 5 November 1815. Deserted in Jamaica 26 May 1819. Rejoined the next day. (No punishment records held.) Discharged Quebec.

Daley/Dailey/Daily, John. 1st Bn 5th Foot. Transported from Portsmouth and confined aboard PS, 14 January 1816. Joined YCs 25 June 1816, and arrived in the WIs 19 December 1816. Discharged Quebec.

Dalton/Dolton, Richard. Carpenter of Hertford. Confined aboard PS, 12 December 1814. Joined YCs 29 June 1815, and arrived in the WIs 5 November 1815. Deserted in Jamaica 8 June 1817. Rejoined 17 June 1817. 300 lashes for being 'Absent without Leave', 19 June 1817. Deserted in Jamaica, 17 July 1817. No record of rejoining.

Daniels/Daniells, Joseph. Potter of Staffordshire. Royal Wagon Train. Marched from Savoy Military Prison and confined aboard PS, 23 January 1814. Joined YCs 25 March 1814, and arrived in the WIs 14 December 1814. Discharged in Jamaica, 10 June 1819.

Daulby/Dalby, James. Carpenter of York. Volunteered as corporal, 2nd Bn 89th Foot, marched from Chelsea, 1 April 1815. Arrived in the WIs 5 November 1815. Reduced 29 February 1816. Died, 1 October 1816.

Davenport, George. Clerk of Leicestershire. Sentenced as a General Service Recruit (date unknown). Arrived in the WIs 21 December 1816. Deserted in Jamaica 19 February 1817. Returned to England, recaptured and confined at Savoy Military Prison, 31 August 1818. No further record.

Davey/Davy, Francis. 2nd Bn 73rd Foot. Marched from Salford and confined aboard PS, 13 March 1814. Joined YCs 25 March 1814, and arrived in the WIs 14 December 1814. 300 lashes for being 'Drunk on Guard', 10 February 1817. Discharged Quebec.

Davies, David. Tinman of Hereford. General Service. Marched from Hereford and confined aboard PS, 12 September 1813. Joined YCs 1 February 1814. Deserted while still at the Isle of Wight, 27 June 1814. No record of rejoining.

Davies/Davis, George. Labourer of Antrim. 25th Foot. Marched from Haverford West and confined at Portchester Castle, 24 January 1817. Joined YCs 3 April 1817, and arrived in the WIs 25 May 1917. Deserted in Jamaica, 6 April 1818. No record of rejoining.

Davies/Davis, James. Labourer of Nottingham. Either 2nd Bn 32nd Foot marched from Lancaster, 14 February 1814, Royals marched from Chester, 24 March 1813, or 49th Foot marched from Danbury and confined aboard PS, 23 April 1813. Joined YCs 1 February 1814. Deserted while still at the Isle of Wight, 27 July 1814. No record of rejoining.

Davies/Davis, John. Labourer of Monmouth. Either 2nd Foot marched from Savoy Military Prison, 21 January 1815, 95th Foot marched from Savoy Military Prison, 12 February 1815, 15th Foot transferred from Regimental Depot, 27 April 1815, or 20th Foot marched from Chester and confined aboard PS, 27 April 1815. Joined YCs 29 June 1815, and arrived in the WIs 5 November 1815. Deserted in Jamaica 13 September 1818. Rejoined 18 September 1818 (No punishment records held.) Discharged Quebec. It is not known which John Davies was sentenced to 'Solitary Confinement for Drunk on Guard', 10 February 1817, or received 150 lashes for 'Leaving limits of Garrison without Leave and being found close to Stony Hill Taverns', 19 March 1817.

Davies/Davis, John. Weaver of Meath. Either 2nd Foot marched from Savoy Military Prison, 21 January 1815, 95th Foot marched from Savoy Military Prison, 12 February 1815, 15th Foot transferred from the Regimental Depot, 27 April 1815, or 20th Foot marched from Chester and confined aboard PS, 27 April 1815. Joined YCs 29 June 1815, and arrived in the West Indies 5 November 1815. Deserted in Jamaica 28 April 1819. No record of rejoining. It is not known which John Davies was sentenced to 'Solitary Confinement for Drunk on Guard', 10 February 1817, or received 150 lashes for 'Leaving limits of Garrison without Leave and being found close to Stony Hill Taverns', 19 March 1817.

Davies/Davis, John. Labourer of Wilbey, Worcestershire. Either 2nd Foot marched from Savoy Military Prison, 21 January 1815, 95th Foot marched from Savoy Military Prison, 12 February 1815, 15th Foot transferred from Regimental Depot, 27 April 1815, or 20th Foot marched from Chester and confined aboard PS, 27 April 1815. Joined YCs 29 June 1815, and arrived in the WIs 5 November 1815. Died Tobago, 14 July 1816.

Davies/Davis, William. Labourer of Lancashire. 3rd Guards. Marched from London and confined aboard PS, 9 April 1815. Joined YCs 29 June 1815, and arrived in the WIs 5 November 1815. Died, 4 October 1816.

Davies/Davis, William. Labourer of Liverpool. 25th Foot. Marched from Haverford West and confined at Portchester Castle, 24 January 1817. Joined YCs 3 April 1817, and arrived in the WIs 25 May 1817. Deserted in Jamaica, 10 April 1818. No record of rejoining.

Dawson, Daniel. General Service. Marched from Gloucester and confined aboard PS, 9 September 1813. Joined YCs 5 February 1814, and arrived in the West Indies 14 December 1814. Discharged Quebec.

Dawson, William. Possibly labourer of Waddleton. Volunteer corporal marched from the Durham District, 25 December 1813. Promoted sergeant, then colour sergeant, 25 February 1814. Arrived in the WIs 14 December 1814. Reduced 29 July 1816. Died Jamaica, 31 May 1818.

Dawson, William. Possible labourer of Waddeton. Either Coldstream Guards marched from St Albans, 28 August 1814, or 1st Foot Guards marched from Savoy Military Prison and confined aboard PS (date unknown) Joined YCs 29 June 1815, and arrived in the WIs as drummer, 5 November 1815. Died Tobago, 20 August 1816.

Deadman/Deldman, Henry. 2nd Bn 45th Foot. Marched from Abingdon and confined aboard PS as Henry Deadman or Delman, 14 November 1814. Joined YCs as Henry Deadman, 29 June 1815. Arrived in the WIs 5 November 1815. Discharged Quebec.

Deaze, William. Cordwainer of Louth. Joined 3rd Foot Guards, 4 December 1811. Marched from Canterbury and confined aboard PS, 25 October 1814. Joined YCs 26 June 1815, and arrived in the WIs 5 November 1815. Deserted in Jamaica 11 February 1819. Rejoined 13 February 1819. Deserted in Jamaica 27 April 1819. Rejoined 5 May 1819. (No punishment records held.) Discharged Quebec.

Delaney, John. Blacksmith of Queen's County. 97th Foot. Marched from Chester and confined aboard PS, 1 May 1815. Joined YCs 29 June 1815, and arrived in WIs 5 November 1815. Deserted in Jamaica 15 March 1818. No record of rejoining.

Dennis, William. Labourer of Huntington. 2nd Bn 79th Foot. Marched from Cambridge and confined aboard PS, 18 January 1814. Joined YCs 7 March 1814, and arrived in the WIs 14 December 1814. Promoted drummer 14 August 1816. 'Reduced and sentenced to 150 lashes for being 'Absent from Parade', 26 September 1816. Corporal punishment remitted. Promoted drummer 3 December 1816. Deserted in Jamaica 8 March 1819. Rejoined as private 15 March 1819. (No punishment records held.) Discharged Quebec.

Derrick, John. 25th Foot. Marched from Shrewsbury and confined at Portchester Castle, 12 January 1817. Joined YCs 3 April 1817, and arrived in the WIs 25 May 1817. Discharged Quebec.

Devine, James. Labourer of Mayo. 79th Foot. Marched from Dover and confined aboard

PS, 4 September 1813. Joined YCs 7 March 1814. Deserted at Falmouth, 19 September 1814. No record of rejoining.

Devlin/Develin, Edward. 13th Foot. Transported from Jersey as Edward Develin and confined aboard PS, 25 September 1815. Joined YCs 19 October 1816 as Edward Devlin and arrived in the WIs 21 December 1816. Discharged Quebec.

Devlin/Develin/Devilon, Thomas. Weaver of Tyrone. Royal Artillery. Marched from Andover and confined aboard PS as Thomas Devilon, 6 December 1814. Joined YCs 29 June 1815, and arrived in the WIs 5 November 1815. Deserted Tobago as Thomas Develin, 18 July 1816. Rejoined 28 July 1816. (No punishment records held.) 1000 lashes for '1. Firing a musket loaded with ball while a prisoner in the Guard Room. 2. Maliciously saying he would complete the purpose for which he fired the musket at a future period', 21 July 1817. Deserted in Jamaica as Thomas Devlin, 20 August 1818. No record of rejoining.

Devon, Charles. 1st Bn 2nd Foot. Marched from Taunton and confined aboard PS, 28 November 1814. Joined YCs 29 June 1815, and arrived in the WIs 5 November 1815. Discharged Quebec.

Dillon, Thomas. Labourer of Roscommon. Joined 32nd Foot, December 1797, transferred to the 4th Garrison Battalion, July 1811. Probably a volunteer who joined YCs 29 June 1815. Arrived in the WIs 5 November 1815. Deserted 16 February 1816. Rejoined 25 February 1816. (No punishment records held.) Deserted in Jamaica 4 April 1819. No record of rejoining.

Dix, John. Volunteered for YCs from 2nd Bn Tower Hamlest Militia, 6 December 1813 (Six Guinea Bounty). Arrived in the WIs 14 December 1814. Promoted corporal 15 January 1815. Reduced 7 August 1816. Discharged Quebec. Possibly returned to England at public expense.

Dixon, John. 68th Foot. Marched from Chester and confined aboard PS, 2 October 1813. Joined YCs 1 February 1814, and arrived in the WIs 14 December 1814. Discharged Quebec.

Dixon, William. Labourer of Lincoln. 2nd Bn 51st Foot. Marched from Savoy Military Prison and confined aboard PS, 1 December 1813. Joined YCs 7 March 1814, and arrived in the WIs 14 December 1814. Deserted in Jamaica 17 April 1818. Rejoined 3 June 1819. Deserted in Jamaica 27 March 1819. Rejoined, date unknown. (No punishment records held.) Discharged Quebec.

Doby, John. Shoemaker of Ayr. 21st Foot. Marched from Bristol and confined aboard PS, 16 August 1815. Embarked Spithead amongst a 300-strong detachment of 'Unattached Deserters' joining the 2nd Foot, 25 April 1816. Arrived WIs 5 June 1816. Transferred into the York Chasseurs 25 August 1816. 300 lashes for being 'Drunk on Guard', 6 March 1817; 900 lashes for being 'Absent without Leave', 23 April 1817. Deserted in Jamaica, 30 June 1817 (two months after his 900 lash flogging). No record of rejoining.

Dodd/Dodds, John. 2nd Bn 34th Foot. Marched from Beverley and confined aboard PS, 18 December 1814. Joined YCs 29 June 1815, and arrived in the WIs 5 November 1815. Died, 26 October 1816.

Dodd/Dodds, Thomas. Weaver of Lanark. 70th Foot. Marched from Glasgow and confined aboard PS, 25 February 1814. Joined YCs 7 March 1814, and arrived in the WIs 14 December 1814. Promoted drummer 25 April 1815. Reduced 12 March 1817. Along with William Dodds, awarded 300 lashes for being 'Drunk & Absent from Parade & found on their way on their way to Stony Hill Taverns', 6 March 1817. Deserted in Jamaica 27 June 1818. Surrendered himself at Glasgow as a deserter from the regiment, February 1819. 'Discharged in consequence of being below the regulated Standard and of bearing Marks of Punishment. Furnished with the necessary protecting Certificate of Discharge'.

Dodd/Dodds, William. Labourer of York. 83rd Foot. Marched from Chester and confined aboard PS, 16 August 1815. Embarked Spithead amongst 300-strong detachment of 'Unattached Deserters' joining 2nd Foot, 25 April 1816. Arrived in the WIs 5 June 1816. Deserted 18 July 1816 Rejoined 30 July 1816. 1,000 lashes and marked with 'D', 25 August 1816. Transferred into the York Chasseurs 25 August 1816. Along with Thomas Dodd, awarded 300 lashes for being 'Drunk & Absent from Parade & found on their way on their way to Stony Hill Taverns', 6 March 1817. Died Jamaica, 17 August 1817.

Donaldson, David. 79th Foot. Marched from Edinburgh and confined aboard PS, 1 January 1815. Joined YCs 29 June 1815, and arrived in the WIs 5 November 1815. Discharged Quebec.

Donaldson, James. Cordwainer of Dundee. Joined 42nd Foot, 20 August 1808. Marched from Chester and confined aboard PS, date unknown. Joined YCs 29 June 1815, and arrived in the WIs 5 November 1815. 300 lashes for 'Offering a pair of shoes for Sale at Port Maria', 10 December 1816. Died Jamaica, 29 May 1817.

Donally/Donnelly/Donnally, Edward. Labourer of Longford. 46th Foot. Marched from Chester and confined aboard PS, 26 September 1813. Joined YCs 5 February 1814, and arrived in the WIs 14 December 1814. 200 lashes for 'Contempt to Capt Daniell', 9 June 1815, 50 lashes remitted; 200 lashes for 'Making away with his Necessaries', 27 June 1815. Deserted 5 December 1816. Rejoined 10 December 1816. Deserted in Jamaica 7 May 1818. Rejoined 10 May 1818. Deserted in Jamaica 2 April 1819. Rejoined 4 April 1819. (No punishment records held.) Discharged Quebec.

Donerhoe/Donoughue/Donohoe/Dunahoe, John. Shoemaker of Galway. 76th Foot. Marched from Horsham and confined aboard PS, 13 September 1813. Joined YCs 5 February 1814, and arrived in the WIs 14 December 1814. 100 lashes for 'Refusing to go to Drill when Ordered', 25 April 1815, 100 lashes remitted. Died, 11 October 1816.

Donnagan/Donaghan/Dunaghan, Patrick. Tobacconist of Dublin. 32nd Foot. Marched from Chester and confined aboard PS, 24 March 1815. Joined YCs 29 June 1815, and arrived in the WIs 5 November 1815. Solitary Confinement for 'Buying Regimental Necessaries', 28 April 1817. Died Jamaica, 4 January 1818.

Donnelly, John. Joined YCs in Jamaica from the 1st European Garrison, 25 May 1817. Discharged Quebec.

Donnovan/Donovan, Daniel. Labourer of Derry. Either 2nd Bn 69th Foot marched from Maidstone, 4 August 1814, or 9th Foot marched from Windsor and confined aboard PS, 27 October 1814. Joined YCs 29 June 1815, and arrived in the WIs 5 November 1815. Deserted in Jamaica 9 September 1818. Rejoined 11 September 1818. Deserted in Jamaica 4 March 1819. Rejoined 7 March 1819. (No punishment records held.) Deserted in Jamaica 18 June 1819. No record of rejoining.

Donnovan/Donavan/Donovan, Patrick. Labourer of Limerick. 88th Foot. Marched from Bristol and confined aboard PS, 28 May 1815. Joined YCs 29 June 1815, and arrived in the WIs 5 November 1815. Died Jamaica, 19 March 1817.

Donohoe/Donoughoe, Patrick. Labourer of Limerick. Embarked Spithead amongst a

300-strong detachment of 'Unattached Deserters' joining the 2nd Foot, 25 April 1816. Arrived in the WIs 5 June 1816. Transferred into the York Chasseurs 25 August 1816. 150 lashes for being 'Drunk and Absenting himself from Parade', 26 December 1816. Deserted in Jamaica 3 March 1819. Rejoined the next day. Deserted in Jamaica 29 April 1819. Rejoined the next day. (No punishment records held.) Discharged Quebec.

Donovan, Hugh. Embarked Spithead amongst a detachment of 300-strong 'Unattached Deserters' joining the 2nd Foot, 25 April 1816. Arrived in the WIs 5 June 1816. Transferred into the York Chasseurs, 25 August 1816. Discharged Quebec.

Doolan, James. Weaver of Neath. 5th Foot. Marched from Chester and confined aboard PS as James Murray or James Doolan, 1 November 1813. Joined YCs 5 February 1814, as James Doolan. Arrived in the WIs14 December 1814. Sentenced 300 lashes but commuted to 16 days solitary confinement for being 'Drunk on Guard', 1 April 1815. Killed in Action at Guadeloupe, 9 August 1815.'

Dore, Robert or **William**. Labourer of Kerry. 81st Foot. Marched from Chester and confined aboard PS as Robert or William Dore, 22 February 1816. Joined YCs 19 October 1816, as Robert Dore. Arrived in the WIs 21 December 1816. Died Jamaica, 3 August 1817.

Dorset/Dorsett, John. 2nd Bn 39th Foot. Marched from Worcester and confined aboard PS, 31 January 1814. Joined YCs 25 March 1814, and arrived in the WIs 14 December 1814. Discharged Quebec.

Dougatt/Duggett/Duggatt, Robert. Weaver of Wicklow. 11th Light Dragoons. Marched from Lewes and confined aboard PS as Robert Dugat or Dougatt, 25 June 1815. Joined YCs 29 June 1815, as Duggatt. Arrived in the WIs 5 November 1815. Died, 9 October 1816.

Dougherty/Dochety/Doughecty, James. Labourer of Wexford. Either 1st Foot or 1st Foot Guards. Marched from Glasgow and confined aboard PS as James Dogherty, 8 June 1815. Joined YCs 29 June 1815, and arrived in the WIs as James Doughecty, 5 November 1815. 300 lashes for 'Theft and Striking Sergeant Alwright', 24 December 1816. Deserted in Jamaica 23 March 1819. Rejoined 17 May 1819. Deserted in Jamaica 21 May 1819. Rejoined the same day. (No punishment records held.) Discharged as James Dougherty at Quebec.

Dougherty/Dogherty/Doghecty, John. Labourer of Mayo. 1st Bn 43rd Foot. Marched from Bristol and confined aboard PS as John Dogherty or Doghecty, 31 October 1814. Joined YCs 29 June 1815, and remained in England as the regiment left for St Vincent. Arrived in the WIs 19 December 1816. Died Jamaica as John Dougherty, 1 November 1817.

Dougherty/Doughecty, Peter or **Patrick**. 28th Foot. Marched from Chester and confined aboard PS as Patrick or Peter Dogherty, 15 May 1815. Joined YCs 29 June 1815, and arrived in the WIs 5 November 1815. Discharged as Peter Dougherty at Quebec.

Douglas, John. Received from the 17th Foot on the Isle of Wight, by Order of the C in C, June 1818. Discharged, 24 December 1818.

Dovey, John. 14th Light Dragoons. Marched from Taunton and confined aboard PS, 18 September 1813. Joined YCs 5 February 1814, and arrived in the WIs 14 December 1814. Discharged Quebec.

Downey/Denahy/Donnely, Edward. Labourer of Limerick. 68th Foot. Marched from

Bristol and confined aboard PS as Edward Denahy, 4 February 1815. Joined YCs as Edward Downey, 29 June 1815. Arrived in the WIs 5 November 1815. Died Jamaica as Edward Donnely, 12 October 1817.

Downs, John. 38th Foot. Marched from Hastings and confined aboard PS, 25 January 1816. Joined YCs 19 October 1816, and arrived in the WIs 21 December 1816. Discharged Quebec.

Downs/ Downes Patrick or **Benjamin.** Weaver of Hereford. 1st Foot Guards. Marched from Monmouth and confined aboard PS as Benjamin Downes, 16 November 1814. Joined YCs 29 June 1815. As Patrick Downs, deserted off Stokes Bay, Gosport, 1 July 1815. No record of rejoining.

Doyle, John. Labourer of Limerick. 17th Dragoons. Marched from Maidstone and confined aboard PS, 8 June 1815. Joined YCs 29 June 1815, and arrived in the WIs 5 November 1815. Died, 11 December 1816.

Doyle, John. Shoemaker of Dublin. Either 87th Foot marched from Chester, 18th January 1816, or 16th Foot marched from Liverpool and confined aboard PS, 5 February 1816. Embarked Spithead amongst a 300-strong detachment of 'Unattached Deserters' joining the 2nd Foot, 25 April 1816. Arrived in WIs 5 June 1816. Deserted 16 July 1816. Rejoined 20 July 1816. 1000 lashes and marked with 'D', 22 July 1816.' Transferred into York Chasseurs, 25 August 1816. Deserted in Jamaica 3 March 1819. No record of rejoining.

Driscoll/Driskell, John. Labourer of Newtown, Ireland. 2nd Bn 89th Foot. Marched from Trowbridge and confined aboard PS as John Driskell, 3 October 1813. Joined YCs 5 February 1814, as John Driscoll and deserted at Bear Haven, Cork, 16 October 1814. No record of rejoining.

Driscoll, John. Butcher of Cork. Joined 2nd Bn 25th Foot 10 April 1817. Transported from Holland to Portsmouth, 21 January 1814, and confined aboard PS, 12 March 1814. Joined YCs 25 March 1814, and arrived in the WIs 14 December 1814. 200 lashes for 'Insolence', 14 July 1815. Deserted at Granada, 14 September 1815. No record of rejoining.

Dudley, Michael. General Service. Marched from Liverpool and confined aboard PS, 3 March 1814. Joined YCs 25 March 1814, and arrived in the WIs 14 December 1814. 300 lashes for 'Forgery', 10 February 1817. Discharged Quebec.

Duffy, Edward. 1st Foot. Marched from Chester and confined aboard PS, 2 August 1813. Joined YCs 5 February 1814, and arrived in the WIs 14 December 1814. Discharged Quebec. Migrated to Murray Township, Northumberland County, and from where he petitioned the War Office (1833) for prize money to which 'He is entitled as a soldier in the engagement at Guadeloupe 9/10th August 1815'. Evidence of prize money has yet to be established. Ironically, with the muster roll and pay list mistakenly recording Edward Duffy, and not John Duffy, as dying, 8 February 1818, if any prize money had been available, Edward Duffy might have struggled to claim it.

Duffy, John. Labourer of Dublin. Monaghan Militia. Marched from Chester Castle and confined aboard PS, 23 January 1816. Joined YCs 16 May 1816, and arrived in the WIs 29 June 1816. Died Jamaica, 8 February 1818.

Duffy, Michael. Weaver of Louth. 71st Foot. Marched from Glasgow and confined aboard PS, 4 June 1815. Joined YCs 29 June 1815, and arrived in the WIs 5 November 1815. Died, 27 September 1816.

Duggan/Dugan/Duggin, John. Labourer of Galway. 19th Light Dragoon. Marched from Chester and confined aboard PS as John Duggin, 28 March 1814. Joined YCs 29 June 1815, and arrived in the WIs as Corporal John Duggan, 5 November 1815. Promoted sergeant 24 September 1816, and colour sergeant 10 November 1817. Reduced 21 March 1819. Discharged from Stony Hill Barracks, Jamaica, as John Dugan 10 June 1819.

Duggan, William. Variously described as carpenter of Kildare, labourer of Donegal or cordwainer of Cork. 2nd Bn 24th Foot. Marched from Maidstone and confined aboard PS, 25 December 1814. Joined YCs 29 June 1815, and arrived in the WIs 5 November 1815. Promoted corporal 18 July 1816. Reduced 10 September 1816. Deserted in Jamaica 14 August 1818. Rejoined the next day. Deserted in Jamaica 4 April 1819. Rejoined 14 April 1819. (No punishment records held.) Deserted in Jamaica, 27 May 1819. No record of rejoining.

Duncan, William. Weaver of Killarney. 86th Foot. Marched from Worcester and confined aboard PS, 12 May 1813. Joined YCs 1 February 1814, and arrived in the WIs 14 December 1814. Died, 20 November 1816.

Dunlop, George. Weaver of Derry. 4th Royals. Marched from Edinburgh and confined aboard PS, 6 January 1814. Joined YCs 29 June 1815. Deserted from Fort Cumberland, Portsmouth, 5 August 1815. No record of rejoining.

Dunn, Edward. Labourer of Worcestershire. Either 44th Foot marched from Bristol, 26 July 1815, or 21st Foot marched from Chester and confined aboard PS, 13 August 1815. Embarked Spithead amongst a 300-strong detachment of 'Unattached Deserters' joining the 2nd Foot, 25 April 1816. Arrived in the WIs 5 June 1816. Deserted 25 July 1816. Rejoined the next day. 1000 lashes and ordered to be marked with 'D', 30 July 1816. Transferred into the York Chasseurs as Edward Dyson, 25 August 1816. Deserted as Edward Dunn, 19 November 1816. Rejoined 24 November 1816. Deserted in Jamaica 22 December 1816. Rejoined 7 January 1817. (No punishment records held.) Deserted in Jamaica 29 March 1817. Rejoined 16 April 1817. 900 lashes for being 'Absent without Leave', 23 April 1817. Deserted in Jamaica 5 July 1817. Rejoined 10 July 1817. 300 lashes for being 'Absent without Leave', 16 July 1817. Deserted in Jamaica 9 August 1818. Rejoined 12 August 1818. Deserted in Jamaica 17 March 1819. Rejoined the next day. (No punishment records held.) Deserted in Jamaica 8 May 1819. No record of rejoining.

Dunn, Patrick. 76th Foot. Marched from Horsham and confined aboard PS, 13 March 1813. Joined YCs 5 February 1814, and arrived in the WIs 14 December 1814. Discharged Quebec.

Dunnett, James. From Caithness. Joined 93rd Foot, 9 July 1800, transferred to 1st Garrison Company, 27 December 1814. Marched from London as volunteer corporal, 1 April 1815. Arrived in the WIs 5 November 1815. Reduced 4 January 1816. Promoted corporal, date unknown. 200 lashes and ordered to be reduced for 'Unsoldierlike Conduct for being Drunk on Escort Duty', 23 August 1817; corporal punishment remitted. Discharged Quebec 24 September 1819. Returned to England and discharged at Chatham to a pension, 12 October 1819. 'Conduct on Discharge – Good'.

Dunning, John. 51st Foot. Marched from Bristol and confined aboard PS, 20 January 1815. Joined YCs 29 June 1815, and arrived in the WIs 5 November 1815. Solitary Confinement for 'Drunk on Guard', 10 February 1817. Promoted corporal 14 October 1817. Reduced 2 September 1818. Discharged Quebec.

Dunning, Peter. Labourer of Louth. 6th Dragoons. Marched from Chester and confined aboard PS, 25 June 1815. Joined YCs 29 June 1815, and arrived in the WIs 5 November 1815. Died, 7 October 1816.

Dwyer, John. Carpenter of Dublin. 5th Dragoon Guards. Marched from Bristol and confined aboard PS as John Carroll or John Dwyer, 20 November 1813. Joined YCs as John Dwyer, 5 February 1814, and arrived in the WIs 14 December 1814. Deserted in Jamaica 22 August 1818. Rejoined 28 April 1819. (No punishment records held.) Discharged Quebec.

Dwyer, John. Labourer of Kildare. Joined YCs 29 June 1815, and arrived in the WIs 5 November 1815. Died Stony Hill, Jamaica, 10 September 1816.

Easden/Heasden, Randol or **Randell.** 12th Light Dragoons. Marched from Winchester and confined aboard PS as Randell William Easden, 25 November 1814. Joined YCs 29 June 1815, and arrived in the WIs as Randol Easden or Heasden, 5 November 1815. 'Left in the Windward Command' as Randol Heasden, June 1816. No further record.

Eccles, Benjamin. Labourer of Buckinghamshire. 48th Foot. Marched from Hartfield and confined aboard PS, 26 September 1813. Joined YCs 7 March 1814, and arrived in the WIs 14 December 1814. 'Drowned whilst a prison-ship guard', 1 March 1815.

Edwards, Edward. 63rd Foot. Marched from Wolverhampton and confined aboard PS, 10 December 1813. Joined YCs 1 February 1814, and arrived in the WIs 14 December 1814. Awarded 200 lashes for 'Theft', 25 April 1815, 50 lashes remitted. Died Grenada, 14 December 1815.

Edwards, James. Boat builder of Cardiff. 51st Foot. Marched from Rochester and confined aboard PS, 25 March 1816. Joined YCs 16 May 1816, and arrived in the WIs 25 June 1816. Died, 12 October 1816.

Edwards, John. Labourer of Guildford. 24th Foot. Marched from Chelmsford and confined aboard PS, 27 July 1813. Joined YCs 1 February 1814. Died Isle of Wight, 21 June 1814.

Edwards, John. 23rd Foot. Sentenced at Portsmouth to 'General Service' 30 August 1814, 'For Desertion from his Regiment on or about the 2nd day of February 1814 when the Battalion was Cantoned in the Village of Ustaritz, France'. Embarked for Guernsey and the York Chasseurs, December 1814. No further record.

Edwards, Moses. Labourer of Carnarvon. 2nd Bn 25 Foot. Marched from Ludlow and confined aboard PS, 27 February 1816. Joined YCs 16 May 1816, and arrived in the WIs 25 June 1816. Died Jamaica, 12 July 1817.

Edwards, William. Labourer of Kent. Royal Artillery Driver. Marched from Carmarthen and confined aboard PS, 22 June 1816. Joined YCs from Portchester Castle, 3 April 1817 and arrived in the WIs 25 May 1817. Died Jamaica, 12 December 1818.

Elliott, James. Either 28th Foot marched from Bristol, 4 February 1815 or 84th from Chester and confined aboard PS, 18 May 1815. Joined YCs 29 June 1815, and 'Left on Detachment' as regiment departed for St Vincent. Arrived in the WIs 19 December 1816. 300 lashes for 'Unsoldierlike Conduct in Threatening the Life of a Sergeant', 29 December 1817; 21 days solitary confinement for 'Unsoldierlike Conduct in Refusing to go to Drill and Striking an NCO', 9 February 1818. Discharged Quebec.

Elliott/Elliot, William. Wheelwright of Newham, Herts. 2nd Dragoons. Marched from Chester and confined aboard PS, 15 October 1813. Joined YCs 7 March 1814, and arrived in the WIs 14 December 1814. Died Barbados, 20 February 1815.

Ellis, John. 86th Foot. Marched from Maidstone and confined aboard PS, 23 December 1813. Joined YCs 5 February 1814. Died Isle of Wight, 17 June 1814.

Ellis, Joseph. 3rd Kings Own Dragoons. Confined aboard PS, 23 December 1813. Joined YCs 7 March 1814, and arrived in the WIs 14 December 1814. Died Jamaica, 22 December 1818.

Ellis, Samuel. 40th Foot. Marched from Bristol and confined aboard PS, 26 May 1815. Joined YCs 29 June 1815, and arrived in the WIs 5 November 1815. Discharged Quebec.

Ellison/Allison, Joseph. Cutler of Sheffield. 2nd Foot. Transported from Gosport and confined aboard PS as Joseph Allison, 8 December 1814. Joined YCs as Joseph Ellison, 29 June 1815, and arrived in the WIs 5 November 1815. 300 lashes for 'giving False Evidence at a Courts-Martial', 2 February 1818. Deserted in Jamaica, 4 April 1819. No record of rejoining.

Emery, Jacob. Labourer of York. 2nd Bn 95th Foot. Marched from Lewes and confined aboard PS, 8 February 1815. Joined YCs 29 June 1815 and arrived in the WIs 5 November 1815. Died, 19 October 1816.

Englefield, Thomas. Hosier of Gloucestershire. Transferred to YCs in Jamaica from 6th Bn 60th Foot, 25 May 1817. Died Jamaica, 19 September 1817.

Epworth, Robert or **George.** From Sheffield. Volunteered for YCs at the Isle of Wight as Robert Epworth, 8 May 1816. Arrived in the WIs 25 June 1816. Discharged Quebec 24 September 1819. Returned to England to enlist for the 5th Royal Veteran Battalion at Plymouth as George Robert Epworth, 30 December 1819. Granted pension – 'Disbandment of the Battalion and General Bad Health'. Conduct as a Soldier – 'Good'. June 1821, aged 26.

Erskey, Joseph. Joined 6th Bn 60th Foot, 31 August 1809. Transferred into York Chasseurs in Jamaica, 25 May 1817. Discharged Quebec.

Evans, David. Labourer of Montgomery. 1st Bn 95th Foot. Marched from Canterbury and confined aboard PS, 22 October 1813. Joined YCs 1 February 1814. Deserted while still at the Isle of Wight, 7 July 1814. No record of rejoining.

Evans, Edward. 2nd Foot Guards. Marched from Savoy Military Prison and confined aboard PS, 3 November 1813. Joined YCs 29 June 1815. Left sick at the Isle of Wight when regiment departed for St Vincent. Discharged, 8 January 1816.

Evans, Paul. 3rd Bn Royal Artillery. Marched from St Albans and confined aboard PS, 6 March 1814. Joined YCs 25 March 1814 and arrived in the WIs 14 December 1814. Discharged 2 December 1816, 'as per instructions from Horse Guards to Lieutenant General Sir James Leith, dated 10th September 1816'.

Evans, Thomas. Labourer of St James, Pembroke. 2nd Bn 34th Foot. Marched from Brecon and confined aboard PS, 1 March 1814. Joined YCs 25 March 1814, and arrived in the WIs 14 December 1814. Deserted 27 May 1815. Rejoined 30 May 1815. Deserted in Jamaica 15 September 1817. Rejoined 25 September 1817. (No punishment records held.) Discharged Quebec.

Evans, Thomas. Labourer of Longford. 2nd Bn 96th Foot. Marched from Bath and confined aboard PS, 9 December 1814. Discharged Quebec.

Everett/Everitt, James. Sailor of Middlesex. 59th Foot. Marched from St Albans and confined at Portchester Castle, 17 December 1816. Joined YCs 3 April 1817, and arrived in the WIs 25 May 1817. Deserted in Jamaica, 1 August 1817. No record of rejoining.

Exton, William. Labourer of Melton Mowbry, Leicestershire. South Lincoln Militia. Marched from Chester and confined aboard PS, 3rd March 1814. Joined YCs 25 March 1814. Deserted while still at the Isle of Wight, 7 June 1814. (Query date of rejoining and punishment received). Arrived in the WIs 14 December 1814. Deserted 17 March 1815. Rejoined 23 March 1815. 300 lashes for being 'Absent without Leave', 1 April 1815; 250 lashes remitted. Deserted 19 May 1815. Rejoined 30 May 1815. 'SENTENCED TO BE SHOT TO DEATH AT ST VINCENT FOR DESERTION', 26 June 1815.

Fagen, John. On muster roll of York Chasseurs at Albany Barracks as private from 16th October 1815 until transferred to the 2nd West India Regiment as sergeant, 25 September 1817. Sergeant Major, 2nd West India Regiment, until transferred to Isle of Wight Staff as Sergeant, 25 September 1822. To pension, 'Establishment being Discontinued and Chronic Affliction of Liver', 10 October 1826, aged 33.

Fairbrother, Jacob. 51st Foot. Marched from Rochester and confined aboard PS, 17 January 1816. Joined YCs 19 October 1816, and arrived in the WIs 21 December 1816. Discharged Quebec.

Fanning, Patrick. Hatter of Roscria, King's County. Joined YCs 29 June 1815, and arrived in the WIs 5 November 1815. Early 1816 at Guadeloupe, Fanning, along with John Glossop, made confessions of murder committed back in Britain. Though still on passage to England, Fanning's confession to the murder of Tobias Roe, June 1806, near Roscar, was already under investigation by the Chief Clerk of Tipperary, who concluded that 'Fanning's confession does not agree with the circumstances attending that murder he alluded'. Deciding that Fanning's confession had been merely a means of achieving his removal from both regiment and the West Indies, the Commander in Chief then ordered 'he be sent back as a Prisoner to his regiment'. Rejoining the regiment in Jamaica, 25 May 1817, Fanning had soon again been in trouble: 200 lashes for 'Theft', commuted to 'One Months Drill', 4 July 1817; 250 lashes for 'Selling his Necessaries', 2 September 1817, 25 lashes remitted; 250 lashes for 'Having in his possession a pair of trowsers not his own possession', 10 January 1818, 25 lashes remitted. Deserted in Jamaica 4 October 1818. Rejoined 13 October. (No punishment records held.) Deserted in Jamaica 2 March 1819. No record of rejoining.

Fanning, Garrett. Labourer of Warwick. 4th Dragoon Guards. Marched from Chester and confined aboard PS, 26 October 1814. Joined YCs 29 June 1815, and arrived in the WIs 5 November 1815. Died Stony Park, Jamaica, 19 September 1816.

Fannon/Farnon, John. Hatter of Rosclare. 54th Foot. Marched from Nottingham and confined aboard PS as John Fannon, 3 September 1813. Joined YCs as John Farnon, 5 February 1814. Deserted while still at the Isle of Wight, 7 July 1814. No record of rejoining.

Farnley, Robert. Royal Horse Artillery. Marched from Chester and confined aboard PS, 26 September 1813. Joined YCs 1 February 1814, and arrived in the WIs 14 December 1814. Sentenced at St Vincent 'To be Shot for Mutinous Conduct', 5 June 1816. Commuted to Solitary Confinement on board the Flag Ship at Port Royal, Jamaica. Transported to Portchester Castle in the company of William James, Michael Low and Andrew Hay to await further disposal, 25 May 1817. Regiment notified of Farnley's transfer to Royal African Corps, 31 March 1818.

Farrel/Farrell, John. 61st Foot. Marched from Preston and confined aboard PS, 14 November 1813. Joined YCs 5 February 1814. Deserted while still at the Isle of Wight, 7 July 1814. No record of rejoining.

Farrell, Patrick. Victualler of Devon. Joined 28th Foot, 3 May 1809. Marched from Bristol and confined aboard PS, 15 January 1815. Joined YCs 29 June 1815, and arrived in the WIs 5 November 1815. Died, 12 October 1816.

Farrell/Foley, William. Labourer of Longford. 54th Foot. Marched from Ipswich and confined aboard PS as William Farrell or Foley, 17 July 1814. Joined YCs as William Farrell, 29 June 1815, and arrived in the WIs 5 November 1815. Died Jamaica, 3 January 1819.

Feeney/Finay/Fierney, Patrick. 21st Foot. Marched from Bristol and confined aboard PS as Patrick Feeney, 1 February 1816. Joined YCs 16 May 1816, and arrived in the WIs as Patrick Finay, 29 June 1816. Deserted as Patrick Fierney, 21 July 1816. No record of rejoining.

Fenton/Fullton, Thomas. Brazier of Warwick. 1st Bn 51st Foot. Marched from Coventry and confined aboard PS as Thomas Fullton or Fenton, 30 March 1816. Joined YCs 3 April 1817, and arrived in the WIs 25 May 1817. Promoted corporal as Fenton, 29 November 1817. Reduced 18 June 1818. Deserted in Jamaica 20 July 1818. Rejoined 13 August 1818. (No punishment records held.) Deserted in Jamaica, 27 May 1819. No record of rejoining.

Ferguson, James. 2nd Dragoon Guards. Marched from Nottingham and confined aboard PS, 2 May 1813. Joined YCs 1 February 1814, and arrived in the WIs 14 December 1814. Promoted corporal 25 February 1814, sergeant March 1814. Reduced June 1814. Promoted corporal,25 September 1814. Reduced 30 April 1814. 300 lashes for being 'Drunk on Guard but FORGIVEN', 11 July 1815. Promoted corporal 25 October 1816. Reduced 1 May 1817. Discharged Quebec.

Fidler, Samuel. Hatter of Chester. 10th Bn Royal Artillery. Marched from Savoy Military Prison and confined aboard PS, 13 February 1814. Joined YCs 7 March 1814, and arrived in the WIs 14 December 1814. Promoted corporal 25 May 1816. 200 lashes and ordered to be reduced for 'Contemptuously taking off his Badge as Corporal', 25 October 1816. Corporal punishment remitted. Deserted in Jamaica 26 May 1819. Rejoined the same day. (No punishment records held.) Discharged Quebec.

Field, Charles. Labourer of Worcestershire. 2nd Bn 62nd Foot. Marched from Worcester and confined aboard PS, 9 December 1813. Joined YCs 1 February 1814, and arrived in the WIs 14 December 1814. 14 days solitary confinement for 'Making Away with a Pair of Trowsers', 22 May 1815, but 'Forgiven'; 200 lashes for being 'Absent on Parade and Making Away with his Blankets', 25 May 1815, 50 lashes remitted. Deserted in Jamaica, 27 May 1819. No record of rejoining.

Field, Thomas. Labourer of Middlesex. 2nd Dragoons. Marched from Salford and confined aboard PS, 17 October 1813. Joined YCs 5 February 1814, and arrived in the WIs 14 December 1814. 100 lashes for 'his Highly Disrespectful Language', 20 April 1815. Died, 11 April 1816. Willed his effects, one shilling and sevenpence ha'penny, to his mother Catherine, a resident of the Whitechapel Workhouse.

Finch, Richard. Embarked Spithead amongst a 300-strong detachment of 'Unattached Deserters' joining the 2nd Foot, 25 April 1816. Arrived in the WIs 5 June 1816. Transferred into the York Chasseurs, 25 August 1816. 200 lashes for 'Loosing or making away with a pair of Shoes', 17 October 1816' Died in the Regimental Hospital 29 October 1816, under sentence but prior to any corporal punishment being inflicted.

Fines, Patrick. Labourer of Kildare. Joined YCs 7 March 1814. Deserted at Cove of Cork, 8 October 1814. No record of rejoining.

Finlay/Findlay, Michael. 23rd Light Dragoons. Marched from Chester and confined aboard PS as Michael Finlay, 16 April 1815. Joined YCs 29 June 1815, and arrived in the WIs as corporal, 5 November 1815. Reduced 7 May 1816. Promoted corporal 25 August 1817. Reduced 16 December 1817. Discharged as Michael Findlay at Quebec.

Fisher, Robert. Labourer of Wiltshire. 4th Dragoons. Marched from Chester and confined aboard PS, 28 December 1814. Joined YCs 29 June 1815, and arrived in the WIs 5 November 1815. Died Stony Hill, Jamaica, 6 September 1816.

Fitzgerald, Andrew. Shoemaker of Dublin. 11th Foot. Marched from Dartford and confined aboard PS, 24 October 1813. Joined YCs 1 February 1814, and arrived in the WIs 14 December 1814. Died Jamaica, 28 November 1817. Willed his effects, six shillings and sevenpence ha'penny to his brother, Thomas Fitzgerald of 28 Edge Street, Manchester.

Fitzgerald/Fitzpatrick, Michael. 97th Foot. Transported from Quebec to Portsmouth and confined aboard PS, 29 August 1815. Embarked Spithead amongst a 300-strong detachment of 'Unattached Deserters' joining the 2nd Foot, 25 April 1816. Arrived in the WIs 5 June 1816. Transferred into the York Chasseurs, 25 August 1816. Deserted, 14 September 1816. No record of rejoining.

Fitzgerald, Morris. 31st Foot. Confined aboard PS, 20 November 1813. Joined YCs 5 February 1814. Left sick at the Isle of Wight as the regiment departed for the WIs. Remained at Albany Barracks until his 7 June 1815 transfer into the 23rd Foot, followed shortly by the 1st Garrison Company.

Fitzgerald, William. Labourer of Longford. 94th Foot. Marched from Bristol and confined aboard PS, 7 February 1816. Arrived in the WIs 16 June 1816. Deserted 29 September 1816. Rejoined 14 October 1816. (No punishment records held.) Deserted 5 December 1816. No record of rejoining.

Flanaghan/Flannagan, Bernard. 2nd Bn 53rd Foot. Marched from Winchester and confined aboard PS, 10 November 1814. Joined YCs 29 June 1814, and arrived in the WIs 5 November 1815. 90 lashes for 'Selling his Necessaries', 2 September 1817, 40 lashes remitted. Discharged Quebec.

Flanagan/Flannagan/Flannigan, John. Labourer of Clare. 1st Bn 21st Foot. Marched from Bristol and confined aboard PS as Flanagan or Flannagan, 14 March 1814. Joined YCs 25 March 1814. Deserted at Bear Haven, Cork, as Flannigan, 30 September 1814. No record of rejoining.

Flanders, Elias. Labourer of Glamorgan. 77th Foot. Marched from Hythe and confined aboard PS, 3 October 1813. Joined YCs 5 February 1814. Deserted while still at the Isle of Wight, 7 July 1814. No record of rejoining.

Fleming, James. 72nd Foot. Marched from Chester and confined aboard PS, 2 August 1813. Joined YCs 7 March 1814, and arrived in the WIs 14 December 1814. In Jamaica, deserted and rejoined the very day regiment had been due to embark for Quebec, 24 June 1819. (No punishment records held.) Discharged Quebec. It is not known which Fleming received 300 lashes for being 'Drunk on Guard', 17 February 1817.

Fleming, John. Labourer of Middlesex. 45th Foot. Marched from Bristol and confined aboard PS, 22 November 1814. Joined YCs 29 June 1815, and arrived in the WIs 5 November 1815. Deserted in Grenada 11 March 1816. 300 lashes for 'Absenting himself 5 months without leave', 26 September 1816; 'Loosing or making off with a shirt', 24 December 1816. Discharged Quebec. It is not known which Fleming received 300 lashes for being 'Drunk on Guard', 17 February 1817.

Fletcher, Joseph. Cabinet maker of Derby. Royal Artillery. Marched from Derby and confined aboard PS, 4 September 1813. Joined YCs as corporal, 1 February 1814. Promoted sergeant 25 February 1814. Reduced 1 May 1814. Arrived in the WIs 14 December 1814. Died Barbados, 24 May 1815.

Fletcher, William. Labourer of Barton, Nottinghamshire or Somerset. 4th Dragoon Guards. Marched from Chester and confined aboard PS, 3 March 1815. Joined YCs 29 June 1815, and arrived in the WIs 5 November 1815. Died, 22 October 1816.

Flinn/Flynn, Edward. Labourer of Dublin. 36th Foot. Marched from Chester and confined aboard PS as Edward Flynn, 26 September 1813. Joined YCs as Edward Flinn, 1 February 1814. Remained sick at Albany Barracks as the regiment left for the WIs. Arrived WIs 5 November 1815. Deserted in Jamaica 27 April 1819. Rejoined 6 May 1819. (No punishment records held.) Discharged Quebec as Edward Flinn.

Flinn/Flynn, Michael. Labourer of Louth. Joined YCs as Michael Flynn, 5 February 1814. Remained sick at Cork General Hospital as the regiment left for the WIs. Arrived in the WIs 5 November 1815. 300 lashes for 'Neglect of Duty on his Post', 28 April 1817. Deserted in Jamaica 27 April 1819. Rejoined 8 May 1819. (No punishment records held) Discharged Quebec as Michael Flinn.

Flinn/Flynn, Patrick. Labourer of Rosscommon. Either Royal Artillery marched from Savoy Military Prison, 11 May 1813, or 2nd Bn 69th Foot marched from Maidstone and confined aboard PS, 10 August 1813. Joined YCs 7 March 1814, and arrived in the WIs 14 December 1814. Died Jamaica, 3 September 1817.

Flinn/Flynn, Patrick. Weaver of Kildare. 101st Foot. Marched from Chester and confined aboard PS, 2 October 1813. Joined YCs 1 February 1814. Remained sick at Guernsey as the regiment left for the WIs. Arrived in the WIs 5 November 1815. Died Stony Hill, Jamaica, 17 September 1816.

Foley, Michael. 46th Foot. Sentenced at the Isle of Wight, to 'General Service' and transferred into the York Chasseurs, 25 March 1816. Arrived in the WIs 25 June 1816. Deserted, 21 July 1816. No record of rejoining.

Foley, Thomas. Sailor of America. 64th Foot. Marched from Preston and confined at Portchester Castle, 20 January 1817. Joined YCs 3 April 1817, and arrived in the WIs 25 May 1817. Deserted in Jamaica, 4 July 1817. No record of rejoining.

Folkett/Falkett, William. 23rd Light Dragoons. Marched from Chester and confined aboard PS, 8 December 1813. Joined YCs 1 February 1814, and arrived in the WIs 14 December 1814. 200 lashes for being 'Absent from Tattoo', 10 July 1815; 200 lashes for being 'Drunk and Insolent to Corporal Smith', 14 September 1815. Discharged Quebec.

Forbes, Alexander. Labourer of Middlesex. Either 10th Foot confined, 19 March 1815, or General Service/67th Foot, confined aboard PS, 19 March 1815. Joined YCs 29 June 1815, and arrived in the WIs 5 November 1815. Deserted in St Vincent 8 March 1816. Rejoined 14 May 1816. (No punishment records held.) Deserted at Tobago 19 July 1816. No record of rejoining.

Ford, Peter. Labourer of Kerry. 76th Foot. Marched from Fisherton and confined aboard PS, 26 February 1815. Joined YCs 29 June 1815, and arrived in the WIs 5 November 1815. Died, 28 September 1815.

Ford, Thomas. Papermaker of Middlesex. 2nd Bn 50th Foot. Marched from Lewes and confined aboard PS, 12 December 1813. Joined YCs 1 February 1814. Promoted corporal 25 June 1814. Reduced 25 December 1814. Arrived in the WIs 14 December 1814. Deserted 17 August 1816. Rejoined 12 October 1816. (No punishment records held.) Deserted in Jamaica 26 June 1817. Rejoined 10 July 1817. 300 lashes for being 'Absent without Leave', 25 July 1817. Promoted drummer March 1819. Deserted in Jamaica 11 June 1819. No record of rejoining.

Foster, Isaac. Shipwright of St Thomas's, Liverpool. 18th Light Dragoons. Marched from Brighton and confined aboard PS, 19 December 1813. Joined YCs 1 February 1814. Deserted while still at the Isle of Wight, 14 May 1814. No record of rejoining.

Foster, John. 21st Foot. Marched from Savoy Military Prison and confined aboard PS, 16 February 1814. Joined YCs 7 March 1814, and arrived in the WIs 14 December 1814. 300 lashes for being 'Drunk on Duty', 30 October 1817, 150 lashed remitted. Discharged Quebec.

Foster, John. Labourer of Derry. 48th Foot. Marched from Derby and confined at Portchester Castle, 20 January 1817. Joined YCs 3 April 1817, and arrived in the WIs 25 May 1817. Deserted in Jamaica 30 November 1817. Rejoined 12 February 1818. (No punishment records held.) Discharged Quebec.

Fowle, John. 57th Foot. Marched from Maidstone and confined aboard PS, 22 October 1813. Joined YCs 5 February 1814. Deserted while still at the Isle of Wight, 30 March 1814. Recaptured by George Cox (Forty Shillings Bounty). Rejoined 9 April 1814, following hospitalisation. (No punishment records held.) Arrived in the WIs 14 December 1814. Discharged Quebec.

Fowles/Folds, William. Royal Artillery. Marched from Chester and confined aboard PS as William Folds, 18 May 1815. Joined YCs 29 June 1815 and arrived in the WIs as William Fowles, 5 November 1815. Promoted corporal 25 June 1817. Reduced 10 October 1817. Died Jamaica, 20 December 1818.

Fox, Charles. Labourer of Exeter. 2nd Bn 14th Foot. Marched from Oxford and confined aboard PS, 22 November 1813. Joined YCs 29 June 1815, and arrived in the West Indies 5 November 1815. Died Jamaica, 23 November 1818.

Fox, Henry. 88th Foot. Marched from Chester and confined aboard PS, 25 May 1815. Joined YCs 29 June 1815. 'Left on Detachment' as the regiment departed for St Vincent. Discharged from Albany Barracks, 20 December 1816.

Fox, John. 47th Foot. Marched from Chester and confined aboard PS, 25 December 1815. Joined YCs 16 May 1816, and arrived in the WIs 29 June 1816. Deserted 29 July 1816. Rejoined 31 December 1816. (No punishment records held.) Discharged Quebec.

Frayney/Frieny, Michael. Labourer of Mayo. 2nd Bn 21st Foot. Marched from Bristol and confined aboard PS as Michael Frieny, 21 August 1813. Joined YCs 7 March 1814, and arrived in the WIs 14th December 1814. 'Died of Wounds at Guadeloupe' as Michael Frayney, 17 August 1815.

Frazer/Fraser, Alexander. Labourer of Mayo. 2nd Bn 18th Foot. Transported from

Jersey and confined aboard PS, 14 October 1814. Joined YCs 29 June 1815, and arrived in the WIs 5 November 1815. Promoted drummer 12 March 1817. Deserted in Jamaica 26 May 1819. No record of rejoining.

Frederic/Frederick, John. Tailor of Hanover. 3rd Bn 95th Foot. Marched from Hythe and confined aboard PS, 2 February 1816. Joined YCs 19 October 1816, and arrived in the WIs 21 December 1816. Deserted in Jamaica 13 July 1817. Rejoined 24 July 1817. 300 lashes for being 'Absent without Leave', 31 July 1817. Deserted in Jamaica 23 October 1817. Rejoined 25 October 1817. 300 lashes for being 'Absent without Leave', 30 October 1817. Deserted in Jamaica 8 July 1818. Rejoined 16 July 1818. (No punishment records held.) Deserted in Jamaica 31 March 1819. No record of rejoining.

Frier, Valantine or **Valentine**. Embarked Spithead amongst a 300-strong detachment of 'Unattached Deserters' joining the 2nd Foot, 25 April 1816. Arrived in the WIs 5 June 1816. Transferred into the York Chasseurs, 25 August 1816. Discharged Quebec.

Fulford, Thomas. 16th Foot. Marched from Haddington and confined PS, 25 August 1813. Joined YCs 7 March 1814, and arrived in the WIs 14 December 1814. Discharged Quebec.

Fuller, Joseph. 8th Bn Royal Artillery. Marched from Savoy Military Prison and confined aboard PS, 26 September 1813. Joined YCs 1 February 1814, and arrived in the WIs 14 December 1814. Discharged Quebec.

Gain, William. Labourer of Northumberland. Royal Artillery Driver. Marched from Maidstone and confined aboard PS, 24 December 1813. Joined YCs 5 February 1814. Deserted while still at Isle of Wight, 7 July 1814. Recaptured by Henry A Brook (Twenty Shillings Bounty). Confined at Newport Gaol, Isle of Wight, rejoined 22 July 1814. (No punishment record held.) Arrived in the WIs 14 December 1814. Died Jamaica, 3 November 1817.

Gallagher, John. Either from the Royal Artillery marched from Aberystwyth, 11 May 1814, or Royal Artillery transported from Ostende, 11 May 1815, 2nd Bn 3rd Foot marched from Savoy Military Prison, 7 August 1814, or Royals marched from Newcastle and confined aboard PS, 7 August 1814 . Joined YCs 29 June 1815, and arrived in the WIs 5 November 1815. Discharged Quebec.

Gallagher, Pheonix or **Peter.** Labourer of Sligo. 27th Foot. Marched from Chester and confined aboard PS as Peter Gallagher, 1 November 1813. Joined YCs as Pheonix Gallagher, 1 February 1814. Deserted while still at Isle of Wight 9 July 1814. Rejoined 17 July 1814. (No punishment record held.) Arrived in the WIs 14 December 1814. Gallagher recorded as with the regiment until December 1815, then no further mention.

Gallagher, Richard. Weaver of Longford. 2nd Bn 9th Foot. Marched from Glasgow and confined aboard PS, 14 November 1813. Joined YCs 1 February 1814. 'Killed by a fall on the Isle of Wight', 16 May 1814.

Galvin, Michael. Labourer of Tipperary. Joined 40th Foot, 9th September 1808. Present at Waterloo. Claimed soldier's privilege to commute punishment to 'Service Abroad' while encamped about half a mile outside the gates of Paris, in the grounds of Neuilly Park. (June–September 1815). Joined YCs 19 October 1816, and arrived in the WIs 21 December 1816. 150 lashes for 'Selling his Necessaries', 21 March 1817; 150 lashes for being 'Drunk & Absent from Parade', 28 April 1817. Deserted in Jamaica, 30 March 1819. Rejoined,1 April 1819. (No punishment records held.) Discharged Quebec.

Gardner/Gardiner, George. 33rd Foot. Marched from Hythe and confined aboard PS as George Jennings or George Gardner, 11 August 1813. Joined YCs 1 February 1814, as George Gardner, and arrived in the WIs 14 December 1814. Discharged Quebec as George Gardiner.

Garney, William. Labourer of Norfolk. 1st Bn 54th Foot. Marched from Wisbech and confined aboard PS, 9 April 1815. Date of joining not known. Deserted at Stokes Bay, Gosport, 4 July 1815. Recaptured and marched from Norwich to Portchester Castle 16 December 1816. No further record.

Garrathy/Garithy, Edward. Labourer of Clare. 2nd Bn 87th Foot. Transported from Gosport and confined aboard PS as Edward Garithy, 19 May 1816. Joined YCs 19 October 1816, and arrived in the WIs 21 December 1816. 300 lashes for being 'Absent from Tattoo and Striking Sergeant Dyson', 6 March 1817. Deserted in Jamaica 1 March 1819. Rejoined 7 March 1819. (No punishment records held) Discharged Quebec as Edward Garrathy.

Garrett, John. Framework knitter of Nottingham. 7th Hussars. Marched from Chelmsford and confined aboard PS, 1 August 1813. Joined YCs 1 February 1814, and arrived in the WIs 14 December 1814. Died, 22 October 1816.

Garrity, Martin. 27th Foot. Confined aboard PS, 5 September 1813. Joined YCs 1 February 1814. Remained sick at the Isle of Wight when the regiment left for WIs. Regiment notified by Mr Kirkland (Agent) of Garrity's desertion, June 1817. No further record.

Garry, Edward. Served with Royal Marines, 1 November 1806 to 11 September 1815. Volunteered for YCs at the Isle of Wight, 21 December 1815. Arrived in the WIs 25 June 1816. Discharged Quebec. Allocated Concession 11. Lot SW 13, Beckwith. No evidence found of him settling there.

Garvin, James. Either Royal Artillery, 8 July 1814, or 3rd Bn 14th Foot marched from St Albans and confined aboard PS, 7 October 1814. Joined YCs 29 June 1815, and arrived in the WIs 5 November 1815. Discharged Quebec, 24 September 1819. Possibly returned to England at public expense.

Gee, Robert. Received into YCs from 1st Bn Royal Scots, June 1814. Probably as 'condemned' rather than 'volunteer'. Arrived in the WIs 14 December 1814. Promoted corporal 16 March 1816, sergeant 30 May 1816. Reduced 14 March 1818. Discharged Quebec.

Gehagan, James. 17th Light Dragoons. Marched from Chester and confined aboard PS, 8 December 1813. Joined YCs 1 February 1814. Sick at Cork's General Hospital as the regiment left for WIs. Regiment notified by Mr Kirkland (Agent) of Gehagan's desertion, June 1817. No further record.

George, Thomas. Collier of Monmouth. 2nd Bn Foot Guards. Marched from Aylesbury and confined aboard PS, 2 August 1813. Joined YCs 1 February 1814. Deserted while still at Isle of Wight, 4 July 1814. No record of rejoining.

Getties/Gettis, James. Labourer of Bridgenorth, Shropshire. 69th Foot. Marched from Warwick and confined aboard PS, 6 December 1814. Joined YCs 29 June 1814, and arrived in the WIs 5 November 1815. 'Private Charles Rogers sentenced to 200 lashes for 'Selling a shirt not his Own and Gettis received the same for Purchasing the Above shirt', 14 February 1817. Died Jamaica, 24 May 1819.

Gilchrist, Peter. Recorded as 1st Bn Guards when marched from Savoy Military Prison and confined aboard PS, 27 November 1814. Joined YCs 29 June 1815, as 1st Bn 58th Foot. Arrived in the WIs 5 November 1815. Discharged Quebec.

Gillespie, George. 2nd Bn 28th Foot. Marched from Pendenis Castle and confined aboard PS, 5 September 1814. Joined YCs 29 June 1815, and arrived in the WIs as drummer, 5 November 1815. Discharged Quebec.

Gilmore, John. Labourer of Dublin. 37th Foot. Marched from Bristol and confined at Portchester Castle, 23 December 1816. Joined YCs 3 April 1817, and arrived in the WIs 25 May 1817. Deserted in Jamaica, 5 June 1818. No record of rejoining.

Gilray, William or **Robert.** Agent informed regiment in Jamaica of William Gilray's Isle of Wight voluntary enlistment, September–December 1817. Remained in Europe and discharged as Robert Gilray, December 1817–March 1818.

Gilroy, Bernard. 1st Bn 52nd Foot. Marched from St Albans and confined aboard PS, 11 December 1814. Joined YCs 29 June 1815. Deserted from Portsmouth's Fort Cumberland, 31 August 1815. No record of rejoining.

Gilroy, Bernard. Possible Royal Scots volunteer. Embarked Isle of Wight for Guernsey, 1 January 1816. No further record.

Gingley, Dennis. 2nd Bn 47th Foot. Marched from Savoy Military Prison and confined aboard PS, 14 April 1813. Joined YCs 1 February 1814, and arrived in the WIs 14 December 1814. 200 lashes for 'Having in his possession a Knife belonging to the Officers Mess', 7 June 1815, commuted to 10 days solitary confinement. Discharged Quebec. Allocated Concession 10. Lot 11. Beckwith. 'Sold to Duncan Campbell for £25, 4th October 1827'.

Gladden/Gladdon, Samuel. Labourer of Harlow. 2nd Bn 44th Foot. Marched from Chelmsford and confined aboard PS, 23 November 1814. Joined YCs 29 June 1815, and arrived in the WIs 5 November 1815. Deserted in Jamaica 13 May 1819. Rejoined the same day. (No punishment records held.) Discharged Quebec.

Gladden, William. Tailor of Stafford. 31st Foot. Transported from Genoa and confined aboard PS, 22 November 1815. Joined YCs 17 May 1816, and arrived in the WIs 25 June 1816. Deserted 1 August 1816. Rejoined 25 January 1817. 300 lashes for 'Absenting himself six months Without Leave', 29 January 1817. Died Jamaica, 8 September 1817.

Gleeson, Daniel. Carpenter of Somerset. 83rd Foot. Marched From Chester and confined aboard PS, 10 September 1815. Embarked Spithead amongst a 300-strong detachment of 'Unattached Deserters' joining the 2nd Foot, 25 April 1816. Arrived in the WIs 5 June 1816. Transferred into the York Chasseurs, 25 August 1816. Promoted corporal 17 November 1816. 200 lashes and ordered to be reduced for 'Drunk on Guard', 24 December 1816. Deserted in Jamaica 23 March 1817. Rejoined 30 March 1817. 300 lashes for 'Absenting himself without Leave', 12 April 1817. 300 lashes 'On suspicion of Theft', 28 April 1817. Deserted in Jamaica, 2 February 1819. Rejoined the next day. No further record.

Gleeson, John. Labourer of Lancashire. 44th Foot. Marched from Chester and confined aboard PS, 27 April 1815. Joined YCs 29 June 1815, and arrived in the WIs 5 November 1815. Deserted at Tobago, 4 May 1816. No record of rejoining.

Glenn/Glinn, James. Cabinet maker of Middlesex. Royal Artillery. Marched from Maidstone and confined aboard PS, 19 March 1813. Joined YCs 5 February 1814, and arrived in the WIs 14 December 1814. 14 days solitary confinement for 'Making away with his Necessaries', 15 May 1815, 11 days remitted. Died, 14 November 1816.

Glossop, John. Labourer of Woodham, Essex. Pay and muster lists for 'Unattached Deserters' records Glossop as being of the 69th Foot, yet no record in either 1st or 2nd Battalions. Marched from Eye and confined aboard prison ships, 24 September 1813. Joined YCs 7 March 1814. Deserted while still at the Isle of Wight, 10 July 1814. Rejoined 20 July 1814. (No punishment record held.) Arrived in the West Indies 14 December 1814. Early 1816 at Guadeloupe, Glossop confessed to murder in Suffolk, 1812, and, along with Fanning on passage back to England, confession investigated by Suffolk magistrate, Mr Carthew. His conclusion, 'that the Story is considered as a fabrication and leading to the conclusion that the confession was some desperate contrivance in getting removed from the West Indies'. Ordered back to the West Indies by the Commander in Chief, Glossop rejoined in Jamaica, 19 December 1816. Deserted in Jamaica 4 January 1818. No date of rejoining. Deserted in Jamaica 9 March 1818. No date of rejoining. Deserted in Jamaica 18 April 1818. Rejoined 27 April 1818. Deserted in Jamaica 29 August 1818. Rejoined 23 October 1818. (No punishment records held.) Deserted in Jamaica 27 January 1819. Returned to England, recaptured and confined at Dartford, Kent, 16 April 1819, before 'Ordered to be sent to Portchester Castle for the purpose of being attached to a Corps serving in the West Indies'. No subsequent record of Glossop at Portchester Castle.

Glover, Soloman. Labourer of Worcestershire. 4th Dragoons. Marched from Gloucester and confined aboard PS, 1 May 1815. Joined YCs 29 June 1815, and arrived in the WIs 5 November 1815. Deserted in Jamaica 28 February 1817. No record of rejoining.

Golding/Goulding, John. 9th Bn Royal Artillery. Marched from Dartford and confined aboard PS as John Golding, 6 March 1814. Joined YCs 25 March 1814, and arrived in the WIs 14 December 1814. Died Guadeloupe as John Goulding, 10 August 1815. 'One of Seven rank and file supposed to have been poisoned'.

Golinkowitze, Joseph. Varnisher of Cracow, Poland. Transferred to YCs from 6th Bn 60th Foot in Jamaica, 25 May 1817. Deserted in Jamaica 6 May 1818. Rejoined 9 May 1818. Deserted in Jamaica 25 September 1818. Rejoined 3 February 1819. No further record.

Goodall, Richard. Royal Artillery. Marched from Wolverhampton and confined aboard PS, 2 February 1815. Joined YCs 29 June 1815, and arrived in the WIs 5 November 1815. Discharged Quebec.

Goodfellow, Andrew. Royal Horse Artillery. Marched from Savoy Military Prison and confined aboard PS, 17 September 1813. Joined YCs 1 February 1814, and arrived in the WIs 14 December 1814. Discharged Quebec.

Goodwin, Thomas. Joiner of Boston. Royal Artillery. Marched from Peterborough and confined aboard PS, 18 February 1815. Joined YCs 29 June 1815, and arrived in the WIs 5 November 1815. Deserted in Jamaica, 17 June 1819. No record of rejoining.

Gordon, John. 1st Bn 20th Foot. Marched from Exeter and confined aboard PS, 9 August 1814. Joined YCs 29 June 1915, and arrived in the WIs 5 November 1815. Promoted corporal 17 March 1816, sergeant, 25 March 1816. Reduced October 1816. Promoted corporal 10 May 1818. Reduced 1 December 1818. Discharged Quebec.

Gordon, Thomas. Shoemaker of St Ann's, Lancashire. 48th Foot. Marched from Nottingham and confined aboard PS as Thomas Jackson or Thomas Gordon, 7 October 1813. Joined YCs as Thomas Gordon, 1 February 1814. Deserted while still at the Isle of Wight, 22 September 1814. No record of rejoining.

Gould, Thomas. Blacksmith of Carrington, Bedfordshire. 30th Foot. Marched from Wisbech and confined aboard PS, date unknown. Joined YCs 29 June 1815, and arrived in the WIs 5 November 1815. Deserted in Tobago 10 August 1816. Rejoined December 1816. (No punishment records held.) Deserted in Jamaica 11 May 1818. No record of rejoining. It is not known which Gould received 200 lashes for 'Making or attempting to strike Sergeant William Anderson', 21 December 1816.

Gould, William. Watchmaker of Winchfield, Hampshire. Joined Royal Horse Guards, 13 March 1807. Marched from Windsor and confined aboard PS, 8 November 1813. Joined YCs 29 June 1815, and arrived in the WIs 5 November 1815. Died Jamaica, 26 September 1817. It is not known which Gould received 200 lashes for 'Making or attempting to strike Sergeant William Anderson', 21 December 1816.

Goulding, Ambrose. Nailor of Cheshire. Joined 4th Dragoons, 30 January 1805. Marched from Chester and confined aboard, PS 3 March 1815. Joined YCs 29 June 1815, and arrived in the WIs 5 November 1815. Died on passage to Quebec, 7 July 1819.

Goulding, Robert. Labourer of Antrim. Royal Artillery. Marched from Savoy Military Prison and confined aboard PS, 7 December 1813. Joined YCs 1 February 1814, and arrived in the WIs 14 December 1814. Promoted corporal 25 February 1814. 200 lashes and ordered to be reduced for being 'Drunk on Guard', 25 October 1816, corporal punishment remitted 'Due to his previous Good Character'. Promoted corporal 9 December 1817. Reduced 4 March 1819. Discharged from Stony Hill Barracks, Jamaica, 10 June 1819.

Gowan/Gowing, John. Labourer of York. 1st Life Guards. Marched from Savoy Military Prison and confined aboard PS as John Gowing, 27 October 1814. Joined YCs as John Gowan, 29 June 1815. Arrived in the WIs 5 November 1815. Died Jamaica,15 September 1818.

Gradwell, John. Framework knitter of Argyle. Royal Artillery Driver. Marched from Glasgow and confined aboard PS, 19 September 1813. Joined YCs 7 March 1814, and arrived in the WIs14 December 1814. Deserted in Jamaica 29 April 1819. Rejoined 6 May 1819. (No punishment records held.) Discharged Quebec.

Grady, Peter or **Michael.** 28th Foot. Marched from Chester and confined aboard PS as Peter Brady or Grady, 27 April 1814. Joined YCs as Peter Grady, 29 June 1815, and arrived in the WIs 14 December 1815. Discharged Quebec. Census Returns (1822). Bathurst Township, Lanark County. Lot 14. Michael Grady, ex-York Chasseurs, wife Ann and infant daughter.

Graham, Robert. 9th Light Dragoons. Marched from Savoy Military Prison and confined aboard PS, 24 December 1813. Joined YCs 5 February 1814, and arrived in the WIs 14 December 1814. Promoted corporal 25 March 1814. Reduced August 1814. Promoted corporal September 1814. Reduced for 'Drunk on passage at Bridge Town, Barbados', 1 April 1815. 14 days solitary confinement for 'Drunk on Piquet', 10 April 1814, 8 days remitted. Discharged Quebec.

Graham, Thomas. 68th Foot. Marched from Carlisle and confined aboard PS, 25 June 1815. Joined YCs 29 June 1815, and arrived in the WIs 5 November 1815. Discharged Quebec.

Grant, Thomas. 12th Foot. Marched from Chester and confined aboard PS, 16 August 1815. Joined YCs 29 June 1815. Remained on the Isle of Wight as regiment left for St Vincent. Transferred to the Royal African Corps, 1817.

Gray, John. Hairdresser of Stockport. 76th Foot. Marched from St Albans and confined aboard PS, 8 September 1813. Joined YCs 5 February 1814, and arrived in the WIs 14 December 1814. Died Grenada, 30 November 1815.

Gray/Grey, William. Waiter of London. 73rd Foot. Marched from Savoy Military Prison and confined aboard PS, 26 December 1813. Joined YCs 7 March 1814, and arrived in the WIs 14 December 1814. Died, 11 October 1816. Willed his effects, eleven shillings and ten pence to his wife Mary, the Kings Arms, Horsley Down.

Green, John. Hatter of Wicklow. 16th Foot. Marched from Salford and confined aboard PS, 23 January 1814. Joined YCs 25 March 1814. Left sick at the Isle of Wight as the regiment left for WIs. Arrived in the WIs 8 May 1815. Died St Vincent, 7 November 1815.

Green, Silus. Labourer of Bath. 63rd Foot. Marched from Newport Gaol, Isle of Wight, and confined aboard PS, 1 February 1815. Joined YCs 17 May 1816, and arrived in the WIs 25 June 1816. 150 lashes for being 'Drunk and Absent from Evening Parade', 26 December 1816; 200 lashes for 'Making Away with Articles of his Necessaries', 7 January 1817; 14 days solitary confinement for 'Selling his Regimental Necessaries', 30 January 1818. Died on passage to Quebec, 27 July 1819.

Green, Thomas. Labourer of Birmingham. 1st Foot Guards. Marched from Savoy Military Prison and confined aboard PS, 3 March 1815. Joined YCs 29 June 1815, and arrived in the WIs 5 November 1815. Died Grenada, 2 December 1815.

Greville/Grenville/Gravell, John. Labourer of Limerick. King's County Militia. Marched from Chester as John Grenville and confined aboard PS , 25 May 1815. Joined YCs 29 June 1815, and arrived in the WIs 5 November 1815. Deserted 26 December 1816. Rejoined 14 January 1817. 300 lashes for 'Absenting himself two weeks without leave'; 300 lashes for 'Offering a pair of Shoes for Sale', 17 February 1817. Deserted in Jamaica as John Gravell, 26 June 1817. No record of rejoining.

Greyson, William. Painter of York. Joined 2nd Bn 95th Foot in Spain 10 January 1810. Returned to Shorncliffe Barracks, late 1812, as sergeant. Court-martialled for 'Conduct tending to produce insubordination in the Regiment'. Ordered to be reduced and sentenced to 250 lashes, 21 November 1813. Allowed to commute his corporal punishment to that of 'Foreign Service'. Marched from Shorncliffe and confined aboard PS, 19 December 1813. Joined YCs as schoolmaster sergeant, 1 February 1814, and arrived in the WIs 14 December 1814. Reduced 24 February 1816. Died Jamaica, 12 November 1817.

Griffin, John. Labourer of St Johns, America. Transferred to YCs from 1st European Garrison in Jamaica as sergeant, 25 May 1817. Reduced 3 August 1817. Died Jamaica, 22 June 1818.

Griffiths, James. 23rd Foot. Transported from France and confined aboard PS, 16 July 1816. Joined YCs 19 October 1816, and arrived in the WIs 21 December 1816. Discharged Quebec. It is not known which Griffiths received 300 lashes for being 'Drunk on Guard', 17 February 1817.

Griffiths, Robert. 92nd Foot. Marched from Bristol and confined aboard PS, 28 May 1815. Joined YCs 29 June 1815, and arrived in the WIs 5 November 1815. Discharged Quebec. It is not known which Griffiths received 300 lashes for being 'Drunk on Guard', 17 February 1817.

Griffiths, Robert. Weaver of Middlesex. 2nd Bn 83rd Foot. Marched from Chelmsford and confined aboard, PS 29 September 1813. Joined YCs 7 March 1813. Deserted while still at the Isle of Wight, 7 July 1814. No record of rejoining.

Griffiths, Thomas. Royal Artillery driver. Marched from Dartford and confined aboard PS, 31 October 1813. Joined YCs 5 February 1814, and arrived in the WIs 14 December 1814. Discharged Quebec. It is not known which Griffiths received 300 lashes for being 'Drunk on Guard', 17 February 1817.

Griffiths, William. Either 2nd Bn 50th Foot marched from Hastings, 6 December 1814, or 'General Service' transported from Hilsea, Portsmouth, and confined aboard PS, 6 December 1814. Joined YCs 29 June 1815, and arrived in the WIs 5 November 1815. Promoted corporal 5 January 1817. Reduced 9 May 1818. Discharged Quebec.

Griffiths, William. Marched from 36th Foot Depot and confined aboard PS, 15 October 1815. Joined YCs 19 October 1816, and arrived in the WIs 21 December 1816. 14 days Solitary Confinement for 'Drunk & Riotous in Barracks', 30 January 1818. Discharged Quebec. It is not known which Griffiths received 300 lashes for being 'Drunk on Guard', 17 February 1817.

Grindwick/Grindrick, Timothy. 23rd Dragoons. Marched from Wakefield and confined aboard PS as Timothy Grindrick, 13 March 1814. Joined YCs as Timothy Grindwick, 25 March 1814, and arrived in the WIs 14 December 1814. Discharged Quebec. Allocated Concession 9. Lot SW 8. Bathurst, as Timothy Grindrick. No evidence of him settling there.

Groves, John. Tailor of Dublin. 6th Dragoons. Marched from Chester Castle and confined aboard PS, 5 February 1814. Joined YCs 7 March 1814, and arrived in the WIs 14 December 1814. Deserted, 15 February 1816. No record of rejoining.

Guest, John. Labourer of Warwick. 2nd Bn 24th Foot. Marched from Coventry and confined aboard PS, 25 February 1815. Joined YCs 29 June 1815. Deserted from Portsmouth's Fort Cumberland, 12 August 1815. Rejoined 23 August 1815. (No punishment records held.) Ordered 'To be confined on board the Prison-ship as opposed to Fort Cumberland, which offers better security until an opportunity occurs for him being embarked for Foreign Service'. Arrived in the WIs 5 November 1815. Died Jamaica, 6 December 1817.

Gurley, Henry. With Mr Charles Willis 'taken on the strength of the regiment as Volunteers in Jamaica from 25th May 1816'. Recorded as being 'Absent without Leave' from St Vincent, September 1816. No record of rejoining.

Gwilliams, Henry. Blacksmith of Gloucestershire. Joined 1st Dragoon Guards, 25 September 1804. Marched from Bristol and confined aboard PS, 1 November 1814. Joined YCs 29 June 1815 and arrived in the WIs 5 November 1815. Discharged from Stony Hill, Jamaica, 10 June 1819.

Hackett, Maurice or **Morris.** Sadler of Tipperary. 95th Foot. Marched from Dover and confined aboard PS, 15 November 1814. Joined YCs 29 June 1815, and arrived in the WIs 5 November 1815. 200 lashes for 'Having a pair of trowsers not his own and resisting Corporal and File of the Guard in the execution of their Duty', 27 December 1817. Deserted in Jamaica 2 March 1818. Rejoined 5 March 1818. Deserted in Jamaica 3 March 1819. Rejoined the next day. (No punishment records held.) Deserted in Jamaica 10 April 1819. No record of rejoining.

Hacking, John. Weaver of Lancashire. 3rd Bn Royal Artillery. Sentenced at Woolwich to 'General Service Abroad for Desertion', 28 June 1813. Marched from Woolwich and confined aboard PS, 31 July 1813. Joined YCs 1 February 1814. Deserted while still at the Isle of Wight, 9 July 1814. Taken the next day and rejoined 22 July 1814. (No punishment records held.) Arrived in the WIs 14 December 1814. Discharged Quebec.

Hagerman/Hageman, Christopher. From Tenby. Transferred to YCs from 6th Bn 60th Foot in Jamaica , 25 May 1817. Died Jamaica, 30 December 1817.

Haley/Holley/Holly, Joseph. 5th Foot. Marched from Taunton and confined aboard PS, 7 November 1812. Joined YCs as Joseph Haley, 25 March 1814, but arrived in the WIs as Joseph Holly or Holley, 14 December 1814. Deserted in Tobago 16 August 1816. Rejoined 23 August 1816. (No punishment record held.) 150 lashes for being 'Drunk & Absent from Evening Parade', 10 February 1817. Punishment remitted. Discharged as Joseph Holly or Haley at Quebec.

Hall, John. Tailor of Staffordshire. 103rd Foot. Marched from Winchester and confined aboard PS, 15 February 1814. Joined YCs 7 March 1814. Deserted while still at the Isle of Wight, 7 July 1814. Rejoined 20 July 1814. (No punishment record held.) Arrived in the WIs 14 December 1814. Discharged Quebec.

Hall, Myles or **Miles.** Labourer of Dublin. 16th Dragoons. Marched from Chester and confined at Portchester Castle as Myles Hall, 7 December 1816. Joined YCs 3 April 1817, and arrived in the WIs 25 May 1817. Deserted in Jamaica 28 June 1818. Rejoined 6 July 1818. (No punishment record held.) Discharged as Miles Hall at Quebec.

Hallings, Thomas. From Holland. Transferred to YCs from 6th Bn 60th Foot in Jamaica, 25 May 1817. Died on passage to Quebec, 27 July 1819.

Halton. Samuel. Joiner of Sutton, Warwickshire. 84th Foot. Marched from Dartford and confined aboard PS, 3 October 1813. Joined YCs 1 February 1814. Deserted while still at the Isle of Wight, 29 April 1814. No record of rejoining.

Hamilton, George. Carpenter of Dungannon or labourer of Tyrone. Transferred from 6th Bn 60th Foot in Jamaica, 25 May 1817. Deserted in Jamaica 19th June 1817. Rejoined 25 June 1817. 300 lashes for being 'Absent without Leave'. Deserted in Jamaica 16 August 1817. Rejoined 24 September. 1817. 300 lashes for being 'Absent without Leave'; 300 lashes for 'Theft', 2 October 1817. Deserted in Jamaica 2 December 1817. Rejoined 9 December 1817. 300 lashes for being 'Absent without Leave', 15 December 1817. Deserted in Jamaica 4 September 1818. Rejoined 7 September 1818. (No punishment records held.) Deserted in Jamaica 13 February 1819. Rejoined 15 February 1819. (No punishment record held.) Deserted in Jamaica 2 March 1819. Rejoined 19 March 1819. (No punishment records held.) Discharged Quebec.

Hamilton, Thomas. 16th Foot. Marched from Edinburgh and confined aboard PS, 17 August 1813. Joined YCs 1 February 1814, and arrived in the WIs 14 December 1814. Died Barbados, 20 February 1815.

Hamilton, William. Weaver of Armagh. Royals. Marched from Marlborough and confined aboard PS, 8 October 1813. Joined YCs 7 March 1814. Deserted while still at the Isle of Wight, 5 July 1814. No record of rejoining.

Hamilton, William. Weaver of Dumfries. Royal Artillery. Marched from Dumfries and confined aboard PS, 24 December 1813. Joined YCs 5 February 1814. Did not arrive in the WIs until 5 November 1815. Died Jamaica, 25 January 1817.

Hammersly/Hammersley, John. 83rd Foot, Marched from Warwick and confined aboard PS, 9 January 1814. Joined YCs 7 March 1814, and arrived in the WIs 14 December 1814. Discharged Quebec.

Hamrough, James. 66th Foot. Marched from Chester and confined aboard PS, 14 November 1813. Joined YCs 5 February 1814, and arrived in the WIs 14 December 1814. Discharged Quebec.

Handley/Hanley, Joseph. 2nd Bn 38th Foot. Marched from Coventry and confined aboard PS as Joseph Hanley, 17 June 1813. Joined YCs 1 February 1814, and arrived in the WIs 14 December 1814. Discharged as Joseph Handley at Quebec.

Hannigan/Hannington, Robert. Weaver of Lanark. 8th Foot. Marched from St Albans and confined aboard PS, 25 September 1813. Joined YCs as Robert Hannington, 1 February 1814. Arrived in the WIs 14 December 1814. Died as Robert Hannigan, 15 November 1816.

Harding, John. Labourer of Somerset. 1st Bn 9th Foot. Marched from Savoy Military Prison and confined aboard PS, 10 October 1814. Joined YCs 29 June 1815, and arrived in the WIs 5 November 1815. Died Tobago, 11 July 1816.

Harper, Daniel. Cutler of Warwick. 32nd Foot. Marched from Winchester and confined aboard PS, 4 March 1815. Joined YCs 29 June 1815, and arrived in the WIs 5 November 1815. Died Jamaica, 17 July 1818.

Harris, Thomas. Woolcomber of Leicestershire. 33rd Foot. Marched from Derby and confined aboard PS, 24 October 1813. Joined YCs 5 February 1814. Deserted while still at the Isle of Wight, 4 July 1814. No record of rejoining.

Harrison, John. 2nd Bn 2nd Foot Guards. Marched from Maidstone and confined aboard PS, 16 May 1813. Joined YCs 7 March 1814, and arrived in the WIs 14 December 1814. Discharged Quebec.

Harrison, John. Cordwainer of Whitby. 1st Bn 3rd Foot Guards. Marched from Tower of London and confined aboard PS, 8 November 1814. Joined YCs 29 June 1815, and arrived in the WIs 5 November 1815. Deserted in Jamaica, 28 April 1819. No record of rejoining.

Harrison, William. Labourer of Lancashire. 23rd Foot. Marched from Chester and confined aboard PS, 4 August 1814. Joined YCs 29 June 1815, and arrived in the WIs 5 November 1815. Died Jamaica, 3 April 1818.

Hart, John. Labourer of Roscommon. 88th Foot. Marched from Chester and confined aboard PS, 25 May 1814. Joined YCs 29 June 1815, and arrived in the WIs 5 November 1815. Died Jamaica, 18 October 1818.

Hart, William. Labourer of Gloucestershire. Either 2nd Foot Guards marched from Gloucester, 2 February 1814, or 29th Foot marched from Maidstone and confined aboard PS, 6 March 1814. Joined YCs 25 March 1814. Promoted corporal 25 April 1814. Reduced, date unknown. Arrived in the WIs 14 December 1814. 300 lashes for 'Absenting himself from Piquet and remaining out of Barracks all Night', 10 April 1815, 150 lashes remitted. Died St Vincent, 17 September 1815.

Hartigan, James. Weaver of Waterford. 102nd Foot. Marched from Bristol and confined aboard PS, 14 March 1814. Joined YCs 25 March 1814. Deserted while still at the Isle of Wight, 7 July 1814. No record of rejoining.

Hartley, John. Cotton Weaver of Lancashire. 76th Foot. Marched from Bristol and confined aboard PS, 5 June 1813. Joined YCs 29 June 1815, and arrived in the WIs 5 November 1815. Died Jamaica, 13 June 1817.

Hartley, Samuel. Weaver of Yorkshire. 33rd Foot. Marched from Wakefield and confined aboard PS, 22 October 1813. Joined YCs 1 February 1814, and arrived in the WIs 14 December 1814. Died Jamaica, 19 February 1817.

Hartshorn, John. Schoolmaster of Warwickshire. Sergeant volunteer, 2nd Bn 89th Foot. Marched from Windsor to Isle of Wight, 6 May 1815. Arrived in the WIs 5 November 1815. Reduced for 'Unsoldierlike Conduct', 27 April 1817. Promoted corporal 4 October 1817. 300 lashes and reduced for 'Unsoldierlike conduct being repeatedly drunk whilst Hospital Steward', 10 December 1817, corporal punishment remitted. Discharged from Stony Hill Barracks, Jamaica, 10 June 1819.

Hartshorn, William. Two years with 14th before enlisting for the 32nd, 24 April 1807. Marched from Bristol and confined aboard PS, 26 March 1815. Joined YCs 29 June 1815, and arrived in the WIs 5 November 1815. Promoted corporal 7 October 1816, sergeant 14 December 1816. Reduced for 'Drunk and Absent from Parade', 28 April 1817. Discharged Quebec.

Haswell, William. From Yorkshire. 48th Foot. Marched from Southwall and confined aboard PS, 16 October 1814. Joined YCs 29 June 1815, and arrived in the WIs 5 November 1815. Promoted drummer 11 May 1816. Reduced 24 May 1816. Transferred to 58th Regiment in Jamaica, March 1819.

Hawkins, John. Labourer of Hertford. 3rd Foot Guards. Transported from France and marched from Canterbury and confined aboard PS, 12 December 1815. Joined YCs 15 May 1816, and arrived in the WIs 25 June 1816. Died, 5 December 1816.

Hawkins, Thomas. Joined 89th Foot, 7 January 1809. Transferred from Regimental Depot and confined aboard PS, 12 May 1815. Joined YCs 29 June 1815, and arrived in the WIs 5 November 1815. Sentenced to solitary confinement in the Windward Command, September 1816. Discharged Quebec.

Hay, Andrew. 2nd Bn 92nd Foot. Marched from Ayr and confined aboard PS, 24 October 1813. Joined YCs 5 February 1814. Deserted while still at the Isle of Wight, June 1814. Rejoined and hospitalised. (No date of return or knowledge of punishment received). Arrived in the WIs 14 December 1814. Promoted corporal 25 April 1815. Reduced 2 October 1815. Sentenced at St Vincent 'To be Shot for Mutinous Conduct', 5 June 1816. Commuted to solitary confinement on board the flag ship at Port Royal, Jamaica. In company with William James, Michael Low and Robert Farnley, transported from Jamaica and confined at Portchester Castle to await further disposal, 25 May 1817. No further record.

Hay, Owen. Labourer of Monaghan. 73rd Foot. Marched from Savoy Military Prison and confined aboard PS, 23 December 1813. Joined YCs 1 February 1814. Deserted while still at the Isle of Wight, 7 July 1814. Recaptured by Henry A Brook, 13 July 1814 (Twenty Shillings Bounty). Rejoined 22 July 1814. (No punishment record held.) Died Jamaica, 12 March 1817.

Hay, Robert. 25th Foot. Marched from Tilbury Foot and confined aboard PS, 13 March 1816. Joined YCs 3 April 1817, and arrived in the WIs 25 May 1817. Discharged Quebec.

Hay/Hays/Hayes, Thomas. 88th Foot. Marched from Bristol and confined aboard PS, 28 October 1815. Joined YCs 16 May 1816, and arrived in the WIs 25 June 1816. Discharged Quebec. *Census of Household Heads and Count of Family Members, Beckwith Township*, complied by Duncan Campbell, Town Clerk, 4 June 1820, records Thomas Hays, ex-York Chasseur, and wife. Concession 10. Lot 9NE.

Haydon, Richard. Labourer of Limerick, Queen's County. 97th Foot. Marched from Bristol and confined aboard PS as Richard Haydon or Hodgins, 29 September 1813. Joined YCs as Richard Haydon, 1 February 1814, and arrived in the WIs 14 December 1814. Deserted in Jamaica 11 April 1819. Returned to England, recaptured and confined at Savoy Military Prison, 23 August 1819. Discharged to 2nd Foot, 22 December 1819. Transferred to 35th Foot, 25 March 1821. Discharged to a pension, 23 October 1834. 'Suffering from General Disability, Scars on the skin from Frequent Ulceration rendering him permanently inefficient'. The Principle Medical Officer of the Dublin Medical Board considered him unfit for further military service 'due his Asthma and associated Pulmonary Attacks'.

Hayfield, William. Labourer of Warwick. 2nd Bn 55th Foot. Marched from Warwick and confined aboard, PS 29 November 1814. Joined YCs 29 June 1815, and arrived in the WIs 5 November 1815. Died Jamaica, 6 September 1817.

Hayman/Haymen, Richard. Labourer of Devon. 2nd Bn 2nd Foot Guards. Marched from Exeter and confined aboard PS, 29 July 1813. Joined YCs 1 February 1814. Deserted while still at the Isle of Wight, 25 June 1814. No record of rejoining.

Haywood, Joseph. Labourer of Ellington. 54th Foot. Transported from Foveaux and confined aboard PS, 8 November 1813. Joined YCs 29 June 1815, and arrived in the WIs 5 November 1815. Deserted 11 October 1816. Rejoined the next day. 800 lashes for 'Desertion', 21 October 1816. Died Jamaica, 9 October 1817.

Hazledine, Joseph. General Service Recruit. Transferred to YCs from 63rd Depot and confined aboard PS, 6 November 1813. Joined YCs 5 February 1814, and arrived in the WIs 14 December 1814. 30 days solitary confinement for 'Taking Rum into the Naval Guard at Barbados', 17 April 1815, 20 days remitted. Discharged Quebec. Allocated Concession 10. Lot NE 13 Bathurst. No evidence found of him settling there.

Healey, Bartley or **Bartholomew.** Labourer of Roscommon. 84th Foot. Marched from Chester and confined aboard PS, 2 October 1813. Joined YCs as Bartley Healey, 5 February 1814, and arrived in the WIs 14 December 1814. Promoted corporal as Bartholomew Healey, 25 March 1814. Reduced 25 May 1814. Promoted corporal 18 October 1815. Reduced 31 May 1816. Promoted corporal 18 June 1816. Reduced 17 July 1816. Promoted corporal 29 September 1817. Reduced 17 December 1817. Deserted in Jamaica 1 August 1818. Rejoined 3 August 1818. (No punishment record held.) Deserted in Jamaica as Bartholomew Healey, 9 May 1819. No record of rejoining.

Healey/Healy, John. Cloth or leather stainer of Limerick. 83rd Foot. Marched from Chester and confined aboard PS, 19 July 1815. Joined YCs 29 June 1815. Promoted sergeant and remained at Regimental Depot until reduced, 2 October 1816. Arrived in the WIs 21 December 1816, and promoted corporal. Deserted 4 July 1817. Rejoined 27 July 1817 as private. (No punishment record held.) Promoted corporal 20 April 1818. Reduced 26 January 1819. Deserted in Jamaica, 9 February 1819. No record of rejoining.

Heals, John. Joined YCs 19 October 1816, and arrived in the WIs 21 December 1816. Deserted in Jamaica 29 March 1817. Rejoined 18 April 1817. 800 lashes for being 'Absent without Leave', 23 April 1817. Discharged Quebec.

Heath, John. 19th Light Dragoons. Marched from Andover and confined aboard PS, 29 September 1813. Joined YCs 5 February 1814, and arrived in the WIs 14 December 1814. Discharged Quebec.

Heaveran/Haffern, John. Carpenter of Antrim. Royal Artillery. Marched from

Woolwich and confined aboard PS as John Haffern or Heaveran, 20 February 1814. Joined as John Heaveran, 25 March 1814. Deserted while still at the Isle of Wight, 7 July 1814. No record of rejoining.

Henderson, Henry. Weaver of Tyrone. 9th Bn Royal Artillery. Sentenced at Woolwich to General Service for 'Desertion', 23 September 1813. Marched from Woolwich and confined aboard, PS 10 October 1813. Joined YCs 5 February 1814, and arrived in the WIs 14 December 1814. 'Killed in action at Guadeloupe', 9 August 1815.

Henderson, Thomas. Bleacher of Cavan. 2nd Bn 50th Foot. Marched from Eastbourne and confined aboard PS, 19 December 1813. Joined YCs as corporal, 7 March 1814, sergeant 25 March 1814. Reduced 5 July 1814. Arrived in the WIs 14 December 1814. Promoted corporal 25 December 1814, sergeant 25 February 1815. Reduced 13 March 1815. Promoted corporal 10 June 1815, sergeant 19 August 1815. Reduced 28 December 1815. Promoted corporal 25 August 1816. Reduced for 'Drunk on Guard,' 21 March 1817. Deserted in Jamaica, 15 July 1818. No record of rejoining.

Hennessy, James. Seaman of Louth. 2nd Bn 88th Foot. Marched from Plymouth Docks and confined aboard PS, 24 September 1814. Joined YCs 29 June 1815, and arrived in the WIs 5 November 1815. Died, 22 October 1816.

Henry, John. 2nd Bn 24th Foot. Marched from Savoy Military Prison and confined aboard PS, 29 September 1813. Joined YCs 1 February 1814. Deserted Cove of Cork, 25 October 1814. Captain Joseph Anderson's 'loyal servant' successfully evaded recapture.

Henry, Thomas. Tailor of Louth. 25th Light Dragoons. Marched from Savoy Military Prison and confined aboard PS. 10 September 1813. Joined YCs 1 February 1814, and arrived in the WIs 14 December 1814. Deserted 4 February 1815. Rejoined 13 March. (No punishment records held.) Deserted Barbados 25 March 1815. Date of return not known. 'Solitary Confinement from 25th July 1815 until 25th September 1815'. Sick in General Hospital, Barbados, 10 November to 24 December 1815. Discharged Quebec.

Hewitt, John. Farrier of Warwick. Royal Horse Guards. Marched from Stafford and confined aboard PS, 7 April 1815. Joined YCs 29 June 1815, and arrived in the WIs 5 November 1815. Died Jamaica, 27 June 1817.

Hewitt, Joseph. 2nd Foot Guards. Marched from Salford confined aboard PS, 3 March 1815. Joined YCs 29 June 1815, and arrived in the WIs 5 November 1815. Discharged Quebec.

Hickey, James. Labourer of Tipperary. Either 35th Foot marched from Bristol, 22 November 1814, or 20th Foot marched from Bristol and confined aboard PS, 3 May 1815. Joined YCs 29 June 1815, and arrived in the WIs 5 November 1815. Died Jamaica, 17 February 1818.

Hicks, Richard. Fisherman of Dorset. Either 97th or 84th Foot. Transferred from Newport Gaol, Isle of Wight, as Richard Rix or Hicks and confined aboard PS, August 1813. Joined YCs as Richard Hicks, 1 February 1814. Deserted while still at the Isle of Wight, 25 June 1814. No record of rejoining.

Higgins, John. Glass grinder of Bath. 21st Foot. Marched from Chester and confined aboard PS, 25 January 1816. Embarked Spithead amongst a 300-strong detachment of 'Unattached Deserters' joining the 2nd Foot, 25 April 1816. Arrived in the WIs 5 June 1816. Transferred into York Chasseurs, 25 August 1816. Deserted, 6 October 1816. No record of rejoining.

Higgins, Thomas. Gardener of Tipperary. 94th Foot. Marched from Leith and confined aboard PS, 1 October 1814. Joined YCs 29 June 1815, and arrived in the WIs 5 November 1815. 300 lashes for 'Forgery' 4 November 1816; 300 lashes for 'Theft', 26 December 1816; 300 lashes 'On suspicion of Theft', 28 April 1817. Died Jamaica, 24 February 1819.

Hill, George. Labourer of Hitchin, Herts. 5th Foot. Marched from Savoy Military Prison and confined aboard PS, 15 December 1813. Joined YCs 7 March 1814. Deserted while still at the Isle of Wight, 28 April 1814. Rejoined 4 September. (No punishment records held) Arrived in the WIs 14 December 1814. Deserted at Barbados, 20 February 1815. No record of rejoining.

Hill, George. Labourer of Antrim. 25th Foot. Marched from Bristol and confined at Portchester Castle, 21 January 1817. Joined YCs 3 April 1817, and arrived in the WIs 25 May 1817. Accused of 'Selling his Regimental Necessaries', 18 August 1817, found 'Not Guilty'. Deserted in Jamaica, 31 March 1819. Rejoined 3 May 1819. (No punishment records held.) Discharged Quebec.

Hilsay/Hilsey, Richard. Transferred to YCs from 1st European Garrison in Jamaica, 25 May 1817. Discharged Quebec.

Hilton, Francis. Labourer of Northumberland. Royal Artillery. Marched from Savoy Military Prison and confined aboard PS, 23 January 1814. Joined YCs 25 March 1814, and arrived in the WIs 14 December 1814. Deserted in Jamaica 17 February 1818. Rejoined 24 March 1818. (No punishment records held.) Deserted in Jamaica 10 February 1819. No record of rejoining.

Hinds/Hines, John. Labourer of Grantham. 1st Bn 7th Foot. Marched from Louth and confined aboard PS as John Hines, 6 December 1814. Joined YCs as John Hinds, 29 June 1815, and arrived in the WIs 5 November 1815. Died Jamaica, 30 September 1817.

Hoddell/Hoddle, Joseph. Coach painter of Hereford. Embarked Spithead amongst a 300-strong detachment of 'Unattached Deserters' joining the 2nd Foot, 25 April 1816. Arrived in the WIs 5 June 1816. Transferred to the York Chasseurs 25 August 1816. Deserted in Jamaica 29 March 1817. Rejoined 16 April 1817. 900 lashes for being 'Absent without Leave', 23 April 1817. Accused of 'Selling his Regimental Necessaries' but acquitted, 5 August 1817. Deserted in Jamaica, 6 April 1818. No record of rejoining.

Hodkin, William. 1st Foot Guards. Marched from Worcester and confined at Portchester Castle, 31 December 1816. Joined YCs 3 April 1817, and arrived in the WIs 25 May 1817. Discharged Quebec.

Hoffer/Haffer, Edward. From Routh, Somerset. 32nd Foot. Marched from Bristol and confined aboard PS, 15 January 1815. Joined YCs 29 June 1815, and arrived in the WIs 5 November 1815. Discharged Quebec. Re-enlisted for the 19th Foot, 19 October 1820. (? Canada or England). 23 October 1838, and at the age of 47 years, discharged to a pension. 'His disability from Muscular Debility and Varicose Veins of the Legs, from Chronic Cough and Weakened Constitution, those are the effects of Long Service and not Fraud or Design. He is unfit for any active service, might serve a few years at Home. Conduct on Discharge – A Good and Efficient Soldier'.

Hogan, Dennis. 13th Foot. Marched from Bristol and confined aboard PS 21, August 1813. Joined YCs 1 February 1814, and arrived in the WIs 14 December 1814. Discharged Quebec.

Hogan, Patrick. Labourer of Wicklow. 92nd Foot. Marched from Bristol and confined aboard PS, 28 May 1815. Joined YCs 29 June 1815, and arrived in the WIs 5 November 1815. Died Jamaica, 3 March 1819.

Holding, Philip. Labourer of Coddenham, Suffolk. 2nd Bn 3rd Foot. Marched from Abingdon and confined aboard PS, 9 September 1813. Joined YCs 7 March 1814, and arrived in the WIs 14 December 1814. Died, 3 December 1816.

Holley/Haley, Joseph. Labourer of Kildare, 5th Foot. Marched from Taunton and confined aboard PS as Joseph Holley, 7 November 1812. Joined YCs as Joseph Haley, 25 March 1814, and arrived in the WIs as Joseph Holley, 14 December 1814. Deserted in Tobago 6 August 1816. Rejoined 23 August. 1816. (No punishment records held.) 150 lashes for being 'Drunk and Absent from Evening Parade', 10 February 1817, punishment remitted. Discharged Quebec. Allocated Concession 9. Lot NE 8. Bathurst. No evidence found of Holley, wife and daughter, settling there.

Hollis, John. Weaver of Prestwick. 83rd Foot. Marched from Chester and confined aboard PS, 25 June 1814. Joined YCs 29 June 1815, and arrived in the WIs 5 November 1815. Promoted corporal 3 October 1816. 'Resigned in consequence of Mental Derangement', 6 October 1818.

Hollister, John. Joined as volunteer, 1st Bn Tower Hamlets Militia, 9 December 1813 (Eight Guinea Bounty). Promoted sergeant 2 February 1814, and arrived in the WIs 14 December 1814. Appointed drum-major May 1815 (Drum-Major Thomas Stewart reduced to private). Reverted to sergeant on the arrival of Drum-Major Bailey, 5 November 1815. Reduced 1 September 1817. Promoted corporal 17 December 1817. Reduced 19 March 1819. Discharged Quebec.

Hooper, Thomas. Labourer of Chorley, Devon. East Devon Militia. Sentenced at Plymouth Docks to 'General Service for Desertion', 15 November 1813. Confined aboard PS, 23 December 1813. Joined YCs 1 February 1814, and arrived in the WIs 14 December 1814. Deserted in Jamaica 2 April 1819. Rejoined 7 April 1819. (No punishment records held.) Deserted in Jamaica, 28 May 1819. No record of rejoining.

Hooper, William. Labourer of Somerset. Coldstream Guards. Marched from Glasgow and confined aboard PS, 24 March 1815. Joined YCs 29 June 1815, and arrived in the WIs 5 November 1815. Died Jamaica, 30 May 1819.

Hope, Robert. Labourer of Northumberland or Northamptonshire. 1st Foot or 1st Foot Guards. Marched from Bristol and confined aboard PS, 28 May 1815. Joined YCs 29 June 1815, and arrived in the WIs 5 November 1815. Deserted in Jamaica 9 October 1818. Rejoined the next day. Deserted in Jamaica 20 October 1818. Rejoined 25 December 1818. Deserted in Jamaica 16 May 1819. Rejoined the next day. (No punishment records held.) Discharged Quebec.

Horan, John. 21st Foot. Marched from Chester and confined aboard PS, 3 February 1814. Joined YCs 29 June 1815, and arrived in the WIs 5 November 1814. Discharged Quebec. Allocated Concession 10. Lot SW 12. Bathurst. No evidence found of settling there.

Hosch/Hosche/Osche, Frederic or **Frederick.** 8th Bn 60th Foot. Transported from Gibraltar and confined aboard PS as Frederic Osche, 9 December 1815. Joined YCs as Frederic Hosch, 17th May 1815, and arrived in the WIs 25 June 1816. Discharged at Quebec as Frederick Hosche.

Houghan/Haugher/Haughen, Dennis. Nailer of Ireland. 86th Foot. Confined aboard

PS as Dennis Houghan or Haugher, 3 February 1814. Joined YCs as Dennis Haugher, 25 March 1814, and arrived in the WIs 14 December 1814. Died St Vincent as Dennis Haughen, 8 September 1815.

Houghy/Houghey/Haughey, Terrence. Royal Artillery. Marched from Woolwich and confined aboard PS as Terence Haughey, 19 September 1813. Joined YCs as Terrence Houghy, 5 February 1814, and arrived in the WIs 14 December 1814. Discharged Quebec as Terrence Houghey.

Howard, Samuel. Shoemaker of Warrington. 2nd Bn 34th Foot. Marched from Bristol and confined aboard PS, 1 December 1814. Joined YCs 29 June 1815, and arrived in the WIs 5 November 1815. Deserted in Jamaica 3 February 1819. Rejoined 5 March 1819. Deserted in Jamaica 3 April 1819. Rejoined 7 April 1819. (No punishment records held.) Discharged Quebec.

Howie, John. Weaver of Forfar. 2nd Bn 91st Foot. Marched from Edinburgh and confined aboard PS as John Howie or Thompson, 23 December 1813. Joined YCs 7 March 1814, as John Howie. Deserted while still at the Isle of Wight, 2 July 1814. No record of rejoining.

Hughes, James. Labourer of Armagh. 18th Foot, Marched from Gosport and confined at Portchester Castle, 7 January 1817. Joined YCs 3 March 1817, and arrived in the WIs 25 May 1817. Deserted in Jamaica, 10 July 1818. No record of rejoining.

Hughes, Jeremiah. Labourer of Carlow. Joined 30th Foot, 3 October 1803. Marched from Savoy Military Prison and confined aboard PS, 7 September 1814. Joined YCs 29 June 1815, and arrived in the WIs as drummer, 5 November 1815. Reduced 16 December 1815. Re-appointed drummer 14 February 1817. Solitary confinement for 'Drunk on Parade', 17 November 1817. Deserted in Jamaica 3 March 1819. Rejoined 9 March 1819. (No punishment records held.) Deserted in Jamaica 13 April 1819. No record of rejoining.

Hughes, John. Spinner of Manchester. 2nd Bn 25th Foot. Marched from Maidstone and confined aboard PS, 8 September 1813. Joined YCs 1 February 1814, and arrived in the WIs 14 December 1814. Died Guadeloupe, 9 August 1815. One of seven men 'Supposed to have been poisoned'.

Hughes, John. Spinner of Lancashire. Transferred to YCs from 101st Foot in Jamaica, 25 December 1816. Accused but found 'Not Guilty of Theft', 18 August 1817. Deserted in Jamaica, 15 April 1818. No record of rejoining.

Hughes, Richard. Blacksmith of Great Ness, Shropshire. 7th Hussars. Transported from Portsmouth and confined aboard PS. 1 September 1813. Joined YCs 1 February 1814, and arrived in the WIs 14 December 1814. Promoted corporal 29 May 1816. Reduced 12 November 1818. Deserted in Jamaica 2 December 1818. Rejoined 23 December 1818. Deserted in Jamaica 15 February 1819. Rejoined 19 March 1819. (No punishment records held.) Discharged Quebec.

Hughes, Richard. Papermaker of Middlesex. Either 1st Bn Royals marched from Andover, 27 November 1814, General Service Recruit transported from Portsmouth, 25 June 1815 or 56th Foot confined aboard PS, 20 February 1815. Joined YCs 29 June 1815, and arrived in the WIs 5 November 1815. Promoted corporal 24 February 1816. Deserted, 18 August 1816. Rejoined at St Vincent as private, 25 May 1817. (No punishment records held.) 200 lashes for 'Making away with Regimental Necessities', 125 lashes remitted, 31 July 1817; 200 lashes for 'Making away with Regimental Necessities', 10 December 1817. Solitary confinement for 'Absent without Leave', 15 January 1818. Deserted in Jamaica, 27 April 1819. No record of rejoining.

Hull, John. Labourer of County Down. 54th Foot. Marched from Chelmsford and confined aboard PS, 24 October 1813. Joined YCs 1 February 1814, and arrived in the WIs 14 December 1814. Promoted sergeant 23 December 1815. Reduced 24 July 1816. Died Jamaica, 3 February 1817.

Humberston, John. Cooper of Middlesex. 86th Foot. Marched from Savoy Military Prison and confined aboard PS, 18 September 1814. Joined YCs 29 June 1815, and arrived in the WIs 5 November 1815. Died Jamaica, 20 January 1818.

Humble, Peter. 2nd Bn 7th Foot. Marched from Chichester and confined aboard PS, 1814 (? date) Joined YCs 29 June 1815, and arrived in the WIs 5 November 1815. Discharged Quebec.

Humphries, David. 1st Bn Grenadier Guards. Marched from Wrexham and confined aboard PS, 7 November 1815. Joined YCs 6 May 1816, and arrived in the WIs 25 June 1816. Died, 30 October 1816.

Humphries, James. Labourer of Kerry. 63rd Foot. Marched from Plymouth and confined aboard PS, 21 May 1815. Joined YCs 29 June 1815, and arrived in the WIs 5 November 1815. Deserted 5 September 1816. Rejoined 14 September 1816. (No punishment records held.) Discharged Quebec.

Hunter, John. 14th Light Dragoons. Marched from Ilchester and confined aboard PS, 19 November 1813. Joined YCs 5 February 1814, and arrived in the WIs 5 November 1814. Discharged Quebec.

Hunter, Thomas. Painter of Northumberland. 2nd Bn 25th Foot. Marched from Edinburgh and confined aboard PS, 13 October 1813. Joined YCs as drummer, 1 February 1814, and arrived in the WIs 14 December 1814. Reduced 24 April 1815. Died Jamaica, 10 July 1818.

Hutchins/Hutchings, John. Labourer of York. 7th Foot. Marched from Kingston and confined aboard PS, 22 September 1814. Joined YCs 29 June 1815, and arrived in the WIs 5 November 1815. Died Tobago, 4 August 1816.

Hutchinson, Alexander. 3rd Bn 14th Foot. Marched from Plymouth and confined aboard PS, 11 November 1814. Joined YCs 29 June 1815, and arrived in the WIs 5 November 1815. Discharged Quebec.

Hutchinson, John. Labourer of Linton. 40th Foot. Marched from Cambridge and confined aboard PS, 3 March 1815. Joined YCs 29 June 1815, and arrived in the WIs 5 November 1815. Deserted in Jamaica 21 July 1817. Rejoined the next day. 300 lashes for being 'Absent without Leave', 26 July 1817. Deserted in Jamaica 26 August 1817. Rejoined 28 August 1817. 300 lashes for being 'Absent without Leave', 2 September.' Died Jamaica, 29 April 1818.

Hutchinson/Hutchins, Thomas. Tailor of Roxborough. 4th Royal Veteran Bn. Marched from York Hospital and confined aboard PS as Thomas Hutchins, 14 September 1813. Joined YCs as Thomas Hutchinson, 1 February 1814, and arrived in the WIs 14 December 1814. 200 lashes for being 'Drunk and Absent from Parade', 12 April 1815, 100 lashes remitted. Deserted in Jamaica 28 April 1819. Rejoined 15 May 1819. (No punishment records held.) Discharged Quebec.

Iggs, Edward. Labourer of Chelmsford. 88th Foot. Marched from Bristol and confined aboard PS, 3 May 1815. Joined YCs 29 June 1815, and arrived in the WIs 5 November

1815. Deserted in Tobago 6 May 1816. Rejoined 10 May 1816. Deserted in Jamaica 31 August 1818. Rejoined 4 September 1818. (No punishment records held.) Deserted in Jamaica, 11 June 1819. No record of rejoining.

Ingram, Henry. A West Indian. 81st Foot. Marched from Savoy Military Prison and confined aboard PS, 12 February 1815. Joined YCs 29 June 1815, and arrived in the WIs 5 November 1815. 300 lashes for being 'Absent from his Guard', 13 October 1816. Deserted in Jamaica, 13 October 1818. Rejoined 16 October 1818. (No punishment records held.) Discharged Quebec.

Ireland, Samuel. Labourer of Nottingham. 1st Foot Guards. Marched from Tower of London and confined aboard PS, 25 October 1814. Joined YCs 29 June 1815, and arrived in the WIs as drummer, 5 November 1815. Died Jamaica, 4 September 1817.

Ironmonger/Ironsmonger, John. Labourer of London. Embarked Spithead amongst a 300-strong detachment of 'Unattached Deserters' joining the 2nd Foot, 25 April 1816. Arrived in the WIs 5 June 1816. Deserted 17 July 1816. Rejoined 28 July 1816. Transferred into the York Chasseurs, 25 August 1816. Deserted 31 August 1816. Rejoined the same day. (No punishment records held.) Died, 30 September 1816. Four weeks after an unsuccessful desertion attempt for which he was most likely flogged.

Irwin, James. 2nd Bn 48th Foot. Marched from Ipswich and confined aboard PS, 1 February 1814. Joined YCs 25 March 1814, and arrived in the WIs 14 December 1814. Died St Vincent, 2 September 1815.

Irwin, Thomas. Transferred to YCs from 6th Bn 60th Foot in Jamaica, 25 May 1817. Discharged Quebec.

Jackson, James. Weaver of Harrington. 41st Foot. Marched from Winchester and confined aboard PS, 16 August 1813. Joined YCs 1 February 1814, and arrived in the WIs 14 December 1814. Died Jamaica, 4 March 1819.

Jackson, James. Brush maker of London. 2nd Bn 84th Foot. Marched from Nottingham and confined aboard PS, 10 February 1816. Joined YCs 16 May 1816, and arrived in the WIs 25 June 1816. Deserted 11 November 1816. No record of rejoining.

Jackson, Samuel. Framework knitter of Nottingham. 2nd Bn 24th Foot. Marched from Salford and confined aboard PS, 7 October 1813. Joined YCs 1 February 1814, and arrived in the WIs 14 December 1814. Discharged Quebec.

Jackson, Samuel. Hatter of Odiham. 33rd Foot. Marched from Middlewich and confined aboard PS, 30 August 1813. Joined YCs 5 February 1814, and arrived in the WIs 14 December 1814. Died, 19 November 1816.

Jackson, Thomas. 55th Foot. Marched from Kendal and confined aboard PS, 1 August 1813. Joined YCs 7 March 1814, and arrived in the WIs 14 December 1814. No record after December 1815.

Jackson, William. Joined 11th Light Dragoons, 22 February 1808. Marched from Canterbury and confined aboard PS, 26 February 1815. Joined YCs 29 June 1815, and arrived in the WIs 5 November 1815. Discharged Quebec.

James, William. Gunsmith of Birmingham. 4th Bn Royal Artillery. Marched from Dartford and confined aboard PS, 16 February 1814. Joined YCs 7 March 1814, and arrived in the WIs 14 December 1814. 12 Months solitary confinement in irons for

'Mutinous Conduct', 5 June 1816. Imprisoned aboard the flag ship at Port Royal, Jamaica. In the company of Andrew Hay, Michael Low and Robert Farnley, transported to England and confined at Portchester Castle to await further instructions, 25 May 1817. No further record.

Jarman, James or **John**. Millwright of Montgomery. 81st Foot. Marched from Savoy Military Prison and confined aboard PS as James Jarman, 1 August 1813. Joined YCs 1 February 1814. Deserted as John Jarman while still at the Isle of Wight, 3 July 1814. No record of rejoining.

Jarvis/Jarvies/Jervis, James. Labourer of Nottingham. 2nd Bn 25th Foot. Marched from Maidstone and confined aboard PS as James Jarvis, 15 December 1813. Joined YCs as James Jarvies, 1 February 1814. Deserted while still at the Isle of Wight, 7 July 1814. Recaptured by Henry A Court (Twenty Shillings Bounty). Rejoined 24 July 1814. (No punishment records held.) Arrived in the WIs 14 December 1814. 300 lashes for being 'Drunk on Barrier Beach Guard', 28 April 1815. Deserted in Jamaica 7 August 1817. Rejoined 13 August 1817. 300 lashes for being 'Absent without leave', 15 August 1817. Deserted in Jamaica as James Jervis, 27 April 1819. No record of rejoining.

Jennings, Alexander. Flax dresser of Dundee. Royal Horse Artillery. Marched from Chester and confined aboard PS, 15 October 1813. Joined YCs 1 February 1814. Deserted from Sandown, Isle of Wight, 22 February 1814. Retaken 25 February 1814 by 19th Foot Corporal Samuel Stewart (Twenty Shillings Bounty). Hospitalised and confined aboard PS until regiment's WIs departure. (No punishment records held.) Deserted at Guernsey, 19 September 1814. No record of rejoining.

Johnson/Johnston, Hugh. Weaver of either Antrim or Ayr. 5th Dragoon Guards. Marched from Nottingham and confined aboard PS as Hugh Johnson or William Boyd, 22 January 1816. Embarked at Spithead as Hugh Johnson, amongst a 300-strong detachment of 'Unattached Deserters' joining the 2nd Foot 25 April 1816. Arrived in the WIs 5 June 1816. Deserted 10 August 1816. Rejoined the next day. Transferred into the York Chasseurs as Hugh Johnston, 25 August 1816. Deserted 30 September 1816. Rejoined 11 October 1816. 800 lashes for 'Desertion', 21 October 1816. Deserted in Jamaica 19 June 1819. No record of rejoining.

Johnson, Jacob Isaac. Labourer of Woodbridge, Suffolk. 2nd Bn 87th Foot. Marched from Kingston and confined aboard PS as Isaac Johnson, 13 January 1814. Joined as Jacob Johnson, 25 March 1814. Deserted while still at the Isle of Wight, 30 March 1814. Recaptured by George Cox (Twenty Shillings Bounty) and rejoined 9 April 1814. (No punishment records held.) Arrived in the WIs 14 December 1814. Promoted drummer 25 May 1816. Died Jamaica, 13 February 1817.

Johnson, James. Carpenter of Tyrone. Royal Sappers and Miners. Marched from Savoy Military Prison and confined aboard PS, 16 February 1814. Joined YCs 7 March 1814. Deserted while still at the Isle of Wight, 29 June 1814. No record of rejoining.

Johnson, James. Labourer of Derry. 18th Dragoons. Marched from Chester and confined aboard PS, 3 March 1815. Joined YCs 29 June 1815, and arrived in the WIs 5 November 1815. Deserted at Grenada, 12 March 1816. No record of rejoining.

Johnson, John. Miner of Cornwall. Joined Royal Artillery, 28 November 1808. Marched from Woolwich and confined aboard PS, 25 February 1815. Joined YCs 29 June 1815, and arrived in the WIs 5 November 1815. Deserted 17 November 1816. No record of rejoining.

Johnson, John. Labourer of Kildare. 78th Foot. Marched from Glasgow and confined at Portchester Castle, 20 January 1817. Joined YCs 3 April 1817, and arrived in the WIs 25 May 1817. Deserted in Jamaica 7 August 1817. Rejoined 28 August 1817. 300 lashes for being 'Absent without Leave', 2 September 1817. Discharged Quebec.

Johnson, John. Weaver of Paisley. Embarked Spithead amongst a 300-strong detachment of 'Unattached Deserters' joining the 2nd Foot, 25 April 1816. Arrived in the WIs 5 June 1816. Deserted 16 July 1816. Rejoined the next day. 1,000 lashes and ordered to be marked with 'D', 25 July 1816. Transferred into York Chasseurs, 25 August 1816. Deserted in Jamaica, 16 April 1819. No record of rejoining.

Johnson, Richard. Fisherman of Cromarty. 34th Foot. Marched from York and confined aboard PS, 7 December 1813. Joined YCs 29 June 1815, and arrived in the WIs 5 November 1815. Died, 19 October 1816.

Johnson, Thomas. Joined 4th Dragoons, 18 December 1807. Marched from Chester and confined aboard PS, 3 March 1815. Joined YCs 29 June 1815, and arrived in the WIs 5 November 1815. Discharged Quebec.

Johnson, William. Dyer of Edinburgh. 94th Foot. Marched from Edinburgh and confined aboard PS, 8 August 1813. Joined YCs 5 February 1814. 'Given to Civil Powers in consequence of having acknowledged accessory to a murder committed in Edinburgh', 30 March 1814. No further record.

Jones, David. General Service. Marched from Hereford and confined aboard PS as David Davies or David Jones, 12 September 1913. Joined YCs as David Jones, 25 March 1814, and arrived in the WIs 14 December 1814. Promoted corporal 25 December 1814. Reduced for 'Drunk on Guard Duty', 27 April 1815. Discharged Quebec.

Jones, David. Labourer of Shropshire. 2nd Bn 84th Foot. Marched from Warwick and confined aboard PS, 15 December 1814. Joined YCs 29 June 1815, and arrived in the WIs 5 November 1815. Died Jamaica, 18 November 1818.

Jones, George. 1st Foot Guards. Marched from Leicester and confined aboard PS, 24 September 1813. Joined YCs 5 February 1814. 'Given to Royal Marines', 6 July 1814.

Jones, John. Cotton Spinner of Dublin. Either 56th Foot marched from Savoy Military Prison, 15 January 1815, 5th Foot marched from Reading, 13 April 1814, Royal Sappers and Miners marched from Chester, 18 May 1815 or 4th Foot transported from Portsmouth and confined aboard PS, 22 April 1815. Joined YCs 29 June 1815, and arrived in the WIs 5 November 1815. Promoted corporal December 1815, sergeant 25 February 1816. Reduced 14 April 1816. Died, 25 September 1816.

Jones, John. Weaver of Skerkin. Either 56th Foot marched from Savoy Military Prison, 15 January 1815, 5th Foot march from Reading, 13 April 1814, Royal Sappers and Miners marched from Chester ,18 May 1815 or 4th Foot transported from Portsmouth and confined aboard PS, 22 April 1815. Joined YCs 29 June 1815, and arrived in the WIs 5 November 1815. Discharged Quebec.

Jones, Robert. Weaver of Armagh. 2nd Bn 1st Foot Guards. Marched from Liverpool and confined aboard PS, 8 December 1813. Joined YCs 29 June 1815, and arrived in the WIs 5 November 1815. Died, 5 February 1816.

Jones, Robert. Labourer of Denbigh or Denby. Warwick Militia. Marched from Maidstone and confined aboard PS, 24 March 1815. Joined YCs 29 June 1815, and arrived in the WIs 5 November 1815. Deserted in Jamaica 31 August 1818. Rejoined 4 September 1818. (No punishment records held) . Deserted in Jamaica 25 September 1818. No record of rejoining.

Jones, Samuel. Labourer of Worcestershire. Transferred to YCs in Jamaica from 6th Bn 60th Foot, 25 May 1817. Discharged from Stony Hill, Jamaica, 10 June 1819.

Jones, Thomas. Hatter of Lanark. Either 69th Foot marched from Norwich, 12 December 1813, or 2nd Bn 90th Foot marched from Hereford and confined aboard PS, 8 December 1813. Joined YCs as drummer 5 February 1814. Promoted corporal 24 February 1814, sergeant 25 March 1814. Arrived in the WIs 14 December 1814. Reduced for 'Exchanging his Regimental Trowsers', 3 June 1815.' Died St Vincent, 2 September 1815.

Jones, Thomas. Labourer of Chester. Either 69th Foot marched from Norwich, 12 December 1813, or 2nd Bn 90th Foot marched from Hereford and confined aboard PS, 8 December 1813. Joined YCs 5 February 1814, and arrived in the WIs 14 December 1814. Died of wounds received in action at Guadeloupe, 11 August 1815.

Jones, Thomas. Clerk of Gloucestershire. Two years with Royal Marine before joining 15th Foot, 22 April 1814. Volunteered at the Isle of Wight, 22 April 1815. Arrived in the WIs as corporal 5 November 1815. Appointed schoolmaster sergeant March 1816. Reverted to sergeant 30 July 1816. Reduced 7 December 1818. Deserted in Jamaica 28 April 1819. Rejoined 9 May 1819. (No punishment records held.) Discharged Quebec.

Jones, William. Blacksmith of Stafford. 22nd Foot. Marched from Shrewsbury and confined aboard PS, 30 January 1814. Joined YCs 25 March 1814, and arrived in the WIs 14 December 1814. Died Jamaica, 18 November 1817.

Jordan/Jordon, Edward. Joined 21st Foot, 21st November 1807. Volunteered as sergeant, 25 December 1813, and immediately promoted colour sergeant. Reduced 19 May 1814. Promoted corporal then sergeant, August 1814. Sick at Cork General Hospital as the regiment left for the WIs. Arrived in the WIs as colour sergeant, 8 May 1815. Reduced and awarded solitary confinement for 'Striking Captain Byrne and challenging a private soldier to fight', 10 February 1817. Promoted corporal 1 May 1817, sergeant 13 October 1817. Reduced 2 May 1819. Discharged Quebec.

Jordan, John. Labourer of Gloucestershire. 2nd Bn 62nd Foot. Transported from Hilsea, Portsmouth, and confined aboard PS, 20 February 1814. Joined YCs 7 March 1814, and arrived in the WIs 14 December 1814. Deserted in Grenada 17 October 1815. Rejoined 5 January 1816. (No punishment records held.) Died Jamaica, 15 June 1817. It is not known which John Jordan received 300 lashes for being 'Drunk on Guard', 24 December 1816.

Jordon, John. Labourer of Amargh. Either 4th Dragoons marched from Chester, 28 December 1814, or 2nd Foot transported from Portsmouth and confined aboard PS, 12 November 1814. Joined YCs 29 June 1815, and arrived in the WIs 5 November 1815. Discharged Quebec. It is not known which John Jordan received 300 lashes for being 'Drunk on Guard', 24 December 1816.

Jordan, John. Labourer of Chester. Either 4th Dragoons marched from Chester, 28 December 1814, or 2nd Foot transported from Portsmouth and confined aboard PS, 12 November 1814. Joined YCs 29 June 1815, and arrived in the WIs 5 November 1815. Discharged Quebec. It is not known which John Jordan received 300 lashes for being 'Drunk on Guard', 24 December 1816.

Joyce, Charles. Frame Work Knitter of Leicestershire. 2nd Bn 24th Foot. Marched from

Savoy Military Prison and confined aboard PS 13 October 1814. Joined YCs 29 June 1815 and arrived in the WIs 5 November 1815. Deserted Tobago, 18 August 1816. General Courts-martial 5 December 1816 – 'That the Long Confinement the prisoner had undergone was sufficient punishment'. 300 lashes for 'Neglect of Duty on his Post', 28 April 1817; 300 lashes for 'Making Away with his Necessaries', 25 July 1817; 300 lashes for 'Unsoldierlike Conduct in Forging a Sergeants name',17 November 1817, 25 lashes remitted. Deserted in Jamaica 8 May 1818. Rejoined 14 May 1818. Deserted in Jamaica 26 August 1818. Rejoined 14 September 1818. Deserted in Jamaica 21 January 1819. Rejoined 28 January 1819. (No punishment records held.) Deserted in Jamaica 16 June 1819. No record of rejoining.

Joyce/Joice, Edward. 59th Foot. Marched from Chester and confined aboard PS as Edward Joice, 15 October 1815. Joined YCs as Edward Joyce, date unknown, and arrived in the WIs 25th June 1816. Deserted 21 July 1816. No record of rejoining.

Joyce, Richard. 51st Foot. Marched from Canterbury and confined aboard PS, 26 November 1813. Joined YCs 7 March 1814, and arrived in the WIs 14 December 1814. Discharged Quebec.

Kane, James. Either 6th Dragoons marched from Chester, 11 August 1813, or 55th Foot marched from Savoy Military Prison and confined aboard PS, 14 November 1813. Joined YCs 7 March 1814, and arrived in the WIs 14 December 1814. Drowned when bathing at Barbados, 27 December 1814.

Kane, James. Either 6th Dragoons marched from Chester, 11 August 1813, or 55th Foot marched from Savoy Military Prison and confined aboard PS, 14 November 1813. Joined YCs 7 March 1814, and arrived in the WIs 14 December 1814. Promoted corporal 24 February 1814. Reduced 31 January 1815. 150 lashes for 'Insolent Language', 12 June 1815. Promoted corporal 30 January 1816. Reduced 11 April 1816. Promoted corporal 5 August 1817. Reduced 15 January 1818. Discharged Quebec.

Kane, Thomas. 50th Foot. Marched from Preston and confined at Portchester Castle, 27 December 1816. Joined YCs 3 April 1817, and arrived in the WIs 25 May 1817. Discharged Quebec.

Kearney, John. Bleacher of Derry. 58th Foot. Marched from Savoy Military Prison and confined aboard PS, 27 November 1814. Joined YCs 29 June 1815, and arrived in the WIs 5 November 1815. Deserted 11 August 1816. General Courts-martial, 5 December 1816 – 'That the Long Confinement the prisoner had undergone was sufficient punishment'. Deserted in Jamaica, 23 March 1817. Rejoined (date unknown). 300 lashes for being 'Absent without Leave', 9 May 1817. Deserted in Jamaica 22 February 1818. Rejoined 27 February 1818. Deserted in Jamaica 29 June 1818. Rejoined the same day. Deserted in Jamaica 17 November 1818. Rejoined 26 November 1818. Deserted in Jamaica 26 January 1819. Rejoined the next day. Deserted in Jamaica 2 April 1819. Rejoined the same day. (No punishment records held.) Discharged Quebec.

Kearns, James. Labourer of Wicklow. Warwick Militia. Sentenced at Bristol 'To seven years General Service for Desertion', 2nd May 1815. Confined aboard PS, 8 May 1815. Joined YCs 29 June 1815, and 'Left on Detachment' when regiment left for St Vincent. Arrived in the WIs 19 December 1816. Deserted in Jamaica 26 January 1819. No record of rejoining.

Keenan, Francis. Weaver of Monaghan. 2nd Bn 27th Foot. Transferred from the Army Depot and confined aboard PS, 26 September 1814. Joined YCs 29 June 1815, and arrived in the WIs 5 November 1815. Deserted in Jamaica 18 December 1816. No record of rejoining.

Keipe, William or **Keep, Philip.** Transferred to YCs from 1st European Garrison in Jamaica as William Keipe, 25 May 1817. Discharged Quebec as Philip Keep.

Kelligher/Keleher/Kellagher, John. 45th Foot. Marched from Winchester and confined aboard PS as John Keleher or Keligher, 4 March 1815. Joined YCs as John Kelligher, 29 June 1815. 'Left on Detachment' as regiment left for WIs. Discharged from Isle of Wight as John Kellagher, 8 June 1816.

Kelly, Daniel. Labourer of Galway. 6th Bn 60th Foot. Marched from Savoy Military Prison and confined aboard PS, 22 September 1814. Joined YCs 29 June 1815, and arrived in the WIs 5 November 1815. Died Jamaica, 19 January 1817.

Kelly, James. Carpenter of Cork. 101st Foot. Marched from Chester and confined aboard PS, 23 January 1816. Joined YCs 17 May 1816, and arrived in the WIs 25 June 1816. 300 lashes for 'Absenting himself two weeks without leave', 21 January 1817; 300 lashes for being 'Drunk on Duty', 28 April 1817; 300 lashes for being 'Absent without Leave', 2 August 1817; 200 lashes for 'Theft', 30 January 1818. Deserted in Jamaica, 19 March 1819. No record of rejoining.

Kelly, John. Blacksmith of Galway. Either 2nd Grenadier Guards marched from Piershill Barracks, 6 November 1814, or 26th Foot from Brighton and confined aboard PS, 23 November 1813. Joined YCs 29 June 1815, and 'Left on Detachment' as the regiment departed for St Vincent. No further record.

Kelly, John. Labourer of Galway. Either 2nd Grenadier Guards marched from Piershill Barracks, 6 November 1814, or 26th Foot from Brighton and confined aboard PS, 23 November 1813. Joined YCs 29 June 1815, and arrived in the WIs 5 November 1815. Deserted in Jamaica 1 January 1819. No record of rejoining. It is not known which John Kelly was sentenced to 150 lashes for being 'Drunk on Evening Parade', 26 December 1816.

Kelly, John. Shoemaker of Castle Dermont, Kildare. Either 2nd Grenadier Guards marched from Piershill Barracks, 6 November 1814, or 26th Foot from Brighton and confined aboard PS, 23 November 1813. Joined YCs 29 June 1815, and arrived in the WIs 5 November 1815. Deserted in Jamaica 18 May 1819. Rejoined 25 May 1819. Discharged Quebec. It is not known which John Kelly was sentenced to 150 lashes for being 'Drunk on Evening Parade', 26 December 1816.

Kelly, Jonathan. 38th Foot. Marched from Winchester and confined at Portchester Castle, 16 January 1817. Joined YCs 3 April 1817, and arrived in the WIs 25 May 1819. Discharged Quebec, 1819.

Kelly, Michael. Shoemaker of Mayo. 66th Foot. Marched from Chester and confined aboard PS as Michael Kelly or McGuire, 15 October 1813. Joined as Michael Kelly, 1 February 1814. Deserted while still at the Isle of Wight 7 July 1814. Rejoined 17 July 1814, and hospitalised. (No punishment records held.) Arrived in the WIs 14 December 1814. Deserted 29 July 1816. No record of rejoining.

Kelly, Michael. Labourer of Tipperary. 95th Foot. Marched from Bristol and confined aboard PS, 6 February 1816. Joined YCs 16 June 1816, and arrived in the WIs August 1816. Died Jamaica, 23 July 1817.

Kelly, Patrick. Labourer of County Down. 37th Foot. Marched from Savoy Military Prison and confined PS, 22 April 1815. Joined YCs 29 June 1815, and arrived in the WIs 5 November 1815. Died, 6 September 1816.

Kendal/Kendall, George. Either 2nd Foot or 2nd Dragoons Guards. Marched from Newcastle and confined aboard PS, 7 October 1813. Joined YCs 1 February 1814, and arrived in the WIs 14 December 1814. Deserted 29 September 1816. Rejoined October 1816. Sentenced to 400 lashes, 22 November 1816, for 'Desertion' (29 September 1816– October 1816). Punishment remitted. Discharged Quebec.

Kendrick, John. Blacksmith of Matlock. 23rd Dragoons. Marched from Liverpool and confined aboard PS, 5 March 1816. Joined YCs 17 May 1816, and arrived in the WIs 25 June 1816. Deserted 8 August 1816. Rejoined 15 December 1816. (No punishment records held.) Deserted in Jamaica 11 May 1818. No record of rejoining.

Kenny, Thomas. Tailor of Roscommon. 23rd Foot. Marched from Chester and confined aboard PS, 28 December 1814. Joined YCs 29 June 1815, and arrived in the WIs 5 November 1815. Deserted in Jamaica 9 May 1819. Rejoined 13 May 1819. (No punishment records held.) Discharged Quebec.

Kenyon, John. 2nd Bn 43rd Foot. Marched from Liverpool and confined aboard PS, 8 December 1813. Joined YCs 1 February 1814, and arrived in the WIs 14 December 1814. Discharged Quebec.

Kindler, William. Weaver of County Down. 1st Bn 95th Foot. Marched from Savoy Military Prison and confined aboard PS, 3 March 1815. Joined YCs 29 June 1815, and arrived in the WIs 5 November 1815. Deserted 30 September 1816. Rejoined 28 October 1816. (No punishment records held.) Deserted in Jamaica 1 March 1817. Rejoined 12 April 1817. 300 lashes for 'Absenting himself without Leave', 12 April 1817. Deserted in Jamaica 22 August 1817. Rejoined 19 January 1818. Deserted in Jamaica 1 April 1819. Rejoined 22 May 1819. (No punishment records held.) Discharged Quebec.

King, Charles. Wheelwright of Devon. 2nd Foot Guards. Marched from Gloucester and confined aboard PS, 2 February 1814. Joined YCs 25 March 1814, and arrived in the WIs 14 December 1814. Deserted 12 October 1816. No record of rejoining.

King, George. Gardener of Tyrone. 2nd Bn 44th Foot. Sentenced at Ostend to General Service and ordered to be marked with a 'D' for 'Desertion', 14 April 1814. Marched from Savoy Military Prison and confined aboard PS, 12 February 1815. Joined YCs 29 June 1815 and arrived in the WIs 5 November 1815. Deserted in Jamaica 20 January 1819. Rejoined the next day. (No punishment records held.) Deserted in Jamaica 21 April 1819. Returned to England, recaptured and confined in Savoy Military Prison, 28 August 1819. No further record. It is not known which King was sentenced to 300 lashes for 'Presenting a Forged Order knowing it to be so', 2 December 1816.

King, James. Royal Artillery Driver. Marched from Chester and confined aboard PS, 3 March 1815. Joined YCs 29 June 1815, and arrived in the WIs 5 November 1815. Discharged Quebec. It is not known which King was sentenced to 300 lashes for 'Presenting a Forged Order knowing it to be so', 2 December 1816.

King, Richard. Guards. Marched from Savoy Military Prison and confined aboard PS, 28 April 1815. Joined YCs 29 June 1815, and arrived in the WIs 5 November 1815. Promoted corporal 29 May 1816, sergeant 16 February 1817, and colour sergeant 28 December 1818. Reduced 14 June 1819. Discharged Quebec.

Kingsley, Thomas. Tallow chandler of Carlow. 18th Foot. Marched from Chester and confined aboard PS, 26 September 1813. Joined YCs 1February 1814. Deserted at Cove of Cork, 30 September 1814. No record of rejoining.

Kinnier/Kennair, John. Labourer of Leeds. 92nd Foot. Marched from Bristol and confined aboard PS, 3 May 1815. Joined YCs 29 June 1815, and arrived in the WIs 5 November 1815. Died, 22 October 1816.

Kinsela/Kinsella, Tobias. Labourer of Carlow. 2nd Bn 95th Foot. Marched from Newbury and confined aboard PS, 18 August 1814. Joined YCs 29 June 1815, and arrived in the WIs 5 November 1815. Deserted in Jamaica 27 April 1819. No record of rejoining.

Kinsella, Patrick. Carpenter of Carlow. 25th Foot. Marched from Bristol and confined aboard PS, 9 September 1813. Joined YCs 7 March 1814. Deserted while still at the Isle of Wight, 7 July 1814. No record of rejoining.

Kirby, Joseph. 19th Foot. Marched from Ripon and confined aboard PS, 11 November 1813. Joined YCs 1 February 1814, and arrived in the WIs 14 December 1814. Discharged Quebec.

Kirkman, William. 77th Foot. Marched from Chester and confined aboard PS, 28 December 1814. Joined YCs 29 June 1815, and arrived in the WIs 5 November 1815. Discharged Quebec.

Knott, John. Labourer of Kent. 34th Foot. Marched from Chester and confined aboard PS, 9 June 1815. Joined YCs 29 June 1815, and arrived in the WIs 5 November 1815. Deserted in Jamaica 6 June 1817. Rejoined the same day. Deserted in Jamaica 11 April 1819. Rejoined 19 May 1819. (No punishment records held.) Discharged Quebec.

Krutzhous/Krutzlious/Kourlzhou, William. 2nd Bn 60th Foot. Confined aboard PS as William Urtzhouse or Krutzhouse, December 1815. Joined 6th Bn 60th Foot in Jamaica, 7 February 1816. Transferred into York Chasseurs as William Kourlzhou, 25 May 1817. Promoted drummer, March 1819. Discharged Quebec as William Krutzlious.

Kyle, Thomas. Stocking weaver of Roxburgh. 2nd Dragoon Guards. Marched from Derby and confined aboard PS, 1 February 1814. Joined YCs 25 March 1814, and arrived in the WIs 14 December 1814. Promoted corporal 20 July 1815. Reduced 30 November 1815. Died, 11 October 1816.

Lacey/Lacy, John. 88th Foot. Marched from Chester and confined aboard PS as John Lacy, 2 October 1813. Joined YCs as John Lacey, 1 February 1814. Arrived in the WIs 14 December 1814. Discharged Quebec.

Laker/Lacher, Thomas. Labourer of Leeds. 52nd Foot. Transported from Foveaux and confined aboard PS as Thomas Lacher or Laker, 8 November 1814. Joined YCs as John Laker 29 June 1815. Arrived in the WIs 5 November 1815. Died St Vincent, 17 January 1816.

Lamb, Israel. Labourer of Maidstone. 1st Bn 52nd Foot. Marched from Maidstone and confined aboard PS, 15 November 1814. Joined YCs 29 June 1815, and arrived in the WIs 5 November 1815. Died Tobago, 27 April 1816.

Lambeth, Thomas. Jeweller of Warwick. 3rd Foot Guards. Marched from Savoy Military Prison and confined at Portchester Castle, 14 December 1816. Joined YCs 3 April 1817, and arrived in the WIs 25 May 1817. Discharged from Stony Hill, Jamaica, 10 June 1819.

Land, Edward. Chair maker of Kent. 2nd Bn 43rd Foot. Marched from Savoy Military Prison and confined aboard PS, 13 October 1814. Joined YCs 29 June 1815, and arrived in the WIs 5 November 1815. Died Jamaica, 10 December 1817.

Lane, William. Labourer of Gloucestershire. 23rd Light Dragoons. Marched from Gloucester and confined aboard PS, 9 February 1814. Joined YCs 25 March 1814. Deserted while still at the Isle of Wight, 7 July 1814. Rejoined 27 July 1814. (No punishment records held.) Arrived in the WIs 14 December 1814. Promoted corporal 4 September 1815. Reduced 10 September 1818. Discharged Quebec.

Laroyd/Learoyd, George. Labourer of Yorkshire. 84th Foot. Marched from Bristol and confined aboard PS as George Heywith or Laroyd, 9 September 1813. Joined YCs as George Laroyd, 5 February 1814. Deserted while still at the Isle of Wight, 9 July 1814; seized by Henry A Brook (Twenty Shillings Bounty). Rejoined 22 July 1814. (No punishment records held.) Arrived in the WIs 14 December 1814. Discharged Quebec as George Learoyd.

Latham, George. 2nd Dragoon Guards. Marched from Hythe and confined aboard PS, 20 February 1814. Joined YCs 7 March 1814. 'Lost on passage to Barbados'.

Latiene/Latine, Joseph. Labourer of Tornau, Hungary. Joined 7th Line Bn, King's German Legion as John Latine, 31 December 1813. Deserted in Palermo, Sicily, 1 November 1814. Rejoined 10 December 1814. Sentenced to be 'Transferred for life to any Corps Abroad', 25 January 1815. Marched from Chatham and confined aboard PS, 14 May 1815. Joined the 6th Bn 60th Foot in Jamaica, 7 February 1816. Transferred into the York Chasseus as Joseph Latine, 25 May 1817. Deserted in Jamaica, 6 May 1818. Rejoined the next day. (No punishment records held.) Discharged Quebec as Joseph Latiene.

Laurence/Lawrence, William. 83rd Foot. Marched from Northampton and confined at Portchester Castle as William Laurence, 20 January 1817. Joined YCs 3 April 1817, and arrived in the WIs 25 May 1817. Discharged Quebec as William Lawrence.

Laws, William. Stocking weaver of Leeds. 10th Foot. Transported from Hilsea, Portsmouth, and confined aboard PS, 7 April 1816. Joined YCs 19 October 1816, and arrived in the WIs 21 December 1816. Deserted in Jamaica 28 July 1818. Rejoined 2 August 1818. Deserted in Jamaica 17 August 1818. Rejoined 23 August 1818. (No punishment records held.) Deserted in Jamaica, 28 December 1818. No record of rejoining.

Lawson, Robert. Labourer of Dumfries. 1st Foot Guards. Marched from Norwich and confined aboard PS, 29 September 1813. Joined YCs 1 February 1814. Deserted while still at the Isle of Wight, 24 June 1814. No record of rejoining.

Lax/Lay/Lan, John. 24th Foot. Marched from Oxford and confined aboard PS as John Lax, Lay or Lan, 3 December 1814. Joined YCs 29 June 1815, and arrived in the WIs 5 November 1815. Discharged Quebec as John Lax, Lay or Lan.

Laybourne/Leybourne/Leyborne, Lewis. Shoemaker of Kilpatrick. Royal Sappers and Miners. Marched from Savoy Military Prison and confined aboard PS as Lewis Leybourne, 22 October 1813. Joined YCs as Lewis Laybourne, 5 February 1814. Arrived in the WIs 14th December 1814. Died Jamaica as Lewis Leyborne, 21 January 1817.

Leach/Leech, Charles. 55th Foot. Marched from Plymouth and confined aboard PS as Charles Leech, 15 February 1814. Joined YCs 7 March 1814, and arrived in the WIs 14 December 1814. 'In the hands of the Civil Powers in Jamaica' from 23 December 1817 until released back to the regiment, 15 April 1818. Discharged Quebec as Charles Leach.

Leadbetter/Leadbeater, James. Arrived in the WIs as James Leadbetter or Leadbeater, 25 June 1816. Discharged Quebec as James Leadbetter.

Leader, Michael. Shoemaker of Norfolk. 1st Bn 23rd Foot. Marched from Norwich and confined aboard PS, 2 January 1815. Joined YCs 29 June 1815, and arrived in the WIs as drummer, 5 November 1815. Volunteer for the 58th Foot in Jamaica as drummer, 25 March 1819. Deserted in Jamaica 31 May 1819. Rejoined 5 June 1819. (No punishment record held.) Served in WIs until 1822, and Ceylon from 1828 until 1836. Invalided to England 'Suffering from Chronic Dysentery and a Debilitated Constitution', 30 November 1836. Discharged to a pension.

Ledger, James or **Joseph.** 4th Bn Royals. Marched from Haddington and confined aboard PS as James Ledger, 8 September 1813. Joined YCs as Joseph Ledger, 7 March 1814. Arrived in the WIs 14 December 1814. Discharged Quebec as James or Joseph Ledger.

Lee, Andrew. 99th Foot. Marched from Chester and confined aboard PS, 1 May 1815. Joined YCs 29 June 1815, and arrived in the West Indies 5 November 1815. Discharged Quebec.

Lee, James. Labourer of Kings County. 56th Foot. Marched from Dartford and confined aboard PS, 22 January 1816. Embarked Spithead amongst a 300-strong detachment of 'Unattached Deserters' joining the 2nd Foot, 25 April 1816. Arrived in the WIs 5 June 1816. Deserted 5 July 1816. Rejoined same day. 800 lashes for 'Desertion' at Barbados 20 July 1816. Transferred into the York Chasseurs, 25 August 1816. Deserted in Jamaica 28 February 1817. Rejoined 5 March 1817. 300 lashes for 'Absenting himself 1 week without Leave', 6 March 1817. Deserted in Jamaica 28 June 1817. Rejoined 1 July 1817. 300 lashes for 'Absenting himself without Leave', 4 July 1817. Deserted in Jamaica 2 July 1818. Rejoined 25 July 1818. Deserted in Jamaica 9 March 1819. Rejoined 20 March 1819. Deserted in Jamaica 22 May 1819. Rejoined 29 May 1819. (No punishment records held.) Discharged Quebec.

Lee, Thomas. 85th Foot. Marched from Dartford and confined at Portchester Castle, 20 December 1816. Joined YCs 3 April 1817, and arrived in the WIs 25 May 1817. Promoted corporal 4 March 1818. Reduced 2 May 1818. Discharged Quebec.

Leighley/Leighly, John. Labourer of Galway. Galway Militia. Marched from Winchester and confined aboard PS, 9 July 1814. Joined YCs 29 June 1815, and arrived in the WIs 5 November 1815. Died Tobago, 25 April 1816.

Leitner, Peter. Labourer of Prussia. 2nd Bn 28th Foot. Marched from Exeter and confined aboard PS, 18 September 1813. Joined YCs 5 February 1814. Promoted drummer 25 February 1814. Remained sick at Guernsey as the regiment left for Barbados. Arrived in the WIs 5 November 1815. Reduced 24 May 1816. Died St Vincent, 12 June 1816.

Lemmon, Charles. 2nd Bn 5th Foot. Marched from Guildford and confined aboard PS, 30 September 1814. Joined YCs 29 June 1815. 'Left on Detachment' as the regiment departed for St Vincent. Discharged from the Isle of Wight, 18 November 1816.

Lemmon, Thomas. Labourer of Suffolk. Transferred to YCs from the 101st Foot in Jamaica, 17 February 1817. Deserted in Jamaica, 20 January 1819. No record of rejoining.

Leonard, Andrew. 27th Foot. Transferred from Jersey and confined aboard PS, 8 March 1815. Arrived in the WIs 25 June 1816. 'Given over to the Civil Powers and Sentenced to Serve for life in the Royal Navy for Highway Robber', 22 July 1816. No further record.

Leonard, Owen. Painter of Devon. 88th Foot. Marched from Bristol and confined aboard PS, 16 August 1815. Embarked Spithead amongst a 300-strong detachment of 'Unattached Deserters' joining the 2nd Foot, 25 April 1816. Arrived in the WIs 5 June

1816. Transferred into the York Chasseurs 25 August 1816. Deserted 11 November 1816. Rejoined 31 December 1816. 300 lashes for 'Absenting himself 6 weeks without Leave', 7 January 1817. Deserted in Jamaica, 27 April 1819. No record of rejoining.

Lester, David. 39th Foot. Marched from Bath and confined aboard PS, 15 December 1814. Joined YCs 29 June 1815. No further record.

Letts, William. 2nd Bn 63rd Foot. Marched from Coventry and confined aboard PS, 7 February 1814. Joined YCs 29 June 1815, and arrived in the WIs 5 November 1815. Discharged Quebec.

Lewis, Henry. 55th Foot. Marched from Hythe and confined aboard PS, 29 October 1815. Joined YCs 16 May 1816, and arrived in the WIs 25 June 1816. Deserted 9 August 1816. No record of rejoining.

Lewis, John. Labourer of Denbigh or Haverford West. Either 2nd Bn 14th Foot marched from Wrexham, 3 March 1814, or 2nd Bn 5th Foot marched from Chelmsford and confined aboard PS, 27 April 1815. Joined YCs 29 June 1815, and arrived in the WIs 5 November 1815. Died Jamaica, 4 October 1817.

Lewis, John. Labourer of Shropshire or Denbigh or Haverfordwest. Either 2nd Bn 14th Foot marched from Wrexham, 3 March 1814, or 2nd Bn 5th Foot marched from Chelmsford and confined aboard PS, 27 April 1815. Joined YCs 29 June 1815, and arrived in the WIs 5 November 1815. Died Tobago, 6 September 1816.

Lilburne/Leybourne, Daniel. Royal Sappers and Miners. Marched from Maidstone and confined aboard PS as Daniel Lilburne or Leybourne, 22 October 1813. Joined YCs as Daniel Lilburne, 1 February 1814, and arrived in the WIs 14 December 1814. Transferred to Royal York Rangers, 24 February 1815.

Limaghan/Lanaghan, Peter. 95th Foot. Marched from Dover and confined aboard PS as Peter Limaghan or Lenaghan, 15 November 1815. Joined YCs 29 June 1815, and arrived in the WIs as Peter Limaghan, 5 November 1815. 100 lashes for being 'Absent from his Barracks Overnight', 10 December1816. Remitted 'Due to his former Good Character'. Discharged Quebec.

Lindsay/Lindsey, John. Shoemaker of Down or Dover. 3rd Bn 27th Foot. Marched from Ayr and confined aboard PS, 17 August 1813. Joined YCs 7 March 1814. Deserted while still at the Isle of Wight, 10 July 1814. Rejoined 20 July 1814, and hospitalised. (No punishment records held.) Arrived in the WIs 14 December 1814. Died Jamaica, 5 March 1817.

Liptrot, James. Labourer of Lancashire. Royal Artillery. Marched from Canterbury and confined aboard PS, 12 December 1813. Joined YCs 7 March 1814. Deserted while still at the Isle of Wight, 3 July 1814. No record of rejoining.

Lloyd/Loyd, Edward. Button maker of Birmingham. 2nd Bn 44th Foot. Marched from Wakefield and confined aboard PS, 12 January 1814. Joined YCs 25 March 1814, and arrived in the WIs 14 December 1814. Died Jamaica, 10 April 1819.

Logue, James. 21st Foot. Marched from Chester and confined aboard PS, 2 October 1813. Joined YCs 7 March 1814, and arrived in the WIs 14 December 1814. Discharged Quebec.

London/Lowden, David. Weaver of Fife. 75th Foot. Marched from Edinburgh and confined aboard PS, 18 January 1814. Joined YCs 25 March 1814. Deserted while still at the Isle of Wight, 2 July 1814. No record of rejoining.

Long, James. Sadler of Louth. Embarked Spithead amongst a 300-strong detachment of 'Unattached Deserters' joining the 2nd Foot, 25 April 1816. Arrived in the WIs 5 June 1816. Deserted 19 July 1816. Rejoined 21 July 1816. 1,000 lashes, 23 July 1816. Transferred into the York Chasseurs, 25 August 1816. Deserted 22 September 1816. Rejoined 25 October 1816. 300 lashes for 'Absenting himself one month without Leave', 28 October 1816. Died Jamaica, 3 January 1817.

Long, John. Labourer of County Down. 1st Bn 11th Foot. Marched from Plymouth Docks and confined aboard PS, 10 November 1813. Joined YCs 1 February 1814, and arrived in the WIs 14 December 1814. Deserted in Jamaica 26 May 1819. Rejoined 2 June 1819. (No punishment records held.) Deserted 23 June 1819, the day prior to the regiment leaving for Canada. No record of rejoining.

Longworth, John. Labourer of Dean, Lancs. Joined 2nd Dragoon Guards, 21 July 1808, possibly employed in suppressing the 'Luddites,' 1812–1813. With Edward Tarling, marched from Sheffield and confined aboard PS, 19 August 1813. Joined YCs 1 February 1814. Promoted drummer 25 February 1815. Deserted while still at the Isle of Wight, 13 July 1814. Rejoined 26 July 1814. (No punishment records held.) Arrived in the WIs 14 December 1814. 200 lashes for 'Being in possession of a shirt not his own', 4 July 1815. Deserted in Grenada, 31 August 1815. 'Apprehended and detained the next day on Board a brig, by a detachment of the 60th Foot under orders for Guadeloupe'. Transferred to the Bourbon Regiment as sergeant, 25 December 1815. With the Bourbon Regiment disbanded, April 1816, Longworth was transferred to the 1st West India Regiment. 'Reduced and 14 days solitary confinement for Wilful Disobedience of Orders', 5 September 1816. Transferred as a private to the 15th Foot at Grenada, December 1816, and embarked on the troopship *Hydra* for Halifax, Nova Scotia, August 1817. Deserting at Nova Scotia, 7 February 1819, Longworth made his way back to the 15th's Regimental Depot, Isle of Wight, where he surrendered, 26 August 1820. Rejoining his regiment, 31 July 1821, Longworth was next arraigned at Plymouth before a Regimental Court Martial, 25 March 1822, to be awarded '14 days solitary confinement for Refusing to go on Regimental Fatigues, and Repeatedly Refusing to go on Drill'. After which, 13 June 1822 and with the 15th Foot at Hull waiting to embark for service in Ireland, Longworth deserted. Brought before the Derby Assizes, 15 July 1826, and accused of stealing two saddles, Longworth, now 29 years of age and described as farmer, ploughman and sheep shearer from Famworth, Lancashire, and not as a deserter from the 15th, was transported to Van Dieman's Land. In 1854, surviving all the rigours of a transported felon, Longworth, the free man, died falling drunk under the wheels of the brewer's dray he was driving.

Loughman, Patrick. Labourer of Cavan. 88th Foot. Marched from Dover and confined aboard PS, 24 July 1816. Joined YCs 18 October 1816, and arrived in the WIs 21 December 1816. 300 lashes for 'Unsoldierlike Conduct in threatening to make a false report of the Commanding Officer and Adjutant', 2 February 1818. 'EXECUTED AT KINGSTON FOR THE MURDER OF HIS WIFE', 5 September 1818.

Louth, Michael. Labourer of Armagh. North Militia. Marched from Peterborough and confined aboard PS, 10 October 1813. Joined YCs 1 February 1814. Deserted while still at the Isle of Wight, 7 July 1814. No record of rejoining.

Lovell, Henry. Baker of Halifax. 65th Foot. Marched from Savoy Military Prison and confined at Portchester Castle, 9 December 1816. Joined YCs 3 April 1817, and arrived in the WIs 25 May 1817. Deserted in Jamaica 8 May 1818. Rejoined 12 May 1818. (No punishment records held.) Discharged from Stony Hill, Jamaica, 10 June 1819.

Lowe, Michael. 11th Foot. Marched from Bristol and confined aboard PS, 18 May 1815. Joined YCs 29 June 1815, and arrived in the WIs 5 November 1815. Deserted 25 December 1815. Rejoined 19 January 1816. (No punishment records held.) 12 months solitary confinement in irons for 'Mutinous Conduct', 5 June 1816. Imprisoned aboard the Port Royal flag ship, Jamaica. In the company of Andrew Hay, William James and Robert Farnley, transported to England and confined in Portchester Castle to await instructions for his future disposal, 25 May 1817. No further record.

Lowe, Thomas. 1st Bn 1st Guards. Marched from Savoy Military Prison and confined aboard PS, 25 December 1814. Joined YCs 29 June 1815, and arrived in the WIs 5 November 1815. Promoted corporal 25 August 1816. 200 lashes and ordered to be reduced for being 'Drunk on Guard', 4 November 1816. Corporal punishment remitted. Discharged Quebec.

Luck, Richard. Blacksmith. 15th Light Dragoons. Marched from Gloucester and confined aboard PS, 30 September 1813. Joined YCs 1 February 1813. Deserted while still at the Isle of Wight, 13 June 1814. No record of rejoining.

Lupton, John. 33rd Foot. Marched from York Castle and confined aboard PS, 5 June 1815. Joined YCs 29 June 1815, and arrived in the WIs 5 November 1815. Discharged Quebec.

Lurcook, Thomas. 50th Foot. Marched from Maidstone and confined at Portchester Castle, 9 December 1816. Joined YCs 3 April 1817, and arrived in the WIs 25 May 1817. Discharged Quebec.

Lusty, William. Volunteer from 2nd Bn Tower Hamlets Militia, 6 December 1813 (Six Guinea Bounty). Promoted corporal 24 February 1814. Reduced 6 April 1814. Arrived in the WIs 14 December 1814. Promoted corporal 30 December 1814, sergeant 29 November 1817. Reduced 3 March 1818. Discharged at Quebec, 24 September 1819. As a volunteer possibly returned at public expense.

Lynch, Daniel. Labourer of Waterford. 2nd Bn 66th Foot. Transported from Portsmouth and confined aboard PS, 27 August 1816. Joined YCs 19 October 1816, and arrived in the WIs 21 December 1816. Deserted in Jamaica 30 January 1817. No record of rejoining.

Lynch, Francis. 16th Foot. Marched from Chester and confined aboard PS 3 March 1814. Joined YCs 25 March 1814, and arrived in the WIs 14 December 1814. Discharged Quebec.

Lynn/Linn, William. Bricklayer of Brighton. 76th Foot. Marched from Horsham and confined aboard PS as William Linn, 3 September 1813. Joined YCs 28 August 1814. Deserted while still at the Isle of Wight as William Lynn, 28 August 1814. No record of rejoining.

Lynsky, John. Labourer of Galway. Embarked Spithead amongst a 300-strong detachment of 'Unattached Deserters' joining the 2nd Foot, 25 April 1816. Arrived in the WIs 5 June 1816. Transferred into the York Chasseurs, 25 August 1816. Deserted in Jamaica 29 December 1816. Rejoined 1 January 1817. 800 lashes and ordered to be marked with 'D' for 'Desertion when on Main Guard at Stony Hill and not returning until brought back by an Escort', 9 January 1817. Deserted in Jamaica 30 March 1817. Rejoined 6 May 1817. 300 lashes for being 'Absent without Leave', 9 May 1817. Deserted in Jamaica 5 July 1817. Rejoined 21 July 1817. Deserted in Jamaica 15 July 1818. Rejoined 29 July 1818. (No punishment records held.) Deserted in Jamaica, 18 May 1819. No record of rejoining.

Lyons, Joseph or **Joshua.** 10th Foot. Marched from Huntington and confined aboard PS as Joshua Lyons, 7 October 1813. Joined YCs 7 March 1814, and arrived in the WIs as Joseph Lyons, 14 December 1814. Discharged Quebec.

Lyons, Patrick. Labourer of Kilkenny. 30th Foot. Marched from Winchester and confined aboard PS, 4 March 1815. Joined YCs 29 June 1815 and arrived in the WIs 5 November 1815. Deserted at Grenada, 12 February 1816. No record of rejoining.

Lyons, Thomas. Labourer of Galway. Kilkenny Militia. Sentenced to General Service for 'Desertion and making away with his Necessaries', 28 November 1813. Marched from Harwich and confined aboard PS, 31 December 1813. Joined YCs 7 March 1814. Deserted while still at the Isle of Wight, 7 July 1814. No record of rejoining.

Mackay/McKay, John. Labourer of Armagh. 69th Foot. Transported from Portsmouth and confined aboard PS as John Mackay, 10 January 1814. Joined YCs as John McKay, 7 March 1814, and arrived in the WIs 14 December 1814. Died as John Mackey, 5 November 1816. Willed his effects, one pound and tenpence to wife, Mary Mackay of Ballycoston, Ballyclare.

Madras/Madrass, John. Pocketbook maker of Leeds. Arrived in Jamaica as a transfer from 51st Foot, 25 January 1818. Deserted in Jamaica 20 August 1818. Rejoined 23 August 1818. Deserted in Jamaica 25 September 1818. Rejoined 23 December 1818. (No punishment records held.) Discharged Quebec.

Magher/Mahar, Thomas. Labourer of Ardfinnan, Tipperary. 74th Foot. Marched from Chester and confined aboard PS as Thomas Magher or Maher, 3 March 1814. Joined YCs as Thomas Mahar, 25 March 1814. Deserted while still at the Isle of Wight, 17 June 1814. No record of rejoining.

Maher/Meagher, Patrick. Labourer of Tipperary. 43rd Foot. Marched from Plymouth and confined aboard PS as Patrick Meagher, 2 February 1815. Joined YCs 29th June 1815, and arrived in the West Indies 5 November 1815. Promoted drummer 25 April 1816. Deserted in Jamaica 28 November 1817. Rejoined 11 December.1817. Reduced to private 19 December 1817. (No punishment records held.) Promoted drummer 25 January 1818. Deserted in Jamaica 6 February 1819. Rejoined 13 February 1818. (No punishment records held.) Discharged Quebec as Patrick Maher.

Mahon, John. Weaver of Tyrone. Volunteer. Served with Breadalbane Fencibles, 29 May 1793 to 29 May 1800. 71st Foot from 30 May 1800 to 9 March 1813. Royal Veteran Battalion from 10 March 1815 to 10 May 1815. Joined YCs as colour sergeant, 11 May 1815, and arrived in the WIs 5 November 1815. Reduced 18 June 1816. Promoted corporal 25 November 1816, sergeant, 2 December 1816. Reduced 23 August 1817. Died Jamaica, 8 February 1819.

Mahoney/Mahony, Cornelius. Labourer of Antrim. 52nd Foot. Transported from Foveaux and marched from Dover to be confined aboard PS, 4 August 1815. Joined YCs 19 October 1816, and arrived in the WIs 21 December 1816. 300 lashes for being 'Drunk on Duty', 2 October 1817. Deserted in Jamaica 5 June 1817. Rejoined,18 June 1817. Deserted in Jamaica 10 July 1817. Rejoined next day. Deserted in Jamaica 31 March 1819. Rejoined 20 April 1819. (No punishment records held.) Deserted in Jamaica 26 May 1819. No record of rejoining.

Mahoney, Dennis. Labourer of Cork. 2nd Bn 37th Foot. Marched from Maidstone and confined aboard PS, 12 January 1814. Joined YCs 1 February 1814, and arrived in the WIs 14 December 1814. Died at Guadeloupe 9 August 1815. One of seven rank and file 'supposed to have been poisoned'.

Mahoney/Mahony, Dennis. Weaver from Limerick. 85th Foot. Marched from Winchester and confined aboard PS, 6 April 1816. Joined YCs 19 October 1816, and arrived in the WIs 21 December 1816. Solitary confinement for 'Loosing or Making away with his Necessaries', 26 December 1816. Died Jamaica, 19 October 1817.

Mahor/Mahon, Patrick. Labourer of Kilkenny. 37th Foot. Marched from Bristol and confined at Portchester Castle, 21 January 1817. Joined YCs 3 April 1817, and arrived in the WIs 25 May 1817. Deserted in Jamaica 28 November 1817. Rejoined 11 December 1817. Deserted in Jamaica 6 February 1819. Rejoined 13 February 1819. (No punishment records held.) Died Jamaica, 2 March 1819, two weeks after returning from desertion and no doubt punishment.

Main/Maine, William. East Devon Militia. Marched from Bristol and confined aboard PS, 22 February 1814. Joined YCs 25 March 1814. Deserted while still at the Isle of Wight, 7 July 1814. No record of rejoining.

Mains/Maines, John. Gardener of Renfrew. 4th Royals. Marched from Edinburgh and confined aboard PS, 11 November 1813. Joined YCs 5 February 1814, and arrived in the WIs 14 December 1814. Died Tobago, 2 August 1816.

Maloney, Michael. Joined 1st Bn 28th Foot, 13th May 1805. Confined aboard PS, 3 March 1814. Joined YCs 25 March 1814, and arrived in the WIs 14 December 1814. 150 lashes for 'Destroying a Fowle belonging to Capt Anderson', 3 June 1815, 50 lashes remitted; 100 lashes for being 'Absent from Parade' 11 July 1815; 200 lashes for 'Drunkeness' 14 July 1815. Died of wounds received in action at Guadeloupe, 10 August 1815.

Mann, William. Marched from Savoy Military Prison and confined aboard PS, 1 December 1813. Joined YCs 7 March 1814, and arrived in the WIs 14 December 1814. Discharged Quebec.

Manning, Thomas. Labourer of Nottinghamshire. 2nd Bn 32nd Foot. Marched from Devizes and confined aboard PS, 1 November 1814. Joined YCs 29 June 1815, and arrived in the WIs 5 November 1815. Deserted at Grenada 14 November 1815. No record of rejoining.

Marcott, William. Labourer of Derby. 3rd Bn 14th Foot. Marched from Daventry and confined aboard PS, 25 February 1815. Joined YCs 29 June 1815 and arrived in the WIs as drummer, 5 November 1815. Reduced 3 December 1816. 250 lashes for being 'Drunk and Riotous in Barracks', 8 September 1817, 150 lashes remitted. Deserted in Jamaica 23 September 1817. Rejoined 29 September 1817. (No punishment records held.) Solitary confinement for 'Drunk of Parade', 17 November 1817. Deserted in Jamaica 18 June 1818. Rejoined 28 June 1818. (No punishment records held.) Died Jamaica, 23 July 1818, less than a month after rejoining from desertion and no doubt punishment.

Marley, James. 1st Royals. Marched from Chester and confined aboard PS as James Marley, Marly or Gowry, 15 October 1813. Joined YCs as James Marley, 29 June 1815. Deserted from Fort Cumberland, Portsmouth, when left sick as the regiment departed for St Vincent. Recaptured at Winchester and re-confined, 8 April 1816. No further record.

Marshall, John or **Thomas B**. Labourer of Newark. Royal Horse Artillery. Marched from Nottingham and confined aboard PS as John Marshall, 8 February 1814. Joined YCs 7 March 1814, and arrived in the WIs 14 December 1814. As Thomas B Marshall promoted corporal,14 October 1815. Reduced, date unknown. As John B Marshall, sentenced to 300 lashes for 'Unsoldierlike conduct in firing at a negro woman', 1 September 1817. Deserted in Jamaica 4 May 1818. Rejoined 21 May 1818. (No punishment record held.)

Deserted in Jamaica 31 March 1819. No record of rejoining.

Martin, Bernard. 32nd Foot. Marched from Liverpool and confined aboard PS, 28 December 1814. Joined YCs 29 June 1815, and arrived in the WIs 5 November 1815. 150 lashes for 'Absenting himself without leave from Evening Parade', 26 December 1816. Discharged Quebec.

Martin, John. Paper maker of Carnarvon. 1st Bn 52nd Foot. Marched from Carnarvon and confined aboard PS, 21 July 1813. Joined YCs as corporal, 1 February 1814, and promoted sergeant 25 March 1814. Reduced 3 September 1814. Arrived in the WIs 14 December 1814. Deserted in Jamaica, date unknown. Returned to England, recaptured at Liverpool as John Martin alias Vensmore, 22 September 1816. Marched to Portchester Castle 'with a view to his being forwarded from thence, when an opportunity offers to rejoin the York Chasseurs in Jamaica'. Arrived back in the WIs 21 December 1816. Deserted in Jamaica 30 June 1817. No record of rejoining.

Martin, John. Tailor of Down. 2nd Bn 50th Foot. Marched from Savoy Military Prison and confined aboard PS, 14 August 1814. Joined YCs 29 June 1815, and arrived in the WIs 5 November 1815. Promoted drummer 29 September 1816. Died Jamaica 24 March 1818.

Martin/Morton, Joseph. Plaisterer of York. 1st Bn 51st Foot. Marched from Wakefield and confined aboard PS as Joseph Morton or Martin, 23 January 1814. Joined YCs as Joseph Martin, 25 March 1814, and arrived in the WIs 14 February 1814. Died, 14 December 1816.

Martin, Thomas. 7th Dragoon Guards. Marched from Edinburgh and confined aboard PS, 18 August 1814. Joined YCs 29 June 1815. Released to 14th Foot, 11 July 1815.

Mason, Thomas. Labourer of York. 14th Light Dragoons. Marched from Worcester and confined aboard PS, 3 October 1813. Joined YCs 7 March 1814, and arrived in the WIs 14 December 1814. Died, 7 October 1816.

Mason, William. 55th Foot. Marched from Ely and confined aboard PS, 27 July 1813. Joined YCs 7 March 1814, and arrived in the WIs 14 December 1814. Discharged Quebec.

Massey, Edward. Labourer of Worcestershire. 21st Light Dragoons. Marched from Dartford and confined aboard PS, 14 November 1813. Joined YCs 7 March 1814, and arrived in the WIs 14 December 1814. Died St Vincent, 6 October 1815.

Masters/Masterman, John. Calico printer of Dublin. 1st Bn 83rd Foot. Marched from Winchester and confined aboard PS as John Masterman, 10 October 1813. Joined YCs as John Masters, 1 February 1814. Arrived in the WIs 14 December 1814. Deserted in Jamaica 18 May 1819. Rejoined 4 June 1819. (No punishment records held.) Discharged Quebec as John Masters.

Mathews, George. 2nd Bn Foot Guards. Marched from Gloucester and confined aboard PS, 23 January 1814. Joined YCs 25 March 1814, and arrived in the WIs 14 December 1814. 'In the hands of the Civil Power Barbados from 25th June 1815 on suspicion of making and uttering Base-Coin'. Returned to regiment, September 1815. Discharged Quebec.

Mathews, Patrick. 83rd Foot. Marched from Chester and confined aboard PS, 14th November 1813. Joined YCs 1st February 1814. Remained sick in the General Hospital, Cork, when the regiment left for Barbados. Deserted at Cove of Cork, 26 October 1814. No record of rejoining.

Mathews, Peter. Labourer of Louth. 55th Foot. Marched from Savoy Military Prison and confined aboard PS, 14 November 1813. Joined YCs 1 February 1814, and arrived in the WIs 14 December 1814. Deserted in Barbados 4 January 1815. Rejoined 9 January 1815. (No punishment records held.) Died Grenada, 17 December 1815.

Maycock, John. Labourer of Renfrew. 54th Foot. Marched from Eccles and confined aboard PS, 15 August 1813. Joined YCs 1 February 1814. Promoted corporal 28 May 1814. Reduced 30 June 1814. Arrived in the WIs 14 December 1814. Promoted corporal 8 January 1816. Reduced 15 March 1816. Deserted in Jamaica date unknown. Rejoined 20 August 1818. (No punishment record held.) Discharged Quebec.

McCabe, John. Weaver of King's County. 70th Foot. Marched from Chester and confined aboard PS, 8 December 1813. Joined YCs 1 February 1814 and arrived in the WIs 14 December 1814. 300 lashes for being 'Drunk on Guard', 26 December 1816. Died Jamaica, 2 February 1817, less than two months after punishment.

McCabe, Thomas. Weaver of Monaghan. 71st Foot. Transported from Jersey and confined aboard PS, 22 August 1815. Embarked Spithead amongst a 300-strong detachment of 'Unattached Deserters' joining the 2nd Foot, 25 April 1816. Arrived in the WIs 5 June 1816. Transferred into the York Chasseurs 25 August 1816. 150 lashes for 'Telling Corporal Brooks "To Kiss his Arse"', 10 December 1816. Commuted to solitary confinement; 300 lashes for being 'Drunk on Duty', 4 July 1817; 200 lashes for 'Making away with his Regimental Necessities', 31 July 1817, 50 lashes remitted. Deserted in Jamaica 28 April 1819. Rejoined 7 May 1819. (No punishment records held.) Died Jamaica, 18 May 1819, less than two weeks after rejoining from desertion and no doubt punishment.

McCann, John. Labourer of Donegal. 1st Foot. Marched from Bristol and confined aboard PS, 28 May 1815. Joined YCs 29 June 1815. 'Left on Detachment' as the regiment departed for St Vincent. Arrived in the WIs 19 December 1816. Deserted in Jamaica, 22 November 1817. Rejoined, 25 November 1817. Deserted in Jamaica, 10 June 1819. Rejoined the next day. (No punishment records held) Discharged Quebec.

McCarlin/McCarlan, William. Weaver of Tyrone. 26th Foot. Marched from Chester and confined aboard PS as William McCarlan, Kelly or Carr, 18 May 1815. Joined YCs as William McCarlin, 29 June 1815. Arrived in the WIs 5 November 1815. Deserted in Jamaica 5 July 1817. Rejoined 8 July 1817. (No punishment records held.) Deserted in Jamaica 5 September 1817. No record of rejoining.

McCarthy, Cornelius. Shoemaker of Armagh. Arrived in the WIs as corporal, 15 November 1815. Reduced 23 May 1816. Deserted in Jamaica, 13 April 1819. No record of rejoining.

McCarthy, John. Either 2nd Bn 44th Foot 'Sentenced at Ostend to General Service and Ordered to be marked with D as a Deserter', 14 November 1814, or 1st Garrison Bn marched from Bristol and confined aboard PS, 1 May 1815. Joined YCs 29 June 1815, and arrived in the WIs 5 November 1815. Promoted drummer 25 December 1815. Reduced 12 August 1816. Discharged Quebec. Served as drummer in Captain McDonell's Company of Glengary Highlanders during 1839. Settled in Low County, Ontario. Petitioned the Commander in Chief of the British North America Forces, Lieutenant General Sir W F Williams 'Requesting for relief in consideration of my services as Drummer from 1809 to 1819 in the "York Chasseurs" commanded by Colonel Hewit, due to my most destitute condition', 23 January 1865.

McCarthy, John. Labourer of Armagh. Either 2nd Bn 44th Foot 'Sentenced at Ostend to General Service and Ordered to be marked with D as a Deserter', 14 November 1814, or

1st Garrison Bn marched from Bristol and confined aboard PS, 1 May 1815. Joined YCs 29 June 1815, and arrived in the WIs 5 November 1815. Deserted in Jamaica 30 March 1819. Rejoined the next day. (No punishment records held.) Discharged Quebec.

McCasland/MaCasland, John. Royals. Marched from Chester and confined aboard PS as John MaCasland, 2 October 1813. Joined YCs as John McCasland, 25 March 1814. Arrived in the WIs14 December 1814. Discharged Quebec.

McChristie/McCristie, John. Blacksmith of Donoughmore. Joined 80th Foot, 25th May 1808, discharged to pension, 7 August 1813. Joined 18th Light Dragoons, 18 August 1813. Marched from Chester and confined aboard PS as John McCristie, 1 November 1813. Joined as John McChristie 1 February 1814. Promoted sergeant 25 February 1814. Reduced 20 April 1814. Arrived in the WIs 14 December 1814. 12 months solitary confinement at Barbados, 1815; 150 lashes for 'Being Absent from Morning and Evening',11 March 1817. Died Jamaica, 11 October 1817.

McClure, James. Labourer of Armagh. 2nd Bn 36th Foot. Marched from Maidstone and confined aboard PS as James McClure or Quinn, 31 January 1814. Joined YCs as James McLure, 25 March 1814, and arrived in the WIs14 December 1814. 300 lashes for being 'Absent from Morning Parade and making away with his Necessaries', 15 May 1815. Received 50 lashes and the remainder commuted to 20 days solitary confinement; 300 lashes for 'Refusing to go to Guard Duty', 10 July 1815; 1,000 lashes for 'Stabbing Private William Price and Making use of Mutinous and Threatening words to Captain Anderson', 10 December 1816' Deserted in Jamaica 31 March 1819. Rejoined 14 April 1819. (No punishment records held.) Deserted in Jamaica 11 May 1819. No record of rejoining.

McClusky, Arthur. Tailor of Derry. Transferred into the YCs from the 6th Bn 60th Foot in Jamaica, 25 May 1817. Deserted in Jamaica 1 October 1818. No record of rejoining.

McConnell, Alexander. Labourer of Antrim. Royal Artillery Driver. Marched from Chester and confined aboard PS 28 December 1814. Joined YCs 29 June 1815, and arrived in the WIs 5 November 1815. Died Jamaica, 5 May 1818.

McConnell, Michael. 87th Foot Recruit. Transferred from Regimental Depot, 1 April 1815, and 'Left on Detachment.'. Arrived in the WIs 19 December 1816. Discharged Quebec. McConnell, with wife and young son, settled Concession 10. Lot NE 13. Beckwith. 'Sold to Patrick Nowland for £15, 5 January 1833'.

McCormick, Bernard. Labourer of Fermanagh. Transferred into the YCs from the 6th Bn 60th Foot in Jamaica, 21 May 1817. 300 lashes for being 'Drunk on Duty', 1 September 1817. Deserted in Jamaica 27 April 1819. Rejoined 30 April 1819. (No punishment records held.) Discharged Quebec.

McCormick, Francis. Labourer of Armagh. 21st Foot. Marched from Chester and confined aboard PS, 16 April 1815. Joined YCs 29 June 1815 and arrived in the WIs 5 November 1815. Died Tobago, 25 July 1816.

McCormick. John. 96th Foot. Marched from Derby and confined at Portchester Castle, 7 January 1817. Joined YCs 3 April 1817, and arrived in the WIs 25 May 1817. Promoted drummer 11 January 1818. Discharged Quebec.

McCormick, Patrick. Labourer of Mayo. 90th Foot. Marched from Chester and confined aboard PS, 26 September 1813. Joined YCs 5 February 1814. Deserted while still at the Isle of Wight, 9 July 1814. Rejoined 17 July 1814, and hospitalised. (No punishment records held.) Arrived in the WIs 14 December 1814. Discharged Quebec.

McCourt, Owen. 40th Foot. Marched from Dover and confined aboard PS, 26 March 1816. Joined YCs 19 October 1816, and arrived in the WIs 21 December 1816. Discharged Quebec.

McCue, James. Labourer of Armagh. Either 39th Foot marched from Chester, 12 November 1813, or 50th Foot from Bristol and confined aboard PS 20 November 1813. Joined YCs 25 March 1814. Deserted while still at the Isle of Wight, 5 July 1814. No record of rejoining.

McCue, Patrick. Labourer of Fermanagh. 90th Foot. Confined aboard PS, 23 January 1814. Joined YCs 25 March 181,4 and arrived in the WIs 14 December 1814. Deserted in Jamaica 9 May 1819. Rejoined 13 May 1819. (No punishment records held.) Discharged Quebec.

McCullock, Terence. Royal Artillery. Marched from Chester and confined aboard PS, 25 March 1815. Joined YCs 29 June 1815, and embarked for Guernsey 28 November 1815. No further record.

McDonald, Angus. 79th Foot. Sentenced at General Courts-martial convened at Cork 30 August 1814: 'To be Shot for Desertion to the Enemy and Disobedience in going Beyond the Piquets 23rd October 1813'. Commuted to service abroad for life, 30 September 1814. Confined aboard PS 15 January 1815. Joined YCs 29 June 1815, and arrived in the WIs 5 November 1815. Discharged Quebec.

McDonald, Archibald. 79th Foot. Marched from Bristol and confined aboard PS 22 September 1814. Arrived in the WIs 8 May 1815. Discharged Quebec.

McDonald, Charles. Joined 79th Foot, 31 May 1808. Marched from Bristol and confined aboard PS 22 November 1814. Joined YCs 29 June 1815 and arrived in the WIs 5 November 1815. Discharged Quebec.

McDonald, David. Butcher of Perth. 79th Foot. Marched from Bristol and confined aboard PS 15 January 1815. Joined YCs 29 June 1815, and arrived in the WIs 5 November 1815. Deserted in Jamaica 2 February 1818. Rejoined 12 February 1818. Deserted in Jamaica 1 April 1819. Rejoined 5 April 1819. (No punishment records held.) Discharged Quebec.

McDonald, Edward. Weaver of Edinburgh. Either 34th Foot marched from Liverpool, 28 September 1815, or 1st Bn from Savoy Military Prison and confined aboard PS 1 February 1816. Joined YCs 16 June 1816, and arrived in the WIs 25 August 1816. Died Jamaica, 18 December 1816.

McDonald, John. Labourer of Roscommon. Either 28th Foot marched from Chester, 26 October 1814, or 2nd Bn 71st Foot marched from Greenock and confined aboard PS, 7 May 1815. Joined YCs 29 June 1815, and arrived in the WIs 5 November 1815. Deserted 20 May 1816. Rejoined the next day. Deserted in Jamaica 31 March 1819. Rejoined, date unknown. (No punishment records held.) Discharged Quebec. Allocated Concession 10. Lot 8 Beckwith. 'Sold to Richard Edwards for £30, 12th May 1828'.

McDonald, John. Either 28th Foot marched from Chester, 26th October 1814, or 2nd Bn 71st Foot marched from Greenock and confined aboard PS, 7 May 1815. Joined YCs 29 June 1815, and arrived in the WIs 5 November 1815. Promoted corporal 25 February 1816, sergeant 16 March 1816. Reduced 12 August 1816. Discharged Quebec.

McDonald, Thomas. Labourer of Donegal. 2nd Bn 26th Foot. Marched from Glasgow and confined aboard PS, 20 February 1814. Joined YCs 7 March 1814. Deserted while still at the Isle of Wight, 7 July 1814. No record of rejoining.

McDonough, Patrick or **Terrence.** Hosier of Longford. 83rd Foot. Marched from Chester and confined aboard PS as Patrick McDonough, 1 May 1815. Joined YCs 29 June 1815, and arrived in the WIs as Terrence McDonough 5 November 1815. Died Jamaica as Patrick McDonough, 23 August 1818.

McDougal/McDougall, William. Labourer of Sheerness. 70th Foot. Marched from Edinburgh and confined aboard PS, 8 August 1813. Joined YCs 7 March 1814. Deserted Bear Haven, Cork, 15 October 1814. 'Was taken up in Bridge Town, Barbados disguised as a sailor', 13 April 1815. Deserted in Jamaica 10 April 1817. Rejoined 14 April 1817. Deserted in Jamaica 15 May 1817. Rejoined the same day. Deserted in Jamaica 26 January 1818. Rejoined 28 January. Deserted in Jamaica 5 August 1818. Rejoined the next day. (No punishment records held.) Discharged Quebec.

McEntee/Mcintee, Daniel. 20th Dragoons. Marched from Hounslow and confined aboard PS as Daniel Mcintee, 29 May 1816. Joined YCs as Daniel McEntee,19 October 1816. Arrived in the WIs 21 December 1816. Died Jamaica, 23 November 1818.

McFadden, Manus. Labourer of Donegal. Marched from Edinburgh and confined at Portchester Castle, 26 December 1816. Joined YCs 3 April 1817, and arrived in the WIs 25 May 1817. Deserted in Jamaica 28 April 1819. Rejoined 8 May 1819. (No punishments record held) Discharged Quebec.

McGearey/McGeary, Edward. Labourer of Dublin. 6th Dragoons. Marched from Chester and confined aboard PS, 23 March 1815. Joined YCs 29 June 1815, and arrived in the WIs as Edward McGearey, 5 November 1815. Deserted in Grenada 11 March 1816. Rejoined 16 March 1816. (No punishment records held.) Discharged Quebec as Edward McGeary.

McGee/Magee, George. Labourer of Monaghan. 49th Foot, Marched from Chester and confined at Portchester Castle as McGee or Magee, 27 December 1816. Joined YCs as George McGee, 3 April 1816. Arrived in the WIs 25 May 1815. Solitary confinement for 'Loosing or making away with his Greatcoat', 5 January 1818. Deserted in Jamaica 2 March 1819. No record of rejoining.

McGinness, Daniel. Labourer of Cork. 74th Foot. Marched from Chester and confined at Portchester Castle, 26 December 1816. Joined YCs 3 April 181,7 and arrived in the WIs 25 May 1817. Died Jamaica, 7 October 1817.

McGovern, James. Joined YCs 5 February 1814, and arrived in the WIs 14 December 1814. 300 lashes for being 'Absent without Leave', 31 May 1815, 100 lashes remitted. Discharged Quebec.

McGowen/McGovern, Thomas. Weaver of Tyrone. 71st Foot. Marched from Chester and confined aboard PS as Thomas McGowen, 14 November 1813. Joined YCs 5 February 1814. Deserted while still at Isle of Wight, 7 July 1814. Rejoined 24 July. (No punishment records held.) Deserted at Guernsey as Thomas McGovern 22 September 1814. No record of rejoining.

McGrichen/McGonkin/McGuicken, Luke. Servant of Ireland. Londonderry Militia. Marched from Dover and confined aboard PS as Luke McGrichen, date unknown. Joined YCs 29 June 1815. Deserted at Portsmouth as Luke McGonkin or McGuicken, 21 July 1815. No record of rejoining

McGueary/McQuary/McLeary, Laughlin or **Loughilin**. Labourer of Dublin. 12th Light Dragoons. Marched from Chester and confined aboard PS as Laughlin McQuery, 28 December 1814. Joined YCs 29 June 1815, and arrived in the WIs as Laughlin McGueary, 5th November 1815. Deserted as Laughlin McQuary or Loughlin McLeary, 29 August 1816. No record of rejoining.

McIndoe, William. Weaver of Renfrew. 74th Foot. Marched from Chester and confined aboard PS, 16 August 1815. Embarked Spithead amongst a 300-strong detachment of 'Unattached Deserters' joining the 2nd Foot, 25 April 1816. Arrived in the WIs 5 June 1816. Deserted 19 July 1816. Rejoined 21 July 1816. 1,000 lashes, 24 July 1816. Transferred into the York Chasseurs, 25 August 1816. Deserted 30 September 1816. Rejoined 11 October 1816. 800 lashes, 'Desertion, 30 September 1816', 21 October 1816. Deserted in Jamaica, 16 August 1818. No record of rejoining.

McIneny, Laughlin or **Lachlan.** Monmouth and Brecon Militia. Marched from Bristol and confined aboard PS, 14 September 1813. Joined YCs 5 February 1814, and arrived in the WIs 14 December 1814. Died Jamaica, 5 September 1817.

McIver/McIvers/McKever/McIvess, Richard. Labourer of Fermanagh. 88th Foot. Marched from Dover and confined aboard PS, 24 July 1816. Joined YCs as Richard McIver or McIvers, 19 October 1816. Arrived in the WIs 21 December 1816. Deserted in Jamaica as Richard McKever or McIvess, 3 April 1819. No record of rejoining.

McKane, John. 6th Foot. Marched from Chester and confined aboard PS, 3 March 1815. Joined YCs 29 June 1815, and arrived in the WIs 5 November 1815. Discharged Quebec.

McKay/Mackey, Donald. Aberdeen Militia. Sentenced at Tower Barracks as Donald McKay, 'General Service for Desertion', 17 March 1815. Marched from London and confined aboard PS, 9 April 1814. Joined YCs as Daniel Mackey, 29 June 1815. Arrived in the WIs 5 November 1815. Promoted corporal 8 August 1816. Reduced 3 March 1818. Discharged Quebec as Donald McKay.

McKen/McKeir/McKlough, Bryan. 90th Foot. Marched from Savoy Military Prison and confined aboard PS, 11 January 1816. Joined YCs as Bryan McKen, 17 May 1816. Arrived in the WIs 25 June 1816. Deserted as Bryan McKeir 21 July 1816. No record of rejoining.

McKenna, Peter. 25th Foot. Marched from Chester and confined aboard PS, 26 September 1813. Joined YCs 5 February 1814, and arrived in the WIs 14 December 1814. Discharged Quebec.

McKenzie, Roderick. Labourer of Edinburgh. 101st Foot. Transferred into 6th Bn 60th Foot, 4th April 1816. Transferred into York Chasseurs in Jamaica, 25 May 1817. Deserted Jamaica 4 May 1818. Rejoined 11 May 1818. Deserted in Jamaica 9 February 1819. Rejoined 13 February 1819. (No punishment records held.) Discharged Quebec. Allocated Concession 11. Lot NE 12. Beckwith. No record of him settling there.

McKever/Mackiver, Hugh. 5th Dragoon Guards. Marched from Guildford and confined aboard PS as Hugh McKever or Mackiver, 5 September 1813. Joined YCs as Hugh McKever, 5 February 1814. Arrived in the WIs 14 December 1814. Discharged Quebec.

McLinlay, John. Labourer of King's County. 77th Foot. Marched from Bristol and confined at Portchester Castle, 20 January 1817. Joined YCs 3 April 1817, and arrived in the WIs 25 May 1817. Died Jamaica, 16 March 1819.

McKinna/McKinnon/McKennan, Norman. Labourer of Rosshire. 27th Foot. Marched from Dover and confined aboard PS as Norman McKennan, 16 July 1816. Joined YCs as Norman McKinna, 19 October 1816. Arrived in the WIs 21 December 1816. 300 lashes for 'Theft', 6 March 1817. Deserted in Jamaica as Norman McKinnon, 3 June 1819. No record of rejoining.

McLaren, Alexander. Shoemaker of Dublin. 73rd Foot. Marched from St Albans and confined at Portchester Castle, 29 December 1916. Joined YCs 3 April 1817, and arrived in the WIs 25 May 1817. Deserted in Jamaica 27 July 1817. Rejoined the next day. (No punishment records held.) Deserted in Jamaica 9 December 1817. Rejoined 12 December 1817. 300 lashes for 'Absenting himself without Leave', 27 December 1817. Deserted in Jamaica 11 April 1819. Rejoined 13 May 1819. (No punishment records held.) Deserted in Jamaica 17 May 1819. No record of rejoining.

McLaughlin, Duncan. 91st Foot. Marched from Glasgow and confined aboard PS, 25 July 1814. Joined YCs 29 June 1815, and arrived in the WIs 5 November 1815. Discharged Quebec.

McLaughlin, Hugh. Labourer of Clare. Enlisted 16th Foot, 1807. Joined YCs 29 June 1815, and arrived in the WIs 5 November 1815. Deserted in Jamaica 8 July 1818. No record of rejoining.

McLaughlin, James. 89th Foot. Marched from Chester and confined aboard PS, 17 July 1814. Joined YCs 29 June 1815, and arrived in the WIs 5 November 1815. Discharged Quebec.

McLeary, Samuel. Weaver of Armagh. Transferred to YCs from 6th Bn 60th Foot in Jamaica, 25 May 1817. Deserted in Jamaica 14 April 1818. Rejoined 17 April 1818. Deserted in Jamaica 24 January 1819. Rejoined 18 February 1819. Deserted in Jamaica 27 May 1819. Rejoined 3 June 1819. (No punishment records held.) Discharged Quebec.

McLeod, David. 2nd Bn 72nd Foot. Marched from Glasgow and confined aboard PS, 19 September 1813. Joined YCs 5 February 1814, and arrived in the WIs 14 December 1814. Promoted corporal 6 June 1814. Reduced 4 March 1815. 300 lashes for being 'Drunk on Guard', 3 June 1815. Discharged Quebec.

McLeod, John. Labourer of Sutherland. Joined 79th Foot, 5 May 1804, at Waterloo. Marched from Dover and confined aboard PS, 23 June 1816. Joined YCs 19 October 1816, and arrived in the WIs 21 December 1816. Died Jamaica, 12 December 1818.

McLowry, Cornelius. Joined YCs 29 June 1815, and 'Remained on Detachment' as the regiment left for St Vincent. Discharged, 8 June 1816.

McMahon/McMan, George. 1st Bn 52nd Foot. Marched from Savoy Military Prison and confined aboard PS as George McMan, 10 January 1815. Joined YCs 29 June 1815, and arrived in the West Indies as George McMahon, 5 November 1815. Deserted in Jamaica 25 May 1817. Rejoined the same day. (No punishment records held.) 300 lashes for being 'Drunk on Duty and Theft', 25 July 1817; 200 lashes for 'Making away with Regimental Necessities', 27 December 1817. Deserted in Jamaica 16 August 1818. No record of rejoining. It is not known which McMahon received solitary confinement for 'Drunk on Guard', 10 February 1817.

McMahon, Hugh. Labourer of Tyrone. 'General Service'. Marched from Chester and confined aboard PS, 26 September 1813. Joined YCs 25 March 1814. Deserted while still at the Isle of Wight, 11 May 1814. Rejoined 21 September. (No punishment records held.)

Confined aboard PS until regiment left for the WIs. Arrived in the WIs 14 December 1814. Deserted in Jamaica 14 July 1818. Rejoined same day. Deserted in Jamaica 10 November 1818. Rejoined 23 November 1818. Deserted in Jamaica 27 May 1819. Rejoined 5 June 1819. (No punishment records held.) Discharged Quebec. It is not known which McMahon received solitary confinement for 'Drunk on Guard', 10 February 1817.

McMahon, John. Either 32nd Foot marched from Bristol 8th October 1815, or 6th Foot from Bristol and confined aboard PS, 15 November 1815. Joined YCs 16 May 1816, and arrived in the WIs June 1816. Discharged Quebec. It is not known which McMahon received solitary confinement for 'Drunk on Guard', 10 February 1817.

McManus, John. Weaver of Dublin. 87th Foot. Marched from Chester and confined aboard PS, 15 October 1813. Joined YCs 5 February 1814. Deserted while still at the Isle of Wight, 9 July 1814. Recaptured by Henry A Brook (Twenty Shillings Bounty). Rejoined, 22 July 1814. (No punishment records held.) Deserted at Bear Haven, Cork, 15 October 1814. No record of rejoining.

McMenomy/McMiniemy, Neil. Tinker of Carlow. 41st Foot. Transported from Newfoundland and confined aboard PS as Niel McMenomy, 14 August 1813. Joined YCs as Neil McMiniemy, 7 March 1814. Arrived in the WIs 14 December 1814. Died, 10 October 1816.

McNail, William. Labourer of Galway. 37th Foot. Marched from Winchester and confined aboard PS, 1 September 1813. Joined YCs 1 February 1814. Deserted while still at the Isle of Wight, 2 July 1814. No record of rejoining.

McNally, John. 84th Foot. Marched from Bristol and confined aboard PS, 8 August 1813. Joined YCs 5 February 1814, and arrived in the WIs 14 December 1814. 200 lashes for being 'Drunk and Absent from Parade', 11 July 1815. Discharged Quebec.

McNamara, Patrick. Cooper of Neath. Royal York Rangers. Marched from Chester and confined aboard PS, 26 May 1815. Joined YCs 29 June 1815, and arrived in the WIs 5 November 1815. Died Tobago, 11 August 1816.

McNamee/McNemy, Henry. Labourer of Armagh. 58th Foot. Marched from Chester and confined aboard PS as Nicholas Buchanan, Henry McNemy or Henry McNamee, 3 March 1814. Joined YCs as Henry McNamee, 25 March 1814. Deserted while still at the Isle of Wight, 10 July 1814. Rejoined 20 July 1814. (No punishment records held.) Arrived in the WIs 14 December 1814. 300 lashes for 'Insubordinate Conduct', 6 July 1815. Died, 12 November 1816.

McNespie, James. 74th Foot. Marched from Glasgow and confined aboard PS, 31 May 1815. Joined YCs 29 June 1815, and arrived in the WIs 5 November 1815. Discharged Quebec.

McNulty/McNally, John. 85th Foot. Marched from Weedon Barracks and confined aboard PS as John McNulty, 24 July 1816. Joined YCs 18 October 1816, and arrived in WIs 21 December 1816. Discharged Quebec as John McNulty or John McNally.

McQuade, Bernard. Weaver of Monaghan. 12th Foot. Marched from Chester and confined aboard PS, 25 March 1815. Joined YCs 29 June 1815, and arrived in the WIs 5 November 1815. Died, 13 November 1816.

McQuiley/McGrily/McGingley, Peter. 1st Foot. Marched from Maidstone and confined aboard PS as Peter McQuiley or Patrick Carey, 26 March 1815. Joined YCs 29 June

1815, and arrived in the WIs as Peter McGrily or McGiugley, 5 November 1815. Discharged Quebec as Peter McGingley.

McStravick/McStaverick/McStravock, Bernard. From Ireland. Either 1st Foot or 1st Foot Guards. Marched from Bristol and confined aboard PS as Bernard McStraveck, 28 May 1815. Joined YCs as Bernard McStaverick, 29 June 1815. Arrived in the WIs 5 November 1815. Discharged at Quebec as Bernard Stravick. Allocated Concession 11. Lot NE 11. Beckwith, as Bernard McStravock. No evidence found of him settling there.

McSweeny, Dennis. Stonemason of Cork. 2nd Bn 45th Foot. Marched from Lewes and confined aboard PS, 3 August 1813. Joined YCs 5 February 1814, and arrived in the WIs 14 December 1814. Died Grenada, 4 September 1815.

McWade/McQuade, Thomas. Labourer of Armagh. 16th Foot. Marched from Chester and confined aboard PS as Thomas McQuade or McWade, 3 March 1814. Joined YCs as McWade, 25 March 1813. Deserted while still at the Isle of Wight, 10 July 1814. Rejoined 20 July 1814. (No punishment records held.) Arrived in the WIs 14 December 1814. Discharged Quebec.

Meads, Daniel. Labourer of Cork. Arrived in the WIs 21 December 1816. Deserted in Jamaica 1 March 1817. Rejoined, date unknown. (No punishment records held.) Deserted in Jamaica, 31 June 1817. No record of rejoining.

Meigh, Sampson. Hatter of Stafford. 2nd Bn 52nd Foot. Marched from Salford and confined aboard PS as Sampson Meigh or May, 4 September 1814. Joined YCs as Sampson Meigh, 29 June 1815. Arrived in the WIs 5 November 1815. Promoted corporal 3 January 1816, sergeant 25 July 1816. Reduced 16 October 1816. Deserted in Jamaica 30 November 1817. Rejoined 21 December 1817. 300 lashes for 'Making away with Regimental Necessities', 27 December 1817. Remitted 'in consequence of his former Good Character and being strongly recommended by the Court'. Deserted in Jamaica 10 February 1819. Rejoined 7 March 1819. (No punishment records held.) Discharged Quebec.

Melsome, William. Transferred to YCs in Jamaica as sergeant of European Garrison Company, May 1817. Reduced 14 October 1817. Discharged Quebec. Allocated Concession 11. Lot 8. Beckwith. Sold for £50 to ex York Chasseur James Nash, 29 June 1826.

Menzies, James. Labourer of Falkirk. 2nd Dragoons. Marched from Birmingham and confined aboard PS, 31 December 1813. Joined YCs 7 March 1814, and arrived in the WIs 14 December 1814. Died Jamaica, 31 December 1816. Willed his effects, seventeen shillings and threepence to his mother, Mary Menzies of Rainsford, Falkirk.

Merchant, John. Labourer of Ashford. 2nd Bn 52nd Foot. Marched from Canterbury and confined aboard PS, 24 September 1813. Joined YCs 7 March 1814, and arrived in the WIs 14 December 1814. Deserted in Jamaica 29 April 1819. Rejoined 6 May 1819. (No punishment records held.) Discharged Quebec.

Middleton, Samuel. House painter of Chipping Ongar. Either 1st Foot or 1st Foot Guards. Marched from Chesterfield and confined aboard PS, 8 June 1815. Joined YCs 29 June 1815 and arrived in the WIs 5 November 1815. Deserted in Jamaica 15 July 1817. No record of rejoining.

Millage, John. Labourer of Bath. Joined 55th Foot at Bath, 29 November 1816 (Five Pound Bounty). Deserted from Regimental Headquarters, 4 December 1816. Marched from Bath and confined at Portchester Castle, 21 January 1817. Joined YCs 3 April 1817, and arrived in the WIs 25 May 1817. Discharged Quebec. Allocated Lot 11. Concession 9. Beckwith. Sold to Peter McFarlane for £40, 30 June 1830. Moved to Isle of St John (present-day Prince Edward Island), 1834.

Millar/Miller, Oliver. Labourer of Fife. 2nd Bn Royal Artillery. Marched from Glasgow and confined aboard PS, 9th January 1814. Joined YCs 1 February 1814. Deserted while still at the Isle of Wight, 1 July 1814. No record of rejoining.

Miller, Robert. Porter of London. Royal Horse Artillery. Marched from St Augustine's and confined aboard PS, 15 December 1813. Joined YCs 7 March 1814, and arrived in the WIs 14 December 1814. 100 lashes for 'Refusing to be Confined', 6 September 1815. Died, 10 October 1816.

Mills, Isaac. Blacksmith of Dublin. Royal Artillery. Marched from Dartford and confined aboard PS, 16 February 1814. Joined YCs 7 March 1814. Deserted while still at the Isle of Wight, 9 July 1814. Recaptured by Henry A Brook (Twenty Shillings Bounty). Rejoined 24 July 1814. (No punishment records held.) Deserted at Bear Haven, Cork, 15 October 1814. No record of rejoining.

Mills, William. Marched from Devizes and confined aboard PS, 23 December 1814. Joined YCs 29 June 1815, and arrived in the WIs 5 November 1815. Discharged Quebec.

Minshall/Minshull, James. Cordwainer of Kilkenny. 1st Bn 31st Foot. Marched from Middlewich and confined aboard PS, 25 December 1814. Joined YCs 29 June 1815. Deserted at Portsmouth, 6 August 1815. No record of rejoining.

Mist, William. 2nd Bn 62nd Foot. Marched from Lewes and confined aboard PS, 28 August 1814. Joined YCs 29 June 1815, and arrived in the WIs 5 November 1815. Discharged Quebec.

Mitchell, Donald. 25th Foot. Marched from High Wycombe and confined at Portchester Castle, 23 January 1817. Joined YCs 3 April 1817 and arrived in the WIs 25 May 1817. Discharged Quebec.

Mitchell/Mitchel, Hugh. Transferred to YCs from 1st European Garrison in Jamaica, 25 May 1817. Discharged Quebec.

Mitchell, James. Labourer of Huntington. 2nd Bn 1st Guards. Marched from Reading and confined aboard PS, 18 August 1813. Joined YCs 1 February 1814 and arrived in the WIs 14 December 1814. 200 lashes for 'Quitting the Garrison without Leave', 26 December 1816. Punishment remitted. Deserted in Jamaica, 30 January 1818. No record of rejoining.

Mitchell, John. Either 20th Light Dragoons marched from Stafford, 2 October 1813, or 3rd Foot marched from Reading and confined aboard PS, 23 October 1813. Joined YCs 5 February 1814, and arrived in the WIs 14 December 1814. 150 lashes for being 'Drunk and Absenting himself from Parade', 26 December 1816. Discharged Quebec.

Moales/Moule/Mowles, John. Wheelwright of Somerset. 69th Foot. Marched from Ely and confined aboard PS as John Mowles, August 1814. Joined YCs as John Moule, 7 March 1814. Arrived in the WIs 14 December 1814. Deserted in Jamaica as John Moales, 30 June 1817. No record of rejoining.

Monaghan, John. Labourer of Monaghan. Joined YCs 25 March 1814, and arrived in the WIs 14 December 1814. Discharged from Stony Hill, Jamaica, 13 June 1819.

Mooney, Edward. General Service. Confined aboard PS, 28 December 1814. Joined YCs 29 June 1815, and arrived in the WIs 5 November 1815. Discharged Quebec.

Mooney, James. Labourer of Skeen. 44th Foot. Marched from Chester and confined aboard PS, 25 May 1815. Joined YCs 29 June 1815, and arrived in the WIs 5 November 1815. Deserted in Grenada 11 March 1816. Rejoined 14 March 1816. (No punishment records held.) Died, 22 October 1816.

Mooney, James. 15th Hussars. Marched from Nottingham and confined at Portchester Castle, 25 July 1816. Joined YCs 7 October 1816, and arrived in the WIs 21 December 1816. Discharged Quebec.

Moore/Muire, George. Cabinetmaker of Dublin. 2nd Bn 20th Foot. Marched from Carlisle and confined aboard PS as George Muire, 22 August 1814. Joined YCs as Drummer George Moore, 7 March 1814. Arrived in the WIs 14 December 1814. 150 lashes and ordered to be reduced for being 'Absent from Evening Parade', 29 September 1816; reduced, but corporal punishment remitted. Promoted drummer 25 November 1816. Died Jamaica, 20 November 1817.

Moore, Philip. 86th Foot. Marched from Chester and confined aboard PS, 25 May 1815. Joined YCs 29 June 1815, and arrived in the WIs 5 November 1815. Promoted corporal 6 November 1817. Reduced 5 May 1818. Discharged Quebec.

Moore, William. Mason of Durham. 70th Foot. Marched from Durham and confined aboard PS, 24 September 1813. Joined YCs 1 February 1814. Deserted while still at the Isle of Wight, 2 July 1814. Recaptured and detained at Savoy Military Prison, 10 March 1815. Re-confined at the Isle of Wight PS, 22 April 1815. No record of rejoining.

Moorehead/Moorhead/Morehead, Robert. Foot Guards. Marched from Bedford and confined aboard PS, 24 February 1814. Joined YCs 25 March 1814, and arrived in the WIs 14 December 1814. Promoted corporal 25 December 1814. Reduced 10 June 1815. Discharged Quebec.

Moran, James. 29th Foot. Marched from Plymouth and confined aboard PS, 24 September 1814. 'Left on Detachment' as the regiment departed for the WIs. Discharged, 8 June 1816.

Moreau/Moran, Martin. 30th Foot. Transported from Ostend and confined aboard PS, 25 June 1815. Joined YCs as Martin Moran or Moreau, 29 June 1815. Arrived in the WIs 5 November 1815. Died Grenada as Martin Moran, 18 December 1815.

Moreton, Thomas or **Morton, John.** Labourer of Oxford. Royal York Rangers. Marched from Exeter and confined aboard PS as John Morton, 8 April 1815. Joined YCs 29 June 1815, and arrived in the WIs as Thomas Moreton, 5 November 1815. Died, 29 September 1816.

Morgan, Daniel. Labourer of Down. 28th Foot. Marched from Winchester and confined aboard PS, 4 March 1815. Joined YCs 29 June 1815, and arrived in the WIs 5 November 1815. Promoted corporal 17 January 1816. Reduced 5 April 1817. Deserted in Jamaica 5 March 1819. Rejoined 13 March 1819. (No punishment records held.) Discharged Quebec.

Morris, Joseph. Weaver of Monaghan. Either Hereford Militia marched from Chester, 25 January 1816, or 85th Foot from Winchester and confined aboard PS, 5 March 1816. Embarked Spithead with a 300-strong detachment of 'Unattached Deserters' joining the

2nd Foot, 25 April 1816. Arrived in the WIs 5 June 1816. Deserted 5 July 1816. Rejoined 21 July 1816. 1,000 lashes 23 July 1816. Transferred into the York Chasseurs, 25 August 1816. Deserted 18 November 1816. Returned to England, recaptured and confined at Portchester Castle, 1817. Date unknown.

Morris, Michael. Royal Horse Artillery. Marched from Savoy Military Prison and confined aboard PS, 1 March 1814. Joined YCs 25 March 1814, and arrived in the WIs 14 December 1814. Promoted corporal 25 June 1814. Reduced 4 September 1814. Promoted corporal 10 September 1816. Reduced 10 June 1817. Discharged Quebec.

Morris, Richard. Cabinetmaker of Middlesex. East London Militia. Marched from Blackheath and confined aboard PS as Richard Herne or Morris, 1 December 1813. Joined YCs as Richard Morris, 7 March 1814. Arrived in the WIs 14th December 1814. Solitary confinement for 'Coming to Parade improperly dressed and Insolence to an Officer', 17 November 1817. Deserted in Jamaica 31 March 1819. No record of rejoining.

Morris, Thomas. Joiner of Denbigh. Staff Corps. Marched from Maidstone and confined aboard PS as Brown or Morris, 10 August 1813. Joined as Thomas Morris, 5 February 1814. Arrived in the WIs 14 December 1814. Promoted corporal, September 1814. Reduced, 27 January 1815. Died Barbados, 21 March 1815.

Morrissey/Morressey/Morrison, Thomas. Either 18th Foot or 46th Foot. Confined aboard PS, 10 April 1815. Joined YCs 29 June 1815, and arrived in the WIs as Thomas Morrisey or Morrison, 5 November 1815. Promoted corporal 1 June 1816. Reduced 22 October 1816. Discharged Quebec as George Morrison.

Morrow/Morrison, George. Joined from 6th Bn 60th Foot in Jamaica as George Morrow, 25 May 1817. 300 lashes for being 'Drunk on Duty, 4th July 1817.' Discharged Quebec as George Morrison.

Moseley/Mosley, John. 2nd Bn 61st Foot. Marched from Newbury and confined aboard PS, 18 August 1814. Joined YCs 29 June 1815, and arrived in the WIs 5 November 1815. Discharged Quebec. Allocated Concession 8. Lot NE 9. Beckwith. No evidence found of him settling there.

Moulds, Samuel or **Thomas.** Royal Artillery. Marched from Chester and confined aboard PS as Thomas Moulds, 2 October 1813. Joined YCs as Samuel Moulds, 29 June 1815. Arrived in the WIs 5 November 1815. Discharged Quebec.

Mullins, Patrick. Tallow chandler of Armagh. 7th Hussars. Marched from Savoy Military Prison and confined at Portchester Castle, 7 December 1816. Joined YCs 3 April 1817, and arrived in the WIs 25 May 1817. Deserted in Jamaica 8 June 1817 (barely two weeks after arrival). No record of rejoining.

Mullins/Mullings, Thomas. 38th Foot. Marched from Horsham and confined aboard PS as Thomas Molliney or Mullany, 7 December 1813. Joined YCs as Thomas Mullings, 5 February 1814. Left sick at Guernsey as the regiment departed for Barbados. Arrived in WIs 5 November 1815. 'In the hands of the Civil Power in Jamaica from 25th December 1817 until released 15th April 1818'. Discharged Quebec as Thomas Mullins.

Mulvaney/Mulvanny/Mulveany, Thomas. Labourer of Dublin. 32nd Foot. Marched from Bristol and confined aboard PS as Thomas Mulvaney, 22 November 1814. Joined YCs 29 June 1815, and arrived in the WIs as Thomas Mulvanny, 5 November 1815. 150 lashes for being 'Drunk & Absent from Parade', 28 April 1817; 150 lashes for 'Theft' but remitted to solitary confinement, 25 July 1817. Deserted in Jamaica 5 March 1819.

Rejoined in Jamaica 7 March 1819. Deserted in Jamaica 5 May 1819. Rejoined 9 May 1819. (No punishment records held.) Discharged Quebec as Thomas Mulveany.

Murcer/Mercer, Thomas. 2nd Bn 73rd Foot. Marched from Salford and confined aboard PS as Thomas Murcer or Mercer, 13 March 1814. Joined YCs as Thomas Murcer, 25 March 1814. Arrived in the WIs 14 December 1814. Discharged Quebec as Thomas Mercer.

Murphy, Andrew. 87th Foot. Marched from Chester and confined aboard PS as John Wilson or Andrew Murphy, 16 April 1815. Joined YCs as Andrew Murphy, 29 June 1815. Arrived in the WIs 5 November 1815. Discharged Quebec. Allocated either Concession 4. Lot SW 22 or Concession 6. Lot. SW 20. Drummond. No evidence of him settling there.

Murphy, Dennis. Dry salter of Belfast. 2nd Bn 43rd Foot. Marched from Canterbury and confined aboard PS, 8 August 1813. Joined YCs 5 February 1814, and arrived in the WIs 14 December 1814. Deserted in Barbados 6 March 1815. Rejoined 17 March 1815. (No punishment records held.) Died, 11 October 1816.

Murphy, Edward. Ships carpenter of Cross Gates. Arrived in the WIs 25 May 1817. Deserted in Jamaica 3 June 1817 (barely days after arrival). No record of rejoining.

Murphy, Hugh. 25th Foot. Marched from Chester and confined aboard PS as Patrick or Hugh Murphy, 24 June 1813. Joined YCs as Hugh Murphy, 1 February 1814. Arrived in the WIs 14 December 1814. Discharged Quebec.

Murphy, John. Shoemaker of Wexford. 82nd Foot. Marched from Bristol and confined aboard PS, 31 July 1813. Joined YCs 7 March 1814, and arrived in the WIs 14 December 1814. Discharged from Stony Hill, Jamaica, 10 June 1819.

Murphy, Thomas. 71st Foot. Marched from Bristol and confined aboard PS, 26 March 1815. 'Left on Detachment' at Albany Barracks. No further record.

Murphy, Timothy. Labourer of Kerry. 16th Foot. Marched from Edinburgh and confined aboard PS, 3 August 1813. Joined YCs 1 February 1814. Deserted while still at Isle of Wight, 7 July 1814. Recaptured and detained Savoy Military Prison, 25 July 1814. Rejoined at the Isle of Wight, 24 December 1814. (No punishment record held.) Arrived in the WIs 5 November 1815. Deserted in Jamaica 5 March 1819. Rejoined 7 March 1819. (No punishment record held.) Discharged Quebec.

Murphy, William. 88th Foot. Marched from Bristol and confined aboard PS, 24 August 1814. Joined YCs 29 June 1815, and arrived in the WIs 5 November 1815. Discharged Quebec.

Murray, James. Cotton spinner of Nottingham. Either 59th Foot marched from Chester, 1 November 1813, or 2nd Bn 91st Foot from Carlisle and confined aboard PS, 19 December 1813. Joined YCs 5 February 1814, and arrived in the WIs 14 December 1814. Discharged Quebec.

Murray, James. Labourer of Market Lavington. 19th Foot. Marched from Wakefield and confined aboard PS, 29 May 1815. Joined YCs 29 June 1815, and arrived in the WIs 5 November 1815. Deserted in Jamaica 31 March 1819. Rejoined 3 April 1819. (No punishment record held.) Died Jamaica 18 May 1819, six weeks after rejoining from desertion and no doubt punishment.

Murray, John. Labourer of King's County. 76th Foot. Marched from Horsham and confined aboard PS, 12 September 1813. Joined YCs 5 February 1814, and arrived in the WIs 14 December 1814. Died, 26 September 1816.

Murray, Michael. Labourer of Dublin. 4th Veteran Bn. Marched from Savoy Military Prison and confined aboard PS, 27 November 1814. Joined YCs 29 June 1815. and arrived in the WIs 5 November 1815. 250 lashes for 'Absenting himself without Leave for One Night', 17 January 1817; 200 lashes for 'Making away with his Regimental Necessaries', 26 January 1818, 50 lashes remitted. Deserted in Jamaica 1 March 1818. Rejoined 15 March 1818. (No punishment records held.) Deserted in Jamaica 28 August 1818. No record of rejoining.

Myland/Mylan/Mylam, Thomas. Shoemaker of Limerick. Joined YCs as Thomas Myland, 25 March 1814. Arrived in the WIs as Thomas Mylan or Mylam, 14 December 1814. Deserted in Jamaica 10 March 1817. No record of rejoining.

Nailor/Naylor, John. Butcher of York. 2nd Dragoons. Marched from Warwick and confined aboard PS, 27 August 1813. Joined YCs 5 February 1814, and arrived in the WIs 14 December 1814. Died Jamiaca, 21 September 1818.

Nash, James. From Faversham, Kent. Joined 101st Foot, 5 October 1808. Discharged in Jamaica, 24 July 1816. Enlisted into York Chasseurs, Stony Hill, Jamaica, 10 June 1817. Discharged Quebec. Nash, accompanied by wife and two daughters, settled Concession 11. Lot NE 13. Beckwith. 'Awarded Chelsea Out-Pension, five pence per diem, 18th February 1826'.

Nash, Samuel. General Service. Marched from Savoy Military Prison and confined aboard PS, 3 January 1816. Embarked Spithead amongst a 300-strong detachment of 'Unattached Deserters' joining the 2nd Foot, 25 April 1816. Arrived in the WIs 5 June 1816. Transferred into the York Chasseurs, 25 August 1816. Discharged Quebec.

Newall/Newbold, Daniel. 3rd Foot Guards. Marched from Savoy Military Prison and confined aboard PS as Daniel Newall, 23 January 1814. Joined YCs as Daniel Newbold, 25 March 1814. Arrived in the WIs 14 December 1814. Promoted drummer 15 May 1815. Discharged Quebec as Daniel Newall.

Newall, John. Labourer of Hereford. Royal Wagon Train. Marched from Wakefield and confined aboard PS, 1 December 1814. Joined YCs 29 June 1815, and arrived in the WIs 5 November 1815. Deserted in Jamaica 29 March 1818. No record of rejoining.

Newbold, Thomas. Weaver of Lancashire. West Middlesex Militia. Sentenced at Nottingham Court-martial to 'General Service for Desertion', 22 October 1813. Confined aboard PS, 28 December 1813. Joined YCs 7 March 1814, and arrived in the WIs 14 December 1814. Died Jamaica, 7 August 1817.

Newbury, Henry. 2nd Bn 59th Foot. Confined aboard PS, 22 March 1816. Joined YCs 16 May 1816, and arrived in the WIs 25 June 1816. Discharged Quebec.

Newby, William. Labourer of Ross, Galway. 4th Dragoon Guards. Marched from Chester and confined aboard PS, 3 March 1815. Joined YCs 29 June 1815, and arrived in the WIs 5 November 1815. Died St Vincent, 28 February 1816.

Nichols/Nicholls, James. 19th Light Dragoons. Marched from Plymouth Docks and confined aboard PS, 20 December 1813. Joined YCs 7 March 1813, and arrived in the WIs 14 December 1814. Discharged Quebec.

Nichols/Nicholls, John. 91st Foot. Marched from Chester and confined aboard PS as John Nicholls or John Niel, 28 December 1814. Joined YCs 29 June 1815. Arrived in the WIs as John Nichols, 5 November 1815. Discharged Quebec as John Nicholls.

Nixon/Noxon, John. Labourer of Derry. 67th Foot. Marched from Chester and confined aboard PS as John Noxon, 26 October 1814. Joined YCs as John Nixon, 29 June 1815. Arrived in the WIs 5 November 1815. Deserted at Grenada, 12 March 1816. No record of rejoining.

Noble, Joseph. Labourer of Bath. 32nd Foot. Marched from Bristol and confined aboard PS, 28 May 1815. Joined YCs 29 June 1815, and arrived in the WIs 5 November 1815. Deserted in Jamaica 20 April 1819. Rejoined 5 May 1819. (No punishment records held.) Discharged Quebec.

Noonan, Thomas. Labourer of Cork. 95th Foot. Transported from Ostend and confined aboard PS, 15 February 1816. Joined YCs 19 October 1816, and arrived in the WIs 21 December 1816. 100 lashes for 'Passing Rum to a Prisoner' 24 December 1816; 300 lashes for 'Theft', 11 March 1817; 300 lashes for 'Theft', 28 April 1817; 300 lashes 'For Breaking into the Taylors Shop', 10 December 1817. Deserted in Jamaica, 22 February 1819. Rejoined 8 March 1819. (No punishment records held.) Deserted in Jamaica, 29 March 1819. No record of rejoining.

Norman, John. 2nd Bn 37th Foot. Marched from Maidstone and confined aboard PS, 12 September 1813. Joined YCs 1 February 1814, and arrived in the WIs 14 December 1814. Discharged Quebec.

Norman, John. Transferred to YCs from 1st European Garrison in Jamaica, 25 May 1817. Discharged Quebec.

Northan, John. Coldstream Guards. Marched from Nottingham and confined aboard PS, 17 July 1814. Joined YCs 29 June 1815, and arrived in the WIs 5 November 1815. Discharged Quebec.

Nowlan/Nowland, Thomas. Labourer of Queen's County. 2nd Bn 38th Foot. Marched from Fisherton and confined aboard PS, 12 October 1813. Joined YCs 29 June 1815, and arrived in the WIs 5 November 1815. Died, 19 November 1816.

Nowland, Charles. Labourer of Dublin. Transferred to YCs from 6th Bn 60th Foot in Jamaica, 25 May 1817. Deserted in Jamaica 23 August 1817. Rejoined the next day. 300 lashes for 'Absenting himself without Leave', 2 September 1817. Deserted in Jamaica 1 October 1817. Rejoined 6 October 1817. 300 lashes for 'Absenting himself without Leave', 17 October 1817. Deserted in Jamaica 14 November 1817. Rejoined 15 November 1817. 300 lashes for being 'Absent without Leave', 22 November 1817. Deserted in Jamaica 3 March 1818. Rejoined 13 March 1818. Deserted in Jamaica 4 September 1818. Rejoined 19 September 1818. (No punishment records held.) Discharged Quebec.

Nulty, Patrick. Either a baker or labourer of Cavan. 96th Foot. Marched from Chester and confined at Portchester Castle, 9 December 1816. Joined YCs 3 April 1817, and arrived in the WIs 25 May 1817. 200 lashes for 'Making away with his Regimental Necessaries', 2 August 1817, 75 lashes remitted. Deserted in Jamaica 2 November 1817. Rejoined 9 November 1817. Deserted in Jamaica 2 April 1819. Rejoined 7 April 1819. Deserted in Jamaica 1 May 1819. Rejoined 9 May 1819. (No punishment records held.) Died Jamaica, 24 May 1819, two weeks after rejoining from desertion and no doubt punishment.

Nulty, Stephen. Labourer of Roscommon. 53rd Foot. Transported from Portsmouth and confined aboard PS, 29 March 1814. Joined YCs 29 June 1815, and arrived in the WIs 5 November 1815. 300 lashes for being 'Drunk on Duty', 1 September 1817. Deserted in Jamaica 14 April 1819. Rejoined the next day. (No punishment records held.) Discharged Quebec.

Nunn, Henry. 8th Light Dragoons. Marched from Savoy Military Prison and confined aboard PS, 12 December 1813. Joined YCs as sergeant, 1 February 1814 Reduced 25 February 1814. Tried by General Court-Martial, Guernsey, 15 August 1814. CHARGES: '1st. For going over the Barracks Wall of the Canteen/De Lancy Barracks on the 12th August 1814, notwithstanding his being repeatedly ordered to the contrary by the sentry who was posted to prevent the Soldiers going over the Barracks Wall at that place. 2nd. Being absent from evening Parade and Tatoo-Roll call of the same day, and remaining out of Barracks the whole of that Night, and not returning till between the hours of Six and Seven on the following Morning. 3rd. For disobedience of Orders in refusing to take off his Green Clothing and lay by his Great coat when ordered to do so by Ensign McMurran of the said Regt on the morning of the 13th August 1814 at De Lancey Barrack aforesaid, and using at the same time the most insubordinate and Mutinous Language to the said Ensign McMurran in saying he would see the said Ensign McMurran damned before he would do so. 4th For highly mutinous Conduct in using the most threatening Language to the said Ensign McMurran, while in the execution of his duty at De Lancey Barracks aforesaid on the Morning of the 13th August 1814'. One Year Imprisonment in solitary confinement in Caste Cornet, 15 August 1814. Subsequently transferred to Royal African Corps.

Oakley, Timothy. Jeweller of Ford, Shropshire. 1st Foot Guards. Marched from Warwick and confined at Portchester Castle, date unknown. Joined YCs 3 April 1817, and arrived in the WIs 25 May 1817. Promoted corporal 2 March 1819. Reduced 4 March 1819. Deserted in Jamaica 30 April 1819. Rejoined the same day. (No punishment record held.) Discharged Quebec.

O'Brien, Michael. Labourer of Fermanagh. Either 18th Light Dragoons marched from Chichester, 12 February 1815, or 27th Foot marched from Tilbury Fort and confined aboard PS, 6 May 1815. Joined YCs 29 June 1815, and arrived in the WIs 5 November 1815. Died Jamaica, 22 October 1817.

O'Brien, Michael. Labourer of Tipperary or Fermanagh. Either 18th Light Dragoons marched from Chichester, 12 February 1815, or 27th Foot marched from Tilbury Fort and confined aboard PS, 6 May 1815. Joined YCs 29 June 1815, and arrived in the WIs 5 November 1815. Deserted 12 March 1816. No record of rejoining.

O'Brien, Patrick. Labourer of Tipperary. 19th Light Dragoons. Marched from Bristol and confined aboard PS, 16 September 1813. Joined YCs 1 February 1814, and arrived in the WIs 14 December 1814. Deserted in Jamaica, 10 March 1817. No record of rejoining.

O'Brien, Terrence. Labourer of Cork. 54th Foot. Marched from Chelmsford and confined aboard PS, 24 October 1813. Joined YCs 1 February 1814, and arrived in the WIs 14 December 1814. Died Jamaica, 20 February 1818.

Ogden, Robert. Weaver of Oldham. 2nd Bn 24th Foot. Marched from Chelmsford and confined aboard PS, 24 December 1813. Joined YCs 1 February 1814, and arrived in the WIs 14 December 1814. Died Garrison Hospital, Grenada, 30 August 1815.

Ogilvie, David. Royal Artillery. Marched from Edinburgh and confined aboard PS, 19 September 1813. Joined YCs 1 February 1814, and arrived in the WIs 14 December 1814. Employed as 'Orderly in the General Hospital' March–June 1815. Deserted in Jamaica,

May 1819. Rejoined, date and punishment unknown. Discharged Quebec.

O'Hara, Edward. Labourer of Down. Royals. Marched from Chester and confined aboard PS, 1 November 1813. Joined YCs 5 February 1814, and arrived in the WIs 14 December 1814. Died, 2 October 1816.

O'Laughlin, Dennis. 16th Foot. Marched from Bristol and confined aboard PS, 16 April 1815. Joined YCs 29 June 1815, and arrived in the WIs 5 November 1815. Discharged Quebec. Allocated Concession 10. Lot SW 12. Beckwith. No evidence found of O'Laughlin, wife, son and two daughters settling there.

Oldroyd/Oldray, Joshua. Weaver of York. Royal Artillery Driver. Marched from Chester and confined aboard PS as Joshua Oldray, 28 December 1814. Joined YCs as Joshua Oldroyd, 29 June 1815. Arrived in the WIs 5 November 1915. Died Tobago, 16 June 1816.

Oliver, William. Labourer of York. Royal Horse Artillery. Marched from Dartford and confined aboard PS, 3 November 1814. Joined YCs 29 June 1815, and arrived in the WIs 5 November 1815. Deserted in Jamaica 27 April 1819. Rejoined 3 May 1819. (No punishment record held.) Deserted in Jamaica 16 May 1819. No record of rejoining.

Oram, Isaac. Transferred to YCs from 1st European Garrison in Jamaica, 25 May 1817. Discharged Quebec.

O'Reilly/O'Rieley/O'Riley, Edward. Labourer of Roscommon. 18th Foot. Marched from Portsmouth and confined at Portchester Castle, 14 January 1817. Joined YCs 3 April 1817, and arrived in the WIs 25 May 1817. Deserted in Jamaica 2 July 1818. Returned to England, recaptured and confined at Savoy Military Prison. 'Considered unfit for further Military Service in consequence of being subject to an ulcer of the leg'. Furnished with a 'Protecting Certificate' and discharged, 31 October 1818.

Orloff, Alexander. Transferred to YCs from 6th Bn 60th Foot in Jamaica, 25 May 1817. Discharged Quebec.

Ormrod/Ormond, William. Labourer of Aberdeen. 91st Foot. Marched from Canterbury and confined aboard PS as William Ormond, 23 October 1814. Joined YCs as William Ormrod, 29 June 1815. Arrived in the WIs 5 November 1815. Died, 19 October 1816.

Osborne/Osborn, John. Rifle Brigade. Marched from Savoy Military Prison and confined at Portchester Castle, 18 January 1817. Joined YCs 3 April 1817, and arrived in the WIs 25 May 1817. Deserted in Jamaica 12 April 1819. Rejoined 14 April 1819. (No punishment record held.) Discharged Quebec.

Osborne/Osbourne, Michael. Fisherman of Falmouth. 85th Foot. Marched from Winchester and confined aboard PS, 9 April 1816. Joined YCs 19 October 1816, and arrived in the WIs 21 December 1816. Died Jamaica, 27 July 1817.

Osbourne/Osborne, William. Bricklayer of Newport, Isle of Wight. 35th Foot. Transferred from Newport and confined aboard PS, 1 January 1814. Joined YCs 5 February 1814. Deserted while still at the Isle of Wight, 28 August 1814. Recaptured (date unknown) and confined at Portchester Castle. 'Surgically Unfit' and discharged, 3 January 1817.

Osgood, William. Weaver of Hampshire. North Hants Militia. Sentenced at Portsmouth to 'General Service for Desertion' and confined aboard PS, 18 July 1814. Joined YCs 29

June 1815, and arrived in the WIs 5 November 1815. Deserted in Jamaica 10 March 1818. Rejoined 21 March 1818. (No punishment record held.) Discharged Quebec.

Overhand/Overhand, Samuel. Weaver of Leeds. Joined YCs 1 February 1814, and arrived in the WIs 14 December 1814. 'Missing in Action' at Guadeloupe, 9 August 1815.

Owens, Robert. 85th Foot. Marched from Salford and confined aboard PS, 14 September 1813. Joined YCs 7 March 1814, and arrived WIs 14 December 1814. Promoted corporal 12 April 1816. Reduced 22 May 1816. 'On Lieutenant Colonel Ewart's recommendation transferred to the 18th Foot in Jamaica, 24th January 1817, with the additional proviso that Owen was to be permitted to return to England when his new regiment embarked the West Indies'.

Page, William. Labourer of Devizes. 4th Dragoons. Marched from Canterbury and confined aboard PS, 6 August 1813. Joined YCs 25 March 1814. Remained sick at the Isle of Wight as the regiment left for Barbados. Arrived in the WIs May 1815. Died either Guadeloupe or Grenada, 9 August 1815.

Palmer, William. Labourer of Oxford. 11th Light Dragoons. Marched from Horsham and confined aboard PS, 31 May 1815. Joined YCs 29 June 1815, and arrived in the WIs 5 November 1815. Deserted in Jamaica 4 May 1819. Rejoined 6 May 1819. (No punishment record held.) Discharged Quebec.

Parish, Robert. Labourer of Lynn. 77th Foot. Marched from Dorchester and confined aboard PS, 26 November 1813. Joined YCs 1 February 1814. Deserted while still at the Isle of Wight, 14 April 1814. No record of rejoining.

Parker, Richard. 101st Foot. Marched from Dartford and confined aboard PS as Richard Parker or Evans, 26 December 1813. Joined YCs as Richard Parker, 7 March 1814. Arrived in the WIs 14 December 1814. Discharged Quebec.

Parland, James. 22nd Foot. Marched from Middlewick and confined aboard PS, 14 March 1814. Joined YCs 25 March 1814, and arrived in the WIs 14 December 1814. Promoted corporal 25 August 1814, sergeant 25 August 1815. Reduced 5 December 1815. Discharged Quebec.

Parsons, Robert. 3rd Foot Guards. Marched from London and confined aboard PS, 18 May 1816. Joined YCs 19 October 1816, and arrived in the WIs 21 December 1816. Discharged Quebec.

Paterson, Archibald. Labourer of Edinburgh. 70th Foot. Marched from Edinburgh and confined aboard PS, 28 December 1813. Joined YCs 7 March 1814, and arrived in the WIs 14 December 1814. Promoted corporal 22 July 1817. Reduced 25 February 1818. Died Jamaica, 1 September 1818.

Patterson, James. Carpenter of Derry. Royal Artillery. Marched from Chester Castle and confined aboard PS, 26 September 1813. Joined YCs 7 March 1814, and arrived in the WIs 14 December 1814. Died Grenada or Guadeloupe, 31 August 1815.

Pavey/Parry, William. 1st Guards. Marched from Wakefield and confined aboard PS as William Pavey, 19 November 1814. Joined YCs as William Parry, 29 June 1815. Arrived in the WIs 5 November 1815. Discharged Quebec as William Pavey.

Payne, Robert. Royal Horse Artillery. Marched from Dartford and confined aboard PS, 17 September 1814. Joined YCs 29 June 1815, and arrived in the WIs 5 November 1815.

Promoted corporal 17 October 1816, sergeant 28 October 1817. Reduced 12 May 1819. Discharged Quebec.

Paynter/Painter, Francis or **Thomas** Labourer from Essex. 32nd Foot. Marched from Bristol and confined aboard PS as Thomas or Francis Painter, 22 November 1814. Joined YCs as Francis Paynter, 29 June 1815. Arrived in the WIs 5 November 1815. Died Jamaica, 14 December 1817.

Peachee, John. Coldstream Guards. Marched from Chester Castle and confined aboard PS, 4 February 1816. Joined YCs 17 May 1816, and arrived in the WIs 25 June 1816. Discharged Quebec.

Pearce/Pierce, Frederick. Labourer of Surrey. 7th Hussars. Marched from Savoy Military Prison and confined aboard PS as Frederick Pierce, 7 March 1815. Joined YCs as Frederick Pearce, 29 June 1815. Arrived in the WIs as sergeant, 5 November 1815. Promoted colour sergeant 27 April 1817. Reduced 20 February 1818. Promoted corporal 4 May 1818. Reduced 24 June 1818. Deserted in Jamaica, 21 April 1819. No record of rejoining.

Pearce, John. Labourer of Wolverhampton. 2nd Bn 14th Foot. Transported from Gosport and confined aboard PS, 28 September 1813. Joined YCs 1 February 1814. Deserted while still at the Isle of Wight, 7 July 1814. Seized by Thomas Gloge of Hayling (Twenty Shillings Bounty). Rejoined 15 July 1814. (No punishment record held.) Arrived in the WIs 14 December 1814. Deserted in Jamaica 12 December 1818. Rejoined 14 December 1818. (No punishment record held.) Discharged Quebec.

Pearce/Pearse, John. Carpenter of Dublin. 43rd Foot. Marched from Hythe and confined aboard PS as John Pearse or Pearce, 13 March 1814. Joined as John Pearce, 25 March 1814. Deserted while still at the Isle of Wight, 2 June 1814. No record of rejoining.

Pearce, Thomas. Carpenter of Liverpool. 89th Foot. Transferred from Newport, Isle of Wight, and confined aboard PS, 29 May 1815. Joined YCs 29 June 1815, and arrived in the WIs 5 November 1815. Died, 20 January 1816.

Pearson, Charles. Labourer of Antrim. Transferred from 101st Foot in Jamaica, 26 February 1817. Deserted in Jamaica, 29 March 1817. No record of rejoining.

Pearson, Robert. 2nd Bn 67th Foot. Marched from Andover and confined aboard PS, 28 November 1813. Joined YCs 5 February 1814, and arrived in the WIs 14 December 1814. Discharged Quebec.

Pearson, William. Brass founder of Lancashire. Royal Artillery Driver. Marched from Winchester and confined aboard PS, 15 February 1814. Joined YCs 7 March 1814, and arrived in the WIs 14 December 1814. Died, 13 October 1816.

Pearson, William. Labourer of Royston. 7th Dragoon Guards. Marched from Chester and confined aboard PS, 17 October 1815. Joined YCs 16 May 1816, and arrived in the WIs 25 June 1816. Died Jamaica, 5 April 1817.

Peck, Henry. 1st Dragoon Guards. Marched from Henley and confined aboard PS, 30 October 1814. Joined YCs 29 June 1815, and arrived in the WIs 5 November 1815. Promoted sergeant 29 August 1816. Reduced 8 October 1818. Discharged Jamaica, March 1819.

Peckering/Pickering, John. Labourer of Yorkshire. Transferred to YCs from 1st

European Garrison in Jamaica, 25 May 1817. Died Jamaica, 24 October 1817.

Pegler, John. Labourer of Gloucestershire. 2nd Bn 3rd Guards. Marched from Savoy Military Prison and confined aboard PS, 7 August 1814. Joined YCs 29 June 1815, and arrived in the WIs as sergeant, 5 November 1815. Reduced 3 February 1816. Promoted corporal 6 May 1816. Reduced 17 October 1816. Died Jamaica, 27 April 1817. Willed effects, four pounds, ten shillings and sixpence, to Samuel Pegler of Wotton-under-Edge.

Pendleton/Pindleeton/Peadleton, Joseph or **Joshua** or **Jacob.** Labourer of Manchester. Horse Guards. Marched from Middlewich and confined aboard PS as Joseph Pendleton, 4 November 1814. Joined YCs 29 June 1815, and arrived in the WIs as Joshua Pindleton or Peadleton, 5 November 1815. Died Tobago as Jacob Pendleton, 21 June 1816.

Penrose, Edward. Blacksmith of Limerick. 85th Foot. Marched from Bristol and confined aboard PS, 23 January 1814. Joined YCs 25 March 1814. Deserted while still at the Isle of Wight, 7 June 1814. Recaptured and marched from Maidstone to PS, 16 April 1815. No further record.

Perry, Edward. 2nd Bn 23rd Foot. Marched from Devizes and confined aboard PS, 30 November 1814. Joined YCs 29 June 1815, and arrived in the WIs 5 November 1815. Discharged Quebec.

Perry, George. 18th Hussars. Marched from Wakefield and confined aboard PS, 28 April 1815. Joined YCs 29 June 1815, and arrived in the WIs 5 November 1815. Deserted in Tobago, 18 August 1816. No record of rejoining.

Peters, William. 2nd Bn 23rd Foot. Marched from Fisherton and confined aboard PS, 22 September 1814. Joined YCs 29 June 1815, and arrived in the WIs 5 November 1815. Discharged Quebec.

Petty, Joseph. Labourer of Oxford. General Service. Marched from Savoy Military Prison and confined aboard PS, 11 December 1814. Joined YCs 29 June 1815, and arrived in the WIs 5 November 1815. Died Jamaica, 18 September 1817.

Phelan, John. Labourer of Tipperary. 11th Foot. Marched from Woodbridge and confined aboard PS, 19 December 1813. Joined YCs 1 February 1814, and arrived in the WIs 14 December 1814. Promoted corporal 25 April 1814, sergeant 24 May 1814. Reduced 16 March 1816. Promoted corporal 4 March 1817. Reduced 4 May 1818. Deserted in Jamaica, 31 March 1819. No record of rejoining.

Phillips, Robert. Labourer of Cambridge. Transferred to YCs from 6th Bn 60th Foot in Jamaica, 25 May 1817. Deserted in Jamaica, 28 April 1819. No record of rejoining.

Philpot/Philpott, William. Labourer of Shropshire. 2nd Bn 63rd Foot. Marched from Coventry and confined aboard PS, 26 February 1814. Joined YCs 25 March 1814. Deserted while still at the Isle of Wight, 7 July 1814. Rejoined 6 September 1814. (No punishment record held.) Arrived in the WIs 14 December 1814. Died, 15 November 1816.

Philpot/Philpott, William. Royal Artillery. Marched from Savoy Military Prison and confined aboard PS, 12 February 1815. Joined YCs 29 June 1815, and arrived in the WIs 5 November 1815. Discharged Quebec. Allocated Concession 9. Lot NE 5. Beckwith. No evidence found of him settling there.

Pickles, Samuel. Weaver of Leeds. 3rd Bn Royal Artillery. Marched from Wakefield and confined aboard PS, 13 October 1813. Joined YCs 7 March 1814, and arrived in the WIs 14 December 1814. Died Grenada, 7 November 1815.

Pilkington/Pickington, James. Weaver of Lancashire. Royal Horse Artillery. Marched from Preston and confined aboard PS as James Pilkington or Pickington, 14 March 1814. Joined YCs as James Pickington, 25 March 1814. Arrived in the WIs 14 December 1814. 'James Pilkington, Killed in action at Guadeloupe, 9th August 1815'.

Pimlett/Princlett, Thomas. Labourer of Putney. 7th Foot. Marched from Winchester and confined aboard PS as Thomas Princlett or Benjamin Williams, 18 January 1815. Joined YCs 29 June 1815, and arrived in the WIs as Thomas Pimlett, 5 November 1815. Died Tobago, 20 April 1816.

Pincot/Pincott/Prescott, Michael. Labourer of Gloucestershire. North Gloucestershire Militia. Marched from Chester and confined aboard PS as Michael Pincott, 31 December 1813. Joined YCs as Michael Prescott, 25 March 1814. Arrived in the WIs as Michael Pincott, 14 December 1814. Deserted at Barbados, 25 February 1815. No record of rejoining.

Pitt/Pitts, Thomas. 63rd Foot. Marched from Bedford and confined aboard PS, 15 May 1814. Joined YCs 29 June 1815, and arrived in the WIs 5 November 1815. Died, 31 October 1816.

Plymouth, Thomas. Joined 6th Foot, 18 June 1810. Marched from Chelsea as volunteer corporal, 1 April 1815. Reduced 11 August 1815. Arrived in the WIs 5 November 1815. Promoted corporal 25 December 1815, sergeant 26 October 1816. 300 lashes and ordered to be reduced for 'Disobedience of Orders and saying he did not give a damn for the Adjutant', 10 December 1816. Reduced but corporal punishment remitted 'Due to His Previous Good Character'; 300 lashes for being 'Drunk on Guard', 24 December 1816. Punishment remitted; 300 lashes for being 'Drunk on Guard & Playing Cards', 1 March 1817. Commuted to solitary confinement. Discharged Quebec. No record of land allocation, yet letter from Horse Guards to Lieutenant General Dalhousie, Canada, 20 June 1827, clearly indicates that Plymouth's mother considered her son as a 'land owner'. 'Application having been made to this Office by a poor woman named Mary Plymouth, relative to her son Thomas Plymouth who was discharged at Quebec on the 24th August 1819 from the York Chasseurs when that Corps was disbanded, and who she states received a quantity of land in North America in lieu of the Out-Pension'.

Pollard, John. 2nd Bn 9th Foot. Marched from Canterbury and confined aboard PS, 29 December 1814. Joined YCs 29 June 1815, and arrived in the WIs 5 November 1815. Discharged Quebec. Allocated Concession 8. Lot SW 9. Beckwith. No evidence found of him settling there.

Pollett/Powlet, John. Hatter of Manchester. 21st Light Dragoons. Marched from Maidstone and confined aboard PS as John Pollett or Powlett, 6 March 1814. Joined YCs as John Pollett, 25 March 1814. Arrived in the WIs 14 December 1814. 150 lashes for 'Making away with his Necessaries', 9 May 1815, 50 lashes remitted. Died St Vincent, 9 August 1815.

Potter, Alexander. Weaver of Forfar. Royal Artillery. Marched from Guildford and confined aboard PS, 8 September 1813. Joined YCs 5 February 1814, and arrived in the WIs 14 December 1814. Died Jamaica, 26 October 1817.

Potter, Henry. Labourer of Yorkshire. 37th Foot. Transported from Portsmouth and confined aboard PS, 25 March 1815. Joined YCs 29 June 1815, and arrived in the WIs 5 November 1815. Deserted in Jamaica April 1817. Rejoined the same day. Deserted in Jamaica 11 July 1817. Rejoined 14 July 1817. (No punishment records held.) Deserted in Jamaica 2 August 1817. No record of rejoining.

Potter, William. Sailor of Wiltshire. 7th Foot. Marched from Marlborough and confined at Portchester Castle, 19 January 1817. Joined YCs 3 April 1817, and arrived in the WIs 25 May 1817. Deserted in Jamaica, 1 May 1819. No record of rejoining.

Pottinger, Bernard. Labourer of Yorkshire. 14th Foot. Marched from Reading and confined aboard PS, 2 June 1815. Joined YCs 29 June 1815, and arrived in the WIs 5 November 1815. Died, 21 September 1816.

Powell, John. Labourer of Somerset. 85th Foot. Marched from Gloucester and confined aboard PS, 24 July 1814. Joined YCs 29 June 1815, and arrived in the WIs 5 November 1815. Died Jamaica, 17 August 1817.

Power, John. 2nd Bn 59th Foot. Marched from Northampton and confined aboard PS, 19 December 1813. Joined YCs 5 February 1814, and arrived in the WIs 14 December 1814. Deserted 24 August 1816. Rejoined 7 September 1816. (No punishment record held.) 150 lashes for being 'Drunk & Absent from Evening Parade', 10 February 1817. Punishment remitted. Discharged Quebec.

Power, John. 11th Foot. Marched from Chester and confined aboard PS, 1 November 1815. Joined YCs 17 May 1816, and arrived in the WIs 25 June 1816. Deserted, 29 July 1816. No record of rejoining.

Power, William. Labourer of Dublin. 11th Foot. Marched from Chester and confined aboard PS, 1 November 1815. Joined YCs 19 October 1816, and arrived in the WIs 19 December, 1816. Deserted in Jamaica, 26 February 1817. No record of rejoining.

Pratt, Benjamin. Weaver of Stafford. 3rd Dragoons. Marched from Huntington and confined aboard, PS 25 February 1815. Joined YCs 29 June 1815, and arrived in the WIs 5 November 1815. Deserted in Jamaica 30 January 1818. Rejoined 4 February 1818. Deserted in Jamaica 14 August 1818. Rejoined the same day. (No punishment records held.) Discharged Quebec.

Pratt, Joseph. Weaver of Limerick. Kilkenny Militia. Marched from Harwich and confined aboard PS, 13 March 1814. Joined YCs 29 June 1815, and arrived in the WIs 5 November 1815. Deserted in Jamaica 7 April 1819. Rejoined 17 May 1819. (No punishment record held.) Discharged Quebec.

Prenderville, William. Labourer of Kerry. 97th Foot. Marched from Bristol and confined at Portchester Castle, 20 January 1817. Joined YCs 3 March 1817, and arrived in the WIs 25 May 1817. Deserted in Jamaica 5 June 1819. Rejoined 10 June 1819. (No punishment record held.) Discharged Quebec.

Prentice, James. Royal Artillery. Marched from Chester and confined aboard PS, 2 October 1813. Joined YCs 5 February 1814, and arrived in the WIs 14 December 1814. Discharged Quebec.

Price, Daniel. Cooper of Herts. Coldstream Guards. Marched from Oxford and confined aboard PS, 14 September 1813. Joined YCs 7 March 1814, and arrived in the WIs 14 December 1814. Died Jamaica, 15 September 1817.

Price, William. 2nd Bn 53rd Foot. Marched from Oxford and confined aboard PS, 12 September 1813. Joined YCs 5 February 1814, and arrived in the WIs 14 December 1814. 'Private James McClure sentenced to 1000 lashes for Stabbing Private William Price and Making use of mutinous and threatening words to Captain Anderson', 10 December 1816. Discharged Quebec.

Pritchard, Richard. Labourer of Hereford. 39th Foot. Marched from Southampton and confined aboard PS, 15 February 1814. Joined YCs 7 March 1814. Deserted at Guernsey, 22 September 1814. No record of rejoining.

Pritchard, William. Labourer of Hereford. 55th Foot. Marched from Worcester and confined at Portchester Castle, 20 December 1816. Joined YCs 3 April 1817, and arrived in the WIs 25 May 1817. Deserted in Jamaica 1 April 1819. Rejoined 4 April 1819. (No punishment record held.) Deserted in Jamaica 15 May 1819. No record of rejoining.

Privett/Privitt, Joseph. Labourer of Middlesex. 55th Foot. Marched from Shepton Mallett and confined at Portchester Castle, 8 December 1816. Joined YCs 3 April 1817, and arrived in the WIs 25 May 1817. Deserted in Jamaica 24 March 1819. Rejoined 26 March 1819. (No punishment record held.) Deserted in Jamaica 1 May 1819. No record of rejoining.

Prosser, John. Sawyer. 7th Foot. Marched from Newport, Isle of Wight and confined aboard PS, 17 October 1813. Joined YCs 5 February 1814. Left sick at Cork as the regiment departed for Barbados. Deserted, recaptured, and then imprisoned at Portchester Castle, 13 June 1817. Joined Royal West India Rangers, 31 May 1818. Discharged at St Johns, New Brunswick, 24 June 1819. Legacy – 'Prosser's Creek', New Brunswick.

Pugh, John. Labourer of Denby. 1st Foot Guards. Marched from Savoy Military Prison and confined aboard PS, date unknown. Joined YCs 29 June 1815, and arrived in the WIs 5 November 1815. Died Jamaica, 23 September 1817.

Pugh, William. General Service. Marched from Savoy Military Prison and confined aboard PS, 5 March 1816. Joined YCs 16 May 1816, and arrived in the WIs 25 June 1816. 'Delivered to Civil Power – Sentenced to serve in the Royal Navy for Life for Highway Robbery', 22 July 1816.

Quick/Quirk, Nicholas. Blacksmith of Cloghin, King's County. Royal Horse Artillery. Marched from Horsham and confined aboard, PS 18 January 1814. Joined YCs 25 March 1814, and arrived in the WIs 14 December 1814. 300 lashes for being 'Drunk on Barrier Beach Guard', 25 April 1815. Deserted in Jamaica 13 September 1818. Rejoined 18 September 1818. Deserted in Jamaica 23 January 1819. Rejoined 4 February 1819. (No punishment records held.) Deserted in Jamaica, 4 March 1819. No recorded of rejoining.

Quigley, William. 72nd Foot. Marched from Bristol and confined aboard PS, 20 October 1813. Joined YCs 1 February 1814, and arrived in the WIs 14 December 1814. Promoted corporal 2 July 1814, sergeant March 1815. Reduced 6 April 1815. Promoted corporal 10 August 1815. Reduced 13 October 1815. Promoted corporal 3 May 1816. Reduced 30 May 1818. Discharged Quebec.

Quinn, Charles. Labourer of Carlow. 97th Foot. Marched from Bristol and confined aboard PS as Charles Quinn or Smith, 29 September 1813. Joined as Charles Quinn, 5 February 1814. Deserted while still at Isle of Wight, 1 July 1814. Rejoined 20 July 1814. (No punishment record held.) Arrived in the WIs 14 December 1814. 200 lashes for 'Theft', 21 January 1817. Deserted in Jamaica 31 March 1819. Rejoined 1 April 1819. (No punishment record held.) Deserted in Jamaica 15 May 1819. No record of rejoining.

Quinn, Cornelius. Labourer of Cork. 95th Foot. Marched from Rochester and confined at Portchester Castle, 23 December 1816. Deserted in Jamaica 23 September 1817. Rejoined 29 September 1817. 300 lashes for being 'Absent without Leave', 1 October 1817. Died Jamaica, 8 October 1818.

Quinn, John. Labourer of Kent. 1st Bn 95th Foot. Marched from Bedford and confined aboard PS, 22 June 1813. Joined YCs 5 February 1814. Deserted at Guernsey, 22 September 1814. No record of rejoining.

Quinn, John. Labourer of Tyrone. 1st Bn 52nd Foot. Marched from Maidstone and confined aboard PS, 1 January 1815. Joined YCs 29 June 1815, and arrived in the WIs 5 November 1815. Died Jamaica, 27 July 1817.

Quirk, Thomas. 85th Foot. Marched from Winchester and confined aboard PS, 5 March 1816. Joined YCs 19 October 1816, and arrived in the WIs 19 December 1816. 300 lashes for being 'Drunk and absenting himself from his Guard', 12 April 1817, 100 lashes remitted; 150 lashes for 'Selling his Necessaries', 28 April 1817. Punishment remitted to solitary confinement; 300 lashes for 'Theft', 24 June 1817. Discharged Quebec.

Ralph/Rolph, William. 36th Foot. Marched from Bristol and confined aboard PS, 16 September 1813. Joined YCs 5 February 1814, and arrived in the WIs 14 December 1814. 'Detained by the Civil Powers at Barbados, charged with accepting Base-Coin but fully acquitted at the Sessions', September 1815; 1,000 lashes for being 'Drunk and Absenting from his Guard and Refusing to become a Prisoner. Using Mutinous and Insolent Expressions to Captain Parker in the Execution of his Duty and Striking or Attempting to Strike the said Officer', 22 November 1816. Discharged Quebec.

Ramsey, James. From Scotland. 74th Foot. Marched from Bristol and confined aboard PS, 16 September 1813. Joined YCs 7 March 1814, and arrived in the WIs 14 December 1814. Discharged Quebec. Allocated Concession 10. Lot NE 14. Bathurst. No evidence of him settling there. 'Concession re-allocated to Thomas Cook, 24th May 1824'.

Rands, Simon. 2nd Bn 83rd Foot. Marched from Huntingdon and confined aboard PS, 25 August 1813. Joined YCs 7 February 1814, and arrived in the WIs 14 December 1814. Discharged Quebec.

Ratcliff/Ratcliffe, John or **Jonah.** 55th Foot. Marched from Middlewich and confined aboard PS as Jonah Ratcliff, 5 February 1814. Joined YCs as John Ratcliffe, 25 March 1814. Arrived in the WIs 14 December 1814. 300 lashes for being 'Drunk on Barrier Beach Guard', 28 April 1815. Discharged Quebec.

Raybold, John. Coach Painter of Middlesex. 22nd Light Dragoons. Marched from Maidstone and confined aboard PS, 9 January 1814. Joined YCs 7 March 1814. Deserted while still at the Isle of Wight, 1 July 1814. Rejoined 30 July 1814. (No punishment record held.) Arrived in WIs 14 December 1814. 150 lashes for 'Refusing to Drill', 20 April 1815. Received 25 lashes with the remaining 125 commuted to solitary confinement. Died Quebec, 20 August 1819, four days prior to disbandment.

Reardon, John. 3rd Foot. Transported from Ostend and confined aboard PS, 16 February 1816. Joined YCs 19 October 1816, and arrived in the WIs 21 December 1816. Deserted in Jamaica, 24 April 1819. No record of rejoining.

Rease/Rice, Michael. 19th Light Dragoons. Marched from Bristol and confined aboard PS as Michael Rice, 22 October 1814. Joined YCs 29 June 1815, and arrived in the WIs 5 November 1815. Discharged Quebec as Michael Rease.

Recrouche/Recroutch/Recivatch, Ilen or **Illen** or **Ileen.** Labourer of Wallacia, Turkey. Transferred to YCs from 6th Bn 60th Foot in Jamaica, 25 May 1817. Died Jamaica, 31 March 1819.

Redding/Reading/Riding, Charles. Royal Artillery. Marched from Chelmsford and confined aboard PS as Charles Redding, 6 March 1814. Joined YCs as Charles Riding, 25 March 1814. Arrived in the WIs 14 December 1814. Promoted corporal 9 October 1814, sergeant 25 February 1815. Reduced for 'Absent from Morning Parade', 3 August 1815. Died Jamaica as Charles Redding or Reading, 26 November 1817. Willed his effects, One pound, nineteen shillings and a penny to his father, Benjamin Redding of Birmingham.

Redding, Mathew. 17th Foot. Marched from Abingdon and confined at Portchester Castle, 9 January 1817. Joined YCs 3 April 1817, and arrived in the WIs 25 May 1817. Discharged Quebec.

Redding/Reddings/Reading/Readings, Samuel. Labourer of Lancashire. 55th Foot. Marched from Savoy Military Prison and confined aboard PS as Samuel Reading, 11 November 1813. Joined YCs 5 February 1814, and arrived in the WIs 14 December 1814. Promoted corporal September 1814. Reduced 4 April 1815. 300 lashes for being 'Drunk on Guard but FORGIVEN', 31 May 1815. Died Tobago as Samuel Reddings, 10 June 1816.

Redman/Redmond, Thomas. Labourer of Hereford. 95th Foot. Transported from Gosport and confined aboard PS as Thomas Redman, 19 January 1816. Embarked Spithead amongst a 300-strong detachment of 'Unattached Deserters' joining the 2nd Foot, 25 April 1816. Arrived in the WIs 5 June 1816. Deserted 16 July 1816. Rejoined 17 July 1816. 1,000 lashes and ordered to be marked with 'D', 25 July 1816. Transferred into York Chasseurs, 25 August 1816. Died as Thomas Redmond, 1 October 1816.

Reed/Reid, James. Whitesmith of Antrim. Joined Royal Artillery, August 1803. Confined aboard PS, 24 December 1815. Joined YCs 19 October 1816, and arrived in the WIs 21 December 1816. 300 lashes for being 'Drunk on Guard and Playing Cards', 1 March 1817. Punishment remitted. Died Jamaica, 25 March 1819.

Rees/Rease, Michael. 4th Battalion 1st Foot. Marched from Cardiff and confined aboard PS 30 December, 1813. Joined YCs as Michael Rees, 7 March 1814. Arrived in the WIs 14 December 1814. Discharged Quebec as Michael Rease.

Reeve, Humphrey. Shoemaker of Kerry. 2nd Bn 37th Foot. Marched from Maidstone and confined aboard PS, date unknown. Joined YCs 5 February 1814. Deserted while still at the Isle of Wight, 7 July 1814. No record of rejoining.

Reiley/Ryley/Riley, James. Labourer of Mayo. West Essex Militia. Marched from Manchester and confined aboard PS as James Ryley, 19 October 1813. Joined YCs as James Riley, 25 March 1814. Deserted while still at the Isle of Wight, 4 July 1814. Rejoined, 15 July 1814, and hospitalised. (No punishment record held.) Arrived in the WIs as James Reiley, 14 December 1814. Died, 12 August 1815.

Reistrich/Reinstruck, John. 2nd Foot Guards. Marched from Wakefield and confined aboard PS as John Reistrich, 20 March 1814. Joined YCs 29 June 1815, and arrived in the WIs 5 November 1815. Discharged Quebec as John Reinstruck.

Renshaw, James. Labourer of Chester. 1st Foot Guards. Marched from Savoy Military Prison and confined aboard PS, 27 October 1814. Joined YCs 29 June 1815, and arrived in the WIs 5 November 1815. Died Jamaica, 21 May 1819.

Rhodes, Benjamin. Labourer of Leeds. 77th Foot. Marched from Bristol and confined aboard PS, 16 July 1816. Joined YCs 19 October 1816, and arrived in the WIs 21 December 1816. Deserted in Jamaica 8 March 1819. Rejoined 14 April 1819. (No punishment record held.) Died Quebec, 17 August 1819, a week before disbandment.

Rice, Joseph. Labourer of Devon. 2nd Bn 5th Foot. Marched from Henley and confined aboard PS, 7 October 1814. Joined YCs 29 June 1815, and arrived in the WIs 5 November 1815. Deserted in Jamaica 15 November 1817. Rejoined, date unknown. (No punishment record held.) Died Jamaica, 6 December 1817, shortly after returning from desertion and no doubt punishment.

Richards, John. Labourer of Llandwelley, Glamorgan. 32nd Foot. Marched from Plymouth Dock and confined aboard PS, 12 October 1813. Joined YCs 5 February 1814, and arrived in the WIs 14 December 1814. 300 lashes for being 'Drunk on Barrier Beach Guard', 28 April 1815. Died Jamaica, 27 March 1817.

Richards, John. Labourer of Leeds. Either 1st or 3rd Bn 95th Foot. Sentenced at Ypres to 'General Service for Life for Desertion and Stealing', 21 October 1814. Marched from Deal and confined aboard PS, 11 December 1814. Joined YCs 29 June 1815, and arrived in the WIs 5 November 1815. 300 lashes for 'Unsoldierlike Conduct – Attempting to stab his wife', 10 October 1817. Commuted to solitary confinement. Discharged from Stony Hill, Jamaica, 10 June 1819.

Richardson, James. 23rd Light Dragoons. Marched from Bristol and confined aboard PS, 11 April 1815. Joined YCs 29 June 1815, and arrived in the WIs 5 November 1815. Discharged Quebec.

Richardson, John. Weaver of Armagh. 18th Foot. Marched from Chester and confined aboard PS, 28 December 1814. Joined YCs 29 June 1815, and arrived in the WIs 5 November 1815. Deserted 22 September 1816. Rejoined 14 October 1816. 800 lashes for 'Desertion', 22 September 1816, and not returning till brought back a prisoner, 14 October 1816–21 October 1816. Died, 13 November 1816, just three weeks following punishment.

Richardson, Richard. Labourer of Lancashire. 29th Foot. Marched from Woodbridge and confined aboard PS, 10 October 1813. Joined YCs 1 February 1814, and arrived in the WIs 14 December 1814. Deserted in Jamaica 10 July 1818. Rejoined 12 July 1818. (No punishment record held.) Discharged Quebec.

Richardson/Richards, William. Weaver of Cumberland. Royal Artillery Driver. Marched from Hull and confined aboard PS as William Richards, 3 September 1813. Joined YCs 5 February 1814. Deserted while still at the Isle of Wight, 10 February 1814. Retaken 11 February 1814. Rejoined 20 February 1814. (No punishment record held.) Hospitalised and re-confined aboard PS as William Richardson to wait regiment's embarkation. Arrived in the WIs as William Richardson, 14 December 1814. Deserted in Jamaica 30 April 1819. Rejoined the same day. (No punishment record held.) Discharged Quebec. Allocated Concession 6. Lot SW 6. Beckwith. No evidence found of him settling there. 'Concession allocated to Duncan Ferguson, 4th July 1828'.

Richmond, Nathanial. 54th Foot. Marched from Liverpool and confined aboard PS, 3 April 1816. Joined YCs 19 October 1816, and arrived in the WIs 21 December 1916. Promoted drummer 25 November 1817. Discharged Quebec.

Ridge, Anthony. 2nd Bn 5th Foot. Marched from Eton and confined aboard PS, 2 August 1815. Joined YCs 16 May 1816, and arrived in the WIs 25 June 1816. Deserted 21 July 1816. No record of rejoining.

Ridley, George. Shoemaker of Queen's County. Joined 2nd Foot, 24 March 1807. Transported from Haslar Barracks, Gosport, and confined aboard PS, 3 March 1815. Joined YCs 29 June 1815, and arrived in the WIs 5 November 1815. Deserted in Tobago 16 August 1816. Rejoined 25 November 1816. General Court-martial, 4 December 1816, considered 'The Long confinement the Prisoner has undergone was of Sufficient Punishment'. 300 lashes for being 'Drunk on Guard & Playing Cards', 1 March 1817. Died Jamaica, 3 October 1818.

Rieley/Reiley, Peter. 2nd Bn 18th Foot. Transported from Portsmouth and confined aboard PS, 16 June 1814. Joined YCs 29 June 1815, and arrived in the WIs 5 November 1815. Discharged Quebec.

Rielly/Rieley, Thomas. 32nd Foot. Marched from Chester and confined aboard PS, 23 February 1816. Joined YCs 3 April 1817, and arrived in the WIs 25 May 1817. Discharged Quebec.

Riley/Reiley, Thomas. 1st Foot. Marched from Chester and confined aboard PS as Thomas Riley, 3 February 1814. Joined YCs 25 March 1814. Died Guernsey as Thomas Rieley, 2 September 1814.

Rippen/Rippon, William. Royal Artillery. Marched from Chester and confined aboard PS, 25 September 1813. Joined YCs as William Rippen 7 March 1814. Arrived in the WIs 14 December 1814. Promoted corporal 25 December 1814. Reduced 10 January 1815. 300 lashes for being 'Absent from Evening Parade', 29 March 1815, 100 lashes remitted. Discharged Quebec as William Rippon. Allocated Concession 10. Lot SW 14. Bathurst. No evidence found of him settling there. 'Concession allocated to James Foster, 28th March 1827'.

Roach, John. Labourer of Wexford. 54th Foot. Marched from Ipswich and confined aboard PS, 7 October 1813. Joined YCs 7 March 1814, and arrived in the WIs 14 December 1814. Deserted 5 December 1816. Rejoined 10 December 1816. Deserted in Jamaica 8 March 1817. Rejoined 10 March 1817. (No punishment record held.) Discharged Quebec.

Roach, Patrick. Labourer of Cavan. 21st Foot General Service Recruit. Transferred from Albany Barracks and confined aboard PS, 6 November 1813. Joined YCs 5 February 1814. Deserted while still at the Isle of Wight, 10 July 1814. Rejoined 20 July 1814 and hospitalised. (No punishment record held.) Deserted Guernsey, 22 September 1814. Rejoined 9 December 1814. Remained in Europe, and no further record after September 1815.

Roach, Patrick. Labourer of Tullamore. 54th Foot. Marched from Chester and confined aboard PS, 18 May 1815. Joined YCs 29 June 1815, and arrived in the WIs 5 November 1815. Died Tobago, 16 May 1816.

Roberts, Thomas. Labourer of Down. 90th Foot. Marched from Bristol and confined aboard PS, 20 November 1813. Joined as drummer 7 March 1814. Arrived in the WIs 14 December 1814. 200 lashes for being 'Drunk and Absent from Morning Practice', 22 May 1815. 50 lashes remitted; 300 lashes for being 'Drunk and Insolent on Evening Parade', 16 September 1815; 200 lashes and ordered to be reduced for being 'Drunk & Absent from Evening Parade and Leaving Limits of the Garrison', 6 March 1817. Deserted in Jamaica 30 May 1819. Rejoined 6 June 1819. (No punishment record held.) Discharged Quebec.

Robinson/Robison, George. Cotton spinner of Manchester. 2nd Bn. 84th Foot. Marched from Bristol and confined aboard PS, 20 November 1813. Joined YCs 7 March 1814, and arrived in the WIs 14 December 1814. Deserted in Jamaica 5 June 1817. Rejoined the same day. (No punishment record held.) Deserted in Jamaica 10 December 1817. Rejoined 12 December 1817. 300 lashes for 'Absenting himself without Leave', 27 December 1817. Deserted in Jamaica 14 June 1818. Rejoined 21 June 1818. Deserted in Jamaica 28 July 1818. Rejoined 5 August 1818. (No punishment records held.) Deserted in Jamaica 10 November 1818. No record of rejoining.

Robinson, Henry. Framework knitter of Nottinghamshire. 73rd Foot. Marched from Liverpool and confined aboard PS, 28 December 1814. Joined YCs 29 June 1815, and arrived in the WIs as drummer, 5 November 1815. Deserted in Jamaica 1 April 1819. Rejoined 6 May 1819. (No punishment record held.) Discharged Quebec.

Robinson/Robison, James. Weaver of Lancashire. Either Royals marched from Tilbury Fort, 12 September 1813, or 47th Foot marched from Beverly and confined aboard PS, 26 September. Joined YCs 5 February 1814, and arrived in the WIs 14 December 1814. Deserted in Jamaica 30 April 1819. Rejoined 4 May 1819. (No punishment record held.) Discharged Quebec.

Robinson/Robison, James. Book Binder of Edinburgh. Either Royals marched from Tilbury Fort, 12 September 1813 or 47th Foot marched from Beverly and confined aboard PS, 26 September 1813. Joined YCs 5 February 1814, and arrived in the WIs 14 December 1814. Discharged Quebec.

Robinson/Robison/Robertson, John. Labourer of Ayr. Berwick Militia. Marched from Newcastle and confined aboard PS as John Robertson, 10 September 1813. Joined YCs as sergeant, 1 February 1814. Reduced 28 April 1814. Deserted as John Robinson or Robison while still at the Isle of Wight, 24 June 1814. No record of rejoining.

Robinson, John. Labourer of Derby. 88th Foot. Marched from Chester and confined aboard PS, 24 May 1816. Joined YCs 3 April 1817, and arrived in the WIs 25 May 1817. Deserted in Jamaica 1 November 1818. No record of rejoining.

Robinson/Robison, Joseph. Seaman of Lincoln. 7th Light Dragoons. Marched from Savoy Military Prison and confined aboard PS, 22 August 1813. Joined YCs 1 February 1814. Deserted from Sandown, Isle of Wight, 4 February 1814. Rejoined, date unknown. (No punishment record held.) Confined aboard PS until regiment left for Barbados. Remained sick at Cork General Hospital. Arrived in the WIs 11 May 1815. Died, 29 September 1816.

Robinson/Robison, Walter. 2nd Bn 79th Foot. Marched from Edinburgh and confined aboard PS, 20 October 1813. Joined YCs 1 February 1814, and arrived in the WIs 14 December 1814. Discharged Quebec.

Robson, Mathew. Dyer of Northumberland. 1st Bn 95th Foot. Transported from France and confined aboard PS, 16 July 1816. Joined YCs 19 October 1816, and arrived in the WIs 21 December 1816. Deserted in Jamaica 27 May 1819. Rejoined, date unknown. (No punishment record held.) Discharged Quebec.

Rock/Roach, Patrick. Labourer of Cavan. 54th Foot. Marched from Chester and confined aboard PS as Patrick Roach or Rock, 18 May 1815. Joined YCs 29 June 1815 as Patrick Rock. Arrived in the WIs as Patrick Rock, 5 November 1815. Deserted 1 September 1816. Rejoined 14 October 1816. 800 lashes 21 October 1816 for 'Desertion, 1st September 1816, and not returning till brought back 14th October 1816'; 200 lashes for 'Theft', 14 January 1817. Deserted in Jamaica 3 November 1817. No record of rejoining.

Rocklidge/Rockledge, William. Labourer of Hampshire, 2nd Bn 33rd Foot. Transported from Jersey and confined aboard PS, 29 July 1813. Joined YCs 5 February 1814. Promoted corporal 25 April 1814. Reduced 30 June 1814. Deserted while still at the Isle of Wight 7 July 1814. Seized by Thomas Gloge (Twenty Shillings Bounty) and rejoined 15 July 1814. (No punishment record held.) Arrived in the WIs 14 December 1814. 300 lashes for being 'Drunk on Guard', 24 December 1816. Died Jamaica, listed as 'flax dresser' of Selby, 2 October 1817.

Rodgers/Rogers, Charles. Labourer of Antrim. 32nd Foot. Marched from Bristol and confined aboard PS, 3 May 1816. Joined YCs 19 October 1816, and arrived in the WIs 21 December 1816. 200 lashes for 'Selling a shirt not his Own', 14 January 1817; 200 lashes for 'Selling part of his Regimental Necessaries', 17 February 1817. Deserted in Jamaica 8 May 1817. No record of rejoining.

Rodgers/Rogers, John. Labourer of Warwickshire. 17th Foot. Marched from Savoy Military Prison and confined aboard PS, 29 September 1813. Joined YCs 1 February 1814, and arrived in the WIs 14 December 1814. Died Jamaica, 4 December 1816.

Rodgers/Rogers, John. Labourer of Tiverton. 2nd Bn 38th Foot. Marched from Bristol and confined aboard PS, 15 January 1815. Joined YCs 29 June 1815, and arrived in the WIs 5 November 1815. Died, 9 May 1816.

Rodgers/Rogers, Thomas. Labourer of Cheston, Devon. 2nd Bn 14th Foot. Marched from Savoy Military Prison and confined aboard PS, 6 August 1813. Joined YCs 5 February 1814. Deserted while still at the Isle of Wight, 30 March 1814. Recaptured by George Cox (Twenty Shillings Reward Bounty) and confined at Hilsea Barracks, Portsmouth, 5 April 1814. Rejoined 9 April 1814 and hospitalised. (No punishment record held.) Arrived in the WIs 14 December 1814. Promoted corporal 21 September 1814, sergeant 15 April 1815. Reduced 14 October 1815. Discharged from Stony Hill, Jamaica, June 1819.

Roffey/Ruffey, James. 2nd Bn 73rd Foot. Marched from Savoy Military Prison and confined aboard PS as James Roffey, 17 August 1813. Joined YCs 1 February 1814, and arrived in the WIs 14 December 1814. 'Employed as Orderly in General Hospital from 20th April to 20th June 1815. Entitled to 2d per diem in lieu of Salt Rations for that period'. Discharged Quebec as James Ruffey.

Rooney, Patrick. Labourer of Monaghan. 2nd Bn 47th Foot. Marched from Chester and confined aboard PS, 22 September 1814. Joined YCs 29 June 1815, and arrived in the WIs 5 November 1815. 200 lashes for 'Loosing or Making Off with a Shirt', 24 December 1816. Deserted in Jamaica 11 May 1818. Rejoined 21 May 1818. (No punishment record held.) Deserted in Jamaica, 15 May 1819. No record of rejoining.

Rosseau/Rossean, Francis. Shoemaker of Dublin. Transferred to YCs from 6th Bn 60th Foot in Jamaica as Rosseau or Rossean, 25 May 1817. Discharged from Stony Hill, Jamaica, 10 June 1819.

Rosser/Rossier, Francis. Clerk of Middlesex. 1st Foot Guards. Marched from Tower of London and confined aboard PS as Francis Rosser or Rossier, 25 October 1814. Joined YCs as Francis Rosser, 29 June 1815. Arrived in the WIs 5 November 1815. Promoted corporal 25 February 1816, sergeant 25 October 1816. Reduced for 'Unsoldierlike Conduct in stating a Falsehood to Major General Conran', 24 June 1817. Sentenced to solitary confinement for a repetition of his 'Unsoldierlike Conduct', 27 June 1817. Deserted in Jamaica 29 August 1819. No record of rejoining.

Rowe, William. Shoemaker. 85th Foot. Marched from Stafford and confined aboard PS, 8 August 1813. Joined YCs 5 February 1814, and arrived in the WIs 14 December 1814. Died Barbados, 13 April 1815.

Rudd, John. Labourer of Queen's County. Arrived in the WIs 25 May 1817. 200 lashes for 'Making Away with Regimental Necessities', 30 October 1817, 50 lashes remitted. Promoted corporal 25 December 1818. Deserted in Jamaica 27 April 1819. Rejoined as private 6 May 1819. Deserted in Jamaica 16 May 1819. Rejoined 1 June 1819. (No punishment records held.) Discharged Quebec.

Rush, Montague. Shoemaker of Cork. 25th Light Dragoons. Marched from Dorchester and confined aboard PS, 26 September 1813. Joined YCs 5 February 1814, and arrived in the WIs 14 December 1814. Died Grenada, 27 February 1816.

Russell, James. Labourer of Queen's County. 11th Light Dragoons. Confined aboard PS as James Dunn or Russell, 18 January 1814. Joined YCs as James Russell, 25 March 1814. Deserted while still at the Isle of Wight, 17 April 1814. No record of rejoining.

Ryan, James. Either 57th Foot marched from Bristol, 20 October 1813, or 16th Light Dragoons marched from Bristol and confined aboard PS, 19 August 1813. Joined YCs 5 February 1814. Deserted at Cork 27 October 1814. No record of rejoining.

Ryan, Michael. Labourer of Waterford. 83rd Foot. Marched from Berryhead and confined aboard PS, 22 September 1813. Joined YCs 25 March 1814. Deserted while still at the Isle of Wight, 1 May 1814. Rejoined 27 July 1814. (No punishment record held.) Deserted Guernsey 19 September 1814. Recaptured and marched from Chester to Isle of Wight PS, 5 February 1815. Escaped, date unknown, recaptured and marched from Bristol to Portchester Castle, 21 November 1816. No further record.

Sadler, John. Labourer of Berkshire. 1st Foot Guards. Marched from Wallingford and confined aboard PS, 29 January 1814. Joined YCs 29 June 1815, and arrived in the WIs 5 November 1815. Died Guadeloupe, 10 August 1815. 'One of seven rank and file supposed to have been poisoned.'

Sale, William. Brass founder of Kent. 24th Foot. Marched from Chelmsford and confined aboard PS, 23 July 1813. Joined YCs 5 February 1814, and arrived in the WIs 14 December 1814. Promoted corporal, 25 February 1815, sergeant, 13 May 1815. Reduced, 5 August 1816. Died, 24 August 1816.

Salt, George. Shoemaker of Macclesfield. Royal Artillery Driver. Marched from Middlewich and confined aboard PS, 3 February 1814. Joined YCs 25 March 1814. Deserted at Guernsey, 19 September 1814. No record of rejoining.

Sanderson, John. Labourer of Yorkshire. 2nd Bn 53rd Foot. Marched from Oxford and confined aboard PS, 12 September 1813. Joined YCs 5 February 1814. Deserted while still at the Isle of Wight, 7 July 1814. Captured by Thomas Gloge of Hayling Island (Twenty Shillings Bounty). Rejoined 15 July 1814, and hospitalized. (No punishment record held) Discharged Quebec.

Sandwick/Sandwich, Aaron. Tailor of Westmorland. Transferred to YCs from 1st European Garrison in Jamaica, 25 May 1817. Died Jamaica, 24 October.1817. Willed his effects, three shillings and eight pence to his father, Richard Sandwich of Kirkland, Kendal.

Sanger/Sangers, Stephen. Labourer of Wiltshire. 76th Foot. Marched from Horsemongers Gaol and confined aboard PS, 10 October 1813. Joined YCs 7 March 1814, and arrived in the WIs 14 March 1814. Died Jamaica, 7 September 1818.

Saunders/Sanders, Thomas. 2nd Bn 5th Foot. Marched from Windsor and confined aboard PS as Thomas Saunders, 8 November 1814. Joined YCs 29 June 1815, and arrived in the WIs 5 November 1815. Discharged Quebec as Thomas Sanders.

Savage, James. Labourer of Cork. 1st Bn 76th Foot. Marched from Chichester and confined aboard PS, 12 January 1814. Joined YCs 5 February 1814, and arrived in the WIs 14 December 1814. 200 lashes for 'Drunk on Guard', 22 September 1815, 100 lashes remitted. Deserted Jamaica, 5 July 1817. Rejoined, 8 July 1817. (No punishment record held) Died Jamaica, 19 November 1817.

Savage, Thomas. Labourer of Loughenislaid. 4th Garrison Bn. Marched from Chester and confined aboard PS, 2 October 1813. Joined YCs 1 February 1814, and immediately promoted colour sergeant. Reduced, date unknown. Deserted Guernsey 22 September 1814. Recaptured, date unknown, and marched from Warwick to Isle of Wight PS, 24 February 1816. No further record.

Savell/Saveal/Savill, Peter. Labourer of Farnon. 7th Foot. Marched from Savoy Military Prison and confined aboard PS as Peter Saveal or Savell, 6 March 1814. Joined as Peter Savell, 25 March 1814. Arrived in the WIs 14 December 1814. Died Regimental Hospital, St Vincent, as Peter Savell or Savill, 22 July 1815.

Savin, George. 37th Foot. Marched from Savoy Military Prison and confined aboard PS, 8 September 1813. Joined YCs 7 March 1814, and arrived in the WIs 14 December 1814. Discharged Quebec.

Sawyer, Edward. Labourer of Berkshire. 1st Light Dragoon Guards. Marched from Hounslow and confined aboard PS, 21 July 1814. Joined YCs 29 June 1815, and arrived in the WIs 5 November 1815. Died, 28 August 1816.

Saxby, Thomas. Labourer of Yorkshire. 70th Foot. Marched from Savoy Military Prison and confined at Portchester Castle, 3 October 1816. Joined YCs 3 April 1817, and arrived in the WIs 25 May 1817. Deserted Jamaica, 26 June 1817. Returned to England, recaptured and marched from Savoy Military Prison to Portchester Castle 22 September 1819. No further record.

Schwartz, Mathew. Musician from Meitz, Mentz or Kaysers Lottein, Germany. Joined 5th Bn 60th Foot at Novia Scotia, 2 May 1803. 'These men were discharged or entitled themselves, having served their time of capitulation, and have re-enlisted, and on doing so received the above Bounty Money (Five Pounds eight shillings and ten pence ha'penny) at Halifax. Nova Scotia'. As a musician Schwartz frequently recorded on pay and muster lists as 'Band.' 5th Bn returned to England and Haslar Barracks, Gosport, October 1805. Bn transferred to Brabourne Lees Barracks, Kent, where Schwartz again recorded as 'being in the regimental band' 1807–1808. Embarked for Cork and then onto Spain and Portugal, July 1808. Deserted 5 February 1810. Rejoined 28 February 1810 (No punishment records held.) Transported from Portugal 'as a suspected man', 24 July 1810, and confined aboard PS, 25 October 1810. Embarked from Cowes aboard transport vessel *Lloyds*, 18 December 1810, and arrived in Jamaica and 6th Bn 60th Foot, 7 February 1811.

6th Bn 60th Foot

Deserted 29 April 1813. Rejoined 30 April 1813.(No punishment records held.)
Deserted 20 July 1814. Rejoined the same day. (No punishment records held.)
Deserted 13 January 1815. Rejoined16 January 1815. (No punishment record held.)
Deserted19 March 1815. Rejoined 23 March 1815.Awarded 800 lashes, 600 remitted.
Deserted 1 November 1815. 3 November 1815. (No punishment records held.)
Deserted12 January 1816. Rejoined 30 May 1816. (No punishment records held.)
Deserted 29 August 1816. Rejoined 28 September 1816. 600 lashes, 4 October 1816.

Transferred to the York Chasseurs 25 May 1817

Deserted 6 June 1817. Rejoined the same day. (No punishment records held.)
Deserted 25 August 1817. Rejoined the next day. 300 lashes, 2 September 1817.
Deserted 3 October 1817. Rejoined the next day. 300 lashes, 10 October 1817.
Deserted 2 May 1818. Rejoined 13 May 1818. (No punishment records held.)
Deserted 2 October 1818. No record of rejoining.

Scott, William. Either a sailor of Burton or labourer of Boston. Transferred from 65th Regimental Depot and confined at Portchester Castle, 7 January 1817. Joined YCs 3 April 1817, and arrived in the WIs 25 May 1817. Deserted in Jamaica 8 June 1817. Rejoined 13 June 1817. 300 lashes for 'Absent without Leave', 19 June 1817. Deserted in Jamaica 4 August 1817. Rejoined 8 August 1817. 300 lashes for 'Absent without Leave'; 300 lashes for 'Persuading Patrick Tanning to Desert and Stealing a Blanket', 30 October 1817, 50 lashes remitted. Deserted in Jamaica 16 April 1819. Rejoined 6 May 1819. (No punishment records held.) Discharged Quebec.

Scully, Peter. Labourer of Armagh. 33rd Foot. Marched from Colchester and confined aboard, PS 25 August 1813. Joined YCs 1 February 1814, and arrived in the WIs 14 December 1814. Promoted corporal 20 May 1814. Reduced 7 September 1814. Promoted corporal 2 June 1815, sergeant 17 October 1815. Reduced 27 December 1816. Deserted in Jamaica 31 July 1817. Rejoined 2 August 1817. (No punishment records held.) Discharged Quebec.

Seed, James. Royal Artillery Driver. Marched from Colchester and confined aboard PS as James Seed or Ludd, 8 May 1815. Joined YCs as James Seed 29 June 1815. 'Left on Detachment' at Guernsey as the regiment departed for Barbados. Arrived in the WIs 19 December 1816. Discharged Quebec.

Seex, Samuel. 3rd Foot Guards. Marched from London and confined aboard PS, 12 March 1816. Joined YCs 16 May 1816, and arrived in the WIs 25 June 1816. Deserted 1 August 1816. No record of rejoining.

Sellard, John. Weaver of Gloucestershire. 14th Foot. Marched from Exeter and confined aboard PS, 8 March 1815. Joined YCs 29 June 1815, and arrived in the WIs 5 November 1815. Discharged from Stony Hill, Jamaica, 10 June 1819.

Shanaghan/Shanahan, David. 88th Foot. Marched from Bristol and confined aboard PS, 7 February 1816. Joined YCs 16 May 1816, and arrived in the WIs 25 June 1816. Died, 3 November 1816.

Shane/Shaw, Michael. Labourer of Cork. 1st Bn 25th Foot. Marched from Savoy Military Prison and confined at Portchester Castle as Michael Shaw or Shane, 28 January 1816. Joined YCs as Michael Shane, 3 April 1817. Arrived in the WIs 25 May 1817. Deserted in Jamaica 5 July 1817. Rejoined 7 July 1817. 300 lashes for 'Absent without Leave'; 150 lashes for 'Neglect of Duty', 1 September 1817; 200 lashes for 'Drunk on Parade and Making away with 10lbs of his ammunition', 20 January 1818. Deserted Jamaica 3 September 1818. Rejoined 22 September 1818. (No punishment records held.) Deserted in Jamaica 6 March 1819. No record of rejoining.

Shannagan/Shannigan, John. Labourer of Tipperary. 2nd Bn 45th Foot. Marched from Coventry and confined aboard PS, 3 October 1813. Joined YCs 1 February 1814. Deserted at Cove of Cork, 30 September 1814. No record of rejoining.

Shannagan/Shanaghan/Shannaghan, Patrick. Tobacconist of Tipperary. Transferred from General Service Recruit Depot and confined aboard PS, 3 October 1814. Joined YCs 29 June 1815, and 'Left on Detachment' at Guernsey. Arrived in the WIs 19 December 1816. Deserted in Jamaica 13 April 1819. No record of rejoining.

Sharp/Sharpe, John. Labourer of Lincoln. 10th Foot. Marched from Dartford and confined aboard PS as John Sharp or Smith, 31 May 1815. Joined YCs as John Sharp or Sharpe, 29 June 1815. Arrived in the WIs 5 November 1815. Died Jamaica, 5 February 1817.

Sharpley, James. Labourer of Middlesex. Royal West India Rangers. Transported from Portsmouth and confined aboard PS, 24 December 1814. Joined YCs 29 June 1815, and arrived in the WIs 5 November 1815. Died Jamaica, 4 January 1818.

Sharriott/Sherrott, Richard. 2nd Bn 6th Foot, Marched from Liverpool and confined aboard PS, 14 November 1814. Joined YCs 29 June 1815, and arrived in the WIs 5 November 1815. Discharged Quebec.

Shaseby/Shaisby, George. Labourer of Northamptonshire. Joined 3rd Dragoon Guards 21 April 1807. Marched from York and confined aboard PS, 23 November 1814. Joined YCs 29 June 1815, and arrived in the WIs 5 November 1815. Deserted in Jamaica 30 March 1819. Rejoined the next day. (No punishment records held.) Deserted in Jamaica 21 May 1819. No record of rejoining.

Shaw, Benjamin. 19th Light Dragoons. Marched from Dartford and confined aboard PS, 20 February 1814. Joined YCs 25 March 1814, and arrived in the WIs 14 December 1814. 200 lashes for 'Drunk on Parade', 14 September 1815. Discharged Quebec.

Shaw, Joseph. Labourer of Lancashire. 84th Foot. Marched from Bristol and confined aboard PS, 4 February 1815. Joined YCs 29 June 1815, and arrived in the WIs 5 November 1815. Deserted in Jamaica 13 June 1819. Rejoined 18 June 1819. (No punishment records held.) Discharged Quebec.

Shea, John. Labourer of Tipperary. 37th Foot. Marched from Bristol and confined aboard PS, 16 April 1815. Joined YCs 29 June 1815, and arrived in the WIs 5 November 1815. Discharged from Stony Hill, Jamaica, 10 June 1819.

Shea, Patrick. Labourer of Bantry. 33rd Foot. Marched from Bristol and confined at Portchester Castle, 7 January 1817. Joined YCs 3 April 1817, and arrived in the WIs 25 May 1817. Deserted Jamaica, 20 July 1818. Rejoined, 12 August 1818. (No punishment record held) Deserted in Jamaica, 29 April 1819. No record of rejoining.

Sheady/Shady, Daniel. Shoemaker of Limerick. 88th Foot. Marched from Bristol and confined aboard PS as Daniel Shady, 26 May 1815. Joined YCs as Daniel Sheady, 29 June 1815. Arrived in the WIs 5 November 1815. Died, 17 September 1816.

Sheardown, Robert. Printer of Lincoln. 19th Foot. Transported from Jersey and confined aboard PS, 1 February 1815. Joined YCs 29 June 1815, and arrived in the WIs 5 November 1815. Died Jamaica, 23 March 1817.

Shepherd/Sheppard, Joseph. 52nd Foot. Marched from Coventry and confined aboard PS as William Sturgess or Joseph Sheppard, 27 August 1813. Joined YCs as Joseph Shepherd, 1 February 1814. Sick at Guernsey as the regiment left for Barbados. Regiment informed of Shepherd's desertion, June 1817. No further record.

Shipman, William. Labourer of Glasgow. Arrived in the WIs May 1817. Deserted in Jamaica, 8 June 1817. No record of rejoining.

Short, John. Miller of Northumberland. 3rd Foot Guards. Marched from Canterbury and confined aboard PS, 24 March 1815. Joined YCs 29 June 1815, and arrived in the WIs 5 November 1815. Died Jamaica, 15 September 1817.

Sie, Hugh. 2nd Foot. Marched from Exeter and confined aboard PS, 6 January 1815. Joined YCs 29 June 1815. Remained at Albany Barracks as the regiment left for St Vincent. Discharged, 13 June 1816.

Simpson, James. Labourer of London. 2nd Bn 25th Foot. Marched from Edinburgh and confined aboard PS, 11 November 1813. Joined YCs 7 March 1814, and arrived in the WIs 14 December 1814. Promoted corporal 25 February 1815. 200 lashes and ordered to be reduced for 'Theft', 13 April 1815. Reduced but corporal punishment remitted. Died St Vincent, 8 October 1815.

Simpson, John. 1st Foot Guards. Marched from Savoy Military Prison and confined aboard PS, 7 January 1815. Joined YCs 29 June 1815, and arrived in the WIs 5 November 1815. Died, 20 October 1816.

Simpson, John. Plasterer of Derby. Staff Corps. Marched from Hythe and confined aboard PS, 31 December 1813. Joined YCs 5 February 1814. Deserted while still at the Isle of Wight 9 July 1814. Rejoined 24 July 1814. (No punishment records held.) Arrived in the WIs 14 December 1814. Deserted at Barbados 1 February 1815. No record of rejoining.

Singleton, Daniel. Labourer of Cork. Joined YCs 29 June 1815, and arrived in the WIs 5 November 1815. Deserted in Jamaica 12 February 1818. Rejoined the same day. Deserted in Jamaica 21 February 1818. Rejoined 24 March 1818. Deserted in Jamaica 2 June 1819. Rejoined 7 June 1819. (No punishment records held.) Discharged Quebec.

Singleton, Joseph. Labourer of Yorkshire. 77th Foot. Marched from Chester and confined aboard PS, 28 December 1814. Joined YCs 29 June 1815, and arrived in the WIs 5 November 1815. Deserted in Jamaica 28 April 1819. Rejoined 30 April 1819. Deserted in Jamaica 18 May 1819. Rejoined 22 May 1819. (No punishmen t records held.) Discharged Quebec.

Sitwell, James. Tailor of Boston. 16th Foot. Marched from Salford and confined aboard PS, 13 January 1814. Joined YCs 7 March 1814. and arrived in the WIs 14 December 1814. Died St Vincent, 31 July 1815.

Skilhorn/Skellern/Skellorn, Thomas. Whitesmith of Cheshire. Royal Horse Artillery. Marched from Chester and confined aboard PS as Thomas Skellorn or Kilborne, 2 October 1813. Joined YCs as Thomas Skellern, 7 March 1814. Arrived in the WIs 14 December 1814. Died as Thomas Skilhorn, 18 September 1816.

Skilton/Skelton, Abraham. Baker of Shropshire. Joined from Portchester Castle, 3 April 1817, and arrived in the WIs 25 May 1817. Deserted in Jamaica 7 August 1817. Rejoined 13 August 1817. (No punishment records held.) Discharged Quebec.

Slack, Abraham. 1st Bn 55th Foot. Marched from Congleton and confined aboard PS, 19 November 1813. Joined YCs 7 March 1814, and arrived in the WIs 14 December 1814. Died Quebec's Garrison Hospital, 14 September 1819, three weeks after disbandment.

Slade, John. 20th Foot. Marched from Bristol and confined aboard PS, 8 December 1813. Joined YCs 7 March 1814. Remained at Guernsey as the regiment left for Barbados. Regiment informed of Slade's desertion, June 1817. No further record.

Slade, John. Shoemaker of Somerset. 4th Foot. Marched from Savoy Military Prison and confined aboard PS, 14 May 1815. Joined YCs 29 June 1815, and arrived in the WIs 5 November 1815. 300 lashes for 'Forgery', 10 February 1817. Deserted in Jamaica 3 June 1819. Rejoined the next day. (No punishment records held.) Discharged Quebec.

Slattery, James. Framework knitter from Limerick. 95th Foot. Marched from Chester and confined at Portchester Castle, 9 December 1816. Joined YCs 3 April 1817, and arrived in the WIs 25 May 1817. Deserted in Jamaica 6 June 1817. ('3rd November 1817. 25

Deserters & Culprits, of whom 21 have been sent to this Country from Ireland'.) Confined Portchester Castle and rejoined in Jamaica 31 January 1818. Deserted in Jamaica 3 September 1818. Rejoined 21 September 1818. Deserted in Jamaica 18 April 1819. Rejoined 15 May 1819. (No punishment records held.) Discharged Quebec.

Slaven/Slavin, John. Shoemaker of Longford. 35th Foot. Marched from Chichester and confined aboard PS, 3 September 1813. Joined YCs 5 February 1814. Deserted at Sandown, Isle of Wight, 10 February 1814. Seized by William Brading (Twenty Shillings Bounty). Rejoined 20 February 1814. Hospitalised and re-confined aboard PS until regiment left for Barbados. (No punishment records held.) Deserted at Guernsey 19 September 1814. No record of rejoining.

Sleath, John. Baker of London. 48th Foot. Marched from Winchester and confined aboard PS, 28 September 1815. Joined YCs 19 October 1816, and arrived in the WIs 21 December 1816. Deserted in Jamaica 19 December 1818. Rejoined 23 December 1818. (No punishment records held.) Discharged Quebec.

Smith, Alexander. Shoemaker of Salkirk. Royal Wagon Train. Marched from Savoy Military Prison and confined aboard PS, 19 December 1813. Joined YCs 5 December 1814, and arrived in the WIs 14 December 1814. Deserted at St Vincent 1 April 1816. No record of rejoining.

Smith, Benjamin. Cordwainer of Leicestershire. 14th Light Dragoons. Marched from Southwell and confined aboard PS, 18 January 1814. Joined YCs 25 March 1814. Deserted while still at the Isle of Wight, 16 June 1814. Rejoined 20 June 1814 and hospitalised. (No punishment records held.) Arrived in the WIs 14 December 1814. Died Jamaica, 16 September 1817.

Smith, David. Labourer of Glasgow. 71st Foot. Marched from Glasgow and confined aboard PS, 11 September 1814. Joined YCs 29 June 1815, and arrived in the WIs 5 November 1815. Died Jamaica, 18 November 1817. Willed effects, eleven shillings and eleven pence, to his wife Esther of 5 Nicholson Road, Edinburgh.

Smith, John. Clerk of Cornhill, Middlesex. 2nd Bn 88th Foot. Marched from Plymouth and confined aboard PS, 27 October 1813. Joined YCs 25 March 1814, and arrived in the WIs 14 December 1814. Promoted corporal 24 April 1814. Reduced 16 August 1814. Promoted corporal 6 December 1816. Sentenced to solitary confinement and ordered to be reduced for 'Unsoldierlike Conduct Drunk and Riotous in Barracks', 17 June 1817. Solitary confinement remitted. Promoted corporal 6 August 1817, sergeant 27 October 1817. Reduced 23 May 1818. Discharged Quebec.

Smith, John. Framework knitter of Leicester. 13th Foot. Marched from Chester and confined aboard PS, 2 October 1813. Joined YCs 5 February 1814 and arrived in the WIs 14 December 1814. Deserted in Jamaica 27 May 1819. Rejoined,1 June 1819. (No punishment records held.) Discharged Quebec.

Smith, John. Labourer of Dullingham. Either 1st Foot Guards marched from Chester, 1 April 1815, or 1st Foot marched from Newcastle and confined aboard PS, 25 January 1815. Joined YCs 29 June 1815. Died on passage to St Vincent, 29 September 1815.

Smith, John. Labourer of Tavistock. Either 1st Foot Guards marched from Chester, 1 April 1815, or 1st Foot marched from Newcastle and confined aboard PS, 25 January 1815. Joined YCs 29 June 1815 and arrived in the WIs 5 November 1815. Discharged Quebec.

Smith, John. Either Coldstream Guards marched from Savoy Military Prison, 13

September 1815, Royal Scots marched from Nottingham, 17 October 1815, or 10th Dragoons marched from Savoy Military Prison and confined aboard PS, 16 November 1815. Joined YCs 16 May 1816, and arrived in the WIs 25 June 1816. Deserted 8 August 1816. No record of rejoining.

Smith, Stephen. From Ireland. 76th Foot. Marched from Plymouth Docks and confined aboard PS, 6 March 1814. Joined YCs 25 March 1814, and arrived in the WIs 14 December 1814. 300 lashes for 'Drunk on Barrier Beach Guard', 28 April 1815. Promoted corporal 25 January 1818. Reduced 1 May 1818. Discharged Quebec. Allocated Concession 8. Lot NE 13. Bathurst. No evidence found of him settling there. 'Concession granted to Thomas Garrett, 13th March 1828'.

Smith, Thomas. Glazier of Middlesex. Either South Lincolnshire Militia marched from Norman Cross, 14 March 1813, 56th Foot marched from Savoy Military Prison, 11 November 1813, or 61st Foot marched from Stafford and confined aboard PS, 2 October 1813. Joined YCs 5 February 1814, and arrived in the WIs 14 December 1814. Discharged Quebec.

Smith, Thomas. Cabinet maker of Suffolk. Either South Lincolnshire Militia marched from Norman Cross, 14 March 1813, 56th Foot marched from Savoy Military Prison, 11 November 1813, or 61st Foot marched from Stafford and confined aboard PS, 2 October 1813. Joined YCs 25 March 1814, and arrived in the WIs 14 December 1814. Deserted in Barbados 10 March 1815. Rejoined 16 March 1815. (No punishment records held.) Promoted corporal 25 December 1815. Reduced 29 July 1818. Discharged Quebec.

Smith, Thomas. Labourer of Gloucestershire. 39th Foot. Marched from Gloucestershire and confined aboard PS, 29 May 1815. Joined YCs 29 June 1815, and arrived in the WIs 5 November 1815. Discharged Quebec.

Smith, Thomas. Labourer of Gloucestershire. Joined 6th Bn 60th Foot, 5th May 1813. Transferred into the York Chasseurs in Jamaica 25 May 1817. Died Jamaica, 11 September 1818.

Smith, William. Tailor of St Mary's, Dublin. 59th Foot. Marched from St Albans and confined aboard PS, 2 May 1813. Joined YCs 5 February 1814, and arrived in the WIs 14 December 1814. Deserted in Jamaica 1 May 1819. Rejoined 30 May 1819. (No punishment records held.) Discharged Quebec.

Smith, William. Labourer of Northampton. General Service. Marched from Warwick and confined aboard PS, 4 March 1814. Joined YCs 25 March 1814, and arrived in the WIs 14 December 1814. Promoted corporal, date unknown. Reduced 22 August 1815. Discharged Quebec.

Smith, William. Labourer of Warwick. 3rd Foot Guards. Marched from Andover and confined aboard PS, 18 May 1815. Joined YCs 29 June 1815, and arrived in the WIs 5 November 1815. Deserted in Jamaica 29 May 1819. Rejoined 6 June 1819. (No punishment records held.) Discharged Quebec.

Smithson, Thomas. 71st Foot. Marched from Rye and confined aboard PS as Thomas Brown or Smithson, 12 September 1813. Joined YCs as Thomas Smithson, 5 February 1814. Arrived in the WIs 14 December 1814. Promoted corporal 25 February 1818. Reduced 22 December 1818. Discharged Quebec.

Snelling, Henry. Labourer of Easton, Kent. 2nd Bn 73rd Foot. Marched from Savoy Military Prison and confined aboard PS, 1 December 1813. Joined YCs 29 June 1815, and arrived in the WIs 5 November 1815. Died St Vincent, 17 September 1816.

Snowden/Snowdon, Joseph. Printer of Down. 87th Foot. Transported from Guernsey and confined aboard PS, 19 October 1815. Joined YCs 17 May 1816, and arrived in the WIs 25 June 1816. Deserted in Jamaica 10 July 1818. No record of rejoining.

Snoxall, James. Joined 2nd Bn 5th Foot at Huntington, 6 May 1814. Deserted 9 June 1814, rejoined 2 July 1814, and deserted again 9 July 1814. (No date of return or punishment received.) Marched from Bedford and confined aboard PS, 26 January 1815. Joined YCs 29 June 1815, and arrived in the WIs 5 November 1815. Discharged Quebec.

Snoxall, Thomas. Labourer of Bedford. Joined 2nd Bn 5th Foot at Huntington, 14 June 1814. Deserted, 24 July 1814. No date of rejoining or punishment received. Marched from Bedford and confined aboard PS, 26 January 1815. Joined YCs 29 June 1815. 'Left on Detachment' as the regiment embarked for St Vincent. Arrived in the WIs 19 December 1816. Died Jamaica, 18 March 1818.

Snoxall, William. Joined 2nd Bn 5th Foot at Huntington, 6 May 1814. Deserted 9 June 1814. Rejoined 2 July 1814. No punishment record held. Deserted 9 July 1814. (No date of rejoining or punishment received.) Marched from Bedford and and confined aboard PS, 26 January 1815. 'Left on Detachment' as the regiment left for St Vincent. Discharged, 9 February 1817.

Soar, William. Grocer of Keyworth. Horse Guards. Marched from Windsor and and confined aboard PS, 2 August 1813. Joined as corporal 1 February 1814 and promoted sergeant 25 February 1814. Reduced 9 April 1814. Deserted while still at the Isle of Wight, 25 June 1814. Surrendered himself to the Army Depot 24 December 1914. No further record.

Solomon, John. Labourer of Cornwall. 83rd Foot. Marched from Launceston and confined aboard PS, 23 December 1813. Joined YCs 7 March 1814, and arrived in the WIs 14 December 1814. Promoted corporal 27 September 1816. Reduced 30 October 1816. Died Jamaica, 24 August 1817.

South, James. Labourer of Norfolk. 2nd Bn 96th Foot. Marched from Norwich and and confined aboard PS, 17 September 1813. Joined YCs 7 March 1814, and arrived in the WIs 14 December 1814. Died Jamaica, 19 April 1819.

Spearing, Samuel. Labourer of Nottinghamshire. 23rd Light Dragoons. Marched from Chester and and confined aboard PS, 14 November 1813. Joined YCs 1 February 1814, and arrived in the WIs 14 December 1814. Promoted corporal, date unknown. Sergeant 25 January 1815. Reduced 24 February 1815. Deserted in Barbados 26 February 1815. Rejoined 3 March 1815. (No punishment records held.) Promoted corporal 25 July 1816. Reduced 24 January 1818. Discharged Quebec.

Spence, George. Tailor of Newcastle. Either 35th Foot marched from Kingston, Surrey, 26 January 1815, or 37th Foot marched from Hastings and confined aboard PS, 15 November 1814. Joined YCs 29 June 1815, and arrived in the WIs 5 November 1815. 150 lashes for 'Drunk & Absent from Parade', 28 April 1817. Deserted in Jamaica 9 May 1818. Rejoined 12 May 1818. Deserted in Jamaica 6 February 1819. Rejoined 12 February 1819. (No punishment records held.) Deserted in Jamaica 3 March 1819. No record of rejoining.

Spence, George. Labourer of Leeds. Either 35th Foot marched from Kingston, Surrey, 26 January 1815, or 37th Foot marched from Hastings and confined aboard PS, 15 November 1814. Joined YCs 29 June 1815, and arrived in the WIs 5 November 1815. Died, 17 October 1816.

Spencer, Joseph. Labourer of Doncaster. 18th Light Dragoons. Marched from Brighton and confined aboard PS, 31 July 1814. Joined YCs 29 June 1815, and arrived in the WIs 5 November 1815. Died, 5 December 1816.

Spencer, Joseph. 67th Foot. Marched from Chester and confined at Portchester Castle, 27 December 1816. Joined YCs 3 April 1817, and arrived in the WIs 25 May 1817. Discharged Quebec.

Spinks, John. Gunsmith of Warwick. Royal Wagon Train. Marched from Dartford and confined aboard PS, 11 March 1815. Joined YCs 29 June 1815, and arrived in the WIs 5 November 1815. Deserted in Jamaica 19 December 1818. Rejoined 22 December 1818. (No punishment records held.) Discharged Quebec.

Spruce, William. Tailor of Chester. Marched from Chester and and confined aboard PS, 11 August 1813. Joined YCs 5 February 1814. Deserted while still at the Isle of Wight, 27 June 1814. No record of rejoining.

Starr, James. West Essex Militia. Sentenced at Warrington to 'General Service for Desertion', 10 September 1813. Marched from Liverpool and confined aboard PS, 1 November 1813. Joined YCs 7 March 1814, and arrived in the WIs 14 December 1814. Discharged Quebec.

Starr, William. Labourer of Maidstone. 9th Foot. Marched from Canterbury and and confined aboard PS, 11 February 1816. Joined YCs 17 May 1816, and arrived in the WIs 25 June 1816. Deserted, date unknown. Rejoined 31 December 1816. (No punishment records held.) Deserted in Jamaica 21 January 1817. No record of rejoining.

Steele, William. Iron Founder of Fife. 6th Bn Royal Artillery. Marched from Maidstone and confined aboard PS, 13 February 1814. Joined YCs 7 March 1814, and arrived in the WIs 14 December 1814. 200 lashes for 'Insubordinate Language to Commanding Officer' commuted to 20 days solitary confinement, 31 May 1815. Died Garrison Hospital Grenada, 18 September 1815.

Stevens, Jacob. 1st Bn 32nd Foot. Marched from Shepton Mallett and and confined aboard PS, 1 December 1813. Joined YCs 7 March 1814. Died Guernsey, 2 September 1814.

Stevens/Stephens, Samuel. Labourer of Marylebone. 19th Dragoons. Marched from Savoy Military Prison and confined aboard PS as Samuel Stevens, 21 December 1813. Joined YCs 1 February 1814. Deserted from Sandown, Isle of Wight, 4 February 1814. Rejoined 20 February. (No punishment records held.) Hospitalised and re-confined aboard PS to await regiment's embarkation for Barbados. Arrived in the WIs 14 December 1814. 200 lashes for 'Losing a Greatcoat', 29 August 1815, 150 lashes remitted. Deserted in Jamaica as Samuel Stephens, 7 May 1818. No record of rejoining.

Stevens/Stevenson/Stephenson, Richard. 62nd Foot. Marched from Savoy Military Prison and confined aboard PS as Richard Stevens, 15 October 1815. Joined YCs 16 May 1816, and arrived in the WIs 25 June 1816. Deserted 17 July 1816. Rejoined as Richard Stevenson, 9 October 1816. 800 lashes for 'Desertion 10th July 1816–9th October 1816', 21 October 1816, 400 lashes remitted. Discharged Quebec as Richard Stephenson.

Stewart, George. Labourer of Glamorgan. 34th Foot. Transferred from Newport, Isle of Wight, and confined aboard PS, 14 June 1815. Joined YCs 29 June 1815, and arrived in the WIs 5 November 1815. Died Tobago, 18 October 1816.

Stewart, James. Labourer of Perth. 1st Bn 79th Foot. Marched from Haddington and confined aboard PS, 26 November 1813. Joined as corporal 1 February 1814, and arrived in the WIs 14 December 1814. Promoted sergeant 25 February 1814. Reduced 5 April 1814. Promoted corporal 1 July 1814, sergeant 5 July 1814. Deserted Guernsey 9 August 1814. Rejoined as private 14 August 1814. (No punishment records held.) 'Immediately handed over to Island's Civil Authorities'. Arrived in the WIs May 1815. 300 lashes at Guadeloupe 'For having in his Possession a French Coin', 17 August 1815, 200 lashes remitted. Promoted corporal 3 January 1816. Reduced 8 January 1816. Discharged Quebec.

Stewart, James. Labourer of Longford. At Waterloo with the 32nd Foot. Transported from Guernsey and confined aboard PS, 12 July 1816. Joined YCs 19 October 1816, and arrived in the WIs 21 December 1816. Promoted corporal 25 February 1817. 200 lashes and ordered to be reduced for 'Theft', 2 October 1817. Reduced but corporal punishment commuted to solitary confinement. Deserted in Jamaica 27 April 1819. No record of rejoining.

Stewart, John. Labourer of Forfar. 2nd Bn 25th Foot. Marched from Edinburgh and confined aboard PS, 5 September 1813. Joined YCs 7 March 1814. Deserted while still at the Isle of Wight, 9 July 1814. Seized by Henry A Brook (Twenty Shillings Bounty) and rejoined, 24 July 1814. (No punishment records held.) Arrived in the WIs 14 December 1814. Deserted in Barbados, 4 April 1815. Rejoined, 8 April 1815. 300 lashes for 'Absent without Leave', 10 April 1815, 150 lashes remitted. Deserted in Jamaica 9 March 1819. No record of rejoining.

Stewart, Thomas. Iron founder. 70th Foot. Marched from Perth and confined aboard PS, 3 September 1813. Joined as corporal 5 February 1814, and promoted sergeant 16 April 1814. Appointed drum-major 25 September 1814. Reduced, date unknown. Arrived in the WIs as private 14 December 1814. Promoted corporal 4 January 1816. Reduced 7 January 1816. Discharged at Quebec. Returned to England and a pension, 14 December 1819. 'Disbandment of the Corps and Loss of Left Arm from a Wound Above the Elbow'.

Stokes, George. 9th Foot. Marched from Maidstone and and confined aboard PS, 2 June 1815. Joined YCs 29 June 1815, and arrived in the WIs 5 November 1815. 300 lashes for 'Sleeping on his Post while Sentinel', 10 February 1817, 25 lashes remitted. Discharged Quebec.

Stokes, Michael. Probable General Service Recruit 'Volunteer'. Arrived in the WIs 25 June 1816. Discharged Quebec 24 September 1819. As a volunteer possibly returned to England at public expense.

Stone, John. Labourer of Somerset. 32nd Foot. Marched from Bristol and confined aboard PS, 18 May 1815. Joined YCs 29 June 1815, and arrived in the WIs 5 November 1815. Promoted corporal 4 February 1816, sergeant 25 February 1817. Deserted in Jamaica 27 April 1819. Rejoined as private 3 May 1819. (No punishment records held.) Died Jamaica, 29 May 1819, less than a month after returning from desertion and no doubt punishment.

Stone, Thomas. Royal Sappers and Miners. Transported from Portsmouth and confined aboard PS, 6 March 1815. Joined YCs 29 June 1815. 'Left on Detachment' when regiment departed for St Vincent. Discharged, 8 June 1816.

Stone/Stoner, Thomas. Carpenter of Sussex. 2nd Foot. Marched from Lewes and confined aboard PS as Stone or Stoner, 27 July 1813. Joined YCs 7 March 1814. Deserted at Guernsey as Stone or Stoner, 19 August 1814. No record of rejoining.

Street, James. Weaver of Lancashire. 1st West York Militia. Marched from Norman Cross and confined aboard PS as James Street or Buckley, 8 February 1814. Joined as James Street, 7 March 1814. Arrived in the WIs 14 December 1814. 'Died of Wounds' received at Guadeloupe, 22 August 1815. Possibly one of the last fatal casualties from 24 years of war.

Strethers/Stathers, William. Labourer of Armagh. 67th Foot. Marched from Chester and confined at Portchester Castle, 27 December 1816. Joined YCs 3 April 1817, and arrived in the WIs 25 May 1817. 250 lashes for 'Selling his Necessaries', 2 September 1817, 50 lashes remitted. Died Jamaica, 6 November 1817, a little over 2 months after punishment.

Sullivan, Daniel. Labourer of Cork. 2nd Bn 95th Foot. Marched from Plymouth and confined aboard PS, 1 February 1815. Joined YCs 29 June 1815, and arrived in the WIs 5 November 1815. Died St Vincent, 28 March 1816.

Sullivan, John. Labourer of Killarney. Either 37th Foot marched from Battle, 19 November 1813, or 16th Foot, confined aboard PS, 23 January 1814. Joined YCs 25 March 1814, and arrived in the WIs 14 December 1814. Deserted in Jamaica 23 May 1818. Rejoined 29 June 1818. Deserted in Jamaica 20 July 1818. Rejoined 28 July 1818. Deserted in Jamaica 18 December 1818. Rejoined 27 April 1819. (No punishment records held.) Discharged Quebec.

Sullivan, John. Nailer of Cork. 29th Foot. Marched from Southampton and confined aboard PS, 14 February 1814. Joined YCs 7 March 1814. Deserted at Cove of Cork, 10 October 1814. Recaptured and marched from Bristol, re-incarcerated aboard PS, 16 April 1815. (No punishment records held.) Rejoined at St Vincent 5 November 1815. Deserted in Jamaica 29 April 1819. Rejoined 6 May 1819. (No punishment records held.) Discharged Quebec.

Sullivan, John. Miner of Cork. 61st Foot. Transported from Belem (Portugal) and confined aboard PS, 7 November 1813. Joined YCs 5 February 1814. Deserted at Cove of Cork, 8 October 1810. No record of rejoining.

Sullivan, Maurice or **Morris.** Butcher of Limerick. 2nd Bn 62nd Foot. Transported from Portsmouth and confined aboard PS, 12 February 1815. Joined YCs 29 June 1815, and arrived in the WIs 5 November 1815. Deserted in Jamaica 17 April 1817. Rejoined the same day. Deserted in Jamaica 25 June 1817. Rejoined 11 July 1817. Deserted in Jamaica 17 July 1817. Rejoined 3 August 1817. (No punishment records held.) Discharged Quebec.

Sullivan, Timothy. Tailor of Kerry. 96th Foot. Marched from Bristol and confined aboard PS, 14 March 1814. Joined YCs 25 March 1814, and arrived in the WIs 14 December 1814. Discharged Quebec.

Sullivan, Timothy. Labourer of Clonmel. Joined YCs 29 June 1815, and arrived in the WIs 5 November 1815. Died, 13 September 1816.

Summers, Henry. Joined YCs 29 June 1815, and arrived in the WIs 5 November 1815. Discharged Quebec.

Summers, Joseph. Cotton spinner of Bristol. 57th Foot. Marched from Bristol and confined aboard PS, 25 January 1815. Joined YCs 29 June 1815, and arrived in the WIs 5 November 1815. Died Jamaica, 22 January 1818.

Summers, William. Labourer of Berkshire or Kent. 68th Foot. Marched from Rochester and confined at Portchester Castle, 30 December 1816. Joined YCs 3 April 1817, and arrived in the WIs 25 May 1817. Deserted in Jamaica 19 July 1817. Rejoined, date unknown. 300 lashes for 'Absent without Leave', 5 August 1817. Promoted drummer 24 November 1817. Deserted in Jamaica 10 January 1818. Returned to England, recaptured and re-confined at Portchester Castle, 4 May 1818. No further record.

Summers, William. Weaver of Lancaster. Possible 'Bounty Jumper'. Recorded as having joined both 33rd and 101st Foot. Marched from Lancaster and confined aboard PS, 4 May 1813. Joined YCs 5 February 1814, and arrived in the WIs 14 December 1814. Deserted in Jamaica 10 February 1817. Rejoined 1 March 1817. 300 lashes for 'Absenting himself for 3 weeks without leave', 7 March 1817. Deserted in Jamaica 6 March 1819. Rejoined 13 March 1819. (No punishment records held.) Discharged Quebec.

Sutherland, Peter. Labourer of Edinburgh. 92nd Foot. Transported from France and confined aboard PS, 12 December 1815. Joined YCs 19 October 1816, and arrived in the WIs 21 December 1816. Deserted in Jamaica 29 December 1816. Rejoined 29 January 1817. (No punishments record.) 300 lashes for 'Absent without Leave', 4 July 1817; 300 lashes for being 'Absent without Leave', 10 January 1818, 125 lashes remitted. Died Jamaica, 9 April 1818, two months after punishment.

Sweeney/Sweeny, Michael. Labourer of Donegal. 1st Foot Guards. Marched from Winchester and confined aboard PS, 4 March 1815. Joined YCs 29 June 1815, and arrived in the WIs 5 November 1815. Promoted corporal 5 September 1816. 200 lashes and ordered to be reduced for 'Drunk on Guard and Playing Cards', 1 March 1817. Corporal Punishment remitted due to his 'Former Good Character'. Deserted in Jamaica 31 March 1817. Returned to England and claimed 'Proclamation of Clemency' by surrendering himself at the Savoy Military Prison, 24 June 1817. 'Voluntarily surrendered himself as Deserter and should be allowed the benefit of the Proclamation and permitted accordingly to rejoin his respective Regiment or Depot'. Marched to Portchester Castle, October 1817, and transferred to the Royal African Corps, January 1818.

Sweeny, Edward. Labourer of Donegal. 27th Foot, Marched from Glasgow and confined aboard PS as Edward Swany or Sweeny, 8 February 1814. Joined YCs as Edward Sweeny, 25 March 1814. Deserted while still at the Isle of Wight, 5 July 1814. No record of rejoining.

Talman, Patrick. Labourer of Galway. 7th Foot. Transported from Portsmouth and confined aboard PS, 24 September 1813. Joining date unknown. Promoted and reduced from corporal, April 1814. Arrived in the WIs 14 December 1814. Died, 16 November 1816.

Tamblyn/Tomlin, Thomas. Labourer of Cornwall. 67th Foot. Marched from Nottingham and confined aboard PS as Thomas Tomlin, 12 December 1813. Joined YCs as Thomas Tamblyn, 25 March 1814. Deserted while still at the Isle of Wight, 13 June 1814. Rejoined 29 September 1814. (No punishments record held.) Confined aboard PS until regiment left for Barbados. Arrived in the WIs 14 December 1814. Discharged Quebec.

Tanner, George. Shoemaker of Gloucestershire. Embarked Spithead amongst a 300-strong detachment of 'Unattached Deserters' joining the 2nd Foot, 24 April 1816. Arrived in the WIs 5 June 1816. Deserted 16 July 1816. Rejoined,21 July 1816. 1,000 lashes and 0rdered to be marked with 'D', 22 July 1816. Transferred into the York Chasseurs 25 August 1816. Deserted in Jamaica 15 July 1818. Rejoined 19 July 1818 . (No punishment records held.) Died Jamaica, 7 August 1818, less than a month after rejoining from desertion and no doubt punishment.

Tarling, Edward. Sadler of Gloucestershire. 2nd Dragoon Guards. Marched from Sheffield along with John Longworth, and confined aboard PS, 19 August 1813. Joined YCs 5 February 1814, and arrived in the WIs 14 December 1814. 200 lashes for 'Making away with his Necessaries', 15 May 1815. Remitted to 20 days solitary confinement. Deserted in Jamaica, 29 April 1819. No record of rejoining.

Tate, John. 80th Foot. Marched from Wakefield and confined aboard PS, 21 September 1813. Joined YCs 1 February 1814, and remained at Guernsey as the regiment left for Barbados. Regiment notified of Tate's desertion, March 1817. No further record.

Tatham/Tathem, James. Shoemaker of Leith. Royal Artillery. Marched from Stafford and confined aboard PS, 3 February 1815. Joined YCs 29 June 1815, and arrived in the WIs 5 November 1815. Died, 9 November 1816.

Taylor, Charles. 15th Hussars or 15th Light Dragoons. Marched from Savoy Military Prison and confined aboard PS, 22 September 1814. Joined YCs 29 June 1815, and arrived in the WIs 5 November 1815. Discharged Quebec.

Taylor, James. 1st Foot Guards. Marched from Savoy Military Prison and confined aboard PS, 17 October 1813. Joined YCs 29 June 1815, and arrived in the WIs 5 November 1815. Discharged Quebec.

Taylor, Robert. Weaver of Ratcliffe. 2nd Dragoon Guards. Marched from Salford and confined aboard PS, 17 October 1813. Joined YCs 5 February 1814. Promoted corporal 25 March 1814. Reduced 5 June 1814. Arrived in the WIs 14 December 1814. 300 lashes for 'Attempting to Desert', 5 August 1817, 100 lashes remitted. Deserted in Jamaica 1 April 1819. Rejoined 5 April 1819. Deserted in Jamaica 28 April 1819. Rejoined 8 May 1819. (No punishment records held.) Discharged Quebec.

Taylor, Thomas. Labourer of Gloucestershire. Either Royal Wagon Train marched from Wakefield, 1 December 1814, or 61st Foot marched from Chester and confined aboard PS, 25 March 1815. Joined YCs 29 June 1815, and arrived in the WIs 5 November 1815. Deserted in Jamaica 11 July 1817. Rejoined 17 July 1817. (No punishment records held.) Promoted corporal 2 May 1818. Reduced 16 June 1818. Discharged Quebec.

Taylor, Thomas. Cabinet maker of Temple, Cavan. Either Royal Wagon Train marched from Wakefield, 1 December 1814, or 61st Foot marched from Chester and confined aboard PS, 25 March 1815. Joined YCs 29 June 1815, and arrived in the WIs 5 November 1815. Deserted in Tobago 14 August 1816. No record of rejoining.

Taylor, Thomas. Labourer of Chester. 25th Foot. Marched from Devizes and confined at Portchester Castle, 17 December 1816. Joined YCs 3 April 1817, and arrived in the WIs 25 May 1817. Died Jamaica, 23 November 1818.

Taylor, William. 7th Light Dragoons. Joined from Portchester Castle, 3 April 1817, and arrived in the WIs 25 May 1817. Discharged Quebec.

Teague/Toyne, James. Labourer of York. 30th Foot. Marched from Bristol and confined aboard PS as James Teague or Toyne, 22 October 1814. Joined YCs as James Teague, 29 June 1815. Arrived in the WIs 5 November 1815. Died, 30 September 1816.

Tennant, James. Sailor of Northampton. Transported from Hilsea, Portsmouth, and confined aboard PS as Joseph Moody or James Tennant, 5 December 1814. Joined YCs as James Tennant, 29 June 1815. Deserted from Stokes Bay, Gosport, 1 July 1815. No record of rejoining.

Tennant, Peter. 1st Bn 55th Foot. Marched from Glasgow and confined aboard PS, 6 December 1814. Joined YCs 29 June 1815, and arrived in the WIs 5 November 1815. Discharged Quebec.

Tennant, Thomas. Tinman of Bedford. 52nd Foot. Marched from Hythe and confined aboard PS, 12 September 1813. Joined YCs 1 February 1814, and arrived in the WIs 14 December 1814. Deserted in Barbados, 18 May 1815. No record of rejoining.

Thatcher/Thacher, Richard. Painter of Hereford. 34th Foot. Marched from Gloucestershire and confined aboard PS, 21 June 1815. Joined YCs 29 June 1815, and arrived in the WIs 5 November 1815. Died Jamaica, 28 October 1817.

Theison, Joshua or **Joseph.** Labourer of Germany. 7th Line Bn. King's German Legion. Transported from Sicily and confined aboard PS as Joseph or Joshua Theison, 14 May 1815. Joined YCs as Joshua Theison, 29 June 1815. Arrived in the WIs 5 November 1815. Deserted in Tobago, 4 May 1816. No record of rejoining.

Thomas, Daniel. Royal Artillery Driver. Marched from Dartford and confined aboard PS, 1 January 1814. Joined YCs 1 February 1814. Deserted while still at the Isle of Wight, 27 July 1814. Rejoined 31 July 1814. (No punishment records held.) Arrived in the WIs 14 December 1814. 300 lashes for 'Insubordinate Conduct at Drill', 25 April 1815, 100 lashes remitted; 150 lashes 'For being Repeatedly Dirty', 11 July 1815. Discharged Quebec.

Thomas, Robert. Miner of Ellesmere. 36th Foot. Marched from East Grinstead and confined aboard PS, 6 November 1813. Joined YCs 25 March 1814, and arrived in the WIs 14 December 1814. Died Tobago, 13 June 1816.

Thomas, William. 70th Foot. Marched from Newcastle and confined aboard PS, 26 September 1813. Joined YCs 5 February 1814, and arrived in the WIs 14 December 1814. Died Grenada, 7 November 1815.

Thomas, William. Labourer of Middlesex. 95th Foot. Marched from Gloucestershire and confined aboard PS, 7 June 1815. Joined YCs 29 June 1815, and arrived in the WIs 5 November 1815. Deserted in Jamaica, 3 June 1817. No record of rejoining.

Thompson, William. Labourer of Cavan. 86th Foot. Marched from Bristol and confined aboard PS, 20 October 1813. Joined as corporal 5 February 1814. Promoted sergeant 24 February 1814. Reduced 15 April 1814. Arrived in the WIs 14 December 1814. Discharged Quebec. It is not known which William Thompson received 100 lashes for 'Calling Sergeant Anderson a Damned Little Rascal', 21 December 1816.

Thompson, William. Rope maker of Carlow. 30th Foot. Transported from Neuilly, France, and confined aboard PS, 24 February 1815. Joined YCs 29 June 1815, and arrived in the WIs 5 November 1815. Deserted in Jamaica 12 December 1817. Rejoined 21 February 1818. Deserted in Jamaica 20 May 1819. Rejoined 13 June 1819. (No punishment records held.) Discharged Quebec. It is not known which William Thompson received 100 lashes for 'Calling Sergeant Anderson a Damned Little Rascal', 21 December 1816.

Thompson, William. Shoemaker of Waterford. 63rd Foot General Service Recruit. Transferred from Depot and confined aboard PS, 6 November 1813. Joined YCs 1 February 1814, and arrived in the WIs 14 December 1814. Deserted in Barbados 7 January 1815. Rejoined 9 January 1815. (No punishment records held.) Deserted in Grenada 14 September 1815. No record of rejoining.

Thompson, William. Whitesmith of Macclesfield. 82nd Foot. Marched from Boston and confined aboard PS, 31 January 1814. Joined YCs 25 March 1814. Deserted at Falmouth, 27 September 1814. No record of rejoining.

Thompson/Thomson, John. Either Royal Artillery marched from Chelmsford, 27 March 1813, or Royal Artillery Driver John Thompson/Bennett marched from Southwick and confined aboard PS, 7 October 1813. Joined YCs as John Thompson, 7 March 1814. Left sick at Guernsey as the regiment departed for Barbados. Regiment notified of Thompson's desertion, June 1817. No further record.

Thompson/Thomson, Thomas. Labourer of Reading. 2nd Bn 63rd Foot. Marched from Maidstone and confined aboard PS, 23 January 1814. Joined YCs 25 March 1814. Deserted while still at the Isle of Wight, 2 April 1814. No record of rejoining.

Thorn/Thornton, Charles. Wheelwright of Sligo. 16th Light Dragoons. Marched from Taunton and confined aboard PS as Charles Thornton, 22 March 1814. Joined YCs as Charles Thorn, 25 March 1814. Deserted while still at the Isle of Wight, 7 July 1814. No record of rejoining.

Thorn/Thorne, William. Engineer of Warwick. 3rd Dragoons. Marched from Dartford and confined aboard PS, 3 October 1813. Joined YCs 5 February 1814. Deserted from Sandown, Isle of Wight, 22 February 1814. Retaken same day by Archibald Herrin. (Twenty Shillings' Bounty). Rejoined via Garrison Hospital, 6 March 1814. Re-confined aboard PS to await regiment's embarkation to Barbados. (No punishment records held.) Arrived in the WIs 14 December 1814. Deserted in Jamaica 10 December1817. Rejoined 12 December 1817. 300 lashes for 'Making away with Regimental Necessities', 27 December 1817. Deserted in Jamaica, 15 May 1819. (Date of rejoining and punishment unknown.) Discharged Quebec.

Thornton, Samuel. Weaver of Yorkshire. 1st Bn 95th Foot. Marched from Dover and confined aboard PS, 5 February 1815. Joined YCs 29 June 1815, and arrived in the WIs 5 November 1815. 300 lashes for 'Absenting himself without Leave', 10 December 1817. Deserted in Jamaica 31 January 1819. No record of rejoining.

Thorold, Joseph. Labourer of Lincoln. Royal Artillery. Marched from Guildford and confined aboard PS, 8 September 1813. Joined YCs 5 February 1814, and arrived in the WIs 14 December 1814. Died Stony Hill, Jamaica, 3 September 1816.

Thorpe, William. 77th Foot. Marched from Hastings and confined at Portchester Castle, 21 November 1816. Joined YCs 3 April 1817, and arrived in the WIs 25 May 1817. 200 lashes remitted to solitary confinement for 'Absenting himself from his Escort Duty and returning Drunk', 23 August 1817. Discharged Quebec. Settled on Concession 9. Lot 15. Bathurst. 1851 Census records 'William Thorpe to be both single and insane'.

Tierny/Tierney, James. Labourer of Lanark. 97th Foot. Marched from York and confined aboard PS, 15 May 1814. Joined YCs 29 June 1815, and arrived in the WIs 5 November 1815. Deserted in Jamaica 29 April 1819. No record of rejoining.

Till-Lloyd, Thomas. Labourer of Colchester. Coldstream Guards. Marched from London and confined aboard PS, 14 August 1815. Joined YCs 18 October 1816, and arrived in the WIs 21 December 1816. Deserted in Jamaica 23 August 1817. Date of rejoining unknown. 300 lashes for 'Absent without Leave', 2 October 1817. Deserted in Jamaica 4 May 1818. Rejoined 22 May 1818. (No punishment records held.) Deserted in Jamaica 27 April 1819. No record of rejoining.

Tindale/Tindall, Michael. 70th Foot. Marched from Savoy Military Prison and confined aboard PS as Michael Tindale, 11 December 1814. Joined YCs 29 June 1815, and arrived in the WIs 5 November 1815. Discharged Quebec as Michael Tindall.

Tinson, Jacob. Labourer of Swindon. Embarked Spithead amongst a 300-strong detachment of 'Unattached Deserters' joining the 2nd Foot, 25 April 1816. Arrived in the WIs 5 June 1816. Transferred into the York Chasseurs 25 August 1816. Deserted in Jamaica 17 October 1817. No record of rejoining.

Toland, James. 1st Bn 40th Foot. Marched from Hertford and confined aboard PS, 18 December 1814. Joined YCs 29 June 1815, and arrived in the WIs 5 November 1815. Died Jamaica, 4 December 1816.

Toole, Peter. Nailer of Wicklow. 12th Foot. Marched from Wrexham and confined aboard PS, 3 June 1815. Joined YCs 29 June 1815, and arrived in the WIs 5 November 1815. Deserted in Jamaica 29 April 1819. Rejoined 25 May 1819. (No punishment records held.) Discharged Quebec.

Townsend, William. Butcher of Oxford. 2nd Bn 95th Foot. Transported from Gosport and confined aboard PS, 17 December 1813. Joined YCs 5 February 1814. Deserted at Bear Haven, Cork, 15 October 1814. No record of rejoining.

Tracey/Tracy, Francis. Whitesmith of Queen's County. 61st Foot. Marched from Bristol and confined aboard PS, 21 August 1813. Joined YCs 7 March 1814. Deserted while still at the Isle of Wight, 2 July 1814. No record of rejoining.

Tracey/Tracy, Robert. Labourer of Kildare. 19th Light Dragoons. Marched from Chester and confined aboard PS, 25 March 1814. Joined YCs 29 June 1815, and arrived in the WIs as sergeant 5 November 1815. Reduced, 1 June 1816. Died Stony Hill, Jamaica, 10 September 1816.

Trimby/Triniby, Isaac. Prison-ship pay and muster roll records Trimby as 10th Foot – not found on regimental pay and muster lists. Marched from Fisherton and and confined aboard PS, 14 September 1813. Joined YCs 1 February 1814, and arrived in the WIs 14 December1814. Discharged Quebec.

Trimby/Trimbey, Thomas. Labourer of Kingston, Wiltshire. Prison-ship pay and muster roll records Trimby as 10th Foot – not found on regimental pay and muster list. Marched from Fisherton and and confined aboard PS, 14 September 1813. Joined YCs 1 February 1814, and arrived in the WIs 14 December1814. Died Jamaica, 4 December 1816.

Trimmell/Trimnell, John. 28th Foot. Marched from Warwick and confined at Portchester Castle, 22 December 1816. Joined YCs 3 April 1817, and arrived in the WIs 25 May 1817. Discharged Quebec.

Trueman, James or **Thomas**. 53rd Foot. Transported from Portsmouth and confined aboard PS, 6 March 1815. Joined YCs 29 June 1815, and arrived in the WIs 5 November 1815. Discharged Quebec. Allocated Concession 7. Lot SW 11. Bathurst. No evidence found of him settling there. 'Concession granted to James Murphy, 13th March 1840.'

Trusdale/Truesdale, John. Weaver of Down. 2nd Bn 43rd Foot. Marched from Plymouth and confined aboard PS, 23 October 1814. Joined YCs 29 June 1815, and arrived in the WIs 5 November 1815. 200 lashes for 'Drunk on Parade', 25 October 1816, punishment remitted. Deserted in Jamaica 11 March.1818. Rejoined 21 March 1818. Deserted in Jamaica 23 May 1818. Rejoined 30 May 1818. Deserted in Jamaica 7 April 1819.

Rejoined 2 May 1819. (No punishment records held.) Deserted in Jamaica 30 May 1819. No record of rejoining.

Tucker, John. Royal Wagon Train. Marched from Chester and confined aboard PS, 28 January 1815. Joined YCs 29 June 1815, and arrived in the WIs 5 November 1815. Discharged Quebec.

Tuckle, Richard. 11th Light Dragoons. Marched from Doncaster and confined aboard PS, 29 September 1813. Joined YCs 7 March 1814, and arrived in the WIs 14 December 1814. Promoted corporal 5 March 1815. Reduced 3 May 1815. Died Barbados, 13 May 1815, 10 days after reduction.

Tully, John. Joined 6th Foot 30 September, 1806. Transported from Jersey to be confined aboard PS, 20 November 1813. Joined YCs 1 February 1814 and promoted corporal, 25 March 1814. Left sick at Cork General Hospital as the regiment departed for Barbados. Reduced, September 1815. Discharged, 8 June 1816.

Tunnage, Robert. Labourer of Essex. West Essex Militia. Sentenced at Sheffield to 'General Service for Desertion', 4 September 1813. Marched from Manchester and confined aboard PS, 19 October 1813. Joined YCs 7 March 1814, and arrived in the WIs 14 December 1814. Deserted in Barbados 30 March 1815. Rejoined 2 April 1815. 300 lashes for 'Absent without Leave', 3 April 1815, 200 lashes remitted. Discharged Quebec.

Turner, George. Royal Artillery. Marched from Stamford and confined aboard PS, 28 May 1815. Joined YCs 29 June 1815, and arrived in the WIs 5 November 1815. Discharged Quebec.

Turner, James. Labourer of Gloucestershire. 1st Bn Royal Artillery. Marched from Bristol and confined aboard PS, 14 March 1814. Joined YCs 25 March 1814, and arrived in the WIs 14 December 1814. 'Killed by lightening at Grenada, 4th September 1815.'

Turner, John. Labourer of Kent. Confined at Portchester Castle and joined YCs 3 April 1817. Arrived in the WIs 25 May 1817. Deserted in Jamaica, 6 November 1817. No record of rejoining.

Turvey, George. Labourer of Beverley. 55th Foot. Marched from Derby and confined aboard PS as George Turvey or Foster, 1 December 1813. Joined YCs as George Turvey, 5 February 1814. Arrived in the WIs 14 December 1814. Promoted corporal 14 April 1815. Reduced 27 September 1816. Deserted in Jamaica 9 August 1818. Rejoined 13 August 1818. (No punishment records held.) Discharged Quebec.

Tyler, William. Labourer of York. 33rd Foot. Marched from Nottingham and confined aboard PS, 25 February 1815. Joined YCs 29 June 1815, and arrived in the WIs 5 November 1815. Died Jamaica, 19 January 1817.

Undrill/Underhill, Richard. Glover of Worcester. 2nd Bn 41st Foot. Marched from Winchester and confined aboard PS as Richard Underhill, 26 November 1813. Joined YCs as Richard Undrill, 1 February 1814. Deserted while still at the Isle of Wight, 25 June 1814. No record of rejoining.

Usher, William. Labourer of Durham. 65th Foot. Marched from Savoy Military Prison and confined at Portchester Castle, 28 December 1816. Joined YCs 3 April 1817, and arrived in the WIs 25 May 1817. Deserted Jamaica, 23 April 1818. No record of rejoining.

Usile/Usill/Usell, Abraham. Transferred from 15th Foot Depot as Abraham Usell, 22

June 1815. Arrived in the WIs as Abraham Usile, 5 November 1815. 300 lashes for 'Drunk on Guard', 21 December 1816. Discharged Quebec.

Utley, Mark. Labourer of Sheffield. Grenadier Guards. Marched from Worcester and confined at Portchester Castle, 26 December 1816. Joined YCs 3 April 1817, and arrived in the WIs 25 May 1817. Deserted in Jamaica 10 April 1818. Returned to England, recaptured and confined at Savoy Military Prison, 21 May 1819. Marched to Isle of Wight to await embarkation to a regiment in the West Indies. No further record.

Varley, William. Framework knitter of Greasley, Nottinghamshire. 45th Foot. Marched from Stafford and confined aboard PS, 4 March 1814. Joined YCs 25 March 1814. Deserted while still at the Isle of Wight, 13 June 1814. No record of rejoining.

Venner/Vennor, Thomas. 16th Dragoons. Marched from Sandwich and confined at Portchester Castle, 26 December 1816. Joined YCs 3 April 1817, and arrived in the WIs 25 May 1817. 300 lashes for 'Theft', 12 September 1817. Discharged Quebec.

Vidian/Vedians, Richard. 2nd Bn 95th Foot. Marched from Faversham and confined aboard PS, 6 January 1815. Joined YCs 29 June 1815, and arrived in the WIs 5 November 1815. Discharged Quebec.

Victory, Laurence or **Lawrence.** Weaver of Longford. 2nd Bn 36th Foot. Marched from Maidstone and confined aboard PS as Laurence Brown or Victory, 24 March 1814. Joined YCs as Laurence Victory, 25 March 1814. Arrived in the WIs 14 December 1814. Died St Vincent, 15 November 1815.

Wainwright, Joseph. Labourer of Shropshire. 43rd Foot. Marched from Warwick and confined aboard PS, 30 December 1814. Joined YCs 29 June 1815, and arrived in the WIs 5 November 1815. Died, 8 October 1816.

Walker, George. Sailor of Sheerness. 2nd Bn 26th Foot. Marched from Kingston-on-Hull and confined aboard PS, 22 January 1815. Joined YCs 29 June 1815 and arrived in the WIs 5 November 1815. Deserted in Jamaica 11 January 1818. No record of rejoining.

Walker, John. Either 1st Bn 3rd Foot Guards marched from Warwick, 18 October 1814, or 49th Foot marched from the Tilbury Fort and confined aboard PS, 6 May 1815. Joined YCs 29 June 1815, and arrived in the WIs 5 November 1815. Discharged Quebec.

Walker, Joseph. Labourer of Worcestershire. 1st Bn 5th Foot. Marched from Windsor and confined aboard PS, 13 March 1813. Joined YCs date unknown. Deserted while still at the Isle of Wight, 4 July 1814. Rejoined, date unknown. Hospitalised. (No punishment records held.) Arrived in the WIs 14 December 1814. Deserted in Barbados 30 March 1815. Rejoined 2 April 1815. 300 lashes for 'Absent without Leave', 3 April 1815, 150 lashes remitted. Died Jamaica, 31 January 1817.

Walker, Peter. Labourer of Mayo. 1st Bn 55th Foot. Marched from Maidstone and confined aboard PS as Patrick Smith or Peter Walker, 13 February 1814. Joined as Peter Walker, 7 March 1814. Deserted in Guernsey, 19 September 1814. No record of rejoining.

Walker, William. St Ann's, Worcestershire. 1st Bn 2nd Foot. Transported from Gosport and confined aboard PS, 10 February 1815. Joined YCs 29 June 1815, and arrived in the WIs 5 November 1815. Died Tobago, 12 May 1816.

Walmesly/Walmsley/Walmsey, Benjamin. Labourer of Yorkshire. 74th Foot. Marched from Chester and confined at Portchester Castle, 26 December 1816. Joined YCs 3 April

1817, and arrived in the WIs 25 May 1817. Died Jamaica, 30 May 1819.

Walmsley, Joseph. 34th Foot. Marched from Plymouth and confined aboard PS, 24 April 1815. Joined YCs 29 June 1815, and arrived in the WIs as corporal 5 November 1815. Reduced 30 January 1816. Discharged Quebec.

Walsh, David. Painter of Sligo. 88th Foot. Marched from Chester and confined aboard PS, 18 May 1815. Joined YCs 29 June 1815, and arrived in the WIs 5 November 1815. Died Montego Bay, Jamaica, 12 March 1819.

Walsh, George. Royal Artillery. Marched from Bristol and confined aboard PS, 15 October 1815. Joined YCs 16 May 1816 and arrived in the WIs 25 June 1816. Discharged Quebec.

Walsh, Laurence or **Lawrence.** Labourer of Wexford. 68th Foot. Marched from Bristol and confined aboard PS, 16 April 1815. Joined YCs 29 June 1815, and arrived in the WIs 5 November 1815. Died Jamaica, 9 May 1819.

Walsh, Michael. Labourer of Kildare. 48th Foot. Marched from Chester and confined aboard PS, 14 November 1813. Joined YCs 1 February 1814, and arrived in the WIs 14 December 1814. Died, 17 November 1816.

Walsh, Thomas. Labourer of Derry. 77th Foot. Marched from Bristol and confined at Portchester Castle, 7 January 1817. Joined YCs 3 April 1817, and arrived in the WIs 25 May 1817. 200 lashes for 'Making away with Regimental Necessaries', 2 August 1817, 50 lashes remitted; 300 lashes for 'Drunk on Duty', 2 October 1817, 150 lashes remitted. Deserted in Jamaica 7 December 1817. Rejoined the next day. 300 lashes for 'Making away with Regimental Necessaries', 15 December 1817. Deserted in Jamaica 14 June 1818. Rejoined 17 June 1818. Deserted in Jamaica 9 July 1818. Rejoined 18 July 1818. (No punishment records held.) Died Jamaica, 27 July 1818, nine days after rejoining and no doubt punishment.

Walsh, William. Weaver of Neath. 28th Foot. Marched from Chester and confined aboard PS 26 October 1814. Joined 29 June 1815 and arrived in the WIs 5 November 1815. Died, 21 December 1816.

Walter, Joseph. Joined YCs 29 June 1815, and arrived in the WIs 5 November 1815. Deserted, date unknown. Rejoined 5 September 1816. (No punishment records held.) Discharged Quebec.

Wanest/Wanhurst/Warrhurst, Isaac. Labourer of Ashton, Lancs. 2nd Bn 84th Foot. Marched from Manchester and confined aboard PS as Isaac Wanest or Newton, 1 November 1813. Joined YCs as Isaac Warrhurst, 25 March 1814. Deserted while still at the Isle of Wight as Isaac Warrhurst or Wanhurst, 13 June 1814. No record of rejoining.

Ward, Robert. 63rd Foot. Marched from Exeter and confined aboard PS, 21 May 1815. Joined YCs 29 June 1815, and arrived in the WIs 5 November 1815. Discharged Quebec.

Warn/Warne/Waine, Samuel. Bricklayer of Suffolk. 2nd Bn 62nd Foot. Marched from Oxford and confined aboard PS as Samuel Warn, 22 November 1813. Joined YCs as Samuel Waine, 7 March 1814. Arrived in the WIs 14 December 1814. Deserted in Jamaica 13 October 1818. Rejoined 16 October 1818. Deserted in Jamaica 20 January 1819. Rejoined 3 May 1819. (No punishment records held.) Discharged Quebec as Samuel Warne.

Warwick, Guy. 2nd Foot Guards. Marched from Carlisle and confined aboard PS, 16 February 1814. Joined YCs 7 March 1814. Left sick as the regiment departed for Guernsey. Deserted while still at the Isle of Wight, 14 August 1814. No record of rejoining.

Waterman, Charles. Whitesmith or mason of Sheerness. 2nd Bn 67th Foot. Marched from Savoy Military Prison and confined aboard PS, 26 February 1815. Joined YCs 29 June 1815, and arrived in the WIs 5 November 1815. Deserted in Jamaica 12 January 1817. 'Recaptured and returned by a Planter who then refused the bounty on offer, 17th January 1817.' 300 lashes for 'Absenting himself 2 weeks without Leave', 21 January 1817; 200 lashes for 'Making away with his Regimental Necessaries', 30 October 1817. Deserted in Jamaica 13 January 1818. Rejoined 2 February 1818. 300 lashes for 'Absent without Leave', 2 February 1818. Deserted in Jamaica 15 July 1818. Rejoined 18 July 1818. Deserted in Jamaica 14 April 1819. Rejoined, date unknown. (No punishment records held.) Discharged Quebec.

Watkins, John. Labourer of Hereford. 2nd Bn 39th Foot. Marched from Gloucester and confined aboard PS, 22 October 1813. Joined YCs 25 March 1814, and arrived in the WIs 14 December 1814. Deserted in Barbados 10 March 1815. Rejoined 16 March 1815. (No punishment records held.) Died Barbados, 6 June 1815.

Watmore/Whatmore/Wheatmore, James. Royal Artillery Driver. Marched from Uxbridge and confined aboard PS as James Watmore, 4 February 1814. Joined YCs 25 March 1814, and arrived in WIs 14 December 1814. Discharged Quebec as James Whatmore.

Watson, George. 2nd Dragoons. Marched from Shrewsbury and confined aboard PS, 14 November 1813. Joined YCs 7 March 1814, and arrived in the WIs 14 December 1814. Discharged Quebec.

Watson, John. Stocking maker of Leicestershire. 3rd Bn Royal Artillery. Marched from Newark and confined aboard PS, 13 March 1814. Joined YCs 25 March 1814. Deserted at Bear Haven, Cork, 16 October 1814. No record of rejoining.

Watson, Thomas. Labourer of Warnford. 74th Foot. Marched from Bristol and confined aboard PS, 26 July 1815. Embarked Spithead amongst a 300-strong detachment of 'Unattached Deserters' joining the 2nd Foot, 24 April 1816. Arrived in the WIs 5 June 1816. Deserted 16 July 1816. Rejoined 21 July 1816. 1,000 lashes and ordered to be marked with 'D', 24 July 1816. Transferred into the York Chasseurs, 25 August 1816. Died Jamaica, 25 December 1816.

Watson, William. 69th Foot. Marched from Savoy Military Prison and confined aboard PS, 11 November 1813. Joined YCs 7 March 1814, and arrived in the WIs 14 December 1814. Deserted Barbados, 20 June 1815. No record of rejoining.

Watson, William. Sailor of Stonehouse. Coldstream Guards. Marched from Warwick and confined at Portchester Castle, 27 January 1817. Joined YCs 3 April 1817, and arrived in the WIs 25 May 1817. Deserted in Jamaica 5 June 1817, just two weeks after arrival. No record of rejoining.

Watts, Henry. 2nd Bn 3rd Dragoons. Marched from Maidstone and confined aboard PS, date unknown. Joined YCs 29 June 1815 and arrived in the WIs 5 November 1815. Promoted corporal, 13 October 1816. 300 lashes and ordered to be reduced for 'Forgery on Lieutenant Watson', 2 December 1816. Discharged Quebec.

Weaver, Daniel. Miner of Cheadle, Staffordshire. 11th Light Dragoons. Marched from

Staffordshire and confined aboard PS, 21 October 1813. Joined YCs 7 March 1814. Deserted in Guernsey 31 August 1814. Rejoined 4 September 1814. (No punishment records held.) 300 lashes for 'Drunk on Barrier Beach Guard', 28 April 1815. Discharged Quebec.

Weaver/Weavers/Weavis, John. Victualler of London. As John Weaver, marched from Chelsea to Portsmouth as corporal volunteer of the 2nd Bn 89th Foot, 1 April 1815. Arrived in the WIs as Weavis 5 November 1815. Deserted in Tobago 28 August 1816. Rejoined 25 November 1816. 200 lashes commuted to reduction, 4 December 1816. Deserted in Jamaica as John Weavis or Weavers, 4 September 1817. No record of rejoining. Though a deserter it seems that in 1827 Weavis may well have signed indentures with the Van Dieman's Land Company, and, two years later, one of four shepherds accused of killing up to 30 aboriginal people at Cape Grim. It seems, as an indentured servant and not a convicted felon, Weavis later settled at Sandy Bay south of Hobart.[181]

Webb, Thomas. Leather dresser of Lauston, Cambridgeshire. 14th Dragoons. Marched from Windsor and confined aboard PS as James or Thomas Webb, 28 October 1814. Joined as Thomas Webb, 29 June 1815. Arrived in the WIs 5 November 1815. Died Jamaica, 7 December 1816.

Webb, William. Stocking weaver of Leicestershire. 3rd Foot Guards. Marched from Leicester and confined aboard PS, 3 October 1813. Joined YCs 25 March 1814, and arrived in the WIs 14 December 1814. Died Grenada, 6 September 1815.

Webster, Thomas. Cordwainer of Sligo. East India Company. Transferred from East India Company's Isle of Wight Depot to PS, 16 December 1813. Joined YCs as corporal 5 February 1814. Reduced 31 March 1814. Arrived in the WIs 14 December 1814. 200 lashes for 'Refusing to go to Drill when Ordered', 25 April 1815, 100 lashes remitted; 200 lashes for 'Drunk in Barracks', 12 June 1815. Deserted in Barbados, date unknown. Rejoined 30 April 1816. (No punishment records held.) 1,000 lashes for 'Deserting on the 20th June 1816 and Threatening Behaviour and Mutinous Conduct to Capt Anderson and Colour Sergeant Sewell, at Fort Augusta, 25th November 1816', 4 December 1816. Died in Jamaica, 10 April 1817.

Wier, James. Sayer of Lanark. 26th Foot. Transported from Guerney to PS, 1 December 1816. Arrived in the WIs 25 May 1817. Deserted in Jamaica 15 June 1817. Rejoined the next day. 300 lashes for 'Absent without Leave', 19 June 1817. Deserted in Jamaica 25 September 1817. Date of rejoining unknown. Deserted in Jamaica 20 December 1817. Rejoined 13 February 1818. Deserted in Jamaica 23 August 1818. Rejoined the next day. Deserted in Jamaica 2 March 1819. Rejoined the next day. (No punishment records held.) Discharged Quebec.

Wells/Willis, William. Butcher of Tiverton. 2nd Bn 9th Foot. Marched from Ilchester and confined aboard PS, 20 November 1814. Joined YCs 29 June 1815, and arrived in the WIs 5 November 1815. Died Tobago as William Wells or Willis, 21 June 1816.

Wenham, William. Bricklayer of Sussex. 95th Foot. Marched from Maidstone and confined aboard PS as William Titchorn or Wenham, 24 October 1813. Joined YCs as William Wenham, 7 March 1814. Deserted at Guernsey, 19th August 1814. No record of rejoining.

Wennol/Warner, William. 51st Foot. Marched from Petworth and confined at Portchester Castle as William Warner, 13 January 1817. Joined YCs 3 April 1817, and arrived in the WIs as William Wennol, 25 May 1817. Discharged Quebec.

Wenskill/Winskill/Winishell, William. 4th Bn Royals. Confined aboard PS as

Winishell, 19 November 1814. Joined YCs 29 June 1815, and arrived in the WIs as Sergeant Wenskill, 5 November 1815. Reduced 3 February 1816. Promoted corporal 1 April 1816. Deserted in Tobago 20 June 1816. Rejoined as private 22 June 1816. (No punishment records held.) Discharged Quebec as Winskill.

Wesenham, William. Labourer of Norfolk. Royal Artillery. Marched from Woolwich and confined aboard PS, 11 November 1813. Joined YCs 5 February 1814. Deserted while still at the Isle of Wight, 2 April 1814. No record of rejoining.

West, James. Blacksmith of Surrey. 61st Foot. Marched from Chester and confined aboard PS, 18 May 1815. Joined YCs 29 June 1815, and arrived in the WIs 5 November 1815. Deserted in Jamaica 30 May 1819. Returned to England, recaptured and confined at Savoy Military Prison. 'Unfit for Further Service due to a Diseased Ankle', 11 October 1819.

West, Joseph. 38th Foot. Marched from Bristol and confined aboard PS, 1 February 1815. Joined YCs 29 June 1815, and arrived in the WIs 5 November 1815. Discharged following 'Urgent Application' made by Colonel Sir Charles Grenville of the 38th Foot, A payment of £20 was accepted for his discharge', 1 October 1818.

West, Ralph. Transferred to YCs from 6th Bn 60th Foot in Jamaica, 25 May 1817. Discharged Quebec.

West, Thomas. Weaver of Yorkshire. 23rd Light Dragoons. Marched from Chester and confined aboard PS, 26 September 1813. Joined YCs 7 March 1814, and arrived in the WIs 14 December 1814. Royal Barracks, Dublin. 12 January 1814.

> I do hereby certify that Thomas West, late of the Regiment, served nine years and fifty days and I further certify that he was not a Deserter from the regiment, but that he commuted the Punishment awarded him by the Sentence of a Regimental Court Martial for Service Abroad
>
> Signed Samuel Hardman. Lieutenant/Adjutant 23rd Light Dragoons.

150 lashes for 'Insolent Language', 28 July 1815. Died St Vincent, 28 April 1816.

West, William. Royal Artillery Driver. Transported from Belem and confined aboard PS, 7 November 1813. Joined YCs 5 February 1814, and arrived in the WIs 14 December 1814. Promoted drummer, 12 March 1817. Discharged Quebec.

Whalley/Walley, Thomas. 4th Bn Royals. Marched from Shrewsbury and confined aboard PS as James Hassett or Thomas Walley, 8 December 1813. Joined YCs as Thomas Whalley, 7 March 1814. Arrived in the WIs 14 December 1814. Died Jamaica, 29 October 1816.

Wheatley, George. Volunteered from 2nd Bn Tower Hamlets Militia, 10 December 1813 (Six Guinea Bounty). Arrived in the WIs 14 December 1814. Discharged at Quebec, 24 September 1819. As a volunteer possibly returned to Europe at public expense.

Wheeler, Richard. 1st Bn 67th Foot. Marched from Hereford and confined aboard PS, 17 December 1813. Joined YCs 29 June 1815, and arrived in the WIs 5 November 1815. Discharged Quebec.

Wheeler, Robert. 15th Foot. Marched from Savoy Military Prison and confined aboard PS, 21 March 1814. Joined YCs 29 June 1815, and arrived in the WIs 5 November 1815. Discharged Quebec.

Whiakors, Hugh. Joined YCs from PS, 25 March 1814. Deserted while still at the Isle of Wight, 12 May 1814. No record of rejoining.

White, John. 19th Dragoons. Marched from Chichester and confined aboard PS, 15 November 1814. Joined YCs 29 June 1815, and arrived in the WIs 5 November 1815. Discharged Quebec.

White, William. Labourer of Kent. Royal Wagon Train. Marched from Savoy Military Prison and confined aboard PS, 26 December 1813. Joined YCs 7 March 1814, and arrived in the WIs 14 December 1814. Died Jamaica, 4 June 1817.

Whitefield/Whitfield, Robert. 2nd Bn 71st Foot. Marched from Edinburgh and confined aboard PS, 4 February 1814. Joined YCs 25 March 1814, and arrived in the WIs 14 December 1814. Deserted in Barbados 10 March 1815. Rejoined the same day. (No punishment records held.) Discharged Quebec.

Whitehair/Whiteham, Peter. 14th Foot. Marched from Savoy Military Prison and confined aboard PS as Peter Whitehair, 14 May 1815. Joined YCs as Peter Whiteham, 29 June 1815. 'Remanded back to the prison-ship on the Order of Colonel Mainwaring, Commandant of the Isle of Wight'.

Whitehead, John. Joined Royal Horse Artillery, 23 November 1803. Marched from Woolwich and confined aboard PS, 4 February 1814. Joined YCs 7 March 1814, and arrived in the WIs 14 December 1814. Promoted corporal 15 April 1814. Reduced 18 April 1814. Promoted corporal March 1815. 300 lashes for 'Absent without Leave but FORGIVEN', 10 July 1815. Promoted sergeant 4 August 1815. Reduced,15 September 1816. 300 lashes for 'Preferring erroneous charges against Ensign Maxwell', 23 December 1816. Discharged Quebec.

Whitely/Whiteley, Joseph. Coachmaker of York. Staff Corps. Marched from Hythe and confined aboard PS, 17 September 1813. Joined YCs 5 February 1814. Deserted while still at the Isle of Wight, 9 July 1814. Seized by Henry A Brook (Twenty Shillings Bounty). Rejoined 22 July 1814. (No punishment records held.) Arrived in the WIs 14 December 1814. Discharged Quebec.

Whittaker/Whitaker, Miles. Labourer of Yorkshire. 1st Dragoon Guards. Marched from Chester and confined aboard PS, 2 October 1813. Joined YCs 5 February 1814, and arrived in the WIs 14 December 1814. Promoted corporal, 18 March 1814. Reduced, July 1814. '150 lashes for 'Absent from Parade but FORGIVEN', 27 June 1815. Died, 8 August 1816.

Whitton/Whiton/McKwilton, Charles. Carpenter of Middlesex. 8th Bn Royal Artillery. Marched from Savoy Military Prison and confined aboard PS, 26 September 1813. Joined YCs as Drummer Charles Whitton 5 February 1814. Arrived in the WIs 14 December 1814. Died Jamaica as Charles Whitton or McKwilton, 17 November 1817.

Whitty/Whittey/Whittie, Robert. Miner of Cumberland. Coldstream Guards. Marched from Dartford and confined aboard PS, 24 July 1814. Joined YCs 29 June 1815, and arrived in the WIs 5 November 1815. Died Jamaica, 16 February 1818.

Whitworth, Henry. Blacksmith of Stafford. 2nd Bn 10th Foot. Marched from Bedford and confined aboard PS, 10 August 1813. Joined YCs 5 February 1814, and arrived in the

WIs 14 December 1814. Died, 24 November 1816.

Wickers, Ambrose. Labourer of Alstead, Essex. 2nd Bn 3rd Foot. Marched from Brighton and confined aboard PS, date unknown. Joined YCs 29 June 1815, and arrived in the WIs 5 November 1815. Died, 28 November 1816.

Wiggins, John. Joined from PS, 1 February 1814. Deserted while still at the Isle of Wight, 7 July 1814. Rejoined 20 July 1814. (No punishment records held.) 'Arraigned by Special Warrant at Guernsey, 22 August 1814' (Charge unknown). Remained a prisoner at Guernsey as the regiment left for Barbados. Subsequently transferred to either Royal African Corps or Royal York Rangers.

Wilcox, John. Labourer of Nottinghamshire. 34th Foot. Marched from Newark and confined aboard PS, 24 December 1813. Joined YCs 5 February 1814, and arrived in the WIs 14 December 1814. Deserted in Jamaica 3 May 1819. Rejoined 11 May 1819. (No punishment records held.) Discharged Quebec.

Wilkinson, George. Cablemaker of Yorkshire. 2nd Bn 84th Foot. Marched from Wakefield and confined aboard PS, 7 December 1813. Joined YCs 1 February 1814, and arrived in the WIs 14 December 1814. Promoted corpora 25 February 1815. 'Reduced 'For Uttering Abusive Language', 29 July 1815. Deserted in St Vincent, 17 August 181. No record of rejoining.

Wilkinson, John. Labourer of Yorkshire. 29th Foot. Marched from Petworth and confined aboard PS, 24 March 1815. Joined YCs 29 June 1815, and arrived in the WIs 5 November 1815. Deserted in Jamaica 13 September 1818. Rejoined 18 September 1818. Deserted in Jamaica 10 November 1818. Rejoined 23 November 1818. Deserted in Jamaica 29 April 1819. Rejoined 3 May 1819. (No punishment records held.) Discharged Quebec.

Williams, David. Tailor of Midlothian. 2nd Bn 84th Foot. Marched from York and confined aboard PS as David Williams or Carr, 14 November 1813. Joined YCs as David Williams 1 February 1814. Deserted at Guernsey, 22 September 1814. No record of rejoining.

Williams, David or **Daniel.** Labourer of Montgomery. 54th Foot. Marched from Savoy Military Prison and confined aboard PS, 1 August 1813. Joined YCs as David Williams 29 June 1815. Arrived in the WIs 5 November 1815. Recorded variously as Daniel or David Williams. Died Jamaica as David Williams, 15 November 1818.

Williams, Edward. Cordwainer of Radnor. 84th Foot. Marched from Woolwich and confined aboard PS as Edward Williams or Meredith, 4 December 1812. Joined YCs as Sergeant Edward Williams 1 February 1814. Arrived in the WIs 14 December 1814. Reduced 25 December 1814. Died Stony Hill Barracks, Jamaica, 23 September 1816.

Williams, Isaac. Labourer of Monmouth. 2nd Bn 1st Foot Guards. Marched from Kingston and confined aboard PS, 9 June 1815. Joined YCs 29 June 1815, and arrived in the WIs 5 November 1815. Died St Vincent, 15 April 1816.

Williams, James. Labourer of Mayo. Joined 48th Foot, 28 November 1811. Marched from Savoy Military Prison and confined aboard PS, 3 March 1815. Joined YCs 29 June 1815, and arrived in the WIs 5 November 1815. Deserted in Jamaica 3 April 1819. Rejoined the same day. (No punishment records held.) Discharged Quebec.

Williams, John. Carpenter of Whitchurch. Royal Artillery. Marched from Savoy Military

Prison and confined aboard PS, 10 September 1813. Joined YCs 1 February 1814. Promoted corporal 24 February 1814. Reduced 10 August 1814. Arrived in the WIs 14 December 1814. Promoted sergeant 10 February 1817. Reduced 16 February 1917. Died Jamaica, 18 October 1817.

Williams, Joseph. Tailor of Midlothian. Royal Artillery. Marched from Nottingham and confined aboard PS, 17 October 1813. Joined YCs 25 March 1814. Deserted while still at the Isle of Wight, 27 June 1814. No record of rejoining.

Williams, Spencer. Collier of London. Either 8th or 81st Foot. Joined YCs 19 March 1815. One of two 'Substitutes' provided by Thomas Billingsley, a volunteer from King George's Stafford Militia. Arrived in the WIs 5 November 1815. Died Jamaica, 6 January 1817.

Williams, Thomas. 3rd Foot Guards. Marched from Cardiff and confined aboard PS, 13 January 1814. Joined YCs 25 March 1814. Deserted Guernsey, 22 September 1814. No record of rejoining.

Williams, William. Bricklayer of Somerset. 13th Foot. Marched from Bath and confined aboard PS, 20 January 1815. Joined YCs 29 June 1815 and arrived in the WIs 5 November 1815. Deserted in St Vincent 15 June 1816. Rejoined 3 July 1816. Deserted in St Vincent 12 August 1816. Rejoined 25 August 1816. Deserted 2 November 1816. Rejoined 10 November 1816. (No punishment records held.) Deserted in Jamaica 4 August 1817. Returned to England, recaptured and confined at Savoy Military Prison (December 1817–March 1818). Rejoined the regiment in Jamaica 6 June 1818. Deserted in Jamaica 20 June 1818. Rejoined the next day. (No punishment records held.) Deserted in Jamaica 15 July 1818. Returned to England and recaptured, details not known. Still in Europe as the regiment embarked for Canada and disbandment. No further record.

Williamson/Williams/Wilkinson, Michael. Labourer of Wilson. 100th Foot. Marched from Savoy Military Prison and confined aboard PS as Michael Williamson or Wilkinson, 12 February 1815. Joined YCs as Michael Williamson 29 June 1815. Arrived in the WIs 5 November 1815. Died Jamaica as Michael Williams, 6 October 1817.

Willis, Charles. From Headcorn, Kent. 'Mr Charles Willis and Mr Henry Gurly being taken on the strength as Volunteers from 25th May 1816'. 'Charles Willis promoted to Ensign of York Chasseurs, 17th September 1817'.

Willy/Willey, Henry. Labourer of Brunswick. Joined King's German Legion's Depot, 16 April 1804, followed by the 4th Line Bn, King's German Legion at Hilsea Barracks, Portsmouth, 2 February 1805. Embarked for France December 1805. Regiment remained at Verdun until transferred to Ireland, February 1806. Served in Sicily from mid-1808, and Spain, early 1812. Deserted in Alicante, Spain, 14 November 1813. Rejoined 7 December 1813. Deserted in Ondres, France, 20 January 1814. Rejoined 30 April 1814. Deserted in Mons, 2 October 1814. Rejoined 12 October 1814. (No punishment records held.) Transported via Ostend and Deal to PS, 13 February 1815. Arrived in Jamaica to join the 6th Bn 60th Foot, 7 February 1816. Deserted in Jamaica 22 May 1816. Rejoined 15 August 1816. (No punishment records held.) Transferred into the York Chasseurs in Jamaica, 25 May 1817. Deserted in Jamaica 9 June 1817. Rejoined 4 August 1817. (No punishment records held.) Deserted in Jamaica,9 March 1819. Rejoined, no date. Discharged Quebec.

Wilson, Alexander. Labourer of Tyrone. 61st Foot. Marched from Chester and confined aboard PS, 26 September 1813. Joined YCs 5 February 1814. Deserted while still at the Isle of Wight, 9 July 1814. Seized by Henry A Brook (Twenty Shillings Bounty). Rejoined 22 July 1814. (No punishment records held.) Arrived in the WIs 14 December 1814. Died Jamaica, 13 May 1817.

Wilson, George. Labourer of Rutland. 70th Foot. Marched from Dartford and confined aboard PS, 7 July 1814. Joined YCs 29 June 1815, and arrived in the WIs 5 November 1815. Deserted 22 September 1816. Rejoined 14 October 1816. 200 lashes for 'Desertion', 21 October 1816. Punishment remitted. Died Jamaica, 17 June 1818.

Wilson, John. Either 74th Foot marched from Salford, 30 March 1813, 66th Foot marched from Salford, 10 May 1813 or 2nd Bn 31st marched from Battle and confined aboard PS, 11 May 1813. Joined YCs 1 February 1814. Promoted corporal 15 April 1814. Reduced 6 June 1814. Arrived in the WIs 14 December 1814. Deserted in Barbados 20 June 1815. No record of rejoining.

Wilson, John. Tailor of London. 21st Light Dragoon. Marched from Maidstone and confined aboard PS, 20 March 1814. Joined YCs 29 June 1815, and arrived in the WIs 5 November 1815. Died, 14 September 1816.

Wilson, Thomas. Spinner of Preston, Lancashire. 74th Foot. Marched from Carlisle and confined aboard PS, 19 November 1813. Joined YCs 1 February 1814, and arrived in the WIs 14 December 1814. 14 days solitary confinement for 'Drunk on Guard', 10 April 1815, 8 days remitted. Died St Vincent, 9 June 1816.

Wilson, Thomas. Labourer of Fermanagh. Either 3rd Foot marched from Canterbury, 4 February 1816, or 38th Foot marched from Winchester and confined at Portchester Castle, 6 January 1817. Joined YCs 3 April 1817, and 'Remained on Detachment.' Arrived in the WIs 24 January 1818. Deserted in Jamaica 16 April 1818. Rejoined same day. (No punishment records held.) Deserted in Jamaica 5 May 1818. No record of rejoining.

Wilson, Thomas. Labourer of New York. Either 3rd Foot marched from Canterbury, 4 February 1816, or 38th Foot marched from Winchester and confined at Portchester Castle, 6 January 1817. Joined YCs 3 April 1817, and arrived in the WIs 25 May 1817. Deserted in Jamaica 2 May 1818. No record of rejoining.

Wilson, William. Weaver of Ayr. Possible 'Bounty Jumper' from both 71st and 90th Foot. Marched from Dover and confined at Portchester Castle, 29 December 1816. Joined YCs 3 April 1817, and arrived in the WIs 25 May 1817. Deserted in Jamaica 15 August 1817. Rejoined the next day. 300 lashes for 'Absent without Leave', 18 August 1817. Discharged Quebec.

Wilson, William. Butcher or Labourer of Kerry. Either West Kent Militia marched from Windsor, 6 April 1814, 42nd Foot marched from Edinburgh, 16th April 1814, 2nd Bn 64th marched from Colchester, 21st October 1814 or Royal Horse Artillery marched from Nottingham and confined aboard PS, 2 May 1815. Joined YCs 29 June 1815, and arrived in the WIs 5 November 1815. Deserted in Jamaica 9 May 1817. Rejoined 18 May 1817. Deserted in Jamaica 4 January 1819. Rejoined 9 March 1819. (No punishment records held.) Discharged Quebec. It is not known which William Wilson received 300 lashes for 'Striking Sergeant Hartshorn and Corporal Davies', 21 January 1817.

Wilson, William. Tailor or labourer of Tipperary. Either West Kent Militia marched from Windsor, 6 April 1814, 42nd Foot marched from Edinburgh, 16 April 1814, 2nd Bn 64th marched from Colchester, 21 October 1814 or Royal Horse Artillery marched from Nottingham and confined aboard PS, 2 May 1815. Joined YCs 29 June 1815, and arrived in the WIs 5 November 1815. Deserted in Grenada 12 March 1816. Rejoined 16 March 1816. (No punishment records held.) Deserted in Jamaica 5 June 1819. No record of rejoining. It is not known which William Wilson received 300 lashes for 'Striking Sergeant Hartshorn and Corporal Davies', 21 January 1817.

Winwood/Wyndwood, Richard. Miner of Worcestershire. 2nd Bn 43rd Foot. Marched from Worcester and confined aboard PS, 11 September 1813. Joined as Richard Winwood, 7 March 1814. Arrived in the WIs 14 December 1814. Died as Richard Winwood or Robert Wyndwood, 21 October 1816.

Woodhouse, John. 7th Foot. Marched from Savoy Military Prison and confined aboard PS, 6 March 1814. Joined YCs 25 March 1814, and arrived in the WIs 14 December 1814. Discharged Quebec.

Woodson/Woodeson/Woodison, James. Labourer of Berkshire. Royal Wagon Train. Marched from Reading and confined aboard PS, 24 May 1815. Joined as Woodson, 29 June 1816. Arrived in the WIs 5 November 1815. Died Jamaica as Woodeson or Woodison, 22 February 1817.

Wooley/Woolley, Thomas. Labourer of Cheadle. Royal Artillery Driver. Marched from Chester and confined aboard PS, 16 April 1815. Joined YCs 29 June 1815, and arrived in the WIs 5 November 1815. Deserted in Jamaica 3 January 1819. Rejoined 29 January 1819. (No punishment records held.) Deserted in Jamaica 27 April 1819. No record of rejoining.

Worthy, John. Royal Artillery Driver. Marched from Colchester and confined aboard PS, 13 October 1814. Joined YCs 29 June 1815, and arrived in the WIs 5 November 1815. Discharged Quebec.

Wright, Benjamin. Labourer of Kent. 3rd Dragoons. Marched from London and confined aboard PS as Benjamin Wright or Stevens, 25 June 1814. Joined YCs as Benjamin Wright 29 June 1815, and arrived in the WIs as corporal, 5 November 1815. Reduced 3 January 1816. Deserted in Jamaica 30 April 1819. Rejoined the same day. (No punishment records held.) Discharged Quebec.

Wright, John. Either 2nd Bn 14th Foot marched from Savoy Military Prison, 11 November 1813, or Royal Artillery marched from Woolwich and confined aboard PS, 26 November 1813. Joined YCs 1 February 1814, and arrived in the WIs 14 December 1814. Discharged Quebec.

Wright, Joseph. 85th Foot. Marched from Derby and confined aboard PS, 7 October 1813. Joined YCs 29 June 1815 and arrived in the WIs 5 November 1815. Discharged Quebec.

Wright, William. Gardener of Witham, Essex. 63rd Foot. Marched from Colchester and confined aboard PS, 3 August 1813. Joined YCs 1 February 1814, and arrived in the WIs 14 December 1814. Promoted drummer 25 April 1815. Reduced 24 April 1816. Promoted drummer 19 December 1817. Reduced 24 January 1818. Deserted in Jamaica 6 May 1818. Rejoined the next day. (No punishment records held.) Discharged Quebec.

Wright, William. Weaver of York. Arrived in Jamaica, May 1817, and died there, January 1818.

Wrigley, Benjamin. Labourer of Lancashire. 3rd Bn 1st Foot Guards. Marched from Savoy Military Prison and confined aboard PS, 1 January 1815. Joined YCs 29 June 1815, and arrived in the WIs 5 November 1815. Died, 29 August 1816.

Wynne/Wyne, Edward. Gardener of King's County. 2nd Bn 73rd Foot. Marched from Glasgow and confined aboard PS, 29 August 1813. Joined YCs 5 February 1814, and arrived in the WIs 14 December 1814. 300 lashes for 'Drunk on Guard', 24 July 1815. Deserted in Jamaica 14 August 1818. Rejoined the next day. (No punishment records held.) Deserted in Jamaica 30 May 1819. No record of rejoining.

Wyse/Wise, John. Shoemaker of Limerick. 9th Foot. Marched from Chester and confined aboard PS as Wise, 21 April 1815. Joined YCs 29 June 1815, and arrived in the WIs as Wyse, 5 November 1815. Died, 30 November 1816.

Yates, George. Royal Artillery. Marched from Woolwich and confined aboard PS, 14 November 1813. Joined YCs 1 February 1814, and arrived in the WIs 14 December 1814. Discharged Quebec.

Yates, William. Royal Horse Artillery. Marched from Oxford and confined aboard PS, 25 August 1813. Joined YCs 1 February 1814, and arrived in the WIs 14 December 1814. Discharged Quebec.

Young, James. Royal Artillery Driver. Marched from Glasgow and confined aboard PS, 24 December 1813. Joined YCs 5 February 1814, and arrived in the WIs 14 December 1814. Discharged Quebec.

Young, Robert. Framework knitter of Roxborough. 2nd Bn 25th Foot. Marched from Leicester and confined aboard PS, 8 August 1813. Joined YCs 1 February 1814, and arrived in the WIs 14 December 1814. Deserted in Jamaica 23 January 1818. Rejoined 31 January 1818. (No punishment records held.) Deserted in Jamaica 13 March 1819. No record of rejoining.

Young, Thomas. Labourer of Donegal. 2nd Bn 2nd Foot Guards. Marched from Savoy Military Prison and confined aboard PS as John or Thomas Young, 20 March 1814. Joined YCs as Thomas Young 25 March 1814. Deserted while still at the Isle of Wight, 15 June 1814. Rejoined 25 June 1814. (No punishment records held.) Arrived in the WIs 14 December 1814. Deserted at Barbados, 15 March 1815. No record of rejoining.

Young, William. Brass founder of Paisley. 56th Foot. Marched from Kingston and confined aboard PS, 24 February 1814. Joined YCs 25 March 1814. Deserted while still at the Isle of Wight, 2 July 1814. No record of rejoining.

Yund, James. 55th Foot. Marched from Fisherton Onger and confined at Portchester Castle, 3 January 1817. Joined YCs 3 April 1817, and arrived in the WIs 25 May 1817. Discharged Quebec.

Table 45 Men of the York Chasseurs Regiment of Infantry Discharged at Quebec

Name	Regiment	Origin/Occupation
Sgt Maj William Hyland	2nd Battn 12th Foot	Clerk of Mountrath, Queen's County
Paymaster Sgt Robert Seaman	3rd Foot Guards	(Discharged 24 September 1819)
Schoolmaster Sgt Terence Gallagher	45th Foot	School teacher of Innishclose
Colour Sergeants		
Francis Allwright	Coldstream Guards	
George Brown	Royal Horse Artillery	
Cornelius Buyss/Buijss	York Light Infantry Volunteers/ 1st Bn Tower Hamlets Militia	Discharged 24 September 1819 Shoemaker of Amsterdam
Robert Denny	2nd Bn 84th Foot	
Mathew Farlie	70th Foot	
Thomas Leonard	50th Foot	Minor of Gibraltar
William Perry	Volunteer from Albany Staff, previously 87th & 95th Foot	County Tyrone
Abraham Temple	85th Foot	
Sergeants		
Charles Annis	70th Foot	
John Cocker	Royal Artillery Drivers	
Richard Dyson	2nd Bn 84th Foot	
William Edwards	2nd Bn 87th Foot	
James Elliott	Either 28th or 84th Foot	
Patrick Ford	28th Foot	
Michael Halleran	12th Foot	
William Harris	Either 2nd Bn Royals or 7th Royal Veteran Bn	
James McCamus	Volunteered at Dublin	Servant of Neath County
William Mann	Transferred from 1st European Garrison	
William Marwick	2nd Bn 36th Foot	
John Newall	19th Dragoons	
David Oram	7th Dragoons	
Donald Ross	42nd Foot and volunteer, 1st Garrison Staff Company (56th Foot)	Ross, Scotland
John Taylor	2nd Bn 4th Foot	
William Till	76th Foot	

Continued

Patrick Toole	3rd Foot Guards	

Corporals

John Angus	Royal Artillery	
Robert Arnold	61st Foot.	
Thomas Barry		
John Blackie	1st Bn 26th Foot	Butcher of Roxborough
Paul Bloom	23rd Light Dragoons	
William Bygrove	16th Foot	
Robert Clarke	2nd Bn 44th Foot	Weaver of St Luke's, Dublin
Richard Crone	3rd Bn 1st Foot or Foot Guards	
James Davis/Davies	56th Foot	
William Deigan	23rd Light Dragoons	
Charles Devlin	103rd Foot	
Charles Eve	44th Foot	
Patrick Fitzgerald	22nd or 46th Foot	
William Fletcher	Volunteer 2nd Bn Tower Hamlets Militia	(Discharged 24 September 1819)
John Fewkes	Volunteer 2nd Bn Tower Hamlets Militia	(Discharged 24 September 1819)
William Jeffries	32nd Foot	
John Lewis	9th Light Dragoons	
Thomas McGinness	54th Foot	
Anthony Mulhearn	2nd Bn 93rd Foot	
Richard Peckham	2nd Bn 73rd Foot	
Nehemiah Perry	1st Bn 87th Foot	
Thomas Quirke	2nd Bn 55th Foot	
James Rieley	92nd Foot	
Henry Smith	3rd Dragoon Guards.	
Joseph Taylor	2nd Guards.	
James Turner	25th Light Dragoons	Dyer of Bury.
Sampson Vaughan	Coldstream Guards	

Drummers & Fifers

Samuel Bird	East Middx Militia	
George Gillespie	2nd Bn 28th Foot	
William Krutzlious	2nd & 6th Bn 60th Foot	
John McCormick	96th Foot	

Continued

Patrick Maher/Meagher	43rd Foot	Labourer of Ardfinnan, Tipperary
Daniel Newall/Newbold	3rd Foot Guards	
Nathanial Richmond	54th Foot	
William West	Royal Artillery Drivers	
Roderick McKenzie	101st Foot transferred to 6th Bn 60th then York Chasseurs	

Privates

Thomas Abbott	4th Dragoon Guards	
William Addsetts or John Adsetts	19th Foot	
Jonas Abberton or Alberton	38th Foot	
William Aldridge	3rd Foot Guards	
John Aley	2nd Bn 69th Foot	
James Allen	16th Light Dragoons	
Richard Allen	48th Foot	
William Allen	23rd Light Dragoons	
Alexander Allsop	2nd Bn 24th Foot	
John Arnold	11th Veteran Bn	
Joseph Arnold	Royal Artillery	
James Ashbolt/Ashboult	7th Light Dragoons	Labourer of Hampton
John Bachelor	38th Foot	Weaver of Gloucestershire
William Balston	1st Dragoon Guards	
James Banks	22nd Foot	
Robert Barber	2nd Bn 63rd Foot	
James Barlow	Warwick Militia	Cooper of Fermanagh
Thomas Bates	Royal Artillery Drivers	
Richard Beasley	Coldstream Guards	
William Beck	48th Foot	Sailor or Labourer of Gloucestershire
John Bennett	36th Foot	
Patrick Bennett	44th Foot	
John Birkinshaw/ Berkinshaw	Royal Artillery	
Michael Berry	27th Foot	
James Bishop (Died 30 August 1819)	39th Foot	Labourer of Hampshire.
John Blake	2nd Bn 37th Foot	

Continued

Richard Bourdman/ Boardman/Boarman	Coldstream Guards	
Joseph Boddy	19th Foot	
James Boram or Boran	44th Foot	Labourer of Essex
John Bowden/Bowan/ Bowen	Royal West India Rangers	
Thomas Bowden	26th Foot	
George Bowen/Bowden	3rd Bn 95th Foot	
Martin Bowes	Royal Wagon Train & 32nd Foot	
Michael Boyles/ Boyle/Bayle	73rd Foot	
William Boyles/ Bayless/Baylis	2nd Bn 63rd Foot	
John Brogan	28th Foot	Mountrath, Queen's County.
Edward Brown	43rd Foot.	
Hugh Brown	Royal Scots	
William Brown (1)	Royal Artillery, 10th Light Dragoons, 2nd Foot Guards	Weaver of Fife
William Brown (2)	3rd Guards, 2nd Bn 7th Foot,48th Foot, 50th Foot or 6th Bn 60th	Tailor of York
William Brown (3)	95th Foot.	
Thomas Bull	Royal Marines & General Service Volunteer	
William Burke	46th Foot	
John Burns (1)	1st or 40th Foot	
John Burns (2)	1st or 40th Foot	
John Burns (3)	Transferred from 2nd (Queen's)	
Edward Butterfield	Possibly Home Office convict sent to General Service	
John Byers	Royal Scots	
Thomas Byworth	1st Foot Guards	
Michael Cahill	2nd Bn 43rd Foot	
John Callaghan (1)	7th Dragoons or 2nd Bn 37th Foot	Labourer of Tipperary
John Callaghan (2)	7th Dragoons or 2nd Bn 37th Foot	Shoemaker of Cavan
Angus Cameron	2nd Bn 26th Foot	
Archibald Campbell	2nd Foot Guards	
Daniel Campbell		
James Campbell	1st Bn 21st Foot	

Continued

Martin Campbell	1st Bn 51st Foot	
James Canavan/ Cannavan	27th Foot	
Charles Cantrell	86th Foot	
Daniel Carroll	3rd Foot	
James Carroll	28th Foot	Labourer of Trallee
James Carson	From Isle of Wight Army Depot	
Michael Casey	97th Foot	
Thomas Chamberlain	9th Foot	
Joseph Chambers	2nd Bn 5th Foot	
James Clarke (1)	2nd Bn 9th Foot	Labourer of Cavan
James Clarke (2)		Coalminer of Dudley
William Clements	1st Bn Coldstream Guards	Stone cutter of Bath
George Cliff	Life Guards	
Jeremiah Coakley	97th Foot	
William Cockerill	46th Foot	
John Cockings	16th Foot	
Dennis Coffey	16th Foot	
Thomas Coldridge/ Couldridge	East London Militia	
Thomas Cole	57th Foot	
John Coleman	24th Foot	Baker of Sevenoaks
James/Samuel Collingwood	83rd Foot	
Benjamin Collins	95th Foot	Shoemaker of York
William Collins	66th Foot	
Timothy Connell	54th Foot	
Thomas Connors	87th Foot	
William Conroy/ Connery	76th Foot	
James Cooley	23rd Light Dragoons	
George Cooper	77th Foot	Labourer of Clare
Joseph Copesteak	79th Foot	Labourer of Derby
Thomas Costello (1)	6th Dragoons	Watchmaker of Fermanagh
Thomas Costello (2)	2nd Bn 87th Foot	
William Cottle	2nd Bn 3rd Foot	

Continued

Patrick Coughlin/ Coughlan	2nd Bn 50th Foot	
Thomas Counsell (Died 20 August 1819)	17th Light Dragoons	Labourer of Wicklow
John Cowan (Died 24 August 1819)	2nd Bn 9th Foot	Labourer of Cavan
William Cowan		
Andrew Craig	6th Dragoons Guards	
William Craig.	22nd Dragoons	
David Crandon	2nd Bn 45th Foot	
Daniel Creamer	31st Foot	Labourer of Kilkenny
Hugh Croghan/ Groughan	2nd Bn 38th Foot	
John Croker	2nd Bn 53rd Foot	Dawby, Gloucestershire
William Crooks	Royal Artillery	
Edward Croston	Royals	
John Cubiss	3rd Bn 95th Foot	
William Cullen	99th Foot.	
Peter Curley	2nd Bn 3rd Foot, prison-ship, 2nd Queen's	
Thomas Curtis	48th Foot	From London
Thomas Dale	Labourer of Warwick	
John Dailey/Daily/Daley	1st Bn 5th Foot	
Richard Dalton	34th Foot	
Francis Davey	2nd Bn 73rd Foot	
John Davis/Davies	Either 2nd, 15th, 20th or 95th Foot	Labourer of Monmouth
Daniel Dawson	General Service	
Henry Deadman	2nd Bn 45th Foot.	
William Deaze	3rd Foot Guards.	Cordwainer of Louth
William Dennis	2nd Bn 79th Foot	Labourer of Huntington
John Derrick	25th Foot	
Edward Devlin	13th Foot.	
Charles Devon	1st Bn 2nd Foot.	
John Dix (Discharged 24 September 1819)	Volunteer, 2nd Bn Tower Hamlet Militia.	
John Dixon	68th Foot	
William Dixon	2nd Bn 51st Foot	Labourer of Lincoln
David Donaldson	79th Foot	

Continued

Edward Donnally	46th Foot	Labourer of Longford
John Donnelly	Transferred from 1st European Garrison	
Patrick Donoughoe	2nd Queen's	Labourer of Limerick
Hugh Donovan	2nd Queen's	
John Dorsett	2nd Bn 39th Foot	
John Dovey	14th Light Dragoons	
James Dougherty	1st Foot or 1st Foot Guards	Labourer of Wexford
Peter Dougherty	28th Foot	
John Downs	38th Foot	
Michael Dudley	General Service	
Edward Duffy	1st Foot	
Patrick Dunn	76th Foo	
James Dunnett (Discharged 24 September 1819)	Volunteer, 93rd Foot, 1st Garrison Company	From Caithness
John Dunning	51st Foot	
John Dwyer	5th Dragoon Guards	Carpenter of Dublin
James Elliott	28th or 84th Foot	
Samuel Ellis	40th Foot	
Robert Epworth	Possible Volunteer	From Sheffield
Joseph Erskey	6th Bn 60th Foot	
Thomas Evans (1)	2nd Bn 34th Foot	Labourer of St James, Pembroke
Thomas Evans (2)	2nd Bn 96th Foot	Labourer of Longford
Jacob Fairbrother	51st Foot	
William Falkett/Folkett	23rd Light Dragoons	
James Ferguson	2nd Dragoon Guards	
Samuel Fidler	10th Bn Royal Artillery	Hatter of Chester
Michael Findlay	23rd Light Dragoons	
Bernard Flanaghan	2nd Bn 53rd Foot	
James Fleming	72nd Foot	
John Fleming	45th Foot	Labourer of Middlesex
Edward Flynn	36th Foot	Labouer of Dublin
Michael Flynn		
John Foster (1)	21st Foot	
John Foster (2)	48th Foot	Labourer of Derry
John Fowle	57th Foot	

Continued

John Fox	47th Foot	
Valentine Frier	2nd Queen's	
Thomas Fulford	16th Foot	
Joseph Fuller	8th Bn Royal Artillery	
John Gallagher	Royals, Royal Artillery or 2nd Bn 3rd Foot Guards	
Michael Galvin	1st Bn 40th Foot (at Waterloo)	Labourer of Tipperary
George Gardiner	33rd Foot	
Edward Garrathy	2nd Bn 87th Foot	Labourer of Clare
Edward Garry	ex-Royal Marine and volunteer	
James Garvin (Discharged 24 September 1819)	Royal Artillery or 3rd Bn 14th Foot	
Robert Gee	1st Bn Royal Scots	
Peter Gilchrist	1st Bn 58th or 1st Bn Guards	
Dennis Gingley	2nd Bn 47th Foot	
Samuel Gladdon	2nd Bn 44th Foot	Labourer of Harlow
Richard Goodall	Royal Artillery	
Andrew Goodfellow	Royal Horse Artillery	
John Gordon	1st Bn 20th Foot	
John Gradwell	Royal Artillery Drivers	Frame Work Knitter of Argyle
Peter Grady	28th Foot	
Robert Graham	9th Light Dragoons	
Thomas Graham	68th Foot	
James Griffiths	23rd Foot	
Robert Griffiths	92nd Foot	
Thomas Griffiths	Royal Artillery Drivers	
William Griffiths (1)	General Service Recruit or 2nd Bn 50th Foot	
William Griffiths (2)	36th Foot	
Timothy Grindwick	23rd Light Dragoons.	
John Hacking	3rd Bn Royal Artillery	Weaver of Lancashire
John Hall	103rd Foot	Tailor of Staffordshire
Miles Hall	16th Dragoons	Labourer of Dublin
George Hamilton	6th Bn 60th Foot	Carpenter of Dungannon or Labourer of Tyrone
John Hammersley	83rd Foot	
James Hamrough	66th Foot	
Joseph Handley/Hanley	2nd Bn 38th Foot	

Continued

John Harrison/Hannington		2nd Bn 2nd Guards
William Hartshorn	14th & 32nd Foot	
Thomas Hawkins	89th Foot	
Robert Hay	25th Foot	
Thomas Hayes	88th Foot	
Joseph Hazledine	63rd Foot recruit	
John Heals		
John Heath	19th Light Dragoons	Tailor of Louth
Thomas Henry	25th Light Dragoons	
Joseph Hewitt	2nd Foot Guards	
George Hill	25th Foot	Labourer of Antrim
Richard Hilsey/Hilsay	Transferred from 1st European Garrison	
William Hodkin	1st Foot Guards	
Edward Hoffer	32nd Foot	Of Routh, Somerset
Dennis Hogan	13th Foot	
John Hollister	1st Bn Tower Hamlets Militia volunteer	
Joseph Holly/Haley	5th Foot	Labourer of Kildare
Robert Hope	1st Foot or 1st Foot Guards	Labourer of Northumberland
John Horan	21st Foot	
Frederick Hosche/Osche	8th Bn 60th Foot	
Terence Houghey	Royal Artillery	
Samuel Howard	2nd Bn 34th Foot	Shoemaker of Warrington
Richard Hughes	7th Hussars	Blacksmith of Great Ness, Shropshire
Peter Humble	2nd Bn 7th Foot	
James Humphries	63rd Foot	Labourer of Kerry
John Hunter	14th Light Dragoons	
Alexander Hutchinson	3rd Bn 14th Foot	
Thomas Hutchinson	4th Royal Veteran Bn	Tailor of Roxborough
Henry Ingram	81st Foot	A West Indian
Thomas Irwin	6th Bn 60th Foot	
Samuel Jackson	2nd Bn 24th Foot	Frame Work Knitter of Nottingham
William Jackson	11th Dragoons	
John Johnson	78th Foot	Labourer of Kildare
Thomas Johnson	4th Dragoons	

Continued

John Jones	Either 4th, 5th, 56th Foot or Royal Sappers and Miners	Weaver of Skerkin
David Jones	General Service	
Thomas Jones	Royal Marines & 15th Foot Volunteer	Clerk of Gloucestershire
Edward Jordan	21st Foot	
John Jordan (1)	4th Dragoon Guards or 2nd Foot	Labourer of Armargh
John Jordan (2)	4th Dragoon Guards or 2nd Foot	Labour of Chester
Richard Joyce	51st Foot	
James Kane	55th Foot or 6th Dragoons	
Thomas Kane	50th Foot	
John Kearney	58th Foot	Bleacher of Derry
Philip Keep/ William Keipe	Transferred from 1st European Garrison	
John Kelly	Either 26th, 61st or 2nd Grenadier Guards	Shoemaker of Castle Dermont, Kildare
Jonathan Kelly	38th Foot	
George Kendall	2nd Dragoon Guards or 2nd Foot	
Thomas Kenny	23rd Foot	Tailor of Roscommon
John Kenyon	2nd Bn 43rd Foot	
William Kindler	1st Bn 95th Foot	Weaver Of County Down
James King	Royal Artillery Drivers	
Richard King	Guards	
Joseph Kirby	19th Foot	
William Kirkman	77th Foot	
John Knott	34th Foot	Labourer of Kent
John Lacey	88th Foot	
William Lane	23rd Light Dragoons	Labourer of Gloucestershire
Peter Lanaghan	95th Foot	
Joseph Latiene	7th Line Bn, King's GermanLegion 6th Bn 60th Foot	Labourer of Tornau, Hungary
William Lawrence	83rd Foot	
John Lax, Lay or Lan	24th Foot	
Charles Leach	55th Foot	
James Leadbeater/Leadbetter		

Continued

Joseph or James Ledger	4th Bn Royals	
Andrew Lee	99th Foot.	
James Lee	56th & 2nd Foot	Labourer of King's County
Thomas Lee	85th Foot	
George Learoyd/Laroyd	84th Foot	Labourer of Yorkshire
William Letts	2nd Bn 63rd Foot.	
James Logue	21st Foot	
Thomas Lowe	1st Bn 1st Guards	
John Lupton	33rd Foot	
Thomas Lurcook	50th Foot	
William Lusty (Discharged 24 September 1819)	2nd Bn Tower Hamlets Militia	
Francis Lynch	16th Foot	
Joseph or Joshua Lyons	10th Foot	
John McCann	1st Foot	Labourer of Donegal
John McCarthy (1)	44th Foot or 1st Garrison Bn	
John McCarthy (2)	44th Foot or 1st Garrison Bn	Labourer of Armagh.
John McCasland/ MaCasland	Royals	
Michael McConnell	87th Foot Recruit	
Bernard McCormick	6th Bn 60th Foot	Labourer of Fermanagh
Patrick McCormick	90th Foo	Labourer of Mayo
Owen McCourt	40th Foot	
Patrick McCue	90th Foot	Labourer of Fermanagh
Angus McDonald	79th Foot	
Archibald McDonald	79th Foot	
Charles McDonald	79th Foot	
David McDonald	79th Foot	
John McDonald (1)	28th or 2nd Bn 71st Foot	Labourer of Roscommon
John McDonald (2)	28th or 2nd Bn 71st Foot	
William McDougall	70th Foot	Labourer of Sheerness
Manus McFadden	19th Foot	Labourer of Donegal
Edward McGeary	6th Dragoons	Labourer of Dublin
Peter McGingley	1st Foot	
James McGovern		

Continued

John McKane	6th Foot	
Donald McKay	Aberdeen Militia	
Peter McKenna	25th Foot	
Hugh McKever	5th Dragoon Guards	
Samuel McLeary	6th Bn 60th Foot	Weaver of Armagh
Duncan McLaughlin	91st Foot	
James McLaughlin	89th Foot	
David McLeod	2nd Bn 72nd Foot	
John McMahon	6th or 32nd Foot	
Hugh McMahon	General Service	Labourer of Tyrone
John McNally (1)	84th Foot	
John McNally/McNulty	85th Foot	
James McNespie	74th Foot	
Bernard McStravick/ McStaverick	1st Foot or 1st Foot Guards	From Ireland
Thomas McWade	16th Foot	Labourer of Armagh
John Madras/ Madrass	51st Foot	Pocket book maker of Leeds
William Mann	55th Foot	
Bernard Martin	32nd Foot	
William Mason	55th Foot	
John Masters/ Masterman	1st Bn 83rd Foot	Calico printer of Dublin
George Mathews	2nd Bn Foot Guards	
John Maycock	54th Foot	Labourer of Renfrew
Sampson Meigh	2nd Bn 52nd Foot	Hatter of Stafford
William Melsome	1st European Garrison Company volunteer	
Thomas Mercer/Murcer	2nd Bn 73rd Foot	
John Merchant	2nd Bn 52nd Foot	Labourer of Ashford
John Millage	55th Foot	Labourer of Bath
William Mills	4th Foot.	
William Mist	2nd Bn 62nd Foot	
Donald Mitchell	25th Foot	
Hugh Mitchel	1st European Garrison Company volunteer	
John Mitchell	20th Light Dragoons or 3rd Foot	
Edward Mooney	General Service	
James Mooney/Moody	15th Hussars	
Philip Moore	86th Foot	

Continued

Robert Morehead	Foot Guards	
Daniel Morgan	28th Foot	
Michael Morris	Royal Horse Artillery	
Thomas Morrissey	18th or 46th Foot	
George Morrison/ Morrow	6th Bn 60th Foot	
John Mosely	2nd Bn 81st Foot	
Samuel Moulds	Royal Artillery	
Thomas Mullins	38th Foot	
Thomas Mulveany	32nd Foot	Labourer of Dublin
Andrew Murphy	87th Foot	
Hugh Murphy	25th Foot	
Timothy Murphy	16th Foot	Labourer of Kerry
William Murphy	88th Foot	
James Murray	59th or 2nd Bn 91st Foot	Cotton spinner of Nottingham
James Nash	101st Foot. Volunteer	Faversham, Kent
Samuel Nash	2nd Queen's	
Henry Newbury	2nd Bn 59th Foot	
James Nicholls	19th Light Dragoons	
John Nicholls	91st Foot	
Joseph Noble	32nd Foot	Labourer of Bath
John Norman. (1)	2nd Bn 37th Foot.	
John Norman (2)	1st European Garrison volunteer	
John Northan	Coldstream Guards	
Charles Nowland	6th Bn 60th Foot	Labourer of Dublin
Stephen Nulty	53rd Foot	Labourer of Roscommon
Timothy Oakley	1st Foot Guards	Jeweller of Ford, Salop
David Ogilvie	Royal Artillery	
Dennis O'Laughlin	16th Foot	
Isaac Oram	1st European Garrison volunteer	
Alexander Orloff	6th Bn 60th Foot	
John Osborn	Rifle Brigade	
William Osgood	North Hants Militia	Weaver of Hampshire
William Palmer	11th Light Dragoons	Labourer of Oxford
Richard Parker	101st Foot	
James Parland	22nd Foot	

Continued

Robert Parsons	3rd Foot Guards	
William Pavey/Perry	1st Guards	
Robert Payne	Royal Horse Artillery	
John Peachee	Coldstream Guards	
John Pearce	2nd Bn 14th Foot	Labourer of Wolverhampton
Robert Pearson	2nd Bn 67th Foot	
Edward Perry	2nd Bn 23rd Foot	
William Peters	2nd Bn 23rd Foot	
William Philpot(t)	Royal Artillery	
Thomas Plymouth	Corporal volunteer, 6th Foot	
John Pollard	2nd Bn 9th Foot	
John Power	2nd Bn 59th Foot	
Benjamin Pratt	3rd Dragoons	Weaver of Stafford
Joseph Pratt	Kilkenny Militia	Weaver of Limerick
William Prenderville	97th Foot	Labourer of Kerry
James Prentice	Royal Artillery	
William Price	2nd Bn 53rd Foot	
William Quigley	72nd Foot	
Thomas Quirk	85th Foot	
William Ralph/Rolph	36th Foot	
James Ramsey	74th Foot	From Scotland
Simon Rands	2nd Bn 83rd Foot	
John Ratcliff	55th Foot	
John Raybold (Died 20 August 1819)	22nd Light Dragoons.	Coach painter of Middlesex
Michael Rease	19th Light Dragoons	
Mathew Reddings	17th Foot	
John Reinstruck	2nd Guards.	
Benjamin Rhodes (Died 17 August 1819)	77th Foot	Labourer of Leeds
James Richardson	23rd Light Dragoons	
Richard Richardson	29th Foot	Labourer of Lancashire
William Richardson	Royal Artillery Drivers	Weaver of Cumberland
Peter Rieley	2nd Bn 18th Foot	
Thomas Rieley	32nd Foot	
William Rippen/Rippon	Royal Artillery	

Continued

John Roach	54th Foot	Labourer of Wexford
Thomas Roberts	90th Foot	Labourer of Down
Henry Robinson	73rd Foot	Frame work knitter of Nottinghamshire
James Robinson	Royals or 47th Foot	Weaver of Lancashire
Walter Robinson	2nd 79th Foot	
Mathew Robson	1st Bn 95th Foot.	Dyer of Northumberland
James Roffey/Ruffey	2nd Bn 73rd Foot	
John Rudd	Labourer of Queen's County	
John Sanderson	2nd Bn 53rd Foot	Labourer of Yorkshire
Thomas Saunders/ Sanders	2nd Bn 5th Foot	
George Savin	37th Foot	
William Scott	65th Foot	Either sailor of Burton or labourer of Boston
Peter Scully	33rd Foot	Labourer of Armagh
James Seed	Royal Artillery Drivers	
Benjamin Shaw	19th Light Dragoons	
Joseph Shaw	84th Foot	Labourer of Lancashire
Richard Sherrott/ Sherriott/Sharratt	2nd Bn 6th Foot	
Joseph Singleton	77th Foot	Labourer of Cork
Abraham Slack	1st Bn 55th Foot	(Died 14 Sptember 1819)
John Slade	4th Foot	Shoemaker of Somerset
James Slattery	95th Foot	Frame work knitter of Limerick
John Sleath	48th Foot	Baker of London
John Smit. (1)	13th Foot	Frame work knitter of Leicestershire
John Smith (2)	2nd Bn 88th Foot	Clerk of Cornhill, Middlesex
John Smith (3)	1st Foot or 1st Foot Guard	Labourer of Tavistock
Stephen Smith	76th Foot	From Ireland
Thomas Smith (1)	South Lincolnshire Militia, 56th or 61st Foot	Glazier of Middlesex
Thomas Smith (2)	South Lincolnshire Militia, 56th or 61st Foot	Cabinet maker of Suffolk
Thomas Smith (3)	39th Foot	Labourer of Gloucestershire
William Smith (1)	59th Foot	Tailor of St Mary's, Dublin
William Smith (2)	General Service	Labourer of Northampton

Continued

William Smith (3)	3rd Foot Guards	Labourer of Warwick
Thomas Smithson	71st Foot	
James Snoxall	2nd Bn 5th Foot	
Samuel Spearing	23rd Light Dragoons	Labourer of Nottinghamshire
Joseph Spencer	67th Foot	
John Spinks	Royal Wagon Train	Gunsmith of Warwick
James Starr	West Essex Militia	
Richard Stephenson/ Stevenson/Stevens	62nd Foot	
James Stewart	1st Bn 79th Foot	Labourer of Perth
Thomas Stewart	70th Foot	Iron founder
George Stokes	9th Foot	
Michael Stokes (Discharged 24 September 1819)	General Service Recruit volunteer	
John Sullivan (1)	16th or 37th Foot	Labourer of Killarney
John Sullivan (2)	29th Foot	Nailer of Cork
Maurice Sullivan	2nd Bn 62nd Foot	Butcher of Limerick
Timothy Sullivan	96th Foot	Tailor of Kerry
Henry Summers		
William Summers	33rd & 101st Foot	Weaver of Lancashire
Thomas Tamblyn	67th Foot	Labourer of Cornwall
Charles Taylor	15th Hussars/Light Dragoons	
James Taylor	1st Foot Guards	
Robert Taylor	2nd Dragoon Guards	Weaver of Ratcliffe.
Thomas Taylor	61st Foot or Royal Wagon Train	Labourer of Gloucestershire
William Taylor	7th Light Dragoons	
Peter Tennant	1st Bn 55th Foot	
Daniel Thomas	Royal Artillery Drivers	
William Thompson (1)	86th Foot	Labourer of Cavan
William Thompson (2)	30th Foot	Rope maker of Carlow
William Thorn	3rd Dragoons	Engineer of Warwick
William Thorp/Thorpe	77th Foot	
Michael Tindall	70th Foot	
Peter Toole	12th Foot	Nailer of Wicklow
Isaac Trimby	10th Foot	
John Trimnell	28th Foot	

Continued

James Trueman	53rd Foot	
John Tucker	Royal Wagon Train	
Robert Tunnage	Western Bn, Essex Militia	Labourer of Essex
George Turner	Royal Artillery	
George Turvey	55th Foot	Labourer of Beverley
Abraham Usile	15th Foot	
Thomas Vennor/Venner	16th Dragoons	
Richard Vidian	2nd Bn 95th Foot	
John Walker	1st Bn 3rd Guards or 49th Foot	
Joseph Walmsley	34th Foot	
George Walsh	Royal Artillery	
Joseph Walter		
Robert Ward	63rd Foot	
Samuel Warne	2nd Bn 62nd Foot	Bricklayer of Suffolk
Charles Waterman	2nd Bn 67th Foot	Whitesmith or mason of Sheerness
George Watson	2nd Dragoons	
Henry Watts	2nd Bn 3rd Dragoons	
Daniel Weaver	11th Light Dragoons	Miner of Cheadle, Staffordshire
James Weir	26th Foot	Sawyer of Lanark
William Wennol/Warner	51st Foot	
Ralph West	6th Bn 60th Foot	
James Whatmore/ Watmore/Wheatmore	Royal Artillery Drivers	
George Wheatley (Discharged 24 September 1819)	2nd Bn Tower Hamlets Militia volunteer	
Robert Wheeler	15th Foot.	
Richard Wheeler	1st Bn 67th Foot	
John White	19th Dragoons	
Joseph Whitely	Staff Corps	Coachmaker of York
Robert Whitfield/ Whitefield	2nd Bn 71st Foot	
John Whitehead	Royal Horse Artillery	
John Wilcox	34th Foot	
John Wilkinson	29th Foot	Labourer of Yorkshire
James Williams	48th Foot	Labourer of Mayo
Henry Willey	6th Bn 60th Foot	Labourer of Brunswick

Continued

William Wilson (1)	Royal Horse Artillery, West Kent Militia, 42nd or 2nd Bn 64th Foot	Butcher or labourer of Kerry
William Wilson (2)	71st & 90th Foot	Weaver of Ayr
William Winskill	4th Bn Royals	
John Woodhouse	7th Foot	
John Worthy	Royal Artillery Drivers	
Benjamin Wright	3rd Dragoons	Labourer of Kent
John Wright	2nd Bn 14th or Royal Artillery	
Joseph Wright	85th Foot	
William Wright	63rd Foot	Gardener of Witham, Essex
George Yates	Royal Artillery	
William Yates	Royal Horse Artillery	
James Young.	Royal Artillery Drivers	
James Yund	55th Foot	

Bibliography

Anderson, Joseph. C.B., K.H. Lieutenant Colonel. *The Recollections of a Peninsular Veteran*. Edward Arnold. (1913)

Ascoli, David. *A Companion to the British Army*. Harrap, London. (1983)

Barty-King, Hugh. *The Drum*. The Royal Tournament, Horse Guards, London.

Elliott, Bruce S, Walker, Dan & Stratford-Devai, Fawn. *Men of Upper Canada Militia Nominal Rolls 1828–1829*. Toronto Ontario Genealogical Society.

Buckley, Roger Norman. *The British Army in the West Indies. Society and the Military in the Revolutionary Age*. University Press of Florida. (1998)

Buckley, Roger Norman. *Slaves in Redcoats. The British West India Regiments, 1795–1815*. New Haven and London Yale University Press. (1979)

Campbell, Charles. *The Intolerable Hulks. British Shipboard Confinement 1776–1857*. Heritage Books, Maryland. (1994)

Cannon, Richard. *Historic Records of the British Army. The Second Dragoon Guards*. London. (1837)

Chartrand, Rene and Chappell, Paul. *British Forces in the West Indies 1793–1815*. Osprey. (1996)

Claver, Scott. *Under the Lash. A History of Corporal Punishment in the British Armed Forces*. Torchstream Books, London. (1954)

Cooke, John. *A True Soldier Gentleman. The memoirs of Lt. John Cooke 1791–1813*. Edited by Eileen Hathaway. Shinglepicker, Swanage. (2000)

Costello, Edward. *The True Story of a Peninsular War Rifleman*. (Ed. Eileen Hathaway) Shinglepicker, Swanage. (1994)

Cunliffe, Barry and Garratt, Beverley. *Excavations at Portchester Castle. Vol V. Post Medieval 1609–1819*. Society of Antiquaries, London. (1994)

Dupin, Sir Charles. *Tour through Naval and military Establishment of Great Britain in the Years 1816–17–18–9 & 1820*.

Ellis, Major A. B. *The History of the First West India Regiment*. Chapman and Hall, London. (1885)

Esdale, Charles. *The Peninsular War*. Penguin Books. (2003)

Fyler, A. E. Colonel. *The History of the 50th. The Queen's Own Regiment*. Chapman and Hall. (1895)

Gould, Robert. W. *British Campaign Medals. Waterloo to the Gulf.* Arms and Armour. (1994)

Hamilton, Anthony. Sergeant. *Hamilton's Campaign with Moore and Wellington during the Peninsular War*. Troy, N. Y. Press of Prescott & Wilson. (1847) Republished by Spellmount, Staplehurst. (1998)

Hamilton, Robert. *The Duties of a Regimental Surgeon Considered*. (1787)

Harris, Benjamin. *A Dorset Rifleman*. (Ed. Eileen Hathaway) Shinglepicker, Swanage. (1995)

Haythornthwaite, Philip J. *The Armies of Wellington*. Arms and Armour. (1994)

Holloway, Roger. *The Queen's Own Royal West Kent Regiment*. Lee Cooper. (1973)

Holmes, Richard. *Redcoat. The British Soldier in the age of Horse and Musket*. HarperCollins. (2001)

Hughes, Robert. *The Fatal Shore*. Pan Books. (1998)

Lambriere, William. *Practical Observations on the diseases of the Army in Jamaica as occurred between the years 1792–1797*. Longman & Rees. (1799)

Levinge, Sir Richard George Augustus. *Historical Records of the Forty-Third Regiment, Monmouthshire Light Infantry*. W. Clowes & Sons, London. (1868)

Livingston, Mildred R. *Lanark, Perth & Richmond Military Settlement. Vol 2. Census & Assessment. 1817–1822*. Edwin A Livingstone. (June 1987)

Lockwood, Glenn J. *Beckwith: Irish and Scottish Identities in a Canadian Community 181–1991*. Corporation of the Township of Beckwith. (1991)

Lyon, David. *The Sailing Navy List. All the Ships of the Royal Navy – Built, Purchased and Captured 1688–1860*. Conway Maritime Press. (1993)

Marshall, Henry &Tullock, Alexander M. *Statistical Report on the Sickness, Mortality, & Invaliding among the Troops in the West Indies*. Clowes & Son. (1838)

Marshall, Henry. F.R.S.E. *Military Miscellany: A History of the Army, Military Punishments*. John Murray, London. (1846)

Morris, Thomas. *The Recollections of Sergeant Morris*. (Ed. John Selby) Windrush Press, Gloucs. (1967)

Napier, Sir Charles. *Treatise on Military Law*. (1837)

Page, F. C. G. Brigadier. *Following the Drum. Women in Wellington's Wars*. André Deutsh, London. (1986)

Palmer, Roy (Ed.) *The Rambling Soldier*, London (1977)

Partridge, Richard & Oliver, Michael. *Napoleonic Army Hndbook:. The British Army and Her Allies*. Constable, London. (1999)

Pinkard, George. *Notes on the West Indies*. London. Balwin, Craddock & Joy & LB Seeley. (1816)

Sergeant, Robert & Miller, J R Ernest. *Census Records for Lanark County*. Kingston Branch Onterio Genealogical Society. (1987)

Shipp, J. *The Memoirs of John Shipp*; modern edn, published as *The Path of Glory* Shanks, C. J.(Ed.) London (1969)

Sir N. Cantlie. *Lieutenant General. A History of the Army Medical Department*. (2 Vols, 1974) Vol 1. Churchill & Livingston.

The Military General Service Roll, 1793–1814. Mullen, A. L. T. (Ed.) London Stamp Exchange. (1990)

White, Colonel A. C.T. *The Story of Army Education. 1643–1963*. Harrap. (1963)

Wheeler, William. *The Letters of Private William Wheeler 1809–1828*. (Ed. Liddell-Hart) Windrush Press. (1999)

Wicks, H. L. *Regiments of Foot: A Historical Record of all Foot Regiments of the British Army*. Osprey. (1974)

Wilson, John. *Memoirs of West Indian Fever; constituting brief notices regarding the treatment, origin, and the nature of the disease commonly called yellow fever*. London; Burgess and Hill. (1827)

Winstock, Lewis. *Songs & Music of the Redcoats. 1642–1902*. Leo Cooper, London. (1970)

Newpapers
Bathurst Courier, Perth Courier, Hampshire Chronical, Hampshire Telegraph and Sussex Chronicle, Quebec Gazette, Quebec Mercury, The Times

Periodicals and Journals
Annual Register (1803), *London Gazette* (September 1815),

Atkinson C.T. 'A Peninsular Veteran. Letter of Major General Sir F P Robinson. K.C.B. Dealing with the Campaign of 1813'. *JSAHR*. (Vol XXXIV, 1956)

Buckley, Roger Norman. 'The Destruction of the British Army in the West Indies. 1793–1815. A Medical History'. *JSAHR*. (1956) No 226. (Summer 1978)

Dickins Bruce. 'Merchantmen of War in Nelson's Day'. *Mariner's Mirror*. (Vol 53) 1963.

Goulden. R. J. 'Deserter Bounty Certificates'. *JSAHR*. (1972)

Haggard, Denis. The Last Fight for Napolean. Journal Society Army Historical Research. No 56. (Winter 1935)

Hart's Army Lists

Jones K. R. 'Richard Cox, Army Agent and Banker'. *JSAHR*. Vol XXXIV, (1956)

Jones K. R. 'Cox and Co.: Craig's Court: The Nineteenth Century'. *JSAHR*. Vol XL, (1962)

Lines Peter and Dr Maxwell-Stewart, Hamish. 'John Longworth's Story: The Caribbean and the Penal Station Complex'. *Australian Cultural History* (2002)

Maxwell-Stewart, Hamish. 'The Rise and Fall of John Longworth: Work and Punishment in Early Port Arthur. Exiles of Empire'. *Tasmanian Historical Studies*. Vol 6 No 2 (1999)

Senior, Terry. *Colonel Eugene Edouard Boyer de Peireleau*. (Unpublished)

Turner J. D. 'Army Agency'. *JSAHR*. Vol XIII, (1934)

Miscellaneous
Lanark County Land Office Records. Almonte, Onterio.

Notes

Complete citations of sources only for the first occurrence, all subsequent references abbreviated.

HT – *Hampshire Telegraph and Sussex Chronicle.*
TNA – The National Archives.
HC – *Hampshire Chronical*
NAC – National Archives of Canada, Ottawa.

1   Harris Benjamin. *A Dorset Rifleman* (Ed Eileen Hathaway) Shinglepicker Publications, Swanage. (1995) p107.
2   *Hampshire Telegraph and Sussex Chronicle*. Monday, 12 December 1803.
3   *Annual Register* (1803) pp664-5.
4   *HT*. Monday, 12 December 1803.
5   Shipp, John. *The Memoirs of John Shipp.* (9th, 16th, 22nd, 34th, 55th and 65th Regiment of Foot – experimental regiments recruited from boys 13 to 18 years of age).
6   Harris ,Benjamin. *A Dorset Rifleman.*
7   Costello, Edward. *The True Story of a Peninsular War Rifleman* (Ed Eileen Hathaway) Shinglepicker Publications (1994).
8   Morris, Thomas. *The Recollections of Sergeant Morris* (Ed John Selby) Windrush Press, Gloucs (1967)
9   Wheeler, William. *The Letters of Private William Wheeler 1809-1828* (Ed Liddell-Hart, B.H) Windrush Press (1999).
10 Small island off Dakar, French West Senegal providing the centre for the West Africa slave trade.
11 TNA. WO1/637. p149. John Graham/Home Office. 8 January 1808.
12 TNA. WO1/638. Eleazor le Leachant/Lieut General Doyle. 16 May 1808.
13 TNA. WO1/638. Lieut General Doyle/Horse Guards 20 May 1808.
14 *The Times*. 12 March 1812.
15 TNA. WO3/51. Commander in Chief to General Officers. 21 August 1810.
16 Dupin, Sir Charles. *Tour through the Naval and military Establishments of Great Britain in the Years 1816-17-18-19 and 1820.*
17 TNA. WO3/361. Commander in Chief/Regimental Officers. 31 October 1812.
18 TNA. WO3/327. War Office Out Letters. 13 November 1813.
19 TNA. WO3/365. Commander in Chief's Letters to Regimental Officers. 16 December 1813.
20 Formed after the capture of the India Ocean sugar colonies of the Isle of Bourbon and Mauritius, the rank and file being principally composed of ex-sugar plantation slaves. Served primarily on Barbados until amalgamated into the 1st West India Regiment April 1816.
21 TNA. WO4/717. Regimental Establishment Letter Book. 24 November 1813.
22 TNA. WO25/2263. Casualty Returns for the York Chasseurs. 1814–1817.
23 *HT*. Monday, 19 December 1814.
24 TNA. WO25/2263. Casualty Returns for the York Chasseurs. 1814–1817.
25 TNA. WO1/659. Variations in Establishment. 15 June 1814.
26 Lieutenant Colonel Joseph Anderson. *Recollections of a Peninsular Veteran*. Edward Arnold. (1913).
27 TNA. WO25/2263. Casualty Returns. 1814–1817.
28 TNA. WO27/135. Inspection Report, St Vincent. 6 November 1815.
29 Ibid.
30 TNA. WO3/66. C in C to General Officer Commanding at Barbados. 29 January 1817.
31 TNA. WO90/1 Judge Advocate General's Records. General and Regimental Courts-Martial Abroad. 1796–1825.
32 *Hampshire Chronicle*. Saturday, 27 June 1801.

33 Sixth Rate 28 gun frigate. en flute (a vessel of war, carrying only part of her armament, to serve as a transport) Built at Sandgate, Kent 1782 and launched 25 November 1783. Employed mainly on troop carrying duties to the Mediterranean. Hulked as a prison-ship 1804, sold 1817.

34 Built at Deptford, London in 1797 as an armed transport. With a total length of 109 feet, beam 31 feet and a complement of 33 men Buffalo was purchased while still on the stocks and launched 3 November 1797. Hulked as a military prison-ship 1809 and sold 1817.

35 Combatant Class sloop, length 120 feet, beam 28 feet and with a ships complement of 120 men. Variously described as gun vessel or sloop. Launched 1804 and hulked as a military prison-ship 1814.

36 *HT*. Monday 11th September, 1815.

37 TNA. WO3/162. Commander in Chief/Secretary at War. 7 September 1816.

38 Ibid.

39 *HT*. Monday, 16 November, 1812.

40 *HT*. Monday 11 October, 1813.

41 *HT*. Monday 16 September, 1811.

42 TNA. WO12/12962. Pay and Muster Lists. Portchester Castle, 1817.

43 TNA. WO3/64. Commander-in-Chief/Major General Gordon. Isle of Wight. 17 November 1815.

44 Ibid.

45 Ibid.

46 Ibid.

47 TNA. WO3/64. Commander-in-Chief/Major General Gordon. Isle of Wight. 23 December 1815.

48 *HT*. Monday, 30 June, 1817.

49 TNA. WO3/163. C-in-C to Secretary-at-War. 5 November 1817.

50 TNA. WO12/12963.

51 Over the Hills and Far Away.

52 TNA. WO27/141. Inspection Report. 5 April 1817– 17 February 1818.

53 Ibid.

54 Ibid.

55 Ibid.

56 TNA.WO12/11581. Muster Book and Pay Lists of the York Chasseurs. 1817– 1819.

57 TNA. CO318/51 Lieutenant General Sir James Leith/Colonial Office. 11 February 1816.

58 *The Times*. Wednesday, 14 June, 1815.

59 Group of islands of the southwest tip of Guadeloupe with a total area of approximately 5 square miles, the two largest islands being Terre de Bas and Terre de Haut.

60 TNA. CO318/51. Captain Moody/Lieutenant General Sir James Leith. HMS Crescent off Guadeloupe, 13 May 1815.

61 Ibid.

62 Ibid.

63 Ibid.

64 *The Times*. 1 September 1815. Extraordinary and Imperial Gazette of Point-a-Petre.

65 Ibid.

66 Ibid

67 TNA. WO318/51. Durham/ Leith. H.M.S. Venerable off Guadeloupe. 19 June, 1815.

68 TNA. CO318/51. Dispatch to Earl Bathurst from Lieutenant General Sir James Leith. Basse-terre. 12 August, 1815.

69 Ibid.

70 Ibid.

71 Ibid.

72 Ibid.

73 TNA. WO17/297. War Office Monthly Returns, 1815.

74 TNA. WO25/2263. Casualty Returns of NCOs, Drummers & Privates of the York Chasseurs. 1814–1817.

75 *HT*. Monday 17 September, 1804.

76 Senior, Terry. J. *Colonel Eugene-Edouard Boyer de Peireleau*. (Unpublished).

77 *The Times*. 13th March,1816.

78 Ibid.

79 Ibid.

80 Marshall, Henry and Tullock, Alexander M. *Statistical Report on the Sickness, Mortality, and Invaliding among the Troops in the West Indies*. London: Clowes and Son (1838).

81 *The Spanish Bride*.

82 Marshall, Henry and Tullock, Alexander M. *Statistical Report on the Sickness and Invaliding*.

83 TNA. WO27/128. Six Monthly Inspection Report. 9 May, 1814.

84 National Archives of Canada, Ottawa.

85   *HT*. 22 June 1807.
86   *HT*. November 25 1811.
87   *HT*. 23 January 1815.
88   TNA. WO25/227. Six Monthly Inspection Report. 2nd Battalion 95th Foot. 1813– 1814.
89   TNA. WOI3/67. Six Monthly Inspection Report. 1 May 1817.
90   TNA. WO25/2263.
91   TNA. WO25/2263. Casualty Returns. 1814–1817.
92   TNA. WO3/67. Half-Yearly Inspection Report. 23 January 1818.
93   Lampriere, William. *Practical observations on the diseases of the Army in Jamaica as they occurred between the years 1792–1797*. London. Longman & Rees (1799).
94   Marshall Henry. Tullock Alexander. *Statistical Report on the Sickness and Invaliding*.
95   TNA. WO27/141. Inspection Report. 5 April 181– 17 February 1818.
96   Marshal & Tullock. *Statistical Report on Sickness and Invaliding*.
97   *The Times*. Thursday 28 April 1814.
98   A Peninsular Veteran. Letter of Major General Sir F P Robinson. K.C.B. Dealing with the Campaign of 1813. Journal of the Society for Army Historical Research. (Vol XXXIV, 1956) p168. Edited by C.T. Atkinson.
99   *HT*. 20 September 1813.
100 *Times*. Thursday, 28 April 1814.
101 *Times*. Wednesday, 21 June 1815.
102 TNA. WO3/371. Commander in Chief to Regimental Officers. 29 September 1815.
103 TNA. WO3/337. Commander in Chief to Regimental Officers. 15 March 1817.
104 Anderson, Joseph. *Recollections of a Peninsular Veteran*. p75.
105 TNA. WO3/368. Commander in Chief/Regimental Officers. 7 December 1814.
106 *Times*. Monday, 17 November 1817.
107 TNA. WO3/365. Commander in Chief to Regimental Officers. 4 March 1814.
108 TNA. WO91/1. Judge Advocate General Court's Martial. February 1814 – June 1815.
109 Ibid.
110 TNA. WO91/10. Judge Advocate General's Office. General Courts Martial. January 1817– January 1819.
111 Ibid.
112 TNA. WO3/387. Commander in Chief to Regimental Officers. 21 June 1819.
113 TNA. WO3/370. Commander in Chief/Regimental Officers, 15 June 1815.
114 Anderson, Lieutenant Colonel Joseph. *Recollections of a Peninsular Veteran*. p75.
115 Ibid.
116 Hughes, Robert. *The Fatal Shore*. Pan Books. (1988). p480.
117 TNA. WO12/11581. Muster Book and Pay List. 1817 – 1819.
118 Lines, Peter and Maxwell-Stewart, Dr Hamish. *John Longworth's Story: The Caribbean and the Penal Station Complex. Australian Cultural History* (2002). pp 41- 49.
119 Ibid.
120 Ibid.
121 Ibid.
122 Ibid.
123 Ibid.
124 Ibid.
125 Ibid.
126 Ibid.
127 TNA. WO3/65. C-in-C to General Officers.
128 TNA. HO42/151. Home Office Records. Dublin Castle. April 1816.
129 TNA. HO30/5 Home Office Records. Whitehall. 11 May 1816.
130 TNA. WO3/65. C-in-C to General Officers. Horse Guards. 10 August 1816.
131 TNA WO89/4. Judge Advocate General Orders. General Regimental Courts Martial. 1813–1819.
132 Ibid.
133 TNA. WO25/2969. Effects to the Next of Kin.
134 Hamilton, Sergeant Anthony. *Hamilton's Campaign with Moore and Wellington During the Peninsular War*. Published by Prescott & Wilson. Troy. New York. (1847) Re-published by Spellmount Limited, Staplehurst, Kent (1998).
135 Hamilton, Sergeant Anthony. *Hamilton's Campaign with Moore and Wellington During the Peninsular War*. Published by Prescott & Wilson. Troy. New York. (1847) Re-published by Spellmount Limited, Staplehurst, Kent (1998). p14.
136 Ibid p 47.
137 Ibid. p68.
138 Ibid p81/82.

139 Ibid p88
140 Ibid p93.
141 Ibid p111.
142 Ibid. p122.
143 Ibid. pp121/122.
144 Ibid. p126.
145 Ibid. p146.
146 Ibid.
147 Ibid. p148.
148 Ibid. p149.
149 Ibid. p158.
150 Ibid. p159.
151 Ibid.
152 Ibid p159.
153 Ibid. p161.
154 Ibid p3.
155 TNA. WO12/5632. Pay List & Muster Records. (1808–1809) 2nd Battalion 43rd Regiment.
156 TNA. WO12/10692.
157 Levinge, Sir Richard. p88.
158 Ibid. pp 125/126.
159 TNA. WO25/1783.1st Batallion 43rd Regiment Casualty Returns (1809–1817)
160 TNA. WO3/164. Commander in Chief/Secretary at War. 23 November 1818.
161 TNA. WO17/339. War Officer Letters 'Un-numbered Corps'. Deputy Adjutant General's Office, Quebec. 6 September 1819.
162 Canadian missionary Mr D De Perron, *HT*. 18 May 1818.
163 Ibid.
164 NAC. M.G. 9, D8-27. Vol 1. Reel C -4651. pp 42–45.
165 Harris Benjamin. *A Dorset Rifleman*.
166 Fyler, Colonel A. E. *The History of the 50th. The Queen's Own Regiment*. Chapman & Hall. (1895).
167 *HT*. 23 January, 1809.
168 Fyler, A.E. p125.
169 Ibid. pp 160– 161.
170 Damaged typeset document in the possession of Dr Leonard.
171 NA. WO97/1180. Out Pensions Chelsea Hospital.
172 NAC. Reel C2783. RG 8. Vol 206. British Military Records.
173 NAC. 1851 Census. Lanark County. Ontario. Reel C – 11,731.
174 TNA. WO12/3331. Pay and Muster List. 16th Regiment. (March–June 1814)
175 NAC. RG 8. Vol 79. Reel C-26421.
176 NAC RG8 Vol 504. Reel 3042. pp 269– 270. British military Records.
177 NAC RG8. Vol 239. Reel C – 2846. p60.
178 TNA. WO3/67. Half-Yearly Inspection Report. 23January 1818.
179 TNA. WO27/141. Part One.
180 TNA. WO27/144. Part Two.
181 Grateful acknowledgement to Dr Hamish Maxwell-Stewart, University of Tasmania.